# FAIRNESS IN INTERNATIONAL CLIMATE CHANGE LAW AND POLICY

This work analyzes fairness dimensions of the climate regime. A central issue in international law and policy is how countries of the world should allocate the burden of addressing global climate change. With the link between human activities and climate change clearly established, and the first impacts of climate change being felt, there is a renewed sense of urgency in addressing the problem. On the basis of an overview of science and the development of the climate regime to date, this book seeks to identify the elements of a working consensus on fairness principles that could be used to solve the hitherto intractable problem of assigning responsibility for combating climate change. The book demonstrates how an analysis of fairness dimensions of climate change – grounded in practical developments and illustrated with reference to the latest developments – can add value to our understanding of current developments and future options for international climate law and policy.

Dr. Friedrich Soltau joined the United Nations in 2000, working since 2003 on a range of issues related to climate change, energy, and sustainable development. Prior to joining the United Nations, he taught in the Law Faculty at the University of Cape Town. His research interests in the area of climate change focus on issues of fairness and equity, also the subject of his doctoral dissertation, as well as adaptation to climate change and legal and policy issues related to new energy technologies.

*For Nikhil, whose laughter and joy brightens my every day.*

# Fairness in International Climate Change Law and Policy

FRIEDRICH SOLTAU

CAMBRIDGE UNIVERSITY PRESS
Cambridge, New York, Melbourne, Madrid, Cape Town, Singapore,
São Paulo, Delhi, Dubai, Tokyo, Mexico City

Cambridge University Press
The Edinburgh Building, Cambridge CB2 8RU, UK

Published in the United States of America by
Cambridge University Press, New York

www.cambridge.org
Information on this title: www.cambridge.org/9780521111089

© Friedrich Soltau 2009

This publication is in copyright. Subject to statutory exception
and to the provisions of relevant collective licensing agreements,
no reproduction of any part may take place without the written
permission of Cambridge University Press.

First published 2009

*A catalogue record for this publication is available from the British Library*

*Library of Congress Cataloguing in Publication Data*

Soltau, Friedrich, 1972–
Fairness in international climate change law and policy / Friedrich Soltau.
    p.   cm.
Includes bibliographical references.
ISBN 978-0-521-11108-9 (hardback)
1. Global warming – Law and legislation.   2. Climatic changes – Research – Law and legislation.   3. Environmental law, International.   I. Title.
K3593.S668    2009
344.04′6342 – dc22             2009008943
306.4′4–dc20

ISBN 978-0-521-11108-9 Hardback

Cambridge University Press has no responsibility for the persistence or
accuracy of URLs for external or third-party internet websites referred to in
this publication, and does not guarantee that any content on such websites is,
or will remain, accurate or appropriate. Information regarding prices, travel
timetables, and other factual information given in this work is correct at
the time of first printing but Cambridge University Press does not guarantee
the accuracy of such information thereafter.

# Contents

| | | |
|---|---|---|
| *List of Abbreviations and Acronyms* | | *page* ix |
| *Acknowledgments* | | xiii |
| 1 | Fairness in International Climate Law and Policy | 1 |
| | 1.1 Introduction | 1 |
| | 1.2 Why Fairness? | 3 |
| | 1.3 International Political Context of Fairness | 5 |
| | 1.4 Changing Nature | 11 |
| | 1.5 The Importance of Economics | 14 |
| | 1.6 Outline of the Book | 15 |
| 2 | The Science of Climate Change and the Energy Challenge | 21 |
| | 2.1 The Science of Climate Change | 21 |
| | 2.2 Emission Trends | 21 |
| | 2.3 Key Findings of the Intergovernmental Panel on Climate Change (IPCC) | 25 |
| | 2.4 Climate Impacts | 27 |
| | 2.5 Uncertainties and Feedbacks | 33 |
| | 2.6 The Science and the IPCC in Context | 34 |
| |    2.6.1 Stabilization Targets | 39 |
| |    2.6.2 The Energy Challenge | 40 |
| | 2.7 Conclusion | 48 |
| 3 | Development of the International Climate Change Regime | 50 |
| | 3.1 Introduction: United Nations Framework Convention on Climate Change (UNFCCC) | 50 |

|     |     |     |
| --- | --- | --- |
|     | 3.1.1 Genesis of the Convention: Negotiating History | 51 |
|     | 3.1.2 Key Provisions of the UNFCCC | 54 |
| 3.2 | The Kyoto Protocol | 59 |
|     | 3.2.1 Negotiating History | 60 |
|     | 3.2.2 Key Provisions | 63 |
|     | 3.2.3 Flexibility Mechanisms | 70 |
| 3.3 | Finalizing the Protocol: Consolidation and Change – The Long Road to Entry into Force | 92 |
|     | 3.3.1 Conference of the Parties (COP)-4: Attending to Unfinished Business | 93 |
|     | 3.3.2 COP-5: Pause and Prelude | 95 |
|     | 3.3.3 COP-6: Things Fall Apart | 96 |
|     | 3.3.4 COP-6bis: Compromise and Concessions | 97 |
|     | 3.3.5 COP-7: The Marrakech Accords – Hard Bargaining | 100 |
|     | 3.3.6 COP-8: Focus on Adaptation in New Delhi | 102 |
|     | 3.3.7 COP-9: Milan | 103 |
|     | 3.3.8 COP-10: Buenos Aires | 104 |
|     | 3.3.9 COP-11: Breakthrough in Montreal | 106 |
|     | 3.3.10 COP-12: Nairobi – The African Adaptation COP | 109 |
|     | 3.3.11 COP-13: Down to the Wire in Bali | 113 |
|     | 3.3.12 COP-14: Poznań, Poland | 121 |
|     | 3.3.13 International Developments outside the Convention Process | 124 |
| 3.4 | Conclusion and the Road Ahead | 127 |
| 4   | **Theoretical Aspects of Fairness** | 133 |
| 4.1 | Introduction | 133 |
|     | 4.1.1 The Role of Interests | 138 |
| 4.2 | Philosophical Roots | 140 |
|     | 4.2.1 Utilitarianism | 143 |
|     | 4.2.2 Rule-Based Theories of Justice | 144 |
| 4.3 | Distributive Justice: From Abstraction to Burden-Sharing Principles | 149 |
|     | 4.3.1 Egalitarian Principles | 153 |
|     | 4.3.2 Need-Based Principles | 154 |
|     | 4.3.3 Responsibility-Based Principles | 155 |

|  |  | 4.3.4 Capability-Based Principles | 160 |
|  |  | 4.3.5 Principles for a Working Consensus | 162 |
|  | 4.4 | Economics | 163 |
|  | 4.5 | Fairness in International Environmental Law | 168 |
|  |  | 4.5.1 Stockholm, the United Nations Conference on Environment and Development, the Johannesburg Plan of Implementation, and the Commission on Sustainable Development | 172 |
|  |  | 4.5.2 International Water Law | 174 |
|  |  | 4.5.3 Law of the Sea | 175 |
|  |  | 4.5.4 Montreal Protocol | 176 |
|  | 4.6 | Conclusion | 177 |
| 5 | Fairness in the Climate Change Regime | | 179 |
|  | 5.1 | Introduction | 179 |
|  | 5.2 | Differentiation: Entry Point for Fairness or Instrument of Expediency? | 180 |
|  |  | 5.2.1 Conceptual Framework of the Principle of Common but Differentiated Responsibility | 185 |
|  |  | 5.2.2 Common but Differentiated Responsibilities in the UNFCCC | 190 |
|  | 5.3 | Technology Transfer | 193 |
|  |  | 5.3.1 Technology Transfer in Multilateral Environmental Agreements | 194 |
|  |  | 5.3.2 Technology Transfer in Action | 196 |
|  | 5.4 | Sharing the Burden: The Global Environment Facility and the Climate Change Funds | 207 |
|  |  | 5.4.1 Convention and Kyoto Protocol Climate Change Funds | 214 |
|  |  | 5.4.2 World Bank Clean Investment Funds | 222 |
|  | 5.5 | Conclusion | 224 |
| 6 | Evaluation of Proposals for Future Climate Policy | | 228 |
|  | 6.1 | Introduction | 228 |
|  | 6.2 | Assessment Criteria | 232 |
|  |  | 6.2.1 Environmental Effectiveness | 232 |
|  |  | 6.2.2 Cost-Effectiveness | 234 |
|  |  | 6.2.3 Institutional Design | 236 |

| | |
|---|---|
| 6.3 International Climate Policy: Proposals | 242 |
|     6.3.1 Contraction and Convergence | 242 |
|     6.3.2 Greenhouse Development Rights | 246 |
|     6.3.3 Brazilian Proposal | 249 |
|     6.3.4 Multistage, and Graduation and Deepening | 251 |
|     6.3.5 Orchestra of Treaties and Converging Markets | 255 |
|     6.3.6 Global Triptych | 257 |
| 6.4 Conclusion | 258 |
| 7 Conclusion | 261 |
| *Bibliography* | 269 |
| *Index* | 285 |

# List of Abbreviations and Acronyms

| | |
|---|---|
| AAU | assigned amount unit |
| AF | Adaptation Fund |
| AGBM | Ad Hoc Group on the Berlin Mandate |
| AIJ | activities implemented jointly |
| Annex I | Annex I parties to the UNFCCC; industrialized countries that were members of the OECD in 1992, as well as countries with economies in transition |
| Annex II | Annex II parties to the UNFCCC; this group consists of the OECD members of Annex 1, but not the parties with economies in transition |
| Annex B | annex to the Protocol that lists the parties that have assumed binding emission limitation and reduction commitments and that sets out their actual commitments |
| AOSIS | Alliance of Small Island States |
| APEC | Asia-Pacific Economic Cooperation |
| APP | Asia-Pacific Partnership on Clean Development and Climate |
| AWG-KP | Ad Hoc Working Group on Annex 1 Commitments; launched by the Conference of the Parties at its Eleventh Session (COP-11) |
| AWG-LCA | Ad Hoc Working Group on Long-Term Cooperative Action under the Convention |
| CBDR | common but differentiated responsibility |
| CCS | carbon capture and storage |
| CDM | Clean Development Mechanism |
| CER | certified emission reduction unit |

| | |
|---|---|
| CFC | chlorofluorocarbon |
| $CH_4$ | methane; one molecule of methane has a warming potential of approximately 20 times that of $CO_2$ |
| CIF | Clean Investment Fund |
| $CO_2$ | carbon dioxide |
| $CO_2$ equivalent | amount of $CO_2$ that would cause the same amount of radiative forcing as a mixture of $CO_2$ and other gases |
| commitment period | emission limitation and reduction commitments under the Kyoto Protocol, which cover a five-year period from 2008 to 2012 |
| COP | Conference of the Parties |
| COP/MOP | Conference of the Parties serving as the Meeting of the Parties; supreme body of the Kyoto Protocol |
| CSD | Commission on Sustainable Development (UN) |
| CTF | Clean Technology Fund |
| EB | CDM Executive Board |
| EC | European Community |
| EGTT | Expert Group on Technology Transfer |
| EIT | economy in transition; the industrialized countries contained in Annex I or B that are undergoing the transition to a market economy |
| ERT | expert review team |
| ERU | emission reduction unit |
| EU ETS | European Union Emission Trading Scheme |
| G-77 | group of 132 developing countries |
| G-77/China | G-77 and China |
| G-8 | group of eight industrialized countries: Canada, France, Germany, Italy, Japan, Russia, the United Kingdom, and the United States |
| GA | general assembly |
| GATT | General Agreement on Tariffs and Trade |
| GDP | gross domestic product |
| GDRs | Greenhouse Development Rights |
| GEF | Global Environment Facility |
| GHG | greenhouse gas |
| GNP | gross national product |
| GWP | global warming potential |

| | |
|---|---|
| HFC | hydrofluorocarbon |
| ICAO | International Civil Aviation Organization |
| ICJ | International Court of Justice |
| ICSU | International Council of Scientific Unions |
| IEA | International Energy Agency |
| IEL | international environmental law |
| ILA | International Law Association |
| ILC | International Law Commission |
| ILM | International Legal Materials |
| IMO | International Maritime Organization |
| INC | Intergovernmental Negotiating Committee |
| IPCC | Intergovernmental Panel on Climate Change |
| ITL | International Transactions Log |
| ITLOS | International Tribunal for the Law of the Sea |
| JI | joint implementation |
| JPOI | Johannesburg Plan of Implementation |
| JUSCANZ | Japan, United States, Canada, Australia, New Zealand |
| LDC | least developed country |
| LDCF | Least Developed Countries Fund |
| LRTAP | Convention on Long-Range Transboundary Air Pollution |
| LULUCF | land use, land-use change, and forestry |
| MDGs | Millennium Development Goals |
| MEA | multilateral environmental agreement |
| MEM | Major Economies Meeting on Energy Security and Climate Change |
| $N_2O$ | nitrous oxide |
| NAPA | national adaptation programme of action |
| NGO | nongovernmental organization |
| NIEO | New International Economic Order |
| Non–Annex I | parties that do not belong to Annex I of the UNFCCC, i.e., largely but not exclusively developing countries |
| ODA | Official Development Assistance |
| ODS | ozone-depleting substance |
| OECD | Organisation for Economic Co-operation and Development |

| | |
|---|---|
| OPEC | Organization of Petroleum Exporting Countries |
| PAM | policies and measures |
| PFC | perfluorocarbon |
| ppm | parts per million |
| PPP | purchasing power parity |
| QELRO | quantified emission limitation and reduction objective |
| RCI | Responsibility-Capacity Index |
| REDD | reducing emissions from deforestation and degradation |
| RMU | removal unit |
| SAR | Second Assessment Report of the IPCC |
| SBI | Subsidiary Body for Implementation |
| SBSTA | Subsidiary Body for Scientific and Technological Advice |
| SCCF | Special Climate Change Fund |
| SCF | Strategic Climate Change Fund |
| SD | sustainable development |
| $SF_6$ | sulfur hexafluoride |
| SIDS | small island developing states |
| SPM | Summary for Policy Makers |
| TEAP | Technical and Economic Assessment Panel |
| TRIPS | Agreement on Trade-Related Aspects of Intellectual Property Rights |
| UN | United Nations |
| UNCED | UN Conference on Environment and Development |
| UNCLOS | UN Convention on the Law of the Sea |
| UNCTAD | UN Conference on Trade and Development |
| UNDP | UN Development Programme |
| UNEP | UN Environment Programme |
| UNFCCC | UN Framework Convention on Climate Change |
| UNTS | UN Treaty Series |
| WCRP | World Climate Research Programme |
| WG | working group |
| WMO | World Meteorological Organization |
| WRI | World Resources Institute |
| WTO | World Trade Organization |

# Acknowledgments

This book could not have been written without the encouragement, steadfast support, and forbearance of my beloved Saras.

I am indebted to professors Nicholas Robinson and Richard Ottinger of Pace University Law School for seeing me through the initial stages of this venture, well before it became a book. Discussions with United Nations colleagues, past and present, have contributed greatly to my understanding of the interlinked issues of energy, climate change, and sustainable development. I should like to mention, especially, Kathleen Abdalla, Steffen Behrle, Kui-nang (Peter) Mak, David O'Connor, Mohammad Reza Salamat, Ivan Vera, and Ralph Wahnschafft. Naturally, all errors of approach and any omissions are entirely my own.

The views expressed in this document are the author's and do not represent the views of the United Nations.

# 1

# Fairness in International Climate Law and Policy

Those of us who live on small specks of land, ... in the Caribbean, have not agreed to be sacrificial lambs on the altar of success of industrial civilization.[1]

The economy is a wholly owned subsidiary of the environment.[2]

Science is about truth and should be wholly indifferent to fairness or political expediency.[3]

## 1.1. INTRODUCTION

Climate change is forcing decision makers at national and international levels to make difficult choices. Confronted with competing demands and interests, countries are faced with committing significant resources to avoid consequences that, while beginning to be felt now, will only manifest themselves decades and, in some cases, centuries from now. Decisions will need to be taken under conditions of considerable uncertainty as to the exact scope and timing of harm. Moreover, the adverse impacts of climate change will be unevenly distributed, with the countries least responsible for the historical buildup of greenhouse gases (GHGs) bearing the brunt. Under such conditions, values and principles carry added weight in decision making. Science provides information on the status of the climate system and projections of future changes. Economics attempts to present the costs and

---

[1] Statement by Ambassador Lionel Hurst of Antigua and Barbuda, at the International Red Cross Conference on Climate Change and Natural Disasters, the Hague, June 28, 2002, quoted in BENITO MÜLLER, EQUITY IN CLIMATE CHANGE: THE GREAT DIVIDE 45 (2002).
[2] Forward, Robert F. Kennedy Jr., in GAYLORD NELSON, BEYOND EARTH DAY: FULFILLING THE PROMISE xvi (2002).
[3] JAMES LOVELOCK, THE VANISHING FACE OF GAIA: A FINAL WARNING 11 (2009).

benefits of alternative courses of action. Yet observing the global effort to combat climate change reveals that a key part of the discussion revolves around the contested concept of fairness. A juridical analysis of options to combat climate change will benefit from a critical engagement with the principle of fairness.

Fairness claims and discourse are a major part of the climate change regime. The United Nations Framework Convention on Climate Change (UNFCCC), which is the multilateral basis for action to combat climate change, itself assigns a prominent place to equity. Equity and fairness are deep-rooted concepts in human relations, and it is not surprising to find them invoked in a setting where decisions with far-reaching social, economic, and environmental consequences are made. Therefore it is desirable to improve our understanding of the dimensions and application of fairness concepts in climate negotiations. Understanding fairness in climate change is all the more important as negotiators, policy makers, and advocates turn to consider deepening and broadening the climate change regime after the end of the first commitment period of the Kyoto Protocol in 2012.[4] As the science points out, the emission reductions that will result from the Protocol are a very modest first step in the face of the much more extensive reductions that will be required in the coming decades. And fairness can be expected to come to the fore even more because the future stages of the international effort to combat climate change will require some form of GHG control for all countries, not only the group of industrialized countries covered under the Kyoto Protocol.

Questions of fairness are central to the challenge of tackling global climate change. The complexity of the question arises from the global and long-term nature of the problem. At the same time, the impacts are localized and differentiated so that states least able to respond are those that will be hardest hit. Policies and measures to abate – mitigate – GHG emissions demand decision making under conditions of uncertainty and a commitment of resources beyond the time horizon of politics-as-usual. And while international environmental law has achieved notable successes, it has arguably not confronted a challenge with so many dimensions, including lifestyles, energy policies, and inequality in the global community. Some observers

---

[4] Joseph E. Aldy et al., *Addressing Costs: The Political Economy of Climate Change*, in BEYOND KYOTO: ADVANCING THE INTERNATIONAL EFFORT AGAINST CLIMATE CHANGE (2003).

have argued that questions of fairness are of secondary, largely rhetorical significance: willingness to pay is what matters.[5] Such views grow from a realist perspective on the relations between states and skepticism about international law. The argument presented in this book is that a fair distribution of benefits and burdens is at the heart of the matter. Individual and collective responses to the climate change problem are shaped and determined as much by social and political factors as by technical and scientific ones. Normative analysis has a role to play in analyzing the problem of climate change and identifying solutions.

## 1.2. WHY FAIRNESS?

One straightforward reason for considering fairness and equity is that the language of the UNFCCC demands it. The Convention enjoins parties "to protect the climate system for the benefit of present and future generations of humankind, on the basis of equity and in accordance with their common but differentiated responsibilities and respective capabilities."[6] Another principle states that the special needs and circumstances of those countries particularly vulnerable to the adverse impacts of climate change should be given full consideration.[7] It also states that in taking action in circumstances of scientific uncertainty, account should be taken of the need to ensure that measures and policies are cost-effective and achieve global benefits at the lowest possible cost.[8] The guiding principles of the Convention refer explicitly to an equitable and fair approach to the protection of the climate system, with a circumscribed mention of cost-effectiveness and no mention of efficiency. A plain reading of the Convention's guiding principles, which are quite evenly balanced, points the reader in the direction of equity and fairness principles for burden sharing. Taking the language of the Convention seriously gives meaning and purpose to an effort to explore and delimit the meaning of equity and fairness in the climate change context. Because equity is not defined in the Convention, it makes sense to have recourse to background moral or ethical notions of fairness, as would be the case in a domestic

---

[5] *See* DAVID VICTOR, THE COLLAPSE OF THE KYOTO PROTOCOL AND THE STRUGGLE TO SLOW GLOBAL WARMING (2001).
[6] United Nations Framework Convention on Climate Change, adopted on May 9, 1992, Art. 3(1), 1771 UNTS 164 Art. 3(1) (hereinafter referred to as UNFCCC).
[7] UNFCCC, Art. 3(2).
[8] UNFCCC, Art. 3(3).

legal system when giving substance to concepts such as equality and due process.[9]

A substantial body of scholarship and policy advocacy has developed that discusses fairness in the climate change context.[10] References to fairness and equity also abound in intergovernmental forums dealing with climate change. Countries from opposite sides of the climate change divide implicitly or explicitly invoke fairness in their arguments. From one perspective, fairness requires that in addressing a problem, all major contributors should play their part, regardless of their historical contribution to the problem.[11] Another view sees a group of countries as the victims of another group of countries' unwillingness to take responsibility for the consequences of their

---

[9] Roger Shiner, *Law and Morality*, in A COMPANION TO PHILOSOPHY OF LAW AND LEGAL THEORY 438 (Dennis Patterson ed., 1996).

[10] For a selection, *see* ANIL AGARWAL & SUNITA NARAIN, GLOBAL WARMING IN AN UNEQUAL WORLD: A CASE OF ENVIRONMENTAL COLONIALISM (1991); Henry Shue, *The Unavoidability of Justice*, in THE INTERNATIONAL POLITICS OF THE ENVIRONMENT: ACTORS, INTERESTS, AND INSTITUTIONS (Andrew Hurrell & Benedict Kingsbury eds., 1992); Henry Shue, *Subsistence Emissions and Luxury Emissions*, 15 LAW & POLICY 40 (1993); Henry Shue, *After You: May Action by the Rich Be Contingent upon Action by the Poor?* 1 INDIANA JOURNAL OF GLOBAL LEGAL STUDIES 343 (1994); Adam Rose, *Equity Considerations of Tradeable Carbon Emission Entitlements*, in COMBATING GLOBAL WARMING: STUDY ON A GLOBAL SYSTEM OF TRADEABLE CARBON EMISSION ENTITLEMENTS, UN Doc. UNCTAD/RDP/DFP/1 55 (1992); Michael Grubb, *Seeking Fair Weather: Ethics and the International Debate on Climate Change*, 71 INTERNATIONAL AFFAIRS 463 (1995); Tariq Banuri et al., *Equity and Social Considerations*, in CLIMATE CHANGE 1995: ECONOMIC AND SOCIAL DIMENSIONS OF CLIMATE CHANGE, CONTRIBUTION OF WORKING GROUP III TO THE SECOND ASSESSMENT REPORT OF THE INTERGOVERNMENTAL PANEL ON CLIMATE CHANGE 83 (James P. Bruce et al. eds., 1996); Mathew Paterson, *International Justice and Global Warming*, in THE ETHICAL DIMENSIONS OF GLOBAL CHANGE (Barry Holden ed., 1996); Matthew Paterson, *Principles of Justice in the Context of Global Climate Change*, in INTERNATIONAL RELATIONS AND GLOBAL CLIMATE CHANGE 119 (Urs Luterbacher & Detlef F. Sprinz eds., 2001); GLOBAL COMMONS INSTITUTE, CONTRACTION AND CONVERGENCE: A GLOBAL SOLUTION TO A GLOBAL PROBLEM (1997); Adam Rose et al., *International Equity and Differentiation in Global Warming Policy: An Application to Tradeable Emission Permits*, 12(1) ENVIRONMENTAL AND RESOURCE ECONOMICS 25 (1998); FERENC L. TÓTH ED., FAIR WEATHER? EQUITY CONCERNS IN CLIMATE CHANGE 193 (1999), which contains contributions from the fields of economics, social science, and law; MARINA CAZORLA & MICHAEL TOMAN, INTERNATIONAL EQUITY AND CLIMATE CHANGE POLICY, Climate Issue Brief 27, Resources for the Future (December 2000); PETER SINGER, ONE WORLD: THE ETHICS OF GLOBALIZATION (2002); JAMES GARVEY, THE ETHICS OF CLIMATE CHANGE: RIGHT AND WRONG IN A WARMING WORLD (2008).

[11] *See*, e.g., the statement of President G.W. Bush: "I oppose the Kyoto Protocol because it exempts 80 percent of the world, including major population centers such as China and India, from compliance, and would cause serious harm to the U.S. economy... the Kyoto Protocol is an unfair and ineffective means of addressing global climate change concerns." Letter to Members of the Senate on the Kyoto Protocol on Climate Change, 37(11) WEEKLY COMP. OF PRES. DOC. 444 (March. 13, 2001).

actions. Cost is often raised as an objection, but it is evident that cost per se is not the crux of the objection – even if large developing countries participated in the mitigation effort, developed countries would still have to incur potentially substantial costs. Burden sharing is thus the issue. Opposite sides in the debate evidently believe that they derive some advantage by articulating their position in terms of fairness. Unless one believes that statements that countries make mean nothing at all, it is worthwhile examining the language countries use and the context in which they do so.

Combating climate change requires global action based on a consensus among sovereign nations that are more likely to adopt and faithfully implement an agreement that is perceived to be fair and equitable.[12] This is a straightforward notion, clearly applicable in the conduct between persons, and scholars have argued that it also applies to agreements between states.[13]

Global environmental problems bring to the fore the need to arrive at some degree of consensus about the meaning of fairness. A primary reason is that, unlike in other cases, such as international trade, developed countries cannot rely on their unequal power and influence to determine a solution, but rather require the voluntary cooperation of developing countries, particularly those that are rapidly industrializing. This opens the possibility for developed countries to deal on fair and equitable terms with developing countries, taking into account the imperative of poorer countries to pursue economic and social development, while at the same time maintaining the stability of the climate system.[14]

## 1.3. INTERNATIONAL POLITICAL CONTEXT OF FAIRNESS

The UNFCCC, which was adopted in 1992 and came into force three years later, is the foundation of the global response to climate change.[15] The ultimate objective of the Convention is the stabilization of GHG concentrations in the atmosphere at a level that would prevent dangerous human interference with the climate system. It does not contain binding emission targets. For this reason, countries initiated a negotiating process that culminated

---

[12] Marco Grosso, *A Normative Ethical Framework in Climate Change*, 81(3–4) CLIMATIC CHANGE 223 (2007).
[13] THOMAS M. FRANCK, FAIRNESS IN INTERNATIONAL LAW AND INSTITUTIONS (1995).
[14] Henry Shue, *Global Environment and International Inequality*, 75(3) INTERNATIONAL AFFAIRS 531 (1999).
[15] UNFCCC, Art. 3(1).

in the adoption of the Kyoto Protocol in 1997.[16] The Protocol, which entered into force in February 2005, commits industrialized countries – so-called Annex I parties to the UNFCCC – to reduce their GHG emissions by an average of 5.2 percent from 1990 levels during the first commitment period from 2008 to 2012. However, this binding target applies only to some 36 countries, representing about 30 percent of global GHG emissions. The nonparticipation of the United States, coupled with various compromises made in the process of bringing the Protocol into operation, means that the real reduction will be well below 5.2 percent. The Protocol is thus only a modest first step in the direction of stabilizing global emissions.

By some estimates, emissions from developing countries of carbon dioxide, the most important GHG, will in the next decade exceed the share from industrialized countries. Developed countries argue that reduction measures therefore are only meaningful if developing countries are prepared to trim their emissions. In turn, developing countries look forward, contending that they ought not bear the burden of abatement at this critical stage in their development. They point also to the historical responsibility of the developed countries, invoking the *polluter pays principle*. Small islands and other particularly vulnerable developing countries seek to emphasize global solidarity and fairness when pressing claims for assistance to adapt to the adverse impacts of climate change. These are only some of the issues entwined in the debate on climate change that lead, directly or indirectly, to the question of fairness.

Climate change stems from the activities at the very heart of our economies and way of life. Of world energy, around 85 percent is supplied from fossil fuels – coal, gas, and oil.[17] Altogether, carbon dioxide from the combustion of fossil fuels is responsible for much more than half of all GHG emissions; approximately another quarter come from carbon dioxide released in the process of deforestation and from various gases released from agricultural and other activities.[18] Many environmental problems stem from human activity, but none relate so directly to the driving force of modern economies. Stabilizing emissions at the level that would prevent large-scale, irreversible damage to the biosphere will require not merely an incremental adjustment of our energy system, but over time, a full-scale transition to new

[16] Kyoto Protocol to the UNFCCC, December 11, 1997, 37 ILM 22, available at http://unfccc.int/resource/docs/convkp/kpeng.pdf.
[17] INTERNATIONAL ENERGY AGENCY, WORLD ENERGY OUTLOOK (2006).
[18] WORLD RESOURCES INSTITUTE, NAVIGATING THE NUMBERS 5–7 (2005).

## 1.3. International Political Context of Fairness

modes of low-carbon consumption and production. Studies suggest that depending on the stringency of the chosen target, global GHG reductions of 50 to 85 percent below 2000 levels may be necessary by 2050, while global emissions would have to peak in 2015 at the latest.

The discourse on fairness is woven into the political process of the climate change regime. It has been observed that international environmental negotiations among developing countries have frequently cast their arguments in terms of justice and fairness.[19] There are several possible reasons for this. First, arguments framed in terms of fairness or justice appear more binding and forceful than those appealing to charity.[20] Second, arguments appealing to moral and, if applicable, legal obligations possess a universal character. A violation of a right to refrain from conduct that injures another, or responsibility to provide compensation for consequent damages, applies objectively to all who fall within the scope of the rule or principle. For example, although a policy argument relating to economic efficiency in combating climate change may not have much to offer the representative of a small island state, claiming the violation of a right by those responsible for GHG emissions has more traction.

Developing countries have viewed climate change in the context of their economic and social development.[21] Imposing limits on their growth is regarded as unfair, given that they have not yet attained the level of development of industrialized countries. While not ruling out so-called cleaner forms of development, they do not wish to bear any additional cost, particularly when the developed countries achieved their status with few, if any, environmental constraints.[22] Developing countries do not want to be held responsible for remedying a problem largely not of their making. Accordingly, they emphasize industrialized countries' dominant share of cumulative carbon dioxide emissions (76 percent).[23] Developing countries

---

[19] Mark A. Drumbl, *Poverty, Wealth, and Obligation in International Law*, 76 TULANE LAW REVIEW 843, 898 (2002).
[20] *Id.* at 897, citing ANDREW DOBSON, JUSTICE AND THE ENVIRONMENT: CONCEPTIONS OF ENVIRONMENTAL SUSTAINABILITY AND THEORIES OF DISTRIBUTIVE JUSTICE 95 (1995).
[21] MÜLLER, *supra* note 2, at 45. The following draws on the points made by Müller.
[22] *See* Delhi Ministerial Declaration on Climate Change and Sustainable Development, Decision 1/CP.8 UN Doc. FCCC/CP/2002/7/Add.1 ("Reaffirming that economic and social development and poverty eradication are the first and overriding priorities of developing country Parties," preambular para. 3; "Recognizing that climate change could endanger future well-being, ecosystems, and economic progress in all regions," preambular para. 6).
[23] WORLD RESOURCES INSTITUTE, *supra* note 18, at 32.

also point out the difference in per capita emissions: some industrialized countries (Australia, Canada, the United States) have per capita emissions more than 6 times those of China, and 13 times those of India.[24] By some estimates, however, the developing country carbon dioxide emissions will exceed those of industrialized countries by 2012.[25] At the same time, some 140 countries, including small islands and the least developed countries, are responsible for only 10 percent of annual emissions.[26]

The argument from historical responsibility has obvious attractions in the international climate change discourse. At face value, basic notions of fairness seem to suggest that the main contributors to a problem should be the ones carrying out abatement.[27] In this context, Brazil, in 1997, put forward a proposal that would assign relative responsibilities to individual industrialized countries in accordance with their respective contributions to climate change, as measured by the induced change in temperature, based on historical emissions.[28] According to recent research, the average contributions to the global mean surface temperature increase in 2000 are around 40 percent from the Organisation for Economic Co-operation and Development group of industrialized countries, 14 percent from Eastern Europe and the former Soviet Union, 24 percent from Asia, and 22 percent from Africa and Latin America.[29]

Generalizing very broadly, the approach to the problem of climate change by industrialized nations, particularly those in Europe, has been from the perspective of correcting or managing an environmental imbalance. While

---

[24] *Id.* at 21 note 80.
[25] INTERNATIONAL ENERGY AGENCY, *supra* note 17, at 81.
[26] *Id.* at 11 note 80.
[27] A country's historical emissions can be presented in at least three ways: on the basis of simple cumulative emissions, the contribution to current concentrations of GHGs, or the contribution to increases in the global average temperature. *See id.* at 32 note 80 for a succinct explanation. The cumulative approach simply counts all emissions since a particular start date. In assessing a country's contributions to atmospheric concentrations, the second approach takes into account the decay of GHGs over time to give a country's share of emissions presently in the atmosphere.
[28] UN Doc. FCCC/AGBM/1997/MISC.1/Add.3, 3. Although not adopted, the Brazilian recommendation remains on the agenda of the Conference of the Parties to the Convention, whose Subsidiary Body for Technological and Scientific Advice (SBSTA) has sponsored continued research into contributions to climate change. *See* UN Doc. FCCC/SBSTA/2002/INF.14 for a summary of the research efforts carried out by various institutions, while up-to-date information is available at http://www.match-info.net/.
[29] Michel den Elzen et al., *Analysing Countries' Contributions to Climate Change: Scientific and Policy-Related Choices*, 8(6) ENVIRONMENTAL SCIENCE & POLICY 614 (2005).

## 1.3. International Political Context of Fairness

catastrophic images may be summoned in support of policy, by and large, the adverse impacts of climate change will be less severe than in the subtropical countries, and the capacity to adapt is more developed than in poor countries.[30] Framing the problem in these terms may have contributed to the climate regime's focus on mitigating GHG emissions, epitomized in the emission limitations and reductions required by the Kyoto Protocol. From an environmental management perspective, informed by the scientific evidence of GHGs and public concern, the primacy of mitigation on the agenda of the international climate change regime made sense. Increased recognition of the economic and social dimensions of climate change meant greater emphasis on adaptation to the adverse effects of climate change – sea-level rise, potentially greater frequency and intensity of extreme weather events, and so on.[31] Even so, funding for adaptation falls well short of what is needed, while progress on the issue in the climate talks remained bogged down for a number of years.[32]

Adaptation thus constitutes an important dimension of fairness in the context of international climate policy. Adaptation is increasingly being regarded as a twin priority with mitigation. Practically, this stems from the realization that the current concentration of GHGs already commits the planet to further warming, even if emissions were frozen at current levels.[33] (This is primarily due to the thermal inertia of the oceans, which have absorbed vast amounts of heat, which will be slowly released into the atmosphere.) Given their vulnerabilities – a combination of geographical location, reliance on sectors vulnerable to climate shocks (agriculture), and low levels of technology and capital accumulation – developing countries are much less able to cope with the impacts of climate change and climate

---

[30] But cf. the 2004 heat wave in Europe, which was responsible for some thirty thousand deaths. Again, remedial measures, such as air-conditioning and improved preparedness, can be taken relatively easily. Compare this with the impact of drought on countries in the Sahel or populations in low-lying areas such as Bangladesh or the Nile delta.

[31] While the UNFCCC did deal with the question of funding for adaptation at the first Conference of the Parties in 1995 (Decision 11/CP.1), it was only with the adoption of the Marrakech Accords in 2001 that adaptation was addressed as a key area of action.

[32] See slow progress on articulating the Buenos Aires Programme of Work on Adaptation and Response Measures, adopted at the 10th Conference of the Parties to the UNFCCC (COP-10) in 2004.

[33] INTERGOVERNMENTAL PANEL ON CLIMATE CHANGE, CLIMATE CHANGE 2007: THE PHYSICAL SCIENCE BASIS, CONTRIBUTION OF WORKING GROUP I TO THE FOURTH ASSESSMENT REPORT OF THE INTERGOVERNMENTAL PANEL ON CLIMATE CHANGE 23 (Susan Solomon et al. eds., 2007).

variability. A drought in the United States may harm the prospects of farmers (many of whom will be cushioned by insurance), but loss of life is unlikely. For a country in a persistently drought-wracked region, such as Niger, where subsistence agriculture supports a large proportion of the population, the situation is quite different. A World Bank study concluded that progress in fighting poverty is under threat from increasingly severe weather events and climate variability.[34] The report goes on to note that 20 to 40 percent of official development assistance (ODA) and public concessional finance (i.e., US$20 billion to US$40 billion per year) is subject to climate risk and that very little ODA takes this risk into account.[35] There is a risk that climate change could impede the achievement of the United Nations Millennium Development Goals, including those on poverty eradication; child mortality; combating HIV/AIDS, malaria, and other diseases; and environmental sustainability.[36]

Some countries are more vulnerable and less able to take adaptive measures than others. The UNFCCC also addresses issues of equity and solidarity, providing that vulnerable countries, particularly small island developing states and least developed countries (LDCs), should be assisted in adapting to the adverse effects of climate change.[37] From the perspective of developing countries, the promise of these provisions has not been fulfilled.[38] The United Nations currently classifies 50 countries as LDCs. These countries are generally those lowest on the development rung – one criterion is an annual per capita gross national income of less than US$750.[39] The individual and total GHG emissions of this group of countries are almost negligible. Due

---

[34] VICE PRESIDENCY FOR SUSTAINABLE DEVELOPMENT, THE WORLD BANK, AN INVESTMENT FRAMEWORK FOR CLEAN ENERGY AND DEVELOPMENT: A PROGRESS REPORT (2006).
[35] *Id.* at 38.
[36] WORLD BANK GROUP, MANAGING CLIMATE RISK: INTEGRATING ADAPTATION INTO WORLD BANK GROUP OPERATIONS 5 (2006). The Millennium Development Goals and related documents are available at http://www.un.org/millenniumgoals/.
[37] *See* UNFCCC, Art. 4(8)–(9).
[38] As further detailed in Chapter 5, several funds have been established to address the adaptation and technology needs of developing countries. The Least Developed Country Fund and the Special Climate Change Fund, both of which are voluntary funds, have supported studies, capacity building, and planning, but for actual adaptation projects, the Adaptation Fund, which was finally operationalized in 2007, should have greater resources at its disposal.
[39] The other two criteria are human resource weakness and economic vulnerability. See explanation on the Web site of the UN Representative for Least Developed Countries, Landlocked Countries, and Small Island Developing States, available at http://www.un.org/special-rep/ohrlls/ldc/ldc%20criteria.htm.

to their vulnerability to climate impacts, over the long term, LDCs stand to gain from stringent emission limitations by major emitters. In the short to medium term, however, they have less to gain from a climate change agenda dominated by mitigation concerns, including haggling among industrialized and emerging countries over the allocation of emission reductions. For small island states, the issue is even more pressing, and they have been the most vocal in calling for strict emission limitations. Their fairness claims are directly founded on the existential threat posed by climate change.

## 1.4. CHANGING NATURE

In the developed world, technology has permitted humans to remove themselves from the forces of nature so that shelter, food, work, and recreation can be provided, save in rare circumstances, independent of the climate. Today, the climate penetrates the public consciousness predominantly through natural disasters, such as Hurricane Katrina, and droughts and phenomena such as the El Niño effect. Despite its inherently unpredictable and dynamic character, society clings to the belief that like nature in general, climate can be conquered and controlled through technology. Even as the threat of climate change is understood, the reflex on the part of many policy makers and some scientists is to set store first by further research, and second by technology. Both are essential parts of the solution, yet they may also serve to avoid a more searching approach to the problem.

According to the Intergovernmental Panel on Climate Change (IPCC), surface temperatures have increased by 0.7 degrees Celsius over the past century, with current concentrations making some further warming inevitable.[40] Depending on their degree of vulnerability, countries will have to adapt more or less to the impacts of climate change. Adaptation will be particularly challenging for those societies that are already having difficulty providing for their people. Furthermore, the record of human adaptation – in prehistorical and modern eras – to climate change has not been simple or easy.[41] Adaptation requires changes in technology as well as in social and

---

[40] INTERGOVERNMENTAL PANEL ON CLIMATE CHANGE, supra note 33, at 5.
[41] Donald Worster, *Climate Change and History: Lessons from the Great Plains, in* EARTH, AIR, FIRE, WATER 72 (John K. Conway et al. eds., 1999). Worster refers to the efforts to make the Great Plains viable for agriculture and concludes, among other things, that adapting to a volatile environment with technology is a more unreliable strategy than is thought, often

cultural ways of life. Not for nothing is there frequent mention in myths and histories of calamitous climatic events.

Even as climate change serves to make society aware of its renewed vulnerability to extremes of climate – rattling the notion that nature has been tamed – it challenges the very conception of nature. For even as society has built up defenses, channeling and domesticating nature, it has retained a belief in the wildness of nature, with wilderness an iconic value, as evidenced, in banal form, in popular media advertising. As William McKibben notes, our faith in the essential strength of nature endures so long as we consider damage as local. However, shifting from the local to the global destroys that faith[42]:

> The idea of nature will not survive the new global pollution – the carbon dioxide and the chlorofluorocarbons and the like. This new rupture with nature is different not only in scope but also in kind from the salmon tins in an English stream. We have changed the atmosphere, and thus we are changing the weather. By changing the weather, we make every spot on earth man-made and artificial. We have deprived nature of its independence, and it is fatal to its meaning. Nature's independence is its meaning; without it there *is* nothing but us.

While this view is quite stark, it usefully underlines two important points. First, that global climate change, once-and-for-all, dispenses with the illusion that human impact on the climate is confined to the local and can be treated as such. Second, and following from the first, our relationship to, and conception of nature, must be re-evaluated. The notion that humanity's knowledge and technological prowess also implies mastery over the physical world is bumping up against its limits. A related issue concerns fundamental assumptions concerning economic growth and whether there may be limits to growth.[43] Certainly any climate policy predicated on, or implying, any significant limits on growth would be a political nonstarter in developing countries, but also in the industrialized world. Nonetheless, it is not certain that a stringent global climate change target is, in practice, compatible

---

bringing with it unforeseen consequences. He also underlines how we underestimate the challenge of cultural adaptation to the environment.

[42] William McKibben, The End of Nature 58 (1989).

[43] Donella H. Meadows et al., The Limits to Growth (1972). The specific projections of resource shortages in the book were proved wrong, and the analysis adopted in the book was heavily criticized.

with economic growth of the kind to which the world has become accustomed.

The ideas sketched here are a reminder that global climate change presents a fundamental challenge to our social, cultural, and political systems. It is worth bearing in mind that climatic change reaches far back to the origins of humankind, playing a role in the evolution of the human species.[44] Climate change poses a challenge for scientists, philosophers, economists, and most crucially, politicians and policy makers. Climate change is a classical over-the-horizon problem – bold policy steps need to be taken today, with largely no return in the near term, even while scientists are still engaged in putting the precise outlines to the threat. As demonstrated by the halting effort to address it with international legal instruments, climate change poses enormous challenges for international environmental governance. From this perspective, the response to date can be regarded as a failure to fully acknowledge the scale of the problem. The question could justifiably be asked whether decision makers and citizens have faced up to the kinds of decisions that will need to be made.

While there exist a large number of environmental and development challenges (health, water, sanitation) vying for attention, climate change is linked in multiple ways with almost all of them. It has recently been found that climate change will be one of the main causes of biodiversity loss, threatening ecosystems such as coral reefs and subjecting fragile ecosystems to change on time scales that, in many cases, do not permit adaptation. Changes in temperature and precipitation patterns threaten agriculture, settlements, and development efforts. In many cases, the most severe impacts will occur where people are poor, directly dependent on natural systems for survival, and without the capacity or resources to adapt. Climate change is thus relevant to development and poverty alleviation and is likely to worsen existing distributional inequalities.[45]

---

[44] A compelling hypothesis explains the sudden extinction of species and the appearance of new ones, to which the fossil record testifies, with reference to environmental change, specifically climatic change. *See* WILLIAM K. STEVENS, THE CHANGE IN THE WEATHER: PEOPLE, WEATHER, AND THE SCIENCE OF CLIMATE 19 (2001), referring to the work of Elisabeth Vrba, *On the Connections between Paleoclimate and Evolution, in* PALEOCLIMATE AND EVOLUTION, WITH EMPHASIS ON HUMAN ORIGINS 24, 25 (Elisabeth Vrba et al. eds., 1996).

[45] *See* UNITED NATIONS DEVELOPMENT PROGRAMME, HUMAN DEVELOPMENT REPORT 2007/2008, FIGHTING CLIMATE CHANGE: HUMAN SOLIDARITY IN A DIVIDED WORLD (2007).

## 1.5. THE IMPORTANCE OF ECONOMICS

Addressing climate change is, in effect, also a discussion concerning the structure of our economies and the energy systems that drive them. Almost invariably, any debate on response to climate change will refer to costs – either of mitigation measures, or of the likely losses stemming from climate impacts; this is not surprising because the economic implications of climate change are significant, with considerable uncertainty. Traditional economic analysis tends to put a lower value on committing resources to guard against damage in the future, such as climate change, as opposed to other concerns, such as fighting disease and providing access to clean water and sanitation.[46] A recent study commissioned by the United Kingdom comprehensively analyzed the cost of climate change, coming to the conclusion that the early action would be considerably less costly than further delay.[47]

Economic analysis provides very useful tools to evaluate the costs and benefits of various courses of action. Nonetheless, the very dictates of such analysis – focused on what is the most efficient allocation of resources in the present – may imply limitations when considering decisions that may have profound implications on other peoples, now and in the future, and potentially irreversible impacts on systems whose value cannot be captured adequately in monetary terms. The framework of the analysis, while potentially maximizing human welfare in the present, may not account adequately for irreversible impacts on the biosphere such as losses of ecosystems like coral reefs. Decisions on combating climate change cannot be determined by the costs of action alone because the understanding of costs is informed by assumptions about what we value,[48] and those assumptions relate to ethical and moral values that stand outside economics.

---

[46] *See*, e.g., the so-called Copenhagen Consensus, which featured a panel of prominent economists, including three Nobel Prize winners, who were asked to rank the spending priority of a number of development challenges given an extra US$50 million in aid resources. Controlling HIV/AIDS ranked at the top, while measures to combat climate change were ranked at the bottom. *See Putting the World to Rights*, THE ECONOMIST, June 3, 2004. The basic reason for coming to this conclusion is that under a cost-benefit analysis, the economic benefits of reducing global warming are largely not felt until well into the twenty-first century – and the costs are felt immediately. *See also* BJØRN LOMBORG ED., GLOBAL CRISES, GLOBAL SOLUTIONS (2004).
[47] NICHOLAS STERN, THE ECONOMICS OF CLIMATE CHANGE: THE STERN REVIEW (2006).
[48] GARVEY, *supra* note 10, at 101.

## 1.6. OUTLINE OF THE BOOK

The ultimate objective of the UNFCCC is the stabilization of atmospheric GHG concentrations "at a level that would prevent dangerous anthropogenic interference with the climate system," that is, at a safe level.[49] Stabilizing concentrations can be roughly compared to slowly taking your foot off the accelerator pedal of a speeding car. The car will not stop immediately, but rather, will roll on for a long time; in the same way, the earth's climate will continue changing, hundreds of years after atmospheric stabilization has been achieved. The longer the driver waits before decelerating, the greater the distance the car will travel; waiting to cut GHG emissions implies a higher stabilization level and more climate change. Looking forward, this means a finite amount of carbon that can be released into the atmosphere over the next century – the collective carbon budget. Setting a global stabilization target immediately raises the question of burden sharing, or *distributive fairness* – sharing the costs of mitigation, contributing to the costs of adapting to climate change, and allocating allowances to use the remaining atmospheric sink capacity. Emissions need to contract dramatically to meet so-called safe stabilization levels. On what basis will the declining total global emissions be allocated – roughly in proportion to past emissions (acquired rights), inversely related to past emissions (historical responsibility), or in relation to developmental status and attainments (capacity)? How will the mitigation burden be allocated among nation states?

This book maps out some of the fairness principles underpinning debates on the sharing among nations of the burdens and benefits of combating climate change. This raises questions of distributive fairness or justice. Only once there is agreement, however, on the amount of climate change deemed acceptable – expressed as a stabilization target, temperature level, or other metric – is it possible to consider a fair distribution of emissions. That is to say, one should first ask, what is the amount of climate change (represented by the stabilization target) that is considered safe? One part in this determination is scientific and empirical, the other moral and ethical. The European Union has proposed that the increase in global average temperatures should be held to below 2 degrees Celsius above preindustrial levels. Yet holding warming to this level will be a daunting challenge. Consider

[49] UNFCCC, Art. 2.

that *current* atmospheric concentrations of GHGs fall within the range the IPCC projects would result in warming of 2 to 2.4 degrees Celsius.[50] Higher levels of warming are regarded by many as unsafe: warming of between 1.6 and 2.6 degrees Celsius could lead to localized melting of the Greenland ice cap, 10 to 40 percent of species committed to extinction, and increased flooding and drought severity.[51] Warming of 2.6 to 3.6 degrees Celsius, associated with a doubling of preindustrial concentrations of $CO_2$, could trigger a partial or, possibly, a total melting of the Greenland ice cap, a process that could take centuries to millennia and would raise global sea levels by 2 meters, or 7 meters, in the case of a complete melting. Having the scientific knowledge at hand, one needs to ask, what are the relevant principles of justice informing any decision? What ethical and moral standards are used in weighing impacts on lives, now and in the future?

The objective is not to further explore here the ethical and moral questions pertaining to a safe level of climate change; rather, the aim is to underline that a conceptual boundary exists between that enquiry and the fairness of the attendant burden-sharing arrangement (distributive fairness). Although both dimensions raise ethical and moral issues, they are not the same. Ethical and moral standards bearing on the question of an acceptable level of climate change have consequences for the long-term integrity of the biosphere; distributive fairness primarily governs the allocation of economic costs and developmental opportunities. In determining the permissible amount of climate change, what is our responsibility to small islands that will be lost, and how should we value their claim to maintain intact cultures and societies? What is the value of diverse ecosystems? Making and defending moral and ethical claims in cases such as these is different to arguing about which rules should govern how the pie – the burden of combating climate change – is divided. Thus fairness principles prominent in the discussion about burden sharing – historical responsibility for climate change, the wealth and differential technological and institutional capacities of countries – are not of determining importance when assessing

---

[50] The present $CO_2$ concentration is 380 parts per million (ppm). Concentrations in the range of 350–400 $CO_2$ ppm are consistent with warming of 2–2.4 degrees Celsius. *See* INTERGOVERNMENTAL PANEL ON CLIMATE CHANGE, CLIMATE CHANGE 2007: MITIGATION, CONTRIBUTION OF WORKING GROUP III TO THE FOURTH ASSESSMENT REPORT OF THE INTERGOVERNMENTAL PANEL ON CLIMATE CHANGE 229 (Bert Metz et al. eds., 2007).
[51] *Id.* at 230.

## 1.6. Outline of the Book

what amount of warming would be consistent with justice. For example, if island state A has a moral claim to be protected from a certain amount of climate change, then in principle, that claim ought to be weighed quite independently of what would constitute a fair allocation of future emissions between highly developed country X and populous, developing country Y.[52] Although a stringent stabilization target entails a smaller global carbon budget, given the variety of conceivable burden-sharing arrangements, it does not *necessarily* imply anything about the share to be borne by any particular country. Interestingly, empirical studies confirm that – especially for developed countries – the chosen stabilization target, not the particular allocation arrangement, is the determining factor with respect to countries' required mitigation effort.[53]

Careful deliberation is called for when considering what would constitute a fair or just amount of climate change, as expressed in the form of a stabilization target or other metric. I have argued here that this question should be considered independently – but not in isolation from – questions of distributive fairness. Undeniably, justice in stabilization and distributive fairness are linked in important ways. First, any stabilization target that is adopted will entail some further climate change and hence adaptation costs; these costs will be either higher or lower, depending on the stabilization target. Developing countries will face the brunt of climate impacts, but lacking in financial and technological resources, they will need assistance from developed countries. In this context, it may be natural to argue that those with the greatest historical contribution should bear a greater share of such compensatory payments. This issue is pressing; already, emissions to date have committed us to a certain amount of climate change so that adaptation is no longer an option, but a necessity. Second, climate change raises issues of intergenerational justice.[54] Any significant abatement action – that is, deviation in GHG emissions from a business-as-usual scenario – will entail some costs to society, now and in the future. Yet the benefits, in the form of a reduction in climate change, will accrue almost entirely to future generations. Broadly speaking, any global agreement on combating

---

[52] For the purpose of the argument advanced here, I assume that moral/ethical arguments can be advanced in the name of states and/or their populations.
[53] Niklas Höhne & Sarah Moltman, The Distribution of Emission Allowances under the Greenhouse Development Rights and Other Effort Sharing Approaches, report prepared for the Heinrich-Böll-Stiftung 27 (2008).
[54] Edith Brown Weiss, In Fairness to Future Generations (1989).

climate change thus involves an explicit or implicit distribution of burdens and benefits *across* present and future generations. Thus a stringent stabilization target imposes greater burdens on present generations and bestows greater benefits (less climate change) on future generations. In the case of distributive fairness, the choice of burden-sharing arrangement can also have distributional consequences across nations. Thus an arrangement based on historical emissions would shift the greater part of the burden onto current and future generations in developed countries, and away from present and future generations in developing countries. Third, notwithstanding the point that burden-sharing arrangements are conceptually independent of the moral and ethical questions raised by the stabilization target, or long-term vision, countries are more likely to adopt such a target if they have a good idea of their expected shares of the burden. The key here is the relative share of the burden. Thus, in a practical sense, agreement on the framework of distributive fairness constitutes the missing piece of the puzzle in adopting a global, long-term target. This book sets out to deepen the understanding of distributive fairness in the context of the climate change regime.

Agreement on a comprehensive definition of *distributive fairness* is destined to remain elusive. Therefore the approach followed here is to identify and briefly discuss a number of – by no means all – fairness principles. In particular, the objective will be to articulate a number of fairness principles that could potentially constitute the basis for a rough, working ethical consensus in the climate change regime. The following representative fairness principles have been selected and are analyzed in turn: egalitarian, responsibility or contribution, need, and capability based. Naturally, these various principles interact and overlap in the climate change discourse.

The book continues in Chapter 2 with an overview of the key findings of the IPCC. Energy and its various dimensions – sources, growth rates, technology – are at the heart of the climate change problem. Accordingly, Chapter 2 provides an overview of the energy challenge. The intention is to capture a few key aspects without doing a disservice to this complex topic. It will be seen that the politics around the international climate change negotiating process had a major hand in shaping the IPCC, a unique institution that operates on the basis of intergovernmental consensus, but at the same time must maintain its scientific credibility.

## 1.6. Outline of the Book

Chapter 3 provides an overview of the UNFCCC and its Kyoto Protocol in greater detail. The chapter covers the genesis of these two instruments and introduces their key provisions. It then goes on to trace the operation and elaboration of the climate change regime through successive meetings of supreme bodies of these two instruments, respectively, the Conference of the Parties (COPs) of the UNFCCC and the COPs serving as the meeting of the Parties (COP/MOP) to the Kyoto Protocol.

Chapter 4 maps out various approaches and conceptions to fairness. Fairness claims are a major part of the climate change regime. The Framework Convention – the universally accepted legal instrument for action to combat climate change – assigns a prominent place to equity.[55] In December 2007, the parties agreed to launch negotiations on a post-2012 climate agreement, which, to be successful, will need both to deliver bigger emission cuts and engage a wider group of states than is currently the case under the Kyoto Protocol. The climate policy negotiated in the next few years will decide how the burden of responding to climate change will be apportioned. It is no surprise, then, that fairness concerns are moving into the limelight. The analysis in this chapter aims to outline the foundations of fairness, before moving on to identify a number of principles that could contribute to a rough, working consensus on fairness in climate change. While general dimensions of fairness are considered, the analysis focuses on allocating responsibility for addressing climate change through mitigation action.

Having analyzed fairness at a theoretical level in the previous chapter, Chapter 5 proceeds to identify and analyze the fairness and equity principles embedded in the Convention and the Protocol. Extensive reference is made to the principle of common but differentiated responsibilities, which is a mainstay of the international discourse on climate change. As potential examples of fairness in practice, the implementation of provisions relating to technology transfer and financial assistance are also examined in more detail.

Chapter 6 evaluates a selection of proposals for a future climate policy against the fairness principles identified in Chapter 4 as well as a set of

[55] The European Commission and 191 states have ratified or acceded to the Convention, leaving as the only nonparties Andorra, the Holy See, Iraq, and Somalia. *See* Web site of the UNFCCC secretariat, available at http://unfccc.int/files/essential_background/convention/status_of_ratification/application/pdf/unfccc_conv_rat.pdf.

policy criteria. A good, albeit preliminary, indication of the usefulness of fairness principles would appear from the extent to which climate change policy proposals do – or do not – reflect a balance of fairness principles. This chapter also identifies and applies a selection of policy assessment criteria drawn from the literature. At this point, it should be noted that to a considerable degree, the discussion of fairness in Chapters 4 and 5 could be applicable to both adaptation to the impacts of climate change and the mitigation of GHG emissions. Both adaptation and mitigation are undeniably important. The focus in Chapter 6, however, is on mitigation and, in particular, specific proposals for climate policy, the emphasis of which tends to be on mitigation efforts. This word of caution is necessary because adaptation raises equity concerns that, while important, fall outside the scope of this book.[56]

The conclusion seeks to draw together the strands of the analysis and then proceeds to make a number of proposals for future climate policy. It is suggested that these proposals would contribute to a post-Kyoto climate agreement that is consonant with fairness principles, as articulated in the prior analysis, while also being capable of implementation, taking into account prevailing economic and political realities.

---

[56] For a discussion of fairness in the context of adaptation, *see* FAIRNESS IN ADAPTATION TO CLIMATE CHANGE (Neil Adger et al. eds., 2006).

# 2

# The Science of Climate Change and the Energy Challenge

## 2.1. THE SCIENCE OF CLIMATE CHANGE

This chapter provides an overview of the science of climate change, drawing largely on the reports of the Intergovernmental Panel on Climate Change (IPCC), an international, multidisciplinary assessment body established by the United Nations (UN). The material covered is intended to frame and inform the analysis in subsequent chapters. The information is based on the consensus contained in the reports of the IPCC, especially the Fourth Assessment Report (4AR), released in 2007. Science is coming to the fore in new ways and is influencing institutions, including those setting norms at the international level. Science influences how the problem is framed. At the same time, political processes bear on the way in which scientific output is received and used in policy making. The central role of energy in modern life – and its dominance as a source of greenhouse gas (GHG) emissions – means that this is where the battle against climate change must be joined. This chapter thus includes a brief summary of the main features of the energy challenge.

## 2.2. EMISSION TRENDS

The primary contributor to global climate change is carbon dioxide ($CO_2$), which is released by the burning of fossil fuels as well as by land-use change, particularly deforestation. Carbon dioxide emissions from fossil fuel use rose to 26.4 billion metric tons per year in 2000–2005, with the contribution of carbon dioxide emissions from land-use change (mainly deforestation) being estimated at 5.9 billion metric tons per year during the 1990s.[1] Of the GHGs, carbon dioxide is responsible for about 77 percent of the human contribution to warming, followed by methane (14 percent) and nitrous oxide (8 percent).[2]

According to the IPCC, atmospheric concentrations of the three main GHGs – carbon dioxide, methane, and nitrous oxide – have increased sharply as a result of human activities since 1750 and now far exceed preindustrial values determined from ice cores spanning thousands of years.[3] The concentration of carbon dioxide in 2005 stood at 379 parts per million (ppm), an increase of 35 percent over the preindustrial level of about 280 ppm. This exceeds, by far, the natural range over the last 650,000, years as determined from ice cores.[4] Atmospheric concentrations of methane (148 percent) and nitrous oxides (18 percent) have also increased relative to preindustrial levels.[5] These, together with three other fluorine-containing gases, constitute the basket of GHGs controlled under the Kyoto Protocol. Although the industrial fluorinated gases – hydrofluorocarbons (HFCs), which are used as substitutes for ozone-depleting substances, some of which are also GHGs; perfluorocarbons (PFCs); and sodium hexafluoride ($SF_6$) – are only small contributors to warming, their concentrations are increasing rapidly.[6]

The concentration of $CO_2$ in the atmosphere is a function of the amount of $CO_2$ emitted – from the burning of fossil fuels and changes in land use – and the capacity of sinks, such as the oceans and biosphere, to absorb $CO_2$. Over the past 200 years, about half the carbon emitted from fossil fuel use has been absorbed by plants on land and by the oceans.[7] In the long run,

---

[1] INTERGOVERNMENTAL PANEL ON CLIMATE CHANGE, CLIMATE CHANGE 2007: THE PHYSICAL SCIENCE BASIS. CONTRIBUTION OF WORKING GROUP I TO THE FOURTH ASSESSMENT REPORT OF THE INTERGOVERNMENTAL PANEL ON CLIMATE CHANGE 2–3 (Susan Solomon et al. eds., 2007).
[2] WORLD RESOURCES INSTITUTE, NAVIGATING THE NUMBERS 5 (2005).
[3] INTERGOVERNMENTAL PANEL ON CLIMATE CHANGE, *supra* note 1, at 2.
[4] *See id.*
[5] *See id.* at 3.
[6] *See id.* at 13. HFCs have been used as substitute for CFCs in refrigeration, while PFCs are emitted during the production of aluminum. Ozone-depleting substances that are also GHGs are regulated under the Montreal Protocol on Substances That Deplete the Ozone Layer of 1987. The climate impact of such gases has peaked and is declining.
[7] *See* INTERGOVERNMENTAL PANEL ON CLIMATE CHANGE, *supra* note 1, at 512. The uptake of $CO_2$ by the oceans is limited by the rate at which absorbed carbon is transported to the deeper layers, as well as the fact that carbon chemistry of water means that less $CO_2$ is

the absorptive capacity of the oceans and the terrestrial ecosystems marks the ultimate stabilization level for human carbon dioxide emissions.

GHGs remain in the atmosphere for decades, with residency periods for the main gases ranging from decades to hundreds of years.[8] During their residence in the atmosphere, the molecules concerned generally retain their warming potential, meaning that those molecules emitted today will still exert their influence years from now. Furthermore, because the oceans store and release solar energy more slowly than the air – a characteristic known as thermal inertia – some additional warming and sea-level rise is already in the system. For policy makers, this time lag is another reason not to delay action until the consequences of GHG emissions become fully apparent. According to the IPCC, even if GHG concentrations were held steady at 2000 levels, a further warming of 0.1 degrees Celsius per decade would be expected.[9]

Beginning a sharp rise after 1945, global $CO_2$ emissions from fossil fuel combustion increased by over 70 percent between 1973 and 2005.[10] Over the period from 1990 to 2004, overall GHG emissions in industrialized countries as a group experienced a slight decline, but this was largely due to a fall in emissions from countries with economies in transition as a result of economic contraction and restructuring, which offset the rise in emissions from highly industrialized countries.[11] In developing countries, $CO_2$ emissions nearly doubled between 1990 and 2002.[12] The percentage rise in emissions from some developed countries, such as the United States (13 percent) and Canada (22 percent), appears modest alongside the more rapid growth rates of some developing countries, such as China (50 percent), Indonesia (97 percent), and the Republic of Korea (97 percent). However, the sheer size of the United States means that its increase in $CO_2$ emissions was roughly equal to

---

taken up as its $CO_2$ concentration increases. *See id.* at 405. *See also* Christopher L. Sabine et al., *The Oceanic Sink for Anthropogenic $CO_2$*, 305(5682) SCIENCE 367 (2004).

[8] Estimating a single lifetime for $CO_2$ in the atmosphere is difficult because while about 50 percent will be removed from the atmosphere within as little as 30 years, some 20 percent will remain for thousands of years. *See* INTERGOVERNMENTAL PANEL ON CLIMATE CHANGE, *supra* note 1, at 514. *See also* DAVID ARCHER, THE LONG THAW: HOW HUMANS ARE CHANGING THE NEXT 100,000 YEARS OF EARTH'S CLIMATE (2008).

[9] INTERGOVERNMENTAL PANEL ON CLIMATE CHANGE, *supra* note 1, at 12.

[10] INTERNATIONAL ENERGY AGENCY, KEY WORLD ENERGY STATISTICS 44 (2007).

[11] UNFCCC SECRETARIAT, UNITED NATIONS FRAMEWORK CONVENTION ON CLIMATE CHANGE: THE FIRST 10 YEARS 24 (2004).

[12] WORLD RESOURCES INSTITUTE, *supra* note 2, at 13.

the combined increase from Brazil, India, Indonesia, and Mexico over this period.[13] It is worth noting that a comparatively small number of countries produce the largest share of global GHG emissions: 25 countries account for around 83 percent of global emissions.[14] Some 140 countries contribute only 10 percent of annual emissions. Until recently, the United States was the largest emitter in absolute terms, with 21 percent of global $CO_2$ emissions; some analyses suggest that China surpassed the United States in 2006, much earlier than had been expected.[15] On a per capita basis, however, developing regions continue to emit far less $CO_2$ than developed regions. Australia, the United States, and Canada rank in the top 10 countries with the highest per capita emissions: more than twice the emissions of the European Union, 6 times those of China, and 13 times those of India.[16] An individual in sub-Saharan Africa accounts for roughly one-tenth of the $CO_2$ produced by an average person in the developed world.[17]

GHG emissions are closely related to economic growth. An important factor is whether growth is concentrated in sectors with high energy intensity (the ratio of energy use to GDP), such as steel making, or the service sector. Generally, energy intensity often depends on a country's stage of development – energy use per unit of output may rise as a society shifts from traditional to commercial forms of energy, begins to industrialize, and makes greater use of motor vehicles.[18] In turn, as industrialization proceeds, growth in economic output outstrips energy use, and energy intensity declines – this is the path observed in developed countries as well as more recently in developing countries. (Declining energy intensity is not the same as declining energy demand.) To track the extent to which countries are (or are not) decarbonizing their economies, analysts also calculate carbon intensity – the ratio of $CO_2$ emissions to gross domestic product. Generally

---

[13] See id.
[14] See id. at 11.
[15] China Contributing Two Thirds to Increase in $CO_2$ Emissions, press release, Netherlands Environment Assessment Agency, June 13, 2008. See also $CO_2$ Emissions Booming, Shifting East, Researchers Report, press release, Oak Ridge National Laboratory, September, 24 2008. (Reporting latest estimates by the Carbon Dioxide Information Analysis Center of $CO_2$ emissions from fossil fuel combustion and cement production and noting that emissions numbers are subject to some uncertainty – about 5 percent for the United States, but possibly as much as 20 percent for China.)
[16] See id. at 21.
[17] INTERNATIONAL ENERGY AGENCY, supra note 10, at 48.
[18] WORLD ENERGY ASSESSMENT: OVERVIEW 2004 UPDATE 2 (José Goldemberg & Thomas B. Johansson eds., 2004).

declining energy intensity equals declining carbon intensity, but two countries with the same energy efficiency will have different carbon intensities if one of them has a significant share of low- or no-carbon energy sources, such as nuclear and renewables, and the other does not. Declining measures of energy and carbon intensity are thus prerequisite for meeting climate stabilization targets. Disconcertingly, data suggest that nearly constant or slightly increasing trends in the carbon intensity of energy have recently been observed in both developed and developing regions; this represents a reversal of trends in the decade 1990–2000.[19] The greater reliance on coal, which is more carbon-intensive ("dirtier") than oil and gas, was a key contributor in this respect. The data show that over the period from 2000 to 2005, coal use worldwide increased by 4.8 percent in developed countries and 9.5 percent in developing countries, outstripping demand for oil and gas.[20] During this period, for instance, the share of coal in China's energy mix increased from 56 percent to 62 percent, against the backdrop of surging energy demand. The global emissions growth rate since 2000, at 3.3 percent per year, has exceeded that for the most fossil fuel–intensive scenario of the IPCC.[21] Not surprisingly, emissions during this period are also not in line with trajectories that would stabilize atmospheric $CO_2$ at midrange (450 ppm) and higher (650 ppm) levels.

## 2.3. KEY FINDINGS OF THE INTERGOVERNMENTAL PANEL ON CLIMATE CHANGE (IPCC)

The scientific consensus is reflected in the reports of the IPCC. The latest reports date from 2007. The IPCC carries out its scientific assessment via three thematic working groups (WG) addressing (1) the scientific basis for climate change (WGI); (2) impacts, adaptation, and vulnerability (WGII); and (3) mitigation (WGIII). The Second Assessment Report, issued in 1995,

---

[19] Gregg Marland et al., *Global and Regional Drivers of Accelerating CO₂ Emissions*, 104(24) PROCEEDINGS OF THE NATIONAL ACADEMY OF SCIENCES OF THE UNITED STATES OF AMERICA 10288 (2008).
[20] INTERNATIONAL ENERGY AGENCY, WORLD ENERGY OUTLOOK 2007: CHINA AND INDIA INSIGHTS 90 (2007).
[21] MARLAND ET AL., *supra* note 19, at 10289. This is the A1F1 scenario, which represents a world heavily reliant on fossil fuels. *See* INTERGOVERNMENTAL PANEL ON CLIMATE CHANGE, SPECIAL REPORT ON EMISSIONS SCENARIOS (2000).

stated that "the balance of evidence suggests a discernible human influence on global climate."[22] By the time of the Third Assessment Report, issued in 2001, the IPCC concluded that "in the light of new evidence and taking into account the remaining uncertainties, most of the observed warming over the past 50 years is likely to have been due to the increase in greenhouse gas concentrations."[23] (In the parlance of the IPCC, *likely* denotes a 60 to 90 percent likelihood.) The 2007 Fourth Assessment Report described warming of the climate system as "unequivocal," based on increases in global average air and ocean temperatures and other observations.[24] And it is "very likely" in other words, there is a greater than 90 percent likelihood, that most of the warming is due to the increase in the concentration of GHGs from human activities.[25]

Among the other key findings of the IPCC in the fourth assessment report are the following:

- The last 12 years (1995–2006) rank as among the 12 warmest since measurements of surface temperatures began in 1850.
- Warming during the past 100 years was 0.74 degrees Celsius, with most of the warming occurring during the past 50 years. The warming for the next 20 years is projected to be 0.2 degrees Celsius per decade.
- The global increases in atmospheric carbon dioxide concentrations are due to fossil fuel use and land-use changes (deforestation).
- Atmospheric concentrations of carbon dioxide in 2005 exceeded, by far, the natural range over the past 650,000 years.
- Various long-term changes in climate have been observed, including rising Arctic temperatures and reduced sea ice; an increase in the frequency of heavy precipitation events (flooding); and changes in extreme temperatures (more hot days and heat waves).

---

[22] INTERGOVERNMENTAL PANEL ON CLIMATE CHANGE, CLIMATE CHANGE 1995: THE SCIENCE OF CLIMATE CHANGE. CONTRIBUTION OF WORKING GROUP I TO THE SECOND ASSESSMENT REPORT OF THE INTERGOVERNMENTAL PANEL ON CLIMATE CHANGE (John Houghton et al. eds., 1996).
[23] INTERGOVERNMENTAL PANEL ON CLIMATE CHANGE, CLIMATE CHANGE 2001: THE SCIENTIFIC BASIS. CONTRIBUTION OF WORKING GROUP I TO THE THIRD ASSESSMENT REPORT OF THE INTERGOVERNMENTAL PANEL ON CLIMATE CHANGE 10 (John Houghton et al. eds., 2001).
[24] INTERGOVERNMENTAL PANEL ON CLIMATE CHANGE, *supra* note 1, at 5.
[25] *See id.* at 5, 10.

In understanding temperature projections, a number of things ought to be borne in mind: first, this is a global average, meaning that some regions, such as the subarctic regions, have warmed by as much as double that[26]; second, this warming is likely to have been the largest of any century during the past 1,000 years; third, ecological systems, and the social systems dependent on them, are complex and sensitive so that even seemingly small shifts in temperature may have unpredictable consequences.

## 2.4. CLIMATE IMPACTS

Human systems that are sensitive to climate change include water resources, agriculture and forestry, fisheries, human settlements, and human health. Projected impacts are largely negative – aside from increased potential crop yields in some regions at midlatitude, increased water supply in some water-scarce regions, such as Southeast Asia, and reduced energy demand for space heating due to higher winter temperatures.[27] Potential adverse impacts include a general reduction in crop yields in most tropical and subtropical regions; decreased water availability in many water-scarce regions, particularly in the subtropics; an increase in the number of people exposed to vector-borne diseases (malaria) and waterborne diseases, and increases in heat stress mortality; a widespread increase in the risk of flooding from heavy precipitation events and sea-level rise; and increased energy demand for space cooling due to higher summer temperatures.[28]

According to the IPCC, by mid-century, annual average river runoff and water availability will increase at high latitudes and in some wet tropical areas, but will decrease by 10 to 30 percent over some dry regions at midlatitudes and in the dry tropics. Some of the affected areas are water stressed and coincide with regions where poverty is widespread, for example, Africa. Provision of clean drinking water is a key challenge in developing countries, where currently some 1.1 billion people lack access to safe water and 2.6 billion lack access to improved sanitation. Linked to this are 4 billion cases of

---

[26] *See id.* at 7.
[27] INTERGOVERNMENTAL PANEL ON CLIMATE CHANGE, CLIMATE CHANGE 2007: IMPACTS, ADAPTATION AND VULNERABILITY. CONTRIBUTION OF WORKING GROUP II TO THE FOURTH ASSESSMENT REPORT OF THE INTERGOVERNMENTAL PANEL ON CLIMATE CHANGE (Martin L. Parry et al. eds., 2007).
[28] *See id.* at 16.

diarrhea per year, which cause 1.8 million deaths, mostly among children under five.[29]

Climate change will also have an uneven impact on food production. Moderate temperature increases will see a rise in productivity at the global level, but at lower latitudes, especially seasonally dry and tropical regions, crop productivity is projected to decrease for even small local temperature increases (1 to 2 degrees Celsius), increasing the risk of hunger.[30] Increased $CO_2$ concentrations stimulate crop growth and yield, but the negative effects of heat and drought may counteract this effect. Recent research that compared actual data on rice yields and temperatures over 25 years found that crop yields had dropped by 10 percent.[31] In some African countries, yields from rain-fed agriculture could be reduced by up to 50 percent by 2020. Farmers in such areas are unlikely to be able to afford adaptive technologies such as improved irrigation or new cultivars.

There is evidence that climate change is already having adverse impacts on health, for instance, in the case of increased mortality from heat waves.[32] Projected health impacts of climate are likely to affect millions of people, particularly the poor and those lacking access to medical care, through increased deaths resulting from heat waves and a higher incidence of waterborne disease such as diarrhea. While it is true, as is sometimes contended, that public health interventions can cope with the spread of diseases resulting from climate change, this cannot necessarily be said of developing countries characterized by weak public health systems.

A range of natural systems – the IPCC specifically mentions coral reefs, glaciers, atolls, and mangroves – are at risk from climate change. A key factor in determining impact is the rate of change – in many cases, ecosystems that have, in the past, adapted to gradual temperature change may simply

---

[29] UNICEF & WORLD HEALTH ORGANIZATION, MEETING THE MDG DRINKING WATER AND SANITATION TARGET: A MID-TERM ASSESSMENT (2004).

[30] INTERGOVERNMENTAL PANEL ON CLIMATE CHANGE, *supra* note 27, at 11.

[31] The fact that warming leads to increased nighttime temperatures, when rice plants respire, is behind the adverse impact. *See* Fred Pearce, *Rice Yields Plummet Due to Balmy Nights*, NEW SCIENTIST, June 29, 2004, available at http://www.newscientist.com/news/news.jsp?id=ns99996082; Shaobing Peng et al., *Rice Yields Decline with Higher Night Temperature from Global Warming*, 101(27) PROCEEDINGS OF THE NATIONAL ACADEMY OF SCIENCES OF THE UNITED STATES OF AMERICA 9971 (2004).

[32] INTERGOVERNMENTAL PANEL ON CLIMATE CHANGE, *supra* note 27, at 9.

## 2.4. Climate Impacts

not be able to adapt to such comparatively rapid change. Understanding the adaptive capacity of ecosystems is complex, and research indicates that climate change is already having an impact on biodiversity and could rival habitat destruction as a cause of extinctions.[33] In coral reefs, mild temperature changes, in the range of 1 to 2 degrees Celsius, can result in *bleaching* – the expulsion of the symbiotic algae that nourish the coral polyps.[34] A majority of corals are expected to exceed their bleaching thresholds by 2030 to 2050.[35] Furthermore, recent studies suggest that the absorption of $CO_2$ by the oceans has reduced the natural alkalinity of seawater, which could have a negative effect on the reef-building ability of corals and shell production among some mollusks and plankton.[36] On land, fragile mountain ecosystems also face rapid change.[37] The IPCC states that there has been a widespread retreat of mountain glaciers in nonpolar regions during the twentieth century.[38] In the Andes, it is estimated that glaciers have retreated by as much as 25 percent in the last 30 years, which could mean water shortages in the future.[39]

According to the IPCC, the global mean sea level is projected to rise by between 0.18 and 0.59 meters by the last decade of the twenty-first century, largely due to the thermal expansion of the oceans and freshwater

---

[33] James Gorman, *Scientists Predict Widespread Extinction by Global Warming*, NEW YORK TIMES, January 8, 2004, at A4. MILLENNIUM ECOSYSTEM ASSESSMENT, ECOSYSTEMS AND HUMAN WELL-BEING: CURRENT STATE AND TRENDS, FINDINGS OF THE CONDITION AND TRENDS WORKING GROUP (2005).

[34] ROBERT W. BUDDEMEIER ET AL., CORAL REEFS AND GLOBAL CLIMATE CHANGE: POTENTIAL CONTRIBUTIONS OF CLIMATE CHANGE TO STRESSES ON CORAL REEF ECOSYSTEMS, report prepared for the Pew Center on Global Climate Change (2004).

[35] INTERGOVERNMENTAL PANEL ON CLIMATE CHANGE, *supra* note 27, at 235.

[36] Andrew C. Revkin, *Carbon Dioxide Extends Its Harmful Reach to Oceans*, NEW YORK TIMES, July 20, 2004, F3. *See also* SABINE ET AL., *supra* note 7, at 367–71; Richard A. Feely et al., *The Impact of Anthropogenic $CO_2$ on the $CaCO_3$ System in the Oceans*, 305(5682) SCIENCE 362 (2004).

[37] E.g., alpine meadows in the Rocky Mountains are likely to disappear. *See* U.S. DEPARTMENT OF STATE, THE UNITED STATES OF AMERICA'S THIRD NATIONAL COMMUNICATION UNDER THE UNITED NATIONS FRAMEWORK CONVENTION ON CLIMATE CHANGE (2002). Andean cloud forests, a biodiversity hotspot, are another example of an ecosystem at immediate risk. *See* Mark B. Bush et al., *48,000 Years of Climate and Forest Change in a Biodiversity Hot Spot*, 303(5659) SCIENCE 827 (2004).

[38] INTERGOVERNMENTAL PANEL ON CLIMATE CHANGE, *supra* note 1, at 5.

[39] Juan Forero, *As Andean Glaciers Shrink, Water Worries Grow*, NEW YORK TIMES, November 24, 2002, at A3.

inflows from melting glaciers and ice caps.[40] More recent research, drawing on the dynamics of glaciers and ice sheets, suggests that sea-level rise is likely to substantially exceed these projections.[41] Low-lying islands and the megadeltas of Africa (Nile) and Asia (Bangladesh) are most at risk from rising seas. The effects of rising sea levels and storm surges are already being experienced in the form of accelerated coastal erosion, forcing some communities to contemplate retreat from the ocean or the construction of costly coastal defenses.[42] Rising sea levels from thermal expansion are projected to continue for hundreds of years after the stabilization of GHG concentrations (even at present levels), as a consequence of the time it takes for the deep ocean layers to adjust to warming. Similarly, melting ice sheets will feed rising sea levels thousands of years after emissions have stabilized. While recent years have witnessed dramatic collapses of ice shelves – masses of floating ice that are extensions of terrestrial ice sheets – these do not have any effect on sea levels.[43] If fully melted, the Antarctic and Greenland ice sheets hold enough water to raise global sea levels by 64 meters.[44] Recent research suggests that the Antarctic ice sheet appears to be losing mass, in part due to accelerated ice flows, but significant uncertainty remains.[45] There is somewhat greater certainty that loss of ice mass is occurring in Greenland, driven by increased melting and accelerated ice flow.[46]

---

[40] INTERGOVERNMENTAL PANEL ON CLIMATE CHANGE, *supra* note 1, at 13–14. Sea-level estimates from the Fourth Assessment are for 2090–2099.
[41] CLIMATE CHANGE SCIENCE PROGRAM, ABRUPT CLIMATE CHANGE: A REPORT BY THE U.S. CLIMATE CHANGE SCIENCE PROGRAM AND THE SUBCOMMITTEE ON GLOBAL CHANGE RESEARCH (2008). See also Stefan Rahmsdorf, *A Semi-empirical Approach to Projecting Future Sea-Level Rise*, 315 SCIENCE 368 (2007).
[42] *Massachusetts v. EPA*, 127 S. Ct. 1438 (2007). The Court found that the Commonwealth of Massachusetts had standing to sue the Environmental Protection Agency for denial of a rulemaking petition under the Clean Air Act, based on actual and imminent harm, including damage to coastal areas caused by rising sea levels.
[43] The Larsen B ice shelf in Antarctica, 200 meters thick and 3,250 square kilometers in size, collapsed suddenly in March 2002. See Andrew C. Revkin, *Large Ice Shelf in Antarctica Disintegrates at Great Speed*, NEW YORK TIMES, March 20, 2002, at A13.
[44] INTERGOVERNMENTAL PANEL ON CLIMATE CHANGE, *supra* note 1, at 361.
[45] See id. at 361.
[46] Andrew C. Revkin, *An Icy Riddle as Big as Greenland*, NEW YORK TIMES, June 8, 2004, at F1. Research indicates that inland melting can have outsized effects on the ice sheets because meltwater formed on the surface percolates down through cracks in the ice, acting like a lubricant and causing ice to slide more smoothly over the bedrock and onward to the sea.

## 2.4. Climate Impacts

Besides raising sea levels, the inflow of freshwater from the melting Greenland ice cap could contribute to a slowing of the ocean conveyor during the twenty-first century, but a halt is regarded as unlikely.[47] The ocean circulation occurs as cold, dense water near Iceland and Greenland sinks, and flows southward in the deep as warm water from the tropics drifts slowly northward nearer the surface, allowing northern Europe to enjoy a climate significantly milder than it otherwise would given its latitude. A weakening of the circulation would lead to a reduction of heat transport to the Northern Hemisphere, but models nonetheless project a warming over Europe due to increased GHGs.[48] There is some evidence that salinity in the deep water of the North Atlantic and Arctic has decreased, with increased salinity observed in the tropical Atlantic.[49] Other irreversible changes with major impacts but low probabilities include accelerated global warming due to carbon cycle feedbacks in the terrestrial biosphere and releases of terrestrial carbon from permafrost regions and methane from hydrates in coastal sediments.[50]

Potentially serious impacts may also result from the increase in climate extremes, as reflected in the damage caused by droughts, floods, heat waves, and windstorms. The IPCC states that it is very likely (greater than 90 percent likelihood) that hot extremes, heat waves, and heavy precipitation events will increase in frequency.[51] Although it is not possible to establish a clear, deterministic causal link between specific instances of more extreme or frequent extreme events and climate change, it is likely that the increase, in some areas, in droughts and more intense high precipitation events is the result of climate change. Thus it is possible to estimate how much human

---

[47] INTERGOVERNMENTAL PANEL ON CLIMATE CHANGE, *supra* note 1, at 16.
[48] *See id.*
[49] *See* Bob Dickson et al., *Rapid Freshening of the Deep North Atlantic Ocean over the Past Four Decades*, 416 NATURE 832 (2002); Bogi Hansen, *Decreasing Overflow from the Nordic Seas into the Atlantic Ocean through the Faroe Bank Channel since 1950*, 411 NATURE 927 (2001). Researchers found that hydrographic records and other observations show that the flows of cold, dense water from near Greenland and Iceland to the Atlantic had decreased. The water that cools and becomes dense near Greenland sinks, but before it can drive the circulation effectively, it must push cold bottom water over the sills of the Greenland-Scotland ridge and into the deep Atlantic.
[50] INTERGOVERNMENTAL PANEL ON CLIMATE CHANGE, CLIMATE CHANGE 2001: IMPACTS, ADAPTATION, AND VULNERABILITY. CONTRIBUTION OF WG II TO THE THIRD ASSESSMENT REPORT OF THE INTERGOVERNMENTAL PANEL ON CLIMATE CHANGE 6 (Osvaldo F. Canziani et al. eds., 2001).
[51] INTERGOVERNMENTAL PANEL ON CLIMATE CHANGE, *supra* note 1, at 15.

activities may have increased the risk of the occurrence of a heat wave, such as the heat wave of summer 2003, which saw record temperatures across Europe.[52] The heat wave was blamed for unusually high mortality in France and elsewhere in Europe.[53] By the reckoning of the insurance industry, there has been an increase in the frequency of extreme weather events and a concomitant increase in losses from weather-related events.

Climate change will have a disproportionate effect on developing countries, especially the least developed countries. The reasons for this are twofold. First, the ability of human systems to adapt to and cope with climate change depends on factors such as wealth, technology, education, skills, infrastructure, access to resources, and management capabilities. For instance, while the Netherlands, with some half of its surface area below sea level, has the resources to further enhance its very extensive (and expensive) system of dykes and controls, a nation such as Bangladesh simply cannot afford similar protective measures. Developing countries lack adaptive capacity and are more vulnerable to climate change, as they are to other stresses. Second, regional projections, although not perfect, provide an outline of more severe impacts in regions where most developing countries are situated. Examples are the likelihood of increased drying over midlatitude continental interiors, with decreased water availability in water-scarce regions; a reduction in crop yields in most tropical and subtropical regions; and flooding from heavier rainfall as well as sea-level rise, which is already impacting island states. Populations reliant on rain-fed subsistence agriculture that lack access to technology (drought-resistant crops) and live in geographical areas that will be hard hit (such sub-Saharan Africa) are therefore doubly at risk. The distribution of impacts and the relative capacity to adapt squarely raise questions of fairness and sustainable development.

---

[52] Peter A. Stott et al., *Human Contribution to the European Heatwave of 2003*, 432 NATURE 610 (2004).

[53] The French Health Ministry estimated that there were an estimated 11,435 additional deaths during the first two weeks of August than in the same period during recent years. INSTITUT DE VEILLE SANITAIRE, IMPACT SANITAIRE DE LA VAGUE DE CHALEUR D'AOÛT 2003 EN FRANCE: BILAN ET PERSPECTIVES 57 (2004), available at http://www.invs.sante.fr/publications/2003/bilan_chaleur_1103/index.html. According to the insurer Munich Re, the heat wave caused some 20,000 deaths in Europe and resulted in property damages of US$13 billion. *See* MUNICH RE, TOPICSGEO ANNUAL REVIEW: NATURAL CATASTROPHES 2003 23 (2004), available at http://www.munichre.com/publications/302-03971_en.pdf.

## 2.5. UNCERTAINTIES AND FEEDBACKS

Scientists studying climate change are usually quick to acknowledge the uncertainties that accompany their findings. One key area of uncertainty is the precise warming of the climate system in response to the external forcing caused by human-induced GHG emissions. The so-called climate sensitivity can be expressed as the warming for doubled $CO_2$ (i.e., from 280 to 560 ppm); the IPCC currently puts the likely range between 2.0 and 4.5 degrees Celsius, with a best estimate of 3 degrees Celsius.[54] Although much less likely, values above 4.5 degrees Celsius cannot be excluded. Uncertainty about climate sensitivity constitutes a strong basis for near-term mitigation action. Warming at the upper end of this range, more likely for tripling of $CO_2$, could very well trigger large-scale, irreversible events, such as massive flooding from melting of the Antarctic ice sheets, with a dramatic effect on human and natural systems. While future climate change was once regarded as a gradual warming, it is now accepted that abrupt, nonlinear change is a possibility. Abrupt climate change can occur when the earth system is pushed across a threshold, either by a natural occurrence, such as a volcanic eruption, or possibly by forcing from anthropogenic emissions.[55] Scientists and policy makers alike face challenges when dealing with uncertainty. It is difficult to incorporate low-probability, high-impact events into models and assessments so that most researchers produce analyses that are essentially surprise-free.[56]

At times, the media, when they take note of the issue, seize on the remote, catastrophic possibilities, ignoring the less headline-grabbing aspects of climate change. There is also a tendency to equate local experiences of extreme weather events with climate change; global warming entered the public consciousness in the United States in 1988, in the middle of a heat wave, and a more recent surge in interest can probably in part be attributed to Hurricane Katrina as well as to the Al Gore documentary *An Inconvenient Truth*. In

---

[54] INTERGOVERNMENTAL PANEL ON CLIMATE CHANGE, *supra* note 1, at 799.
[55] *See* CLIMATE CHANGE SCIENCE PROGRAM, *supra* note 41. *See also* NATIONAL ACADEMY OF SCIENCES, ABRUPT CLIMATE CHANGE: INEVITABLE SURPRISES (2002).
[56] Stephen H. Schneider & Kirstin Kuntz-Duriseti, *Uncertainty and Climate Change Policy*, *in* CLIMATE CHANGE POLICY: A SURVEY 58 (Stephen H. Schneider et al. eds., 2002).

many cases, scientists, while in agreement that change is occurring, may disagree about whether specific changes are largely or only in part attributable to climate change; the timescales involved; and the probability of projected changes. The process of testing hypotheses leaves specific questions unanswered, with contradictory explanations being posited, to be resolved only through new observations or improved computer modeling. The existence of complex interactions and feedbacks in the climate system sometimes contributes to the lack of ready-made and definitive answers. For example, scientists may be reluctant to conclude that any given temperature is "safe," putting them at odds with policy makers and politicians. This should not, however, detract from the urgent need for action, particularly because in many cases, climate impacts will be irreversible. Early action also constitutes a form of insurance against climate surprises.

## 2.6. THE SCIENCE AND THE IPCC IN CONTEXT

The IPCC is an intergovernmental body, carrying out a scientific assessment function; participation is open to all member countries of the UN Environment Programme (UNEP) and the World Meteorological Organization (WMO).[57] The IPCC was established in 1988 under the auspices of UNEP and WMO as an intergovernmental mechanism to carry out internationally coordinated scientific assessments of the magnitude, impact, and potential timing of climate change.[58] Key among the early decisions made was to

---

[57] PRINCIPLES GOVERNING IPCC WORK, approved at the Fourteenth Session (Vienna, October 1–3, 1998) on October 1, 1998, and amended at the Twenty-First Session (Vienna, November 3 and 6–7, 2003), available at http://www.ipcc.ch/about/procd.htm.

[58] REPORT OF THE THIRTY-NINTH SESSION OF THE EXECUTIVE COUNCIL, JUNE 1–5, 1987, WMO Doc. 687, 7 (1987). UNEP: REPORT OF THE GOVERNING COUNCIL, UN GOAR, Forty-Second Sess., Supp. No. 25, UN Doc. A/42/25 (1987). See also Jack Fitzgerald, *The Intergovernmental Panel on Climate Change: Taking the First Steps towards a Global Response*, 14 SOUTHERN ILLINOIS UNIVERSITY LAW JOURNAL 231 (1990). Ahead of the first meeting of the IPCC in November 1988, Malta introduced an agenda item titled "Conservation of Climate as Part of the Common Heritage of Mankind" in the UN General Assembly, and the resolution adopted endorsed the decision to establish the IPCC and requested the secretary-general of the WMO and the Executive Director of UNEP, through the IPCC, to begin a comprehensive review and make recommendations on, among other things, the state of knowledge of climate change, impacts of climate change, and possible response strategies. GA Res. 43/53, paras. 5 and 10, UN Doc. A/RES/43/53. The draft resolution referred to the climate as the "common heritage of mankind," but this was later changed to refer to climate change as the "common concern of mankind" (para. 1).

## 2.6. The Science and the IPCC in Context

bestow a comprehensive assessment mandate on the IPCC, covering the science, the impacts of climate change, and responses.[59]

Reports of the IPCC are subjected to both peer and government review. The panel, its WGs, and its task forces endeavor to reach decisions on the basis of consensus. Where this is not possible in relation to reports, differing views are explained; disagreements on scientific, technical, or socioeconomic questions are to be appropriately represented in the relevant document.[60] Its plenary (the panel) consists of government representatives, who usually meet at least once a year. As is the norm for UN intergovernmental bodies, the IPCC is headed by a bureau, which includes the chair and three vice chairs. Two co-chairs and a number of vice chairs head each of the three WGs.[61] Membership in the bureaus of the IPCC and its WGs is by election; elections are held approximately every five years. Unlike plenary sessions of the panel, where governmental representatives are present, bureau members are in the first order scientific and technical experts and are not acting under instructions from their countries of nationality. Nonetheless, they are selected on the basis of a regional formula to provide for geographic balance; furthermore, for some time, it has been the practice that one co-chair of each WG should be from a developing country. The work of the IPCC is organized around assessment cycles, with assessment reports being published about twice a decade. Since its establishment, the IPCC has completed four assessment reports – the first in 1990 and the most recent in 2007.

Assessment reports consist of two parts: the scientific and technical analysis, containing details of the science, and the much less technical summary for policy makers (SPM). This summary is intended to be a policy-neutral and more accessible document outlining the key points contained in the underlying report.[62] The two different types of outputs are subject to

---

[59] SHARDUL AGRAWALA, EXPLAINING THE EVOLUTION OF THE IPCC STRUCTURE AND PROCESS, ENRP Discussion Paper E-97-05, Kennedy School of Government 9 (1997). See also Shardul Agrawala, Early Science-Policy Interactions in Climate Change: Lessons from the Advisory Group on Greenhouse Gases, 9(2) GLOBAL ENVIRONMENTAL CHANGE: HUMAN AND POLICY DIMENSIONS 157 (1999).

[60] PRINCIPLES GOVERNING IPCC WORK, supra note 57.

[61] REPORT OF THE NINETEENTH SESSION OF THE INTERGOVERNMENTAL PANEL ON CLIMATE CHANGE, Geneva, Switzerland, September 17–20, 2002, Appendix H, available at http://www.ipcc.ch/meet/rep19session.pdf.

[62] Aside from Assessment Reports, the other materials are Synthesis, Special Reports and Methodology Reports, with the former two also being accompanied by a separate SPM.

different formal levels of endorsement. Thus, in the last part of the review process, IPCC reports are accepted at a session of the relevant WG, where all member countries are represented. Acceptance means that the material has not been subject to a line-by-line discussion and agreement, but that it nevertheless presents a comprehensive, objective, and balanced view of the subject matter. By contrast, the SPM are subject to line-by-line approval by government representatives in plenary sessions of the panel. It is here that governments negotiate over every word in an arduous process.[63]

The point has been made that international environmental agreements are distinguished from most other types of international agreements by their reliance on science and technology.[64] Scientific findings have played a key role in identifying and defining the existence of transboundary environmental issues as well as outlining options for mitigation and protection of the environment. The use of scientific advice and monitoring has a long history in international law.[65] The IPCC may be regarded against the backdrop of the increased implications of science in policy making. This trend has, for some time, been well advanced at the national level in liberal democratic states, as seen in public debates around risks from toxic chemicals and environmental regulation in general. At the international level, the interlinkage between science and policy making reached a new level with the negotiation of the Montreal Protocol.[66] With greater reliance on the output of scientific expert bodies, the working methods and procedures have become increasingly formalized, with application of stricter legal procedures; the IPCC has thus adopted formal peer review procedures.

Efforts also have been made to enhance the diversity of the panel by ensuring balanced representation from developed and developing countries,

---

[63] For a view on the 2007 Fourth Assessment Report, see Andrew C. Revkin, *Melding Science and Diplomacy to Run a Global Climate Review*, NEW YORK TIMES, February 6, 2007.

[64] Sheila Jasanoff, *Contingent Knowledge: Implications for Implementation and Compliance*, in ENGAGING COUNTRIES: STRENGTHENING COMPLIANCE WITH INTERNATIONAL ENVIRONMENTAL ACCORDS 63 (Edith Brown Weiss & Harold K. Jacobson eds., 1998).

[65] *See*, e.g., LEE A. KIMBALL, TREATY IMPLEMENTATION: SCIENCE AND TECHNICAL ADVICE ENTERS A NEW STAGE (1996). She cites as early examples of international scientific bodies the International Council for the Exploration of the Sea, established in 1902 to promote marine observations in the North Atlantic. She also notes that the 1946 International Convention for the Regulation of Whaling appears to be the first to explicitly link the collection and analysis of data to the management of whale fisheries and the first also to require that conservation measures "be based on scientific findings."

[66] RICHARD ELLIOT BENEDICK, OZONE DIPLOMACY 7 (1991).

## 2.6. The Science and the IPCC in Context

which is critical to acceptance by developing countries of the work of the IPCC. After early experiences with the framing of the climate change debate, developing countries are keenly aware of how important it is to participate, to the fullest extent possible, in a body such as the IPCC.[67] It has been pointed out that reliance on peer-reviewed literature potentially discriminates against scientific input from countries whose scientists do not have the opportunity to have their research published in peer-reviewed journals.[68] In its more recent reports, the IPCC also has broadened its consideration of the economic and social dimensions of climate change with respect to both drivers of change and impacts. A genuine attempt has been made to take a multidisciplinary approach to investigate climate change, as evidenced by the use of cross-cutting themes such as sustainable development. This is important because it is increasingly recognized that underlying development pathways – not climate policies on their own – are the most important determinant of future emissions.

The IPCC has been remarkably successful in preparing policy-relevant scientific assessments, even as the area of work with which it is concerned has become politically contentious. In accordance with its mandate as an assessment body charged with periodically taking stock of the latest science, it has consciously steered clear of overtly presenting policy prescriptions. Its assessments have enormous influence and are accepted by most scientists and governments as authoritative. However, its conclusions have been disputed and its working methods attacked by a small group of so-called skeptics as well as by various interest groups.[69] In this politicized atmosphere, it is not surprising that a former Executive Secretary of the Secretariat of the UN Framework Convention on Climate Change (UNFCCC) has stated that "[t]he science has driven the politics.... If the science is to continue guiding the politics, it is essential to keep the politics out of the science."[70]

---

[67] See FRANK BIERMANN, SCIENCE AS POWER IN INTERNATIONAL NEGOTIATIONS: GLOBAL ENVIRONMENTAL ASSESSMENTS BETWEEN NORTH AND SOUTH, ENRP Discussion Paper 2000-17, Belfer Center for Science and International Affairs 2 (2000).

[68] NATIONAL ACADEMY OF SCIENCES, KNOWLEDGE AND DIPLOMACY: SCIENCE ADVICE IN THE UNITED NATIONS SYSTEM 41 (2002).

[69] For details of the relationships between skeptics and industry-funded lobby groups, see ROSS GELBSPAN, THE HEAT IS ON (1998); JEREMY K. LEGGETT, THE CARBON WAR: GLOBAL WARMING AND THE END OF THE OIL ERA (2001).

[70] Michael Zammit Cutajar, quoted in TIM FORSYTH, CRITICAL POLITICAL ECOLOGY: THE POLITICS OF ENVIRONMENTAL SCIENCE 1 (2003).

It is easy to sympathize with this plea. However, one must ask whether an institution – more precisely, an *intergovernmental* panel whose membership includes countries with such divergent interests with respect to climate change as Antigua and Barbuda, China, the European Union, Saudi Arabia, and the United States – can realistically steer clear of politics. Its synthesis reports are subject to line-by-line negotiations by government lawyers. Government representatives elect the chair of the panel as well as the scientists who head up the WGs. The IPCC operates in a political environment.

There is a general conception of science as neutral territory apart from politics, which is consistent with a model of decision making that characterizes science as a source of objective knowledge for informing and rationalizing policy choices.[71] A more recent strand of research on science and technology conceives of them as being socially embedded; that is, science and technology are social institutions, influenced by context.[72] Such conceptions are particularly relevant for understanding and analyzing the IPCC. Although the IPCC is engaged in producing assessments, and not prescriptions, it is situated at the interface between science and politics. Some scholars of science, skeptical of a clear divide between the production of scientific knowledge, on one hand, and policy, on the other, have referred to *coproduction* to explain the mutual evolution of science and politics.[73] The term refers to the ways in which knowledge, including scientific knowledge, is "framed, collected, and disseminated through social interaction" and how such knowledge, in turn, also impacts social change.[74] Importantly, acknowledging the social influence on science does not entail an inevitable descent into relativism and devaluation of the basic precepts of the natural sciences.

The IPCC has managed to maintain credibility in relation to two very different constituencies: the scientists making up its core membership and the global policy community.[75] Independent self-governance, more

---

[71] JASANOFF, *supra* note 64, at 64.
[72] *Id.* at 65.
[73] Sheila Jasanoff, *Beyond Epistemology: Relativism and Engagement in the Politics of Science*, 26(2) SOCIAL STUDIES OF SCIENCE 393, 397 (1996). *See also* SHEILA JASANOFF, THE FIFTH BRANCH: SCIENCE ADVISERS AS POLICYMAKERS (1990).
[74] FORSYTH, *supra* note 70, at 104.
[75] Paul N. Edwards & Stephen H. Schneider, *Self-Governance and Peer Review in Science-for-Policy: The Case of the IPCC Second Assessment Report*, *in* CHANGING THE ATMOSPHERE: EXPERT KNOWLEDGE AND ENVIRONMENTAL GOVERNANCE 225 (Clark A. Miller & Paul N. Edwards eds., 2001).

## 2.6. The Science and the IPCC in Context

specifically, peer review, has proved critical in maintaining the credibility of the IPCC. Thus the IPCC has managed to dynamically straddle the junction between science and politics, on one hand producing syntheses of the latest science that are a balanced reflection of the latest scientific knowledge and, on the other, producing SPMs that satisfy divergent views of member governments and remain consistent with the science. Although some may maintain that this process entails some compromises, the very involvement and final imprimatur of governments gives the reports of IPCC credibility with a very important constituency – governments.

### 2.6.1. Stabilization Targets

The ultimate objective of the UNFCCC is the stabilization of atmospheric GHG concentrations at a safe level; as is often pointed out, the determination of a so-called safe level is guided by the science but remains, in the first place, a moral, ethical, and – in the final analysis – political question. Nonetheless, science can inform, guide, and set some of the parameters within which questions such as this ought to be addressed.[76] In the long run, and in rough terms, the absorptive capacity of the oceans and the terrestrial ecosystems determines the ultimate stabilization level for human carbon dioxide emissions. Importantly, stabilization of GHG concentrations does not equal stabilization of the climate – according to the IPCC, "warming and sea-level rise would continue for centuries due to the time scales associated with climate processes and feedbacks."[77]

The results of climate modeling reported in the IPCC Fourth Assessment provide that stabilization at 445 carbon dioxide equivalent ($CO_{2-eq}$) ppm would require that global emissions peak by 2015 and fall by 50 to 85 percent below 2000 levels by 2050 (see Table 2.1).[78] This represents a radical departure from business as usual, but even then, the resultant increase above preindustrial levels is projected to be in the range of 2 to 2.4 degrees Celsius. For reference, the European Union has proposed that the temperature increase should not exceed 2 degrees Celsius or 3 degrees Fahrenheit. Even

---

[76] Ann Kinzig et al., *Coping with Uncertainty: A Call for a New Science-Policy Forum*, 32(5) AMBIO 330 (2003).
[77] INTERGOVERNMENTAL PANEL ON CLIMATE CHANGE, *supra* note 1, at 16.
[78] Carbon dioxide equivalents, or [$CO_{2-eq}$], is a way of expressing the cumulative effect of $CO_2$ and the other GHGs.

TABLE 2.1. *Characteristics of post-IPCC Third Assessment Report stabilization scenarios*

| $CO_2$ concentration (ppm) | $CO_{2\text{-eq}}$ concentration (ppm) | Global mean temperature increase above preindustrial (degrees Celsius) | Year in which $CO_2$ emissions peak | Change in $CO_2$ emissions in 2050 (% of 2000 emissions) |
|---|---|---|---|---|
| 350–400 | 445–490 | 2.0–2.4 | 2000–2015 | −85 to −50 |
| 400–440 | 490–535 | 2.4–2.8 | 2000–2020 | −60 to −30 |
| 440–485 | 535–590 | 2.8–3.2 | 2010–2030 | −30 to +5 |
| 485–570 | 590–710 | 3.2–4.0 | 2020–2060 | +10 to +60 |

*Source:* Adapted from IPCC, 2007, WGIII, table SPM. 5

if a concentration target of 445 $CO_{2\text{-eq}}$ ppm is attained, the probability of exceeding 2 degrees Celsius still remains at just under 50 percent.[79]

### 2.6.2. *The Energy Challenge*

The energy challenge has a number of dimensions, only two of which will be discussed here. First, access to clean and affordable energy services remains heavily skewed in favor of developed countries, which raises questions of equity. Second, the stabilization of atmospheric GHG concentrations cannot be achieved without the transition to a low-carbon energy system, a shift that will need to take place against the backdrop of the aforementioned inequalities in access to energy services and, more broadly, development opportunities. Let us first turn to the issue of access to energy services.

Even as the early impacts of climate change are beginning to be felt, access to safe energy and effective energy remains largely out of reach in many developing countries. It is estimated that some 2 billion people – one-third of the world's population – rely almost completely on traditional energy sources (wood, charcoal, crop residues, and dung) and are unable to take advantage of modern forms of energy, such as electricity, that are taken

---

[79] Michel den Elzen & Malte Meinshausen, *Multi-gas Emission Pathways for Meeting the EU 2 Degree Celsius Climate Target*, in AVOIDING DANGEROUS CLIMATE CHANGE 299 (Hans Joachim Schellnhuber et al. eds., 2006).

## 2.6. The Science and the IPCC in Context 41

for granted in the developed world.[80] For instance, the combined rural and urban electrification rate for sub-Saharan Africa is 26 percent, while the figure for rural areas is only 8 percent.[81] Lacking access to modern energy services – electric lighting, clean cooking facilities, efficient and nonpolluting fuel supplies – the populations of many developing countries are unable to benefit from opportunities for economic development and increased living standards.[82] Access to modern energy is increasingly widely recognized as crucial to stepping out of poverty and for meeting the Millennium Development Goals (MDGs).[83] The MDGs are the international community's commitment to halving poverty in the world's poorest countries by 2015. Evidence from the field suggests that the benefits of access to modern energy services are real and significant. A recent World Bank cross-country study of rural electrification programs found that the development benefits – improved levels of education, reduced indoor air pollution, improved health services – considerably exceeded the costs of service.[84]

The role of energy in sustainable development and poverty reduction has been recognized in a number of UN declarations and other soft-law instruments. For example, the Johannesburg Plan of Implementation, adopted at the World Summit on Sustainable Development in 2002, refers extensively to energy in the context of sustainable development and highlights the need to enhance access to energy, including from renewable sources.[85] Similarly, the eighth Conference of the Parties to the UNFCCC in New Delhi in 2002 affirmed that "economic and social development and poverty eradication are the first and overriding priorities of developing country Parties" and that energy policies should be supportive of developing countries' efforts to eradicate poverty.[86] The resolution adopted at the 2005 World Summit of

---

[80] UN DEVELOPMENT PROGRAMME ET AL., WORLD ENERGY ASSESSMENT 3 (2000).
[81] INTERNATIONAL ENERGY AGENCY, WORLD ENERGY OUTLOOK 2006 567 (2006).
[82] Adrian Bradbrook et al., *A Human Dimension to the Energy Debate: Access to Modern Energy Services* 26(4) JOURNAL OF ENERGY & NATURAL RESOURCES LAW 526 (2008).
[83] VIJAY MODI ET AL., ENERGY SERVICES FOR THE MILLENNIUM DEVELOPMENT GOALS 1 (2005).
[84] THE WORLD BANK, THE WELFARE IMPACT OF RURAL ELECTRIFICATION: A REASSESSMENT OF COSTS AND BENEFITS, AN IEG IMPACT EVALUATION (2008).
[85] REPORT OF THE WORLD SUMMIT ON SUSTAINABLE DEVELOPMENT, Resolution 2, Annex, Plan of Implementation of the World Summit on Sustainable Development, paras. 19–20, UN Doc. A/CONF.199/20.
[86] Decision 1/CP.8, REPORT OF THE CONFERENCE OF THE PARTIES ON ITS EIGHTH SESSION, Addendum, Part II: Action Taken by the Parties, vol. 1, FCCC/CP/2002/7/Add.1.

TABLE 2.2. *Commercial primary energy use by region*

| Region | Million tonnes of oil equivalent (Mtoe) 2000 | 2007 | 2007 as share of world total (%) | Percentage growth 2000–2007 |
|---|---|---|---|---|
| North America | 2,737.5 | 2,838.6 | 25.7 | 3.37 |
| South and Central America | 456.2 | 552.9 | 5.0 | 20.4 |
| Middle East | 402.9 | 574.1 | 5.2 | 42.8 |
| Africa | 275.8 | 344.4 | 3.1 | 24.7 |
| Europe and Eurasia | 2,829.2 | 2,987.5 | 26.9 | 5.6 |
| Asia Pacific | 2,607.0 | 3,801.8 | 34.3 | 47.3 |
| **World Total** | **9,308.7** | **11,099.3** | **100** | **19.4** |
| EU 27* | 1,709.7 | 1,744.5 | 15.7 | 2 |
| OECD | 5,359.6 | 5,566.4 | 50.2 | 3.8 |
| Former Soviet Union | 941.3 | 1,035.2 | 9.3 | 10.0 |
| United States | 2,311.9 | 2,361.4 | 21.3 | 2.24 |
| Japan | 514.8 | 517.5 | 4.7 | 1.0 |
| Germany | 330.5 | 311.0 | 2.8 | −5.8 |
| China | 966.7 | 1,863.4 | 16.8 | 92.6 |
| India | 320.4 | 404.4 | 3.6 | 37.0 |

\* Member states of the European Union: Austria, Belgium, Bulgaria, Cyprus, Czech Republic, Denmark, Estonia, Finland, France, Germany, Greece, Hungary, Ireland, Italy, Latvia, Lithuania, Luxemburg, Malta, the Netherlands, Poland, Portugal, Romania, Slovakia, Slovenia, Spain, Sweden, and the United Kingdom.
*Source:* Adapted from BP, Statistical Review of World Energy (2008).

Heads of State and Government addresses the question of climate change and underlines that the international community faces "serious and multiple challenges in tackling climate change, promoting clean energy, meeting energy needs and achieving sustainable development."[87]

Developing countries' energy consumption, in both absolute terms and per capita terms, remains low relative to that of developed nations. The Organisation for Economic Co-operation and Development (OECD) countries alone account for 50 percent of world commercial energy use; in comparison, China and India together account for just over 20 percent (see Table 2.2). And per capita energy consumption in developing countries is about one-sixth that in Europe and one-eighth that in North America.[88] The

---
[87] GA Res. 60/1, para. 50, UN Doc. A/RES/60/1.
[88] WORLD RESOURCES INSTITUTE, EARTHTRENDS ENVIRONMENTAL INFORMATION, available at http://earthtrends.wri.org/text/energy-resources/variable-351.html.

## 2.6. The Science and the IPCC in Context

developing countries' share of primary energy demand is forecast to grow from 40 percent in 2004 to 50 percent in 2030.[89] During this period, global energy demand is projected to double, with over 70 percent of the increase coming from developing countries.[90] It is generally assumed that during the coming decades, developing countries will experience quite rapid economic growth, with incomes converging or approaching those of developed countries, in the process leading to increased demand for energy – predominantly fossil fuels – for industrial and transport use. In many cases, diversified economic growth should enable developing countries to make economic transitions from a high dependence on activities that are vulnerable to climate shocks, such as agriculture and fisheries, and the export of primary commodities, for instance, cotton, copper, and other metals, that may be subject to market volatility and declining terms of trade. With rising incomes, developing nations would also be increasingly able to acquire the technological and financial resources to decarbonize their economies. It may, however, be that many developing countries are unable to meaningfully narrow the income gap and match the superior technological expertise and greater wealth of developed countries.[91] If this is the case, then developing countries may be less willing – and able – to implement robust mitigation activities. Fairness would then also seem to suggest that industrialized countries ought to take on a greater share of the mitigation burden; in short, burden-sharing arrangements should remain sensitive to overall socioeconomic progress made by developing countries.

The quest for basic energy services should not become a false sacrifice on the altar of the low-carbon economy. On principle, access to energy for the poor must be distinguished from fossil fuel use in developed countries. Providing access to a basic minimum of energy services for household cooking, heating, and lighting for the poor in Africa and South Asia would have only a modest impact on GHG emissions. For instance, it has been pointed out that[92]

> current fossil fuel consumption levels in tropical sub-Saharan Africa are so low that even if these countries increased at an annual rate of 10 percent

[89] *Id.* at 68.
[90] *Id.* at 68.
[91] Patricia Romero Lankao et al., *Development and Greenhouse Gas Emissions Deviate from the "Modernization" Theory and "Convergence" Hypothesis*, 38 CLIMATE RESEARCH 17 (2008).
[92] MODI ET AL., *supra* note 83, at 30–31 (2005).

(the annual rate at which China's consumption grew during the 1971–97 period) by 2015, the associated per capita GHG emissions will remain at levels that are less than 5 percent of those in the high-income countries today.

In a carbon-constrained future, fairness indicates that developing countries ought to benefit, to the extent possible, from the affordable and reliable sources of energy, which, in many cases, will still be from fossil fuel sources. It would be unfair if developing countries found that social and economic progress is predicated predominantly on the incrementally more expensive – and, in some cases, technically immature – low-carbon energy technologies.

Let us now turn to another dimension of the energy challenge – decarbonizing the global energy system. As we have seen, the transition to a low-carbon economy will need to occur in the face of rising energy demand. Table 2.2 shows that energy consumption has grown in all regions, developed and developing alike, albeit much more slowly in the former. In fact, the only instance in which energy demand has fallen is in the case of economic downturns, as in the case of the states of the former Soviet Union after the end of Communism. Yet, as noted earlier, global energy demand is projected to increase by half by 2030, then go on to double by 2050. Over the same period, a continuation of current trends would see emissions more than doubling from current levels.[93] Stabilizing concentrations at around double preindustrial levels would entail a massive increase in the supply of carbon-free energy, in the order of the entire current global energy demand.[94] A recent report by the International Energy Agency concluded that the accelerated deployment of energy technologies could return energy-related carbon dioxide emissions to their *current* levels by 2050.[95] A strategy to mitigate emissions must begin by improving the efficiency with which energy is produced (e.g., installing more efficient power plants) and consumed by end users (e.g., through more efficient household appliances

---

[93] PRICEWATERHOUSECOOPERS, THE WORLD IN 2050: THE IMPLICATIONS OF GLOBAL GROWTH FOR CARBON EMISSIONS AND CLIMATE CHANGE POLICY 3 (2006), available at http://www.pwc.com/extweb/pwcpublications.nsf/docid/dfb54c8aad6742db852571f5006dd53; INTERNATIONAL ENERGY AGENCY, ENERGY TECHNOLOGY PERSPECTIVES – SCENARIOS AND STRATEGIES TO 2050 25 (2006); NICHOLAS STERN, THE ECONOMICS OF CLIMATE CHANGE: THE STERN REVIEW 176 (2006).

[94] Martin I. Hoffert et al., *Energy Implications of Future Stabilization of Atmospheric $CO_2$ Content*, 395(6704) NATURE 881 (1998).

[95] INTERNATIONAL ENERGY AGENCY, *supra* note 93, at 25.

## 2.6. The Science and the IPCC in Context

or compact fluorescent light bulbs). Improvements in efficiency, along with changes in the source of energy, are the main reason that until recently, carbon dioxide emissions increased at only half the rate of world economic output (1.5 versus 3 percent per year).[96]

Many analyses acknowledge that meeting the need for clean energy will depend on utilizing a number of options in addition to enhanced efficiency, including renewables, nuclear energy, and advanced fossil fuel technologies such as carbon capture and storage.[97] A fundamental restructuring of the global energy system will be required to increase energy from carbon-free energy sources such as renewables. Renewable energy has important co-benefits in that when it is substituted for fossil energy, it reduces air pollution and contributes to energy security, particularly for countries that face high fuel import costs such as small island states. However, as Table 2.3 illustrates, the present contribution to world energy demand of renewables – especially wind, solar, and geothermal – remains very low, meaning that without very dramatic increases in capacity, the overall share is projected to remain fairly modest. Recent years have seen rapid growth – between 2004 and 2007 power generated from renewables excluding large hydropower increased by 50 percent.[98] Some 3.5 percent of power globally is generated from "new" renewables, mostly wind.

Studies of the combined technical potential of bioenergy, wind, geothermal, and hydro suggest that these sources will not be able to meet the global demand for carbon-free energy.[99] Theoretically, solar energy, which has the greatest technical potential of all renewable energies, could meet global energy demand, but it currently faces technical and cost barriers. Moreover, the existing share in 2004 of only 0.039 percent of global energy

---

[96] Roberta Hotinski et al., *Solving the Climate Problem*, 46(10) ENVIRONMENT 10 (2004).

[97] Steven Pacala & Robert Socolow, *Stabilization Wedges: Solving the Climate Problem for the Next 50 Years with Current Technologies*, 305(5686) SCIENCE 968 (2004); INTERGOVERNMENTAL PANEL ON CLIMATE CHANGE, CLIMATE CHANGE 2007: MITIGATION. CONTRIBUTION OF WORKING GROUP III TO THE FOURTH ASSESSMENT REPORT OF THE INTERGOVERNMENTAL PANEL ON CLIMATE CHANGE (Bert Metz et al. eds., 2007). Some prominent environmental thinkers, e.g., John Lovelock, now advocate nuclear energy as crucial to combating climate change. *See* JOHN LOVELOCK, THE REVENGE OF GAIA (2007).

[98] REN21, RENEWABLES 2007: GLOBAL STATUS REPORT 6 (2008).

[99] *See* VACLAV SMIL, ENERGY AT THE CROSSROADS: GLOBAL PERSPECTIVES AND UNCERTAINTIES (2003). RICHARD DOORNBOSCH & SIMON UPTON, DO WE HAVE THE RIGHT R&D PRIORITIES TO SUPPORT THE ENERGY TECHNOLOGIES OF THE FUTURE? International Energy Agency, SG/SD/RT(2006)1 25 (2006).

TABLE 2.3. *World primary energy demand, percentage share*

| | 1980 (%) | 2004 (%) | 2030 (%) | 2004–2030 annual growth (%) |
|---|---|---|---|---|
| Coal | 24.6 | 24.7 | 26.0 | 1.8 |
| Oil | 42.8 | 35.2 | 32.5 | 1.3 |
| Gas | 17.0 | 20.4 | 22.5 | 2.0 |
| Nuclear | 2.6 | 6.4 | 5.0 | 0.7 |
| Hydro | 2.0 | 2.1 | 2.39 | 2.0 |
| Biomass and waste[a] | 10.4 | 10.5 | 9.2 | 1.3 |
| Other renewables[b] | 0.44 | 0.50 | 1.7 | 6.6 |

[a] Includes biomass used for heating and cooking, especially in developing countries.
[b] So-called new renewables like wind, solar, geothermal.
*Source:* Adapted from IEA World Energy Outlook (2006).

supply underlines the challenges faced in scaling up solar energy.[100] However, renewables have made significant inroads in countries that have provided supportive policies, for instance in Germany and Spain. Cost has been the major constraint facing renewable energy, with most technologies, except large hydropower and geothermal energy, not not competitive with prices of wholesale electricity generated from fossil sources.[101] Of course, fossil fuels benefit from a range of explicit and implicit subsidies, not to mention the existence of an established infrastructure for production and delivery. Naturally, once carbon is priced – either through a cap-and-trade scheme or a carbon tax – renewable energy will become more competitive. Economies of scale and technical innovation will, over time, bring down the cost of renewables.

Biofuels as a substitute for fossil fuels in road transportation have been the subject of increased attention and have driven energy security and climate concerns. According to one estimate, biofuels could meet 4 to 7 percent of road-transport fuel demand,[102] but net GHG reductions from displacing fossil fuels depend on the feedstock, with corn ethanol, for instance, delivering significantly lower climate benefits than ethanol produced from sugarcane.[103] Unintended consequences of increased cultivation of crops for

[100] INTERNATIONAL ENERGY AGENCY, RENEWABLES IN GLOBAL ENERGY SUPPLY: AN IEA FACT SHEET 3 (2007).
[101] *Id.* at 6. The subsidies made available for fossil fuels must be borne in mind.
[102] INTERNATIONAL ENERGY AGENCY, *supra* note 10, at 385.
[103] INTERNATIONAL ENERGY AGENCY, BIOFUELS FOR TRANSPORT: AN INTERNATIONAL PERSPECTIVE 13 (2004).

## 2.6. The Science and the IPCC in Context

biofuels production may include rising food prices, impacts on land and water supplies, and increased release of carbon dioxide from land cleared for cultivation.[104]

Carbon capture and storage is regarded by many as a vital part of a clean energy future, and major research and development efforts are under way in the United States and other industrialized countries.[105] This technology involves the separation, compression, and long-term storage of carbon dioxide associated with fossil fuel combustion at power plants.[106] It, while featuring in all modeling of mitigation scenarios, has not yet been demonstrated on a commercial scale in a power plant.

It is widely acknowledged that current expenditures on energy research and development, from both public and private sources, are inadequate.[107] This presents a major challenge. Equally, the cycle running from innovation through commercial deployment will need to be compressed if critical technologies are to be brought into operation at the scale necessary to make a difference.

---

[104] UN-Energy, Sustainable Bioenergy: A Framework for Decision-Makers (2007), available at http://esa.un.org/un-energy/pdf/susdev.Biofuels.FAO.pdf. The clearing of land for palm oil production, in the process, releasing large amounts of carbon dioxide stored in peatlands, is turning out to be one of the unintended consequences of rising demand for biofuels. See, e.g., Elisabeth Rosenthal, *Once a Dream Fuel, Palm Oil May Be an Econightmare*, New York Times, January 31, 2007.

[105] See G8 Hokkaido Toyako Summit Leaders Declaration, July 8, 2008, at para. 31, which expresses support for 20 large-scale CCS demonstration projects globally by 2010, in order to achieve broad deployment by 2020. Available at http://www.mofa.go.jp/policy/economy/summit/2008/doc/doc080714_en.html. See also, e.g., National Energy Technology Laboratory, U.S. Department of Energy, Carbon Sequestration Technology Roadmap and Program Plan 2007 (2007). In February 2003, President Bush announced US$1 billion to construct the world's first coal-based, zero-emissions electricity and hydrogen power plant, also known as FuturGen. See *Statement by President Bush*, White House press release, February 27, 2003, available at http://www.whitehouse.gov/news/releases/2003/02/20030227-11.html. In February 2008, the Department of Energy effectively withdrew its support from the FuturGen project. See Andrew C. Revkin, *A "Bold" Step to Capture an Elusive Gas Falters*, New York Times, February 3, 2008.

[106] International Energy Agency, Prospects for $CO_2$ Capture and Storage (2004); Massachusetts Institute of Technology, The Future of Coal: An Interdisciplinary MIT Study (2007), available at http://web.mit.edu/coal/.

[107] See, for the statistics from the OECD group of industrialized countries, Doornbosch & Upton, *supra* note 99, at 31–32. They note that in most industrialized countries, public sector research and development expenditure has been rising in real terms, while energy research and development has declined steeply from a peak in the early 1980s, although there are recent signs of a rise in spending.

Finally, it must be borne in mind that fossil fuels are presently abundant, as well as convenient, with few ready substitutes in sectors such as transportation, where emissions are growing rapidly. The world's poor, who tend to be on the lowest rung of the energy ladder, are indifferent to the source of improved energy services, fossil or otherwise, provided these are safe, reliable, and affordable. They cannot be expected to pay a premium for more expensive, albeit cleaner, energy. Convenience and cost will always influence energy policies as well as the choices made by households and individuals. New technologies and sources of energy face the challenge of competing with fuels that are ubiquitous, reliable, and supported by well-developed, sophisticated infrastructure. This suggests that greatly accelerated deployment of clean technologies, coupled with a concerted R&D effort, will be required to make the transition to a low-carbon energy system. In order that developing countries can achieve economic and social development without radically adding to the climate problem, industrialized countries will need to provide finance and access to technology.

## 2.7. CONCLUSION

This chapter has briefly outlined some relevant aspects of the science of climate change as well as selected dimensions of the energy challenge. The diligence and dedication has furnished us with an ever deepening knowledge of this most complex of problems – the influence of emissions on the processes of the biosphere, the likely future impacts on the natural resource base underpinning human society, and long-term projections of global change. Yet this sophisticated understanding of the impacts occurring now – and those projected for the future – on its own cannot determine how human society ought to confront the problem of climate change. How to respond remains a question of values – in short, a moral and ethical question, resolved ultimately through a political process, guided and informed by scientific assessments that are clear and useful for policy makers. As we have seen, the IPCC has served this purpose very well so that national decision makers and the international climate negotiation process have benefited from regular assessments of the state of the science, impacts and adaptation, and the opportunities for mitigation of GHGs. Quantifying and communicating uncertainty in climate change presents a significant challenge for scientists in their interactions with decision makers.

The setting of a GHG stabilization target brings to the fore difficult moral and ethical questions as well as tremendous practical challenges. Any attempt to answer the question of what amount of climate change would be compatible with conceptions of fairness and justice leads to a host of sometimes irreconcilable claims about the respective value of development, politics, culture, and the integrity of the environment. Establishing a target immediately raises the related question of burden sharing – how will the effort required be allocated among nation states? How will individual states allocate the burden domestically? Most stabilization targets at the low end, which would still imply temperature rises of above 2 degrees Celsius, can only be attained through an unprecedented decarbonization of the global energy system, in the course of a large-scale transformation of the world economy. As briefly highlighted in this chapter, such a transition will require a portfolio of cleaner technologies, which must be deployed rapidly, while research and development on the next generation of technologies actively are pursued.

# 3

# Development of the International Climate Change Regime

## 3.1. INTRODUCTION: UNITED NATIONS FRAMEWORK CONVENTION ON CLIMATE CHANGE (UNFCCC)

By the end of the 1980s, the threat of climate change had entered the policy arena. The basic scientific conclusions about the causes and dimensions of the potential human impact on the climate were sufficient to bring pressure to bear to take action at the international level.[1] Momentum had begun to build with the release of the first report of the Intergovernmental Panel on Climate Change (IPCC) and the holding of the Second World Climate Conference in Geneva in November 1990. In December of that year, the United Nations (UN) General Assembly established the Intergovernmental Negotiating Committee (INC), tasked with negotiating the Convention. The INC met in five formal sessions, working within a tight deadline to complete a text for adoption before the UN Conference on Environment and Development, commonly known as the Earth Summit. The text of what was called the UN Framework Convention on Climate Change (UNFCCC) was adopted on May 9, 1992, and opened for signature a month later at the summit.[2]

---

[1] The evolving scientific understanding and early policy responses are covered in Chapter 1. The developments prior to the Convention are comprehensively covered by Daniel Bodansky, *The United Nations Framework Convention on Climate Change: A Commentary*, 18 YALE JOURNAL OF INTERNATIONAL LAW 451, 458–71 (1993) (hereinafter referred to as BODANSKY, *Commentary*). *See also* Daniel Bodansky, *Prologue to the Climate Change Convention, in* NEGOTIATING CLIMATE CHANGE: THE INSIDE STORY OF THE RIO CONVENTION 45, 46–60 (Irving L. Minzer & J. Amber Leonard eds., 1994) (hereinafter referred to as BODANSKY, *Prologue*). This and the following section draw on these two sources.

[2] United Nations Framework Convention on Climate Change, adopted on May 9, 1992, Art. 3(1), 1771 UNTS 164, 31 ILM 851 (hereinafter referred to as UNFCCC).

## 3.1. Introduction

According to the author of the leading commentary, the Convention proved disappointing to many.[3] Efforts to include binding stabilization targets, not to mention reductions, were watered down, leaving the Convention only with vague commitments with respect to stabilization.[4] Other shortcomings mentioned included a failure to include an insurance fund and technology transfer mechanism (sought by the developing countries), the absence of market mechanisms such as emissions credits, and the limited-obligations imposed on developing countries. Nonetheless, given the diverging interests of the parties concerned, the Convention was a remarkable achievement. It unambiguously recognizes climate change as a threat and sets the long-term objective to stabilize greenhouse gas (GHG) emissions "at a level that would prevent dangerous anthropogenic interference with the climate system."[5] The process of convening regular conferences of the parties (COPs) is one of the Convention's key features, as it has led to improvements in the collection of information concerning emissions, the reduction of uncertainties, and the work toward international standards. Similarly, it was soon recognized that the Convention needed to be fleshed out, leading to the negotiation of the Kyoto Protocol, under the auspices of the COPs of the Convention, which in effect served as preparatory committees for the Protocol.

This chapter provides a brief account of the genesis of the Convention and an overview of its key provisions. The second section traces the development of the Kyoto Protocol and briefly outlines some of its key provisions.

### 3.1.1. Genesis of the Convention: Negotiating History

The international scientific effort to study climate change was taken up at the intergovernmental level with the formation of the IPCC in 1988, under the auspices of the World Meteorological Organization (WMO) and the UN Environment Programme (UNEP).[6] And while the discussions on an international policy response to the emerging threat of climate change were at an early stage, the UN General Assembly resolution endorsing the

---

[3] See BODANSKY, Commentary, at 454.
[4] See Richard A. Kerr, U.S. Bites Greenhouse Bullet and Gags, 251 SCIENCE 868 (1991); Rose Gutfeld, Climate Change Pact Is Reached by 143 Nations – Treaty Begins Initial Attack on Global Warming, WALL STREET JOURNAL, May 11, 1991, at A7.
[5] See UNFCCC, Art. 2.
[6] See Chapter 2.

establishment of the IPCC made reference to "the identification and possible strengthening of relevant existing international legal instruments having a bearing on climate... [and] elements for inclusion in a possible future international convention on climate."[7] Yet this was far from a definitive call to action. The year 1989 saw support for a convention mount, with a large group of industrialized countries calling for negotiations, in the process, increasing pressure on the United States to change course and support such an initiative.[8] When the United States changed its position, it was not long afterward that the UNEP Governing Council adopted a resolution mandating UNEP to commence preparations for the negotiations. However, as momentum for a treaty grew, so, too, did the view that such negotiations should take place under the broader umbrella of the General Assembly, rather than the technical structures of UNEP and the WMO, in recognition that climate change had implications beyond the environment.[9] Earlier, developing countries had raised concerns that the IPCC process was dominated by developed countries, whose experts were in the majority on the panel.[10]

Discussions also took place on the form a convention might take, with some favoring a general framework agreement modeled on the UN Law of the Sea Convention, supplemented by separate protocols covering particular atmospheric issues, such as climate change and ozone depletion.[11] Even before the onset of formal discussions, however, the alternative approach of a dedicated framework convention on climate change emerged as the preferred option. In a resolution adopted in December 1989, the UN General Assembly expressed support for the initiative to begin preparations for negotiations on a framework convention on climate and called on states to "prepare, as a matter of urgency, a framework convention on climate and associated protocols containing concrete commitments in the light of priorities that may be authoritatively identified on the basis of sound scientific knowledge, and taking into account the specific development needs

---

[7] GA Res. 53, UN GAOR, Forty-Third Sess., UN Doc. A/RES/43/53 (1988).
[8] *See* BODANSKY, *Prologue*, at 54.
[9] Delphine Borione & Jean Ripert, *Exercising Common but Differentiated Responsibility*, in NEGOTIATING CLIMATE CHANGE: THE INSIDE STORY OF THE RIO CONVENTION 81–82 (Irving L. Minzer & J. Amber Leonard eds., 1994).
[10] *See* GA Res. 207, UN GAOR, Forty-Fourth Sess., UN Doc. A/RES/44/207 (1989), at preamble para. 9 and op. para. 9.
[11] *See* BODANSKY, *Prologue*, at 53.

of developing countries."[12] This resolution also foreshadowed some of the themes that would feature in the subsequent negotiation of the Convention and beyond, including the historical responsibility of industrialized countries for anthropogenic climate change and developing countries' need for financial support as well access to, and transfer of, environmentally sound technologies.[13] A year later, the General Assembly established the INC and mandated it to pursue "a single intergovernmental negotiating process under the auspices of the General Assembly," tasked with negotiating a convention incorporating "appropriate commitments."[14]

A number of determining positions stood out and were instrumental in shaping the Convention. First, throughout the negotiations, the United States remained firmly opposed to binding targets for emission stabilization and reduction, which, in various forms, were advocated by the member states of what is now the European Union (EU). Although it favored a pared-down treaty along the lines of the Vienna Convention for the Protection of the Ozone Layer, the United States came to accept a more detailed Climate Convention. The question of targets and timetables bedeviled the process, until before the very last session of the INC, just prior to which it was resolved by means of a compromise crafted by the United Kingdom and the United States, giving rise to what is now Article 4(2) of the Convention, which addresses the mitigation obligations of developed countries.[15] Targets and timetables were replaced with language, according to which industrialized countries would report regularly on policies and measures to reduce emissions, with the aim of returning emissions to their 1990 levels.[16] Arguing that they lacked resources and needed to accord priority to achieving economic growth, developing countries called for access to financial resources and technology to bring about a fair and equitable sharing of the burden of environmental protection.

By and large, the industrialized countries, quite possibly aware of the cost that mitigation efforts would exact from their economies, were unwilling to agree to either specific mitigation targets for themselves or new and

[12] *Supra* note 10, at op. para. 12.
[13] *See id.* preamble para. 7 and op. paras. 14–15.
[14] GA Res. 212, UN GAOR, Forty-Fifth Sess., UN Doc. A/RES/45/212 (1990). *See also* Ahmed Djoghlaf, *The Beginnings of an International Climate Law, in* MINZER & LEONARD, *supra* note 9, at 102.
[15] *See* BODANSKY, *Commentary*, at 491.
[16] UNFCCC, Art. 4(2)(b).

additional resource flows to developing countries. Discussion centered around the role of the Global Environment Facility (GEF), with industrialized countries insisting on designating it as the funding mechanism, while developing countries argued for the creation of a dedicated financial mechanism for the Convention.[17] In the view of developing countries, the governance structure of the GEF meant that it was under the sway of the developed countries. Third, among the developing countries, who underscored the industrialized countries' historical responsibility for emissions, there was generally little support for strong commitments or mechanisms for implementation, with the exception of island and small low-lying states, which banded together under the umbrella of the Alliance of Small Island States (AOSIS). Given their particular and immediate concern with the effects of climate change, this group of states advocated positions considerably more stringent than the bloc of developing countries known as the G-77 and China.[18]

### 3.1.2. *Key Provisions of the UNFCCC*

Bodansky concludes that the Convention falls somewhere between a framework and a substantive convention, establishing more comprehensive obligations than the bare-bones form of a treaty such as the Vienna Convention for the Protection of the Ozone Layer, yet falling short of the detailed commitments contained in the Montreal Protocol to the Vienna Convention.[19] Functionally, the provisions of the Convention can be roughly grouped under four headings: introductory provisions, commitments and associated provisions, institutions established by the Convention, and final or boilerplate provisions relating to amendments, entry into force, and the like. Thus the introductory part consists of the preamble, definitions, the objective of the Convention (Article 2), and principles guiding the implementation of

---

[17] *See* Elizabeth Dowdeswell & Richard J. Kinley, *Constructive Damage to the Status Quo*, in MINZER & LEONARD, *supra* note 9, at 113, 124–25. Initially designated as the financial mechanism on an interim basis only, a later decision of the COP confirmed the status of the GEF as the financial mechanism of the Convention. The establishment and function of the GEF is covered in more detail in Chapter 5.

[18] The G-77 and China, so called for its original number of members, but today a group representing 132 developing countries in various UN fora, including the climate change negotiations. The chairmanship of the G-77 rotates on a six-month basis. For a selection of recent statements made on behalf of G-77, *see* http://www.g77.org/.

[19] *See* BODANSKY, *Commentary*, at 496.

## 3.1. Introduction

the Convention (Article 3). Principles listed include the principle of the protection of the climate system for the benefit of present and future generations of humankind, the principle of equity, the principle of common but differentiated responsibilities, and the precautionary principle. With respect to the latter, it is evident how carefully the provision is balanced – it affirms that lack of full scientific certainty should not be used as a reason to postpone mitigation measures; at the same time, such measures must be cost-effective to ensure global benefits at the lowest possible cost. The principle of the right to sustainable development is included. The linkage between climate change and sustainable development is an important one, underpinning, as it does, so many debates between north and south on the conceptualization of global problems, including climate change. Considered overall, the phrasing of the principles reveals several, sometimes opposing, strands. For example, phrases emphasizing environmental integrity are linked with a reference to cost-effectiveness of measures. Similarly, mitigation measures should not come at the cost of development for the developing countries, and mitigation measures should not constitute an unjustifiable restriction on international trade.[20] The legal status of the principles is difficult to define with certainty. Nonetheless, and despite efforts to dilute their legal implications, the principles stand clearly as interpretive aids to the Convention.[21]

The ultimate objective of the Convention is clearly stated in Article 2 as "the stabilization of greenhouse gas concentrations at a level that would prevent dangerous anthropogenic interference with the climate system." This level "should be achieved within a time-frame sufficient to allow ecosystems to adapt naturally to climate change, to ensure that food production is not threatened and to enable economic development to proceed in a sustainable manner." The recognition of the need to stabilize GHG emissions underlines the serious nature of climate change. The exact legal status of the objective is, however, not entirely clear.[22] While the objective is not phrased as an obligation, it can convincingly be argued that it is akin to a collective commitment, as it encapsulates the rationale of the Convention as a whole.

---

[20] *See*, in relation to trade, UNFCCC, Art. 3(5).
[21] *See* BODANSKY, *Commentary*, at 501 (noting that the United States inserted the word *guide* and replaced the word *States* with *Parties* to undercut the argument that the principles were part of customary international law binding on all parties).
[22] *See* BODANSKY, *Commentary*, at 500.

Various stabilization targets have been proposed, based on the avoidance of major, irreversible events, and at the same time considering what is technologically and economically feasible. The objective cannot be understood as an obligation to meet any such specific target, but rather as a commitment to strive, in good faith, to stabilize GHG concentrations, including through the implementation of the Convention and subsequent protocols. In the final analysis, although the objective is explicit, it retains a Delphic quality. Who is to say precisely what constitutes "dangerous" interference with the climate system, and for whom?[23]

The principle of "common but differentiated responsibilities" finds its most explicit expression in the Convention.[24] The principle is not a new one in international law, finding expression in, among other vehicles, provisions of the General Agreement on Tariffs and Trade and the UN Convention on the Law of the Sea.[25] In the context of the negotiations, the principle served to bridge the positions of most developed countries, which sought some form of targets for stabilization and reduction, and the developing countries, which generally contended that it would be unfair to them to assume such commitments. In the Convention, the principle finds expression in the differentiation in commitments between Annex I, or developed country parties, and non–Annex I parties. Differentiation exists with respect to Annex I parties' nonbinding goal to return their emissions to 1990 levels by 2000; more stringent and frequent reporting obligations of Annex I parties; and provisions concerning the granting of assistance, which also fall within the ambit of differential treatment, as articulated by the principle of common but differentiated responsibilities.[26] The Convention provides that a subset of Annex I parties – essentially the members of the Organisation for Economic Co-operation and Development (OECD) in 1992, listed in Annex II to the Convention – have a special responsibility to assist developing countries in meeting their commitments. Thus Article 4(3) states that parties

---

[23] For a recent scientific contribution addressing this issue, see AVOIDING DANGEROUS CLIMATE CHANGE (Hans Joachim Schellnhuber et al. eds., 2006).
[24] See UNFCCC, Art. 3(1) and Art. 4(1). The principle is further analyzed in Chapter 5. For a detailed analysis of the principle in the climate change regime, see LAVANYA RAJAMANI, DIFFERENTIAL TREATMENT IN INTERNATIONAL ENVIRONMENTAL LAW 176–249 (2006).
[25] Yoshiro Matsui, Some Aspects of the Principle of "Common but Differentiated Responsibilities," 2 INTERNATIONAL ENVIRONMENTAL AGREEMENTS: POLITICS, LAW AND ECONOMICS 151, 151–52 (2002).
[26] RAJAMANI, supra note 24, at 191.

included in Annex II "shall provide new and additional financial resources to meet the agreed full costs incurred by developing country Parties" in complying with their reporting obligations. Parties included in Annex II are, among other things, also required ("shall") to take all practicable measures to promote and finance the transfer of environmentally sound technologies, particularly to developing countries.[27] The notion here is that in the absence of such measures, it would not be fair to expect developing countries to shoulder their share of the mitigation burden.

The commitments contained in Article 4 form the core of the Convention, setting out obligations common to all parties as well as those applicable only to industrialized or Annex I parties. In terms of Article 4(1), all parties must prepare national inventories of anthropogenic emissions by sources and removals by sinks and implement programs containing measures to mitigate climate change as well as measures to facilitate adaptation. The parties are also required to promote sustainable management, conservation, and enhancement of sinks and reservoirs of GHGs, including forests and oceans. Under Article 4(2), the Annex I parties commit themselves to adopting national policies and taking corresponding measures on the mitigation of climate change by limiting anthropogenic emissions of GHGs and protecting sinks. The Annex I parties are also required to report periodically on the preceding policies undertaken by them, "with the aim of returning individually or jointly to their 1990 levels these anthropogenic emissions of carbon dioxide and other greenhouse gases."[28] To the extent that this is a binding legal obligation, it is a rather weak and diluted one.[29] As the record shows, where this obligation was met, it was, by and large, due to economic factors and unrelated to mitigation measures.[30]

Article 12, on reporting ("communication of information") of inventories and applicable methodologies, reinforces, and is closely linked to, Article 4. While all parties must communicate their inventories and describe steps taken to implement the Convention, Annex I countries must also include in their communications detailed descriptions of policies and measures to mitigate climate change. However, the reporting obligation is differentiated

---

[27] UNFCCC, Art. 4(5).
[28] UNFCCC, Art. 4(2)(b).
[29] See BODANSKY, Commentary, at 516 (expressing doubt as to whether they were legally binding and calling them a "quasi-target and quasi-timetable").
[30] Primarily the economic collapse in states of the former Soviet Union and shuttering of inefficient industries in central and Eastern Europe and the reunified Germany.

for developing countries, which shall submit their first national communication within three years of the entry into force of the Convention or of the availability of financial resources in accordance with Article 4(1). Least developed countries (LDCs), a subset of developing countries classified by the UN largely on the basis of very low per capita gross domestic product (GDP), can submit national communications at their discretion.[31] The provision relating to reporting forms a fundamental part of the Convention as reporting and monitoring are vital to measuring progress. They also facilitate the development of common standards and build trust among the parties. Reporting and monitoring is a mainstay of multilateral environmental agreements, as is true of treaties in other spheres such as human rights. And while the Convention does not explicitly empower any of its institutions to review compliance with its provisions, the COP has elaborated a process of in-depth expert reviews of Annex I parties' national communications.[32] Finally, as they serve to facilitate reporting, the provisions covering cooperation on research and observation and education and training should also be mentioned here.[33]

A third key part of the Convention consists of the articles relating to the institutional arrangements, namely, the COP and its subsidiary organs for scientific and technological advice and implementation as well as the financial mechanism. The COP, as the supreme body of the Convention, is empowered to make decisions to promote the effective implementation of the Convention, including to "exercise such other functions as are required for the achievement of the objective of the Convention."[34] Thus, aside from the enumerated functions, the COP is entrusted with such open-ended powers necessary to implement the Convention. It is also provided that the COP shall agree on and adopt by consensus rules of procedure.[35] This stipulation had the result that parties who did not support the objectives of the Convention could block consensus on the adoption of the rules of procedure, which was the case at the first COP, with the result that the rules of procedure have, at every meeting, been applied, without ever

---

[31] UNFCCC, Art. 12(5).
[32] *See* Jacob Werksman, *Compliance and the Kyoto Protocol: Building a Backbone into a Flexible Regime*, YEARBOOK OF INTERNATIONAL ENVIRONMENTAL LAW, vol. 9, 48, 65–66 (Jutta Brunnée & Ellen Hay eds., 1999).
[33] *See* UNFCCC, Art. 5 and Art. 6.
[34] *See* UNFCCC, Art. 7(2)(m).
[35] UNFCCC, Art. 7(2)(k).

having been formally adopted.[36] Exponents of delay and obfuscation were thus handed a veto because – in the absence of voting rules – the rule of consensus applies. Creative accommodation and skilful chairmanship have thus proved key to overcoming this impediment. The Convention's unhappy status quo concerning the rules of procedure was also imported into the Kyoto Protocol.[37]

### 3.2. THE KYOTO PROTOCOL

Adopted in 1997, the Kyoto Protocol had existed in something of a state of limbo after the decision of the United States not to ratify the instrument.[38] A significant new chapter in the field of climate, environment, and energy was opened with the decision, in 2004, of the Russian Federation to ratify the Protocol. With Russia's ratification, the Protocol cleared its final hurdle, entering into force on February 16, 2005.[39] It builds on the UNFCCC by setting binding emission targets for Annex I countries to limit or reduce their GHG emissions. Overall, the Annex I countries that have ratified the Protocol are required to reduce their emissions by 5.2 percent relative to 1990 emissions. Parties must meet their targets at the end of the commitment period, from 2008 to 2012.

The Protocol contains a number of innovations. In terms of institutional design, the mechanism for monitoring and enforcing compliance is unique

---

[36] Sebastian Oberthür & Hermann E. Ott, THE KYOTO PROTOCOL: INTERNATIONAL CLIMATE POLICY FOR THE 21ST CENTURY 40, 46 (1999). Art. 17, concerning protocols to the convention, does not specify procedures for the adoption of such instruments, which meant that parties were referred back to the rules of procedure "applied" but not "adopted." This effectively extended the veto to the decision on the adoption of the Kyoto Protocol. For the text of the draft rules of procedure, see ORGANIZATIONAL MATTERS, ADOPTION OF THE RULES OF PROCEDURE, NOTE BY THE SECRETARIAT, FCCC/CP/1996/2 (1996).

[37] UNFCCC, Art. 13(5), states that "the rules of procedure of the Conference of the Parties . . . shall be applied mutatis mutandis under this Protocol, except as may be otherwise decided by consensus."

[38] Kyoto Protocol to the United Nations Framework Convention on Climate Change, December 11, 1997, 2303 UNTS 148, 37 ILM 22, text available at http://unfccc.int/kyoto_protocol/items/2830.php (hereinafter referred to as the Protocol).

[39] UNFCCC, Art. 25(1), stipulates that entry into force is conditional on ratification of 55 countries and representing at least 55 percent of $CO_2$ emissions in 1990, the base year for the treaty. As of October 16, 2008, 182 countries and one regional integration organization had ratified or acceded to the Protocol. Australia deposited its instrument of accession at the Thirteenth Conference of the Parties in Bali in 2007, leaving the United States the sole industrialized country not to have ratified the Protocol.

among multilateral environmental agreements. To a significant degree, the Protocol itself consists of an outline so that considerable time and effort was required to finalize the rule book necessary to implement its provisions. That process is essentially complete. Under provisions for a "prompt start," key aspects of the Protocol, such as the Clean Development Mechanism (CDM), began to operate before its entry into force. A key innovation of the Protocol is the establishment of the so-called flexibility mechanisms, which consist of emissions trading between Annex I countries, joint implementation (JI) between developed countries, and the CDM, which links carbon reduction efforts with developing countries by making it possible to earn credits for projects implemented in developing countries. Importantly, the CDM is not designed solely to accomplish carbon reductions, but is also intended to help developing countries achieve sustainable development.[40] The next section provides a brief account of the Protocol's negotiating history.

### 3.2.1. Negotiating History

The Protocol is the result of more than two years of preparatory negotiations, culminating in a down-to-the-wire final negotiating session.[41] The seeds for the Protocol were sown by the Convention. Thus UNFCCC Article 4(2) provides that the COP shall, at its first meeting, review the adequacy of the aim to return GHGs to 1990 levels by the year 2000 and to consider next steps. Projections indicated that it was very unlikely that Annex I parties were going to meet that goal.[42] It was also evident that commitments with a horizon of 2000 were not sufficient to combat climate change in a meaningful manner. Given the work of the IPCC, policy makers were also cognizant that stabilizing GHG concentrations would require more aggressive mitigation action. Thus, when the first COP (COP-1) met in Berlin in April 1995, there was a realization that further commitments would be required, a conclusion that was opposed by oil-producing and -exporting countries and some powerful interest groups such as the U.S. industrial

---

[40] Protocol, Art. 12(2).
[41] Two well-known books on the Kyoto Protocol are OBERTHÜR & OTT, *supra* note 36 (hereinafter referred to as OBERTHÜR & OTT, INTERNATIONAL CLIMATE POLICY); MICHAEL GRUBB ET AL., THE KYOTO PROTOCOL: A GUIDE AND ASSESSMENT (1999) (hereinafter referred to as GRUBB ET AL., GUIDE AND ASSESSMENT).
[42] FIRST REVIEW OF INFORMATION COMMUNICATED BY EACH PARTY INCLUDED IN ANNEX I TO THE CONVENTION, UN Doc. A/AC.237/81 (1994).

lobby.[43] Nonetheless, at COP-1, parties reached an agreement coined the Berlin Mandate, which set in motion a process to reinforce the Convention's commitments by means of a protocol or other instrument, with the objective of elaborating policies and measures and setting quantified limitation and reduction objectives ("targets") within specified post-2000 time frames.[44] It was also decided that the negotiations on the protocol should be completed in 1997, with a view to adopting the results at the third session of the COP.

Developing countries contended that in accordance with the principle of common but differentiated responsibilities, the process leading to a new instrument should not introduce any fresh commitments for them. Industrialized countries' (reluctant) acceptance of this position was an important factor in reaching agreement and in shaping the instrument that emerged from the negotiations. (In the explicit exclusion of commitments for developing countries lay seeds of the fateful U.S. Senate's Byrd-Hagel resolution, which, by a vote of 97–0, rejected Senate ratification of any agreement not contemplating commitments for developing countries.) Following the Berlin meeting, a negotiating body, known as the Ad Hoc Group on the Berlin Mandate (AGBM), was established to oversee the negotiation of the new instrument. The AGBM met eight times between 1995 and 1997 and produced a compilation text in time for COP-3 in Kyoto.

Countries participate in the climate change negotiations as members of one or other grouping.[45] The largest, and the oldest, is the G-77, which today counts 132 developing countries as members.[46] China is an associate member and works closely with the group so that statements are usually made "on behalf of the G-77 and China." It is active throughout the UN system, and the country holding the six-month presidency of the group usually appoints individuals as spokespersons on a particular issue, or for certain negotiating

---

[43] See GRUBB ET AL., GUIDE AND ASSESSMENT, at 46.
[44] Decision 1/CP.1, in REPORT OF THE PARTIES TO THE CONVENTION ON ITS FIRST SESSION, Addendum, Part II: Action Taken by the Parties, FCCC/CP/1995/7/Add.1 (1995). For details on the Berlin Mandate and the AGBM, see GRUBB ET AL., GUIDE AND ASSESSMENT, at 43–60; OBERTHÜR & OTT, INTERNATIONAL CLIMATE POLICY, at 43–54.
[45] The UNFCCC secretariat has a useful note on the various groupings on its Web site at http://unfccc.int/parties_and_observers/parties/negotiating_groups/items/2714.php.
More details on the party groups and their negotiating positions and influence can be found in FARHANA YAMIN & JOANNA DEPLEDGE, THE INTERNATIONAL CLIMATE REGIME: A GUIDE TO RULES, INSTITUTIONS AND PROCEDURES 34–46 (2005).
[46] At its founding in 1964, in the context of the UN Conference on Trade and Development, the group had a membership of 77 countries. Membership grew in the following decades, as more countries attained independence and joined the UN.

sessions. The group houses the diverse interests of countries ranging from members of the Organization of Petroleum Exporting Countries (OPEC) to small island states. Sometimes certain developing countries will pursue their interests through smaller groups, such as AOSIS, a grouping of 43 low-lying and island countries, and the LDCs. AOSIS was formed during the negotiations on the UNFCCC. The member states of the EU negotiate as a bloc, led by the country holding the Union's rotating six-month presidency. The Umbrella Group is loosely organized and brings together non-EU industrialized countries, usually Australia, Canada, Iceland, Japan, New Zealand, Norway, the Russian Federation, Ukraine, and the United States. The Umbrella Group evolved out of the JUSSCANNZ coalition (Japan, United States, Switzerland, Canada, Australia, Norway, and New Zealand), which became active during the Kyoto Protocol negotiations at COP-3. The Umbrella Group countries share an interest in advocating for cost-effectiveness and flexibility in the development and implementation of the climate regime. A fairly new grouping is the Environmental Integrity Group, consisting of Mexico, the Republic of Korea, and Switzerland.

The key issues in the negotiating process – the AGBM – that would culminate in the Kyoto Protocol can be grouped under three broad headings: (1) specific policies and measures that might be included; (2) targets, or "quantified emissions limitations and reduction objectives," in the negotiating jargon; and (3) developing country concerns relating to financial support and technology transfer.[47] At the instigation of the EU, the Berlin Mandate committed the parties to elaborate policies and measures for mitigating climate change, ranging from energy efficiency appliance labeling through to carbon taxes. After internal wrangling, the EU submitted a list of policies and measures, some of which were intended to be mandatory, but this "command and control" regulatory approach was rejected by the United States, which preferred to retain flexibility with respect to choice of mitigation mechanisms.[48] The EU proposals did not garner much support, with the OPEC states especially emphatic to exclude carbon taxes. A turning point came at COP-2, when the United States spoke out in favor of binding emission reductions, taking the wind out of the sails of EU's arguments for mandatory policies and measures. The watered-down version of the EU

---

[47] See GRUBB ET AL., GUIDE AND ASSESSMENT, at 62.
[48] For more details, see OBERTHÜR & OTT, INTERNATIONAL CLIMATE POLICY, at 103–6.

proposals is contained in Article 2. A few years later, in an audacious policy about-face, the EU embraced binding targets and market mechanisms, establishing a EU-wide emissions trading scheme in 2005.

COP-2 was held in Geneva in early July 1996. The IPCC's Second Assessment Report (SAR), officially published in June, concluded, "The balance of evidence suggests that there is a discernible human influence on global climate." The Geneva Ministerial Declaration endorsed the SAR and stated that it should provide a scientific basis for strengthening action, particularly action by Annex I parties to limit and reduce emissions of GHGs. The declaration also noted several findings of the SAR, including that achieving a stabilization of atmospheric GHG concentrations at twice preindustrial levels would eventually require global emissions to fall below half of 1995 levels. The Geneva Conference also saw an about-face by the United States, which changed the dynamic of the negotiations when it announced support for legally binding commitments. With this, it became clear that despite some lingering objections, binding commitments would be a feature of whatever instrument eventually was adopted.[49] In retrospect, it is somewhat surprising that, until well into the AGBM process, it was uncertain whether the emission targets would be legally binding or framed as so-called soft targets, similar to those in the Convention.[50]

The next section provides an overview of the key provisions of the Protocol. For practical purposes, the section focuses on analyzing the most relevant provisions, providing details of the negotiations, where relevant.

### 3.2.2. Key Provisions

The basic structure of the Protocol may be summarized briefly as follows. The substantive obligations of industrialized (Annex I) countries are set out in Article 2 (policies and measures), Article 3 (emission target and timetable), Article 4 (joint fulfillment by a group of parties), Article 5 (inventories and methodologies), and Article 7 (reporting). Article 10 largely restates the Convention provisions on cooperation and national communications. Article 11 essentially repeats Convention Articles 4(3) and 11, providing guidance to Annex II parties on financing for developing countries to

---

[49] See GRUBB ET AL., GUIDE AND ASSESSMENT, at 53–55.
[50] See OBERTHÜR & OTT, INTERNATIONAL CLIMATE POLICY, at 49.

carry out their inventory and reporting obligations. The institutional roles of the COP, the Secretariat, the subsidiary bodies, and related matters are dealt with in Articles 9, 13, 14, 15, and 16. The market-based mechanisms designed to assist Annex I parties in meeting their obligations to reduce GHG emissions are covered in Article 6, Article 12, and Article 17. Article 18 requires the development of compliance procedures and mechanisms. Article 19 makes the dispute resolution provisions of the Convention applicable to the Protocol. The legal boilerplate relating to matters such as amendment, entry into force, and so forth is covered in Articles 20 to 28.

Article 2(1) sets out a menu of polices and measures to be adopted by Annex I countries, which are phrased in nonbinding terms and qualified ("in accordance with its national circumstances"). The policies covered include enhancement of energy efficiency, protection and enhancement of sinks and reservoirs, development of renewable forms of energy, and reduction or phasing out of market imperfections and subsidies that run counter to the objectives of the Convention.[51]

Article 2(2) calls on Annex I parties to pursue the limitation or reduction of GHG emissions from aviation and marine bunker fuels, working through the International Civil Aviation Organization (ICAO) and the International Maritime Organization (IMO), which are the international organizations that deal with these sectors. International bunker fuel emissions were not included in Annex I parties' Kyoto targets, largely because no agreement could be reached on how to ascribe responsibility for such emissions.[52] Accordingly, while Annex I parties must tally these emissions in their GHG inventories, they are excluded from national totals and are reported separately. The issue continues to be on the agenda of the Protocol's Subsidiary Body for Scientific and Technological Advice (SBSTA), which has discussed matters related to improving the monitoring and accuracy of emissions international bunker fuels as well as liaising with ICAO and IMO.[53] For their part, these organizations have been studying the issue but have not moved toward control measures.[54] Driven by growth in air travel and international

[51] See UNFCCC, Art. 2(1)(a).
[52] See OBERTHÜR & OTT, INTERNATIONAL CLIMATE POLICY, at 107–8.
[53] See METHODOLOGICAL ISSUES RELATING TO EMISSIONS FROM INTERNATIONAL AVIATION AND MARITIME TRANSPORT, NOTE BY THE SECRETARIAT, FCCC/SBSTA/2004/INF.5 (2004).
[54] The Thirty-Sixth ICAO Assembly established a group to develop a program of action on climate change and international aviation, but parties could not agree on a proposal

## 3.2. The Kyoto Protocol

trade, both aviation and maritime emissions are rising rapidly so that regulation under future international climate policy will be important.[55] Emissions from $CO_2$ rose about 68 percent between 1990 and 2000.[56] In addition, various factors amplify the effect of emissions from air travel: a special report of the IPCC on aviation noted that while aviation was responsible for about 2 percent of $CO_2$ emissions from human activities, it accounted for an estimated 3.5 percent of climate change.[57] Given the lack of available substitutes for aviation and marine bunkers, efficiency improvements are the focus in both transport sectors.[58] With respect to aviation, the IPCC has estimated that fuel burn could be reduced by 6 to 18 percent with better operating measures, particularly air traffic control.

The agreement on binding quantified emissions targets and a timetable for their achievement represents the heart of the Kyoto Protocol. Under Article 3, Annex I parties, as a group, committed themselves to individual and differentiated emission targets, which they would have to meet with a view to reducing their overall emissions of the applicable GHGs by at least 5 percent below 1990 levels. The individual targets, relative to the 1990 baseline, are inscribed in Annex B to the Protocol. During the negotiations, various targets were proposed, some for specific gases, but the introduction

---

to endorse emissions trading. The resolution adopted provides that emissions trading schemes should only be implemented with mutual consent of the states concerned. *See* CONSOLIDATED STATEMENT OF CONTINUING ICAO POLICIES AND PRACTICES RELATED TO ENVIRONMENTAL PROTECTION, Ass. Res. A36-22, appendixes K and L (2007), compiled in RESOLUTIONS ADOPTED AT THE 36TH ASSEMBLY, Provisional Edition (Sept. 2007). At the regional level, the European Commission has proposed bringing aviation, including flights into and out of the EU, under the European Union Emission Trading Scheme. *See* COMMISSION OF THE EUROPEAN COMMUNITIES, PROPOSAL FOR A DIRECTIVE OF THE EUROPEAN PARLIAMENT AND OF THE COUNCIL AMENDING DIRECTIVE 2003/87/EC SO AS TO INCLUDE AVIATION ACTIVITIES IN THE SCHEME FOR GREENHOUSE GAS EMISSION ALLOWANCE TRADING WITHIN THE COMMUNITY, COM(2006) 818 (Dec. 20, 2006). Despite opposition from airlines, it seems that the EU governments will adopt an amended version of the proposal. *See* James Kanter, *Plan on Emissions Hints at U.S.-Europe Rift*, NEW YORK TIMES, December 21, 2007.

[55] MICHEL DEN ELZEN ET AL., AN ANALYSIS OF OPTIONS FOR INCLUDING INTERNATIONAL AVIATION AND MARINE EMISSIONS IN A POST-2012 CLIMATE MITIGATION REGIME, Netherlands Environment Agency Report, MNP Report 500114007/2007, 13 (2007).

[56] INTERGOVERNMENTAL PANEL ON CLIMATE CHANGE, CLIMATE CHANGE 2007: MITIGATION. CONTRIBUTION OF WORKING GROUP III TO THE FOURTH ASSESSMENT REPORT OF THE INTERGOVERNMENTAL PANEL ON CLIMATE CHANGE 330 (Bert Metz et al. eds., 2007).

[57] IPCC SPECIAL REPORT: AVIATION AND THE GLOBAL ATMOSPHERE 6, 8 (Joyce E. Penne et al. eds., 1999).

[58] The use of biofuels in aviation is being explored. *See* Bettina Wassener, *Airline Flies a 747 on Fuel from a Plant*, NEW YORK TIMES, December 30, 2008, at B5.

of differentiated targets helped to bridge the existing differences. While the EU advocated that an early date for meeting targets should be met – 2005 was proposed – the United States preferred 2010. The rump of the EU proposal is to be found in Article 3(2), which provides that each Annex I party should, by 2005, have made "demonstrable progress in achieving its commitments." From a fairness perspective, it is interesting to note that, apparently, there was never much question that targets would be formulated with reference to, and largely on the basis of, historical emissions; alternatives, such as indexes calculating emissions relative to population or GDP, were never seriously considered.[59] In the first place, a recognition of political reality, the selection of 1990 as a base year for emissions can also be seen as an acknowledgment of acquired rights, at the expense of fairness principles based on responsibility (polluter pays) or equal per capita shares. The choice of a base year, against which emission reductions are measured, also has distributional consequences.[60] By the time of the adoption of the Protocol in 1997, the economies of Eastern Europe and the former Soviet Union had undergone severe contraction, with emissions levels much lower than they had been in 1990. Similarly, the reunification of Germany, and the shuttering of less efficient East German industries, acted as a brake on emissions, making 1990 a favorable baseline. The same was not true for less economically advanced developed countries, which were in the process of catching up, such as Ireland or Spain, or the United States, which saw more rapid economic growth after 1990 than most European countries.

Other key issues concerned which sources (gases) would be covered and how to account for sinks (forests). With respect to sources, negotiators opted for a so-called basket of gases, or a comprehensive approach that, in addition to the three GHGs – carbon dioxide, methane, and nitrous oxide – includes three trace gases that have very powerful warming effects. The Protocol thus defined and put into practice the comprehensive approach to GHGs previously adopted in the Convention. The basket of gases approach introduces a degree of "what" flexibility because parties can select the gas or gases on which to concentrate their mitigation activities, enabling them

---

[59] *See* GRUBB ET AL., GUIDE AND ASSESSMENT, at 77. The next section draws heavily on his work.

[60] In accordance with Article 3(5), the historical base year for most Annex I parties is 1990, but parties undergoing the process of transition to a market economy may choose a year or period other than 1990. Parties with a base year other than 1990 are Bulgaria (1988), Hungary (average of 1985–1987), Poland (1988), Romania (1989), and Slovenia (1986).

## 3.2. The Kyoto Protocol

to choose the most cost-effective options. A comprehensive approach thus promotes efficiency. To make reductions of the various gases comparable, negotiators turned to the global warming potentials (GWPs) that the IPCC had developed for the various GHGs. The GWP expresses the greenhouse forcing effect of a gas relative to $CO_2$. Using the GWPs, collective emissions of the applicable GHGs can be calculated as $CO_2$-equivalent emissions, which is the term used in Article 3 of the Protocol.[61] Table 3.1 illustrates the respective GWPs of the GHGs controlled under the Kyoto Protocol as well as their main sources.

The technically very complicated issue of sinks came to prominence quite late in the negotiations.[62] Up to half of the carbon emitted from human sources is quite rapidly absorbed by terrestrial sources (plants) and the oceans through the operation of the natural carbon cycle.[63] Countries with significant forests stood to gain if absorption by sinks was to be counted against $CO_2$ emissions (the so-called net emissions approach). The subject became controversial, not least because counting sinks (forests) appeared to be postponing actual cuts in emissions and seemed to favor some countries over others. While it was agreed that parties should not be able to count natural sinks (existing forests), this begged the question of what constituted an anthropogenic sink.[64] The approach eventually adopted counts "the

---

[61] Although the GWPs are a convenient tool, questions have been raised concerning their scientific soundness and accuracy. See GRUBB ET AL., GUIDE AND ASSESSMENT, at 74 (referring to academic criticisms that GWPs are "uncertain and logically imperfect").

[62] See OBERTHÜR & OTT, INTERNATIONAL CLIMATE POLICY, at 130.

[63] The storage capacity on land and in the oceans is clearly not unlimited. While considerable uncertainties remain, indications are that the oceans absorb about half of anthropogenic carbon. As warming increases, the physical uptake of this carbon is expected to decrease. See Christopher L. Sabine et al., *The Oceanic Sink for Anthropogenic $CO_2$*, 305(5682) SCIENCE 367 (2004). In addition, higher levels of $CO_2$ have also been linked with acidification of the oceans, with yet uncertain consequences for organisms and ecosystems, but it is thought that corals and components of phytoplankton may be affected. See THE ROYAL SOCIETY, OCEAN ACIDIFICATION DUE TO INCREASING ATMOSPHERIC CARBON DIOXIDE, Policy Doc. 12/05 (2005).

[64] It is frequently pointed out that because natural forests are carbon sinks, there ought to be a way to link their protection and preservation to the generation of carbon offset credits. In general, one problem with carbon offsets for avoided deforestation is that alternative land uses, commonly logging or soybean farming, are currently economically more attractive. Within the climate regime, countries with large areas of tropical rainforest that are experiencing significant deforestation (and resultant emissions) have not encouraged discussions of any measures or policies related to preserving forests as natural sinks. This has changed, however, in the past few years, with Indonesia, for instance, joining other smaller tropical rainforest countries in expressing interest in market incentives for reduced

TABLE 3.1. *Greenhouse gases in the Kyoto Protocol*

| Gas | Sources | Emission trends, 1990–2000 | Lifetime (years) | GWP-100 years | % GHG Annex I, 2000 |
|---|---|---|---|---|---|
| Carbon dioxide ($CO_2$) | Fossil fuel burning, cement | Small decrease (<1%), mainly due to reduction in EIT countries, significant increases in some EU and OECD countries | Variable, depending on uptake by sinks, but dominant component up to 100 | 1 | 82 |
| Methane ($CH_4$) | Rice, cattle, biomass burning, land conversion, fossil fuel production | 21% decline, increases in a few countries | 8.4/12 | 23 | 10 |
| Nitrous oxide ($N_2O$) | Fertilizers, fossil fuel burning, land conversion for agriculture | 5% decrease due to sharp drop in EITs | 120/114 | 296 | 6 |
| Perfluorocarbons (PFCs) | Industry, aluminum, electronic and electrical industries, fire fighting, solvents | Decreased | 10,000 to >50,000 | 5,700 ($CF_4$); 11,900 ($C_2F_6$) | 0.30 |
| Hydrofluorocarbons (HFCs) | Industry, refrigerants | Sharp increase due to substitution for ODS controlled by Montreal Protocol | 1.40 to 260 | 120 (HFC-152a); 1,200 (HFC-23) | 1.23 |
| Sulfur hexafluoride ($SF_6$) | Electronic and electrical industries, insulation | Decreased | 3,200 | 22,000 | 0.38 |

*Source:* Adapted from Intergovernmental Panel on Climate Change, *Climate Change 2001: Working Group 1: The Scientific Basis*, table 4.1(a), and *Compilation and Synthesis of Third National Communications*, UN Doc. UNFCCC/SBI/7/Add.1 (2003).

## 3.2. The Kyoto Protocol

net changes in greenhouse gas emissions by sources and removals by sinks resulting from *direct human-induced* land-use change and forestry activities, limited to afforestation, reforestation and deforestation since 1990."[65] This definition left a number of questions open, and the adoption of detailed implementation rules proved difficult and time consuming.[66]

The Protocol does not establish a set of full-fledged institutions.[67] Although not stated explicitly, the supreme governing body is the Conference of the Parties serving as the Meeting of the Parties, or the COP/MOP, as it is known.[68] The COP/MOP is assigned the responsibility of keeping under review the implementation of the Protocol, and it is empowered to make "the decisions necessary to promote its effective implementation."[69] This is consistent with practice in international environmental law of bestowing quite wide legislative (or quasi-legislative) and administrative powers on COPs.[70] The enumerated tasks of the COP/MOP include assessing the implementation of the Protocol and the extent to which progress toward the objective of the Convention is being achieved,[71] periodically

---

deforestation. Costa Rica has pioneered the concept of ecosystem services. Forestry Law No. 7575, adopted in 1996, recognizes four services provided by Costa Rica's forests: carbon sequestration, hydrological services, biodiversity protection, and scenic beauty.

[65] Protocol, Art. 3(3), emphasis added.

[66] Decision 19/CP.9, in REPORT OF THE CONFERENCE OF THE PARTIES ON ITS NINTH SESSION, Addendum, Part II: Action Taken by the Parties, vol. 2, FCCC/CP/2003/6/Add.2 (2004). *See* section 3.3, summarizing the outcomes of COP-9.

[67] *See* OBERTHÜR & OTT, INTERNATIONAL CLIMATE POLICY, at 240–41, detailing why a majority of the parties to the convention preferred not to create new institutions for reasons of economy as well as out of a desire to retain authority in the subsidiary bodies of the convention.

[68] *See id.* at 242–43. That the COP/MOP is a separate entity from the COP appears from Art. 13(2)-(3), providing that in COP/MOP meetings, nonparties may participate as observers, but that decisions under the Protocol may be made only by parties to the Protocol. Similarly, when the COP/MOP meets, bureau members who are not parties to the Protocol shall be replaced by additional members who are parties. (The bureau consists of representatives elected in accordance with the regional groups of the UN and tasked with chairing and coordinating the COP and its various bodies.) *See also* REPORT OF THE SUBSIDIARY BODY FOR IMPLEMENTATION ON ITS EIGHTEENTH SESSION, FCCC/SBI/2003/8, para. 44 (2003): "The SBI recognized that the COP and the COP/MOP are legally distinct with separate agendas."

[69] Protocol, Art. 13(4).

[70] *See* OBERTHÜR & OTT, INTERNATIONAL CLIMATE POLICY, at 243, noting that the elaboration of the compliance regime under Art. 18 may add quasi-judicial powers to the list. *See*, for developments with respect to MEAs generally, Jutta Brunnée, *COPing with Consent: Law-Making under Multilateral Environmental Agreements*, 15 LEIDEN JOURNAL OF INTERNATIONAL LAW 1 (2002).

[71] Protocol, Art. 13(4)(a).

examining the obligations of the parties under the Protocol, considering and adopting reports on its implementation,[72] and carrying out the development and periodic refinement of methodologies for the effective implementation of the Protocol.[73] With respect to subsidiary organs, Article 15 provides that the SBSTA and the Subsidiary Body for Implementation (SBI) established under the Convention shall also serve, respectively, as the SBSTA and SBI for the Protocol. As with the COP/MOP, nonparties to the Protocol may participate as observers, but not in decisions concerning the Protocol.[74] Although the functions of the subsidiary organs are not specifically enumerated in the same manner as in the Convention, the Protocol, in various places, assigns tasks to the subsidiary organs such as mandating the SBSTA to provide advice in relation to sinks and methodologies.[75] Article 13(5) provides that the same rules applied under the Convention will be applicable to the Protocol until such time as otherwise decided by consensus. This has the effect of incorporating the state of affairs existing under the Convention, meaning that decisions under the Protocol are also subject to consensus.[76]

### 3.2.3. Flexibility Mechanisms

The Kyoto Protocol introduces flexibility in several respects. First, and very importantly, three trading mechanisms – JI, CDM, and international emissions trading – provide flexibility regarding the location where emissions reductions can be undertaken.[77] Second, the comprehensive approach, discussed in section 3.2.2, introduces flexibility as to which GHGs count. Third, the provision of a five-year commitment period (2008–2012) allows some

---

[72] See id. Art. 13(4)(b).
[73] See id. Art. 13(4)(3) and Art. 5.
[74] See id. Art. 15(2). Items of the agenda of the SBSTA and SBI will be clearly identified so that it is clear in which capacity the bodies are acting, in other words, under the Convention or Protocol.
[75] See id. Art. 3(4) and Art. 5(2).
[76] See OBERTHÜR & OTT, INTERNATIONAL CLIMATE POLICY, at 100. The reason is that the impasse on the rules of procedure, and the consequent absence of a provision on voting, means that decisions have to be taken by consensus, a state of affairs that gives objectors a veto. In practice, at crucial times, chairmen have managed to carry majority decisions over the objections of a few states.
[77] See, for discussion of various types of flexibility, Jim Skea, *Flexibility, Emissions Trading and the Kyoto Protocol*, in POLLUTION FOR SALE: EMISSIONS TRADING AND JOINT IMPLEMENTATION (Steve Sorrell & Jim Skea eds., 1999).

## 3.2. The Kyoto Protocol

leeway regarding when the commitment must be met. In addition, countries with economies in transition, in other words, the countries of Eastern Europe and the former Soviet Union, were granted flexibility in choosing their baselines.[78] Last, Article 4 of the Protocol allows members of a regional integration organization to fulfill their obligations jointly under a so-called bubble arrangement.[79] The EU assumed an overall reduction commitment of 8 percent below 1990 levels, which was then divided into individual targets for the 15 member states that jointly ratified the Protocol.[80] The arrangement permitted the EU as a whole to advocate for, and assume, a fairly aggressive target, while also providing the flexibility to take account of differences in member states' economic development, generation mix, and so on.[81]

Foremost of the measures allowing for flexibility are the market-based mechanisms elaborated in Articles 6 (joint implementation), Article 12 (clean development mechanism), and Article 17 (international emissions trading). Legally, support for such flexibility can be found in the Convention. Article 3(3) states that policies and measures "should be cost-effective so as to ensure global benefits at the lowest possible cost" and "be comprehensive, cover all relevant sources ... and comprise all economic sectors." It also provides that efforts to address climate change may be carried out cooperatively by interested parties. Article 4(2)(a) states that Annex I parties may implement policies and measures jointly with other parties and cooperate to achieve the objective of UNFCCC Article 4(2)(d), provided that the COP shall decide on criteria for joint implementation. Before considering the

---

[78] Since allowances were effectively grandfathered, being able to select a year when the economy was robust and emissions at a historical high point was potentially of considerable benefit. Among the countries with different base years are Bulgaria (1989) and Poland (1988).

[79] If the group of countries fails to meet its collective target, each of the countries, and the regional integration organization that is a party to the Protocol, will be held liable according to its individual targets under the burden-sharing agreement. See Art. 4(6).

[80] See Jürgen Lefevere, *The EU Greenhouse Gas Emission Allowance Trading Scheme*, in CLIMATE CHANGE AND CARBON MARKETS: A HANDBOOK OF EMISSIONS REDUCTIONS MECHANISMS 75, 77–88 (Farhana Yamin ed., 2005). Internally, the burden-sharing agreement was made binding on the 15 member states of the EU. See Council Decision 2002/358/EC of April 25, 2002, Art. 2, 2002 OJ (L 130) 1, 2. Because Art. 4 of the Protocol does not permit amendments to burden-sharing agreements, the accession of 10 members to the Union in 2004 and a further 2 in 2007 has not altered the EU burden-sharing agreement.

[81] E.g., the EU's economically less developed countries could increase their emissions over the 1990 baseline (Greece +30 percent, Ireland +15 percent, and Portugal +40 percent), while other countries accepted deeper cuts to compensate (Austria −25 percent, Denmark −25 percent, and Germany −25 percent).

market mechanisms in greater detail, it is worth considering their common features and the context in which they operate.

To illustrate how market mechanisms function, it may be useful to consider a hypothetical national cap-and-trade scheme. Under such a scheme, total GHG emissions from the relevant sectors, usually power generation and other large, stationary industrial installations, are limited, or capped, over a given period of time. (In the case of the Protocol, this is the first or 2008–2012 commitment period.) The firms in question are eligible for allowances, which can either be distributed for free ("grandfathered") or auctioned. Allowances correspond to a given unit of emissions, usually a ton of carbon dioxide. The total number of allowances distributed is less than the expected amount of emissions from all covered industries over the period in question. The consequence of this regulated scarcity is a price on carbon; all else being equal, the tighter the cap, the higher the price of allowances. Emission control costs vary across different plants and industries. That is to say, the marginal cost of abatement varies. Some firms may find that they can engage in mitigation activities, for example, by installing more efficient machinery, and then sell excess allowances. Other firms, facing higher abatement costs, may instead find that it is cheaper to purchase emissions allowances. The carbon price acts as an incentive for firms to seek out the least-cost mitigation opportunities, with the result that the overall mitigation effort takes place in the most efficient manner. For this reason, economists prefer market-based instruments over command-and-control regulatory policies, such as design or performance standards, which, it is argued, result in economic losses.[82] The experience in the United States with the 1990 amendments to the Clean Air Act[83] resulted in reductions of sulfur dioxide at much lower cost than had been predicted, providing a major boost to the proponents of trading mechanisms.[84] A larger and more

---

[82] Robert N. Stavins, *What Can We Learn from the Grand Policy Experiment? Lessons from SO₂ Allowance Trading*, 12(3) JOURNAL OF ECONOMIC PERSPECTIVES 69, 69 (1998). Interestingly, Stavins also summarizes reasons why legislators, regulators, and industry favored a command-and-control approach.

[83] Clean Air Act of 1970, 42 USC S § 761b (2003).

[84] The savings are generally estimated to have been about US$1 billion (in 1996 dollars) per year. However, the calculation of savings is sensitive to assumptions about alternative regulatory options. *See* CURTIS CARLSON ET AL., SULFUR DIOXIDE CONTROL BY ELECTRIC UTILITIES: WHAT ARE THE GAINS FROM TRADE?, Discussion Paper 98-44-REV, Resources for the Future 3–5 (2000). According to Office of Management and Budget calculations, for the period 1992 to 1995, the benefits of the Title IV SO₂ trading provisions exceeded the

## 3.2. The Kyoto Protocol

diverse market – with more mitigation opportunities – leads to lower aggregate mitigation costs so that on economic efficiency grounds, larger emission trading markets (national or international) are preferable to smaller ones.[85] Studies demonstrate that developed countries could significantly reduce the cost of meeting their GHG reduction goals by making use of the flexibility mechanisms.[86]

Theoretically, taxes can achieve the same results as a trading scheme, at the same or lower aggregate costs.[87] In fact, economic theory suggests that taxes are more appropriate for addressing climate change, where what counts is not achieving a particular level of pollutants year to year – as in the case of air pollution – but ensuring a change in the long-term trend. In practice, however, carbon taxes have, with the exception of a few European countries, proved politically unpalatable. For their part, regulated industries may prefer emissions trading, in part because such a scheme creates a tradable asset, as opposed to a tax that extracts revenue.[88] If emissions allowances

---

costs 40:1. *See* OFFICE OF MANAGEMENT AND BUDGET, DRAFT 2003 REPORT TO CONGRESS ON THE COSTS AND BENEFITS OF FEDERAL REGULATIONS, 68 Fed. Reg. 5492, 5500 (2003).

[85] Economic studies confirm that global trading, as opposed to domestic action, lowers the cost of meeting commitments under the Kyoto Protocol. *See* John P. Weyant & Jennifer Hill, *Introduction and Overview*, in THE COSTS OF THE KYOTO PROTOCOL: A MULTI-MODEL EVALUATION, SPECIAL ISSUE OF THE ENERGY JOURNAL vii (John P. Weyant ed., 1999). This is one reason why the private sector may prefer a federal cap-and-trade system in the United States, as opposed to a number of overlapping but separate state schemes, for instance, the planned California initiative.

[86] Economic modeling strongly suggests that marginal abatement costs are significantly lower if global trading is instituted. *See* a comparison of the results of two dozen models by Urs Springer, *The Market for Tradable GHG Permits under the Kyoto Protocol: A Survey of Model Studies*, 25(3) ENERGY ECONOMICS 527 (2003).

[87] Economic analysis suggests that price (tax) measures are more suited than permit or trading (quantity) approaches to certain environmental problems. In particular, price measures are more efficient in situations where harmful consequences of the pollution (externality) are a function of a much larger stock accumulating in the environment, rather than an annual flow. The lack of a definite, short-term threshold for severe damage also favors a tax approach. This is the case for ozone-depleting substances, groundwater pollution, and the accumulation of GHGs in the atmosphere. In the case of climate change, because the problem is caused by the total concentration of GHGs, the marginal benefit of reducing a unit of emissions is rather low. In the terminology of economics, the marginal benefits curve is flat relative to the marginal cost of abatement, and hence prices are preferred on efficiency grounds. *See* RICHARD G. NEWELL & WILLIAM A. PIZER, REGULATING STOCK EXTERNALITIES UNDER UNCERTAINTY, Discussion Paper 99-10-REV, Resources for the Future 1–2 (2000). The classic analysis on the merits of prices versus quantities is M. L. Weitzman, *Prices vs. Quantities*, 41(4) REVIEW OF ECONOMIC STUDIES 477–91 (1974).

[88] *See* GRUBB ET AL., GUIDE AND ASSESSMENT, at 90. The "political economy" of trading schemes is covered by Stavins, *supra* note 82, at 74–76. Since permits are almost always

or permits are allocated at no cost – that is, grandfathered, as opposed to auctioned – some firms will extract a benefit, or economic rent. With a tax, revenue is channeled to the government, which, in theory, can recycle it by adjusting other taxes to address distortions in the tax system and fund other desirable activities, like worker retraining in emissions-intensive industries or research on clean energy technologies.[89] Functioning emissions trading markets require careful design and a sophisticated regulatory framework, as demonstrated by the experience of the European Union Emission Trading Scheme (EU ETS) in 2006, when information showing that many firms had benefited from an overallocation of allowances resulted in a dramatic drop in prices.[90] A recent study concluded that the first phase of the EU ETS offered three key lessons: (1) accurate emissions data are essential to setting an effective emissions cap; (2) a cap-and-trade scheme should provide enough certainty to influence technology investment; and (3) the method for allocating allowances may have important economic effects in that free allocation may distribute wealth to covered entities, while auctioning could generate revenue for governments.[91] Availability of full information – actual historical emissions, monitoring of emissions, and realistic calculations of expected growth – are critical for the regulator. Given weaker regulatory frameworks, as well as uncertainty about emissions growth projections, cap-and-trade schemes are generally not regarded as a preferred policy option for most developing countries. Finally, unlike a carbon tax, under an emission trading scheme the price of carbon is subject to volatility – during an economic downturn the fall in output will also depress allowance prices.

freely allocated (grandfathered), regulated industries are able to extract an economic rent. In addition, free initial allocation serves as a barrier to entry for new firms, who would have to purchase permits. For legislators, a permit scheme with a free allocation has the advantage of masking the cost of regulation, unlike a tax. For more on this, *see* Nathaniel O. Keohane et al., *The Choice of Regulatory Instruments in Environmental Policy*, 22 HARVARD ENVIRONMENTAL LAW REVIEW 313–67 (1998).

[89] *See*, e.g., the ecological tax reforms in Germany, which aim to reduce the tax burden on labor and shift a portion of it to environmental consumption. E.g., Mineral Oil Tax Law of December 21, 1992, as amended (*Mineralölsteuergesetz* vom 21 Dezember 1992).

[90] After it became known in April 2006 that firms in several member states held considerably more allowances than actual emissions of the covered installations, the price of EU allowances (EUAs) almost halved. While regulated entities may have an interest in inflating their emissions projections, the integrity of a trading scheme demands that the regulator have access to real emissions data.

[91] U.S. GOVERNMENT ACCOUNTABILITY OFFICE, INTERNATIONAL CLIMATE CHANGE PROGRAMS: LESSONS LEARNED FROM THE EUROPEAN UNION'S EMISSIONS TRADING SCHEME AND THE KYOTO PROTOCOL'S CLEAN DEVELOPMENT MECHANISM, GAO-09-151 (2008).

Volatility may reduce the incentive for firms to make long-term investments in low-carbon infrastructure.

3.2.3.1. Joint Implementation. JI is a project-based mechanism by which emission reductions are achieved in accordance with projects implemented in an Annex I country by investors from another Annex I country. The investor/investing country can then claim the resulting emission reduction to sell on the market or credit it against the investor country's target. The term *joint implementation* has a somewhat tangled history, but under the Protocol, its meaning and ambit are clear and uncontroversial.[92] JI has its roots in Articles 4(2)(a) and (d) of the Convention, under which the COP established a pilot phase for activities implemented jointly (AIJ). Under AIJ, industrialized (Annex I) parties could implement projects reducing emissions of GHGs or enhancing their removal through sinks in other countries, both industrialized and developing.[93] Participation in the AIJ is voluntary, and no credits are granted for any reductions achieved under the program.[94] However, the eligibility requirements for AIJ projects closely tracked those that were later made applicable to JI and the CDM, including that activities should result in real and measurable environmental benefits that would not have occurred in the absence of the project.[95] AIJ enabled countries to gain experience with a project-based mechanism, including an approximation of emissions reduction potential, costs, and likely barriers.[96]

---

[92] *See* Grubb et al., Guide and Assessment, at 87–89.
[93] Decision 5/CP.1, in Report of the Conference of the Parties on its First Session, Addendum, Part II: Action Taken by the Parties, FCCC/1995/7/Add.1 (1995).
[94] The pilot phase of the AIJ continues, with 157 projects in 42 countries. *See* Activities Implemented Jointly under the Pilot Phase: Seventh Progress Report, UNFCCC/SBSTA/2006/8 (2006).
[95] Decision 5/CP.1, in Report of the Conference of the Parties on its Seventh Session, Addendum, Part II: Action Taken by the Parties, para. 1(d), FCCC/1995/Add.1 (1995). *See* Charlotte Streck, *Joint Implementation: History, Requirements, and Challenges*, in Legal Aspects of Implementing the Kyoto Protocol Mechanisms: Making Kyoto Work 108–9 (David Freestone & Charlotte Streck eds., 2005).
[96] *See*, e.g., a study prepared for the government of the Netherlands, which analyzed AIJ projects to estimate the potential market for credits under the CDM, including prices. Netherlands Energy Research Foundation (ECN) et al., Potential and Cost of the Clean Development Options in the Energy Sector: Inventory of Options in Non-Annex I Countries to Reduce GHG Emissions (1999). Jason Anderson & Rob Bradley, *Joint Implementation and Emissions Trading in CEE*, in Climate Change and Carbon Markets, *supra* note 80, at 211–13.

Although there are many similarities, it is important to distinguish JI from its close conceptual cousin, the CDM. JI projects take place between Annex I countries, and the mechanism is intended to assist Annex I parties in complying with their emission reduction obligations under Article 3 of the Protocol. The CDM has a dual purpose: to assist Annex I countries in meeting their emissions limitation and reduction obligations and to promote sustainable development in host countries, for instance, by promoting transfer of clean technology. Because JI projects are implemented in Annex I countries, the credits earned from a given project – known as emission reduction units, or ERUs – are deducted from the host country's Kyoto allowance, known as assigned amount units (AAUs). This means that JI projects do not introduce additional allowances into the system; the overall amount of emissions under the cap does not increase. Environmental integrity is safeguarded by the requirement that a JI host country maintain an appropriate inventory of GHG sources and sinks as well as an accounting system for additions and subtractions from its allocation of AAUs. This contrasts with CDM, where there is no deduction from an allocation of allowances because projects are located in developing countries with no Kyoto target. To maintain the environmental integrity of the CDM – that is, to avoid the issuing of credits not based on real emission reductions – the verification, monitoring, and certification requirements for the CDM are more onerous than the equivalent JI provisions.[97]

The basic eligibility requirements for JI projects are set out in Article 6(1), namely, that projects require the approval of both countries involved (host and investor), that any reduction in emissions by sources or removal by sinks must be additional to any that would otherwise occur, and that countries maintain proper inventories and comply with the Protocol's reporting obligations. Article 6(3) provides that private sector entities may, subject to the authorization of the country concerned, participate in JI projects. During the negotiations, it was envisaged that the private sector would have a key role to play as investor in, and developer of, JI projects. However, since JI projects result in a subtraction from a host country's allocation of AAUs, with potential consequences for compliance with its emission reduction commitments, government supervision is important. Hence the

---

[97] STRECK, *supra* note 95, at 112. The requirements for CDM projects are discussed in greater detail in the next section.

proviso that private sector participation is subject to authorization and the requirement that both the host and the purchasing country must approve the project.

As noted previously, developers of JI projects must demonstrate additionality; in other words, they must make the case that project emissions will be lower than a credible baseline, which would have applied but for the project. The Protocol does not address the process for verifying additionality and other requirements for JI projects, simply stating that the parties "may... further elaborate guidelines for the implementation of this Article, including for verification and reporting."[98] The rules developed to implement JI provide for two variants. The first, known as track 1 JI, is available to host countries that have demonstrated certain reporting and accounting requirements. These countries may themselves – without additional oversight – verify that emissions reductions achieved by the project are, in fact, additional.[99] Such self-verification does not jeopardize environmental integrity because, as noted earlier, reported project reductions, even if nominally inflated, are subtracted from the host country's allocation of AAUs.[100] A second option, involving more oversight, is available for Annex I countries that do not meet the requirements for track 1 JI. In this case, an independent body, the Joint Implementation Supervisory Committee, carries out the tasks of ensuring that project design meets JI requirements, verifying emission reductions, and confirming the issuance of ERUs.

For Annex I countries that are not on track to meet their Kyoto commitments from action alone, the attraction of JI stems from lower mitigation costs in the countries of Eastern Europe, as compared with costs in the more advanced industrialized economies.[101] In the process of transition to market

---

[98] Protocol, Art. 6(2).
[99] 16/CP.7, in REPORT OF THE CONFERENCE OF THE PARTIES ON ITS SEVENTH SESSION, ADDENDUM, PART II: ACTION TAKEN BY THE CONFERENCE OF THE PARTIES, annex, para. 21, 23, FCCC/CP/2001/13/Add.2 (2002). See Jari Väyrynen & Franck Lecoq, Track One JI and "Greening of AAUs": How Could It Work?, in LEGAL ASPECTS OF IMPLEMENTING THE KYOTO PROTOCOL, supra note 95, at 156.
[100] The line separating international emissions trading of AAUs under Article 17 and track 1 JI can become rather blurred. The implications are further explored by VÄYRYNEN & LECOQ, supra note 99.
[101] E.g., the Japanese economy is already very energy-efficient and has a low carbon intensity. Therefore domestic abatement costs are high, and Japan is an active participant in the market to acquire JI and CDM credits.

economies, most of these countries moved away from their earlier reliance on energy-intensive and less efficient heavy industries. With emissions well below their 1990 baselines, several of the economies in transition will have a surplus of AAUs available in the first Kyoto commitment period from 2008 to 2012.[102] For host countries, the advantages of JI over pure emissions trading lie in the transfer of clean energy technology, enhanced energy efficiency, and of course, greater long-term reductions in GHG emissions. From the perspective of investors, JI projects may present fewer regulatory and related risks than the CDM. This is particularly true for track 1 JI projects, for which risks associated with baselines, additionality, and verification can be mitigated in a manner not feasible under the CDM.[103] At the same time, unclear institutional responsibilities in host countries, coupled with a lack of transparent approval procedures, and political uncertainties in some host countries, has meant that the JI market has been slow to reach its full potential.[104] The value of the JI market stood at US$499 million in 2007, up from US$141 million the previous year.[105]

The expansion in membership of the EU in 2004, and again in 2007, has diminished the attractiveness of several Eastern European states as JI hosts. On joining the EU, these countries become subject to the EU ETS. The EU ETS covers some 12,000 installations, accounting for almost 45 percent of $CO_2$ emissions of the 25 European member states.[106] The EU ETS applies to a range of installations, including in the power generation, iron and steel, glass, and cement sectors. The first phase of the EU ETS covered the period 2005–2007, while the second phase coincides with the Kyoto Protocol's first commitment period, from 2008 to 2012. The EU ETS is intended to assist the EU in meeting its Kyoto commitment of an 8 percent reduction below 1990 levels. The EU amended the legislation establishing the EU ETS so that certified emission reductions (CERs) from CDM projects and ERUs from

---

[102] ANDERSON & BRADLEY, *supra* note 96, at 203–5.
[103] STRECK, *supra* note 95, at 125.
[104] John O'Brien, *Optimism amid Uncertainty?*, in KYOTO AND THE CARBON MARKETS: FINANCING CLIMATE POLICY TO 2012 AND BEYOND, A SPECIAL SUPPLEMENT to ENVIRONMENTAL FINANCE AND CARBON FINANCE S38 (2006).
[105] KARAN CAPOOR & PHILIPPE AMBROSI, WORLD BANK, STATE AND TRENDS OF THE CARBON MARKET 1 (2008).
[106] *See* Directive 2003/87/EC of the European Parliament and of the Council of October 13, 2003, establishing a scheme for GHG emission allowance trading within the Community and amending Council Directive 96/61/EC, 2003 OJ (L 275) 32.

*3.2. The Kyoto Protocol* 79

JI projects could be traded in the EU ETS.[107] Subject to some limitations, the so-called linking directive makes it possible to convert project-based credits that meet the Kyoto standards into EU allowances.[108] Firms subject to the EU ETS can thus draw on CDM and JI credits in meeting their targets under the scheme. Interaction of the EU ETS with CDM and JI gives rise to the rather technical issue of double counting, which "refers to a situation in which CERs or ERUs are issued as a result of reductions that also lead to a reduction from emissions from an installation covered by the [Emissions Trading] Directive."[109] To prevent double counting under the EU ETS and the Protocol, installations covered by the EU ETS are not eligible to generate ERUs under JI.

3.2.3.2. Clean Development Mechanism. The second flexibility mechanism is the CDM, which is established by Article 12 to serve the twin goals of assisting developing countries in achieving sustainable development and aiding Annex I parties in meeting their emission limitation and reduction commitments.[110] The CDM has its roots in a proposal for a Clean Development Fund advanced by Brazil, to be financed from fines levied on Annex I parties for noncompliance.[111] As elaborated by the United States in the final Kyoto

---

[107] *See* Directive 2004/101/EC of October 27, 2004, amending Directive 2003/87/EC, establishing a scheme for GHG emission allowance trading within the Community, in respect of the Kyoto Protocol's project mechanisms, 2004 OJ (L 338) 18. For details on the Linking Directive, *see* Lefevere, *supra* note 80, at 126–38.

[108] The directive does not cap the number of CERs and ERUs that member states may introduce into the ETS but provides that inclusion of an amount greater than 6 percent of a member state's EU allowances will trigger a review process. CERs and ERUs from forestry-related projects are excluded.

[109] Lefevere, *supra* note 80, at 138. E.g., double counting would arise, where a JI project is implemented at an installation subject to the ETS. The project will give rise to JI credits – which can be traded in the EU ETS – *as well as* freeing up EU allowances assigned to the particular installation. To prevent double counting, the operator of the installation is required to cancel a EU allowance for every JI credit (ERU) that is issued. For a more detailed discussion of double counting under the EU ETS and JI, *see* Streck, *supra* note 95, at 123–25. The provisions of the Linking Directive relating to double counting are regarded as having made JI projects in EU countries less attractive, leading to criticism from Japan, which felt it was being denied access credits needed to meet its Kyoto obligations. Linking the EU ETS to other cap-and-trade schemes has been mooted from time to time, and if and when such arrangements come into being, double counting will also be an issue.

[110] Mark Kenber, *The Clean Development Mechanism: A Tool for Promoting Long-Term Climate Protection and Sustainable Development?*, in Climate Change and Carbon Markets, *supra* note 80, at 263.

[111] *See* Oberthür & Ott, International Climate Policy, *supra* note 41, at 165–66; FCCC/AGBM/1997/MISC.1/Add.3.

negotiations, the proposal was transformed into what is now the CDM, which incorporates the underlying principle of joint implementation.[112]

Like JI, the CDM is a project-based mechanism, but in this case, credits may be earned for projects executed in developing countries. Every CER is equivalent to a ton of $CO_2$. For each CER purchased, an Annex I party, in effect, increases its cap; unlike under JI projects, the CERs generated by CDM projects are not backed by a subtraction from an Annex I party's assigned basket of allowances. Thus ensuring the environmental integrity of CDM projects is all the more important.[113] Resulting GHG reductions must be real and measurable and "additional to any that would occur in the absence of the certified project activity."[114] Thus developers of CDM projects must demonstrate that a project's reduction in GHG emissions goes beyond business as usual, which involves showing that emission reductions generated by the project are in addition to any that would have occurred in the project's absence (the so-called additionality criterion).[115] CDM projects are also required to contribute to sustainable development, but the determination of whether this criterion has been met rests with the host country. To ensure the environmental integrity of the CDM and its proper administration, the COP has developed detailed rules covering project validation; registration with the Executive Board (EB); and the verification, certification, and issuance of credits from CDM activities.[116]

The implementation of the CDM is overseen by the CDM EB, which is composed of 20 members (10 full-time members and 10 alternates) drawn from among Annex I and non–Annex I (developing) countries.[117] The EB

---

[112] Naoki Matsuo, *CDM in the Kyoto Negotiations: How CDM Has Worked as a Bridge between Developed and Developing Worlds?*, 8 MITIGATION AND ADAPTATION STRATEGIES FOR GLOBAL CHANGE 191, 197 (2003).

[113] Ernestine Meijer & Jacob Werksman, *Keeping It Clean – Safeguarding the Environmental Integrity of the Clean Development Mechanism*, in LEGAL ASPECTS OF IMPLEMENTING THE KYOTO PROTOCOL, *supra* note 95, at 191.

[114] Protocol, Art. 12(5).

[115] For detailed discussion of baselines and additionality, *see* Axel Michaelowa, *Determination of Baselines and Additionality for the CDM: A Crucial Element of the Credibility of the Climate Regime*, in CLIMATE CHANGE AND CARBON MARKETS, *supra* note 80, at 287.

[116] For a summary of the CDM project cycle, *see* Farhana Yamin, *The International Rules of the Kyoto Mechanisms*, in CLIMATE CHANGE AND CARBON MARKETS, *supra* note 80, at 29–52; Maria Netto & Kai-Uwe Barani Schmidt, *CDM Project Cycle and the Role of the UNFCCC*, in LEGAL ASPECTS OF IMPLEMENTING THE KYOTO PROTOCOL, *supra* note 95, at 175.

[117] *See* Decision 17/CP.7, in REPORT OF THE CONFERENCE OF THE PARTIES ON ITS SEVENTH SESSION, ADDENDUM, PART II: ACTION TAKEN BY THE CONFERENCE OF THE PARTIES, VOL. II, ANNEX, MODALITIES AND PROCEDURES FOR A CLEAN DEVELOPMENT MECHANISM,

elaborates the rules and modalities governing the CDM, approves and registers CDM projects, issues CERs, and carries out other functions relating to the CDM.[118] The EB is subject to the "guidance" of the COP/MOP, which is the supreme body of the Protocol. The COP/MOP fulfils this function only in relation to a number of enumerated issues – for instance, the rules of procedure of the EB and the geographical distribution of CDM projects – but it does not serve as a general avenue of appeal for decisions taken by the EB.[119] The EB has established several panels and working groups to assist it in carrying out its functions. The Methodology Panel, tasked with developing project methodologies, has attracted the most attention and scrutiny. Project developers and investors in the carbon market have criticized the EB for supposedly applying overly stringent project approval criteria, lack of transparency, and insufficient resources and capacity, with negative consequences on the ability to cope with its workload.[120] Overall, the registration of projects is accelerating, and the EB's funding shortfalls, resulting from its reliance on voluntary funding, will recede as it begins to benefit from the collection of administrative fees levied on CDM projects. On the other side, studies have pointed to problems with the CDM market, particularly with respect to the additionality of some CDM credits.[121] As it is not possible to ensure that every credit from an offset mechanism like the CDM represents a real, measurable, and long-term reduction in emissions, the use of carbon

---

FCCC/CP/2001/13/Add.2 (2002). Members of the EB serve in their personal capacity, are required to take a written oath of service, and may not have a pecuniary or financial interest in any aspect of a CDM project activity. See supra Decision 17/CP.7, respectively, para. 8(c), (e), and (f), MODALITIES AND PROCEDURES FOR A CLEAN DEVELOPMENT MECHANISM. As a body established under public international law, the decisions of the EB are probably not subject to review under domestic law. The EB is solely subject to the political and legal control of the COP/MOP.

[118] Maria Netto & Kai-Uwe Barani Schmidt, *CDM Project Cycle and the Role of the UNFCCC Secretariat, in* LEGAL ASPECTS OF IMPLEMENTING THE KYOTO PROTOCOL, *supra* note 95, at 177–80.

[119] Decision 17/CP.7, in REPORT OF THE CONFERENCE OF THE PARTIES, *supra* note 117, annex, paras. 2–4. Farhana Yamin, *The International Rules of the Kyoto Mechanisms, in* CLIMATE CHANGE AND CARBON MARKETS, *supra* note 80, at 34.

[120] For an expression of such views, *see* INTERNATIONAL EMISSIONS TRADING ASSOCIATION, 2006 STATE OF THE CDM: IETA POSITION ON THE CDM FOR CoP-12/MoP-2 11–20 (2006). *See also* CAPOOR & AMBROSI, *supra* note 105, at 4–5.

[121] AXEL MICHAELOWA & PALLAV PUROHIT, ADDITIONALITY DETERMINATION OF INDIAN CDM PROJECTS: CAN INDIAN CDM PROJECT DEVELOPERS OUTWIT THE CDM EXECUTIVE BOARD (2007); U.S. GOVERNMENT ACCOUNTABILITY OFFICE, *supra* note 91; David Victor & Michael Wara, *A Realistic Policy on International Carbon Offsets*, PESD Working Paper 74 (2008).

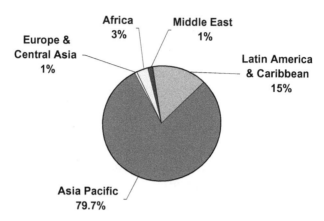

FIGURE 3.1. Projected regional distribution of CERs in 2012. *Source:* Adapted from CDM Pipeline, Jørgen Fenhann, UNEP Risøe Centre (2008).

offsets in a cap-and-trade system can potentially undermine the system's integrity.

The CDM market has generated a great deal of interest on the part of developing countries, who see a potential influx of technology and resources, as well as developed countries, who see cheaper compliance and opportunities for their private sectors in banking, advising, and legal services. The value of CDM credit purchases in 2007 reached US$8.2 billion, a figure that dwarves other multilateral investments in climate mitigation.[122] As is evident from Table 3.1, the geographic distribution of CDM projects is very uneven, with Asia and Latin America accounting for the lion's share. An analysis by the UN Development Programme estimated that Asia and Latin America are expected to generate around 95 percent of CERs through 2012; Africa is expected to garner only 3 percent of CERs by that date.[123] Countries from regions that have so far benefited less from the CDM, such as sub-Saharan Africa, have called for measures to promote a more equitable distribution of projects. Given the high transaction costs associated with the CDM, project size (more tons abated equals more credits), and economies of scale (many similar projects), it is unsurprising that China and India lead in the number of projects. Because the ability to attract CDM investment depends significantly on existing emissions reduction potential, as between

---

[122] CAPOOR & AMBROSI, *supra* note 105, at 19.
[123] UNDP, THE CLEAN DEVELOPMENT MECHANISM: AN ASSESSMENT OF PROGRESS 11–12 (2006).

developing countries, it may tend to reinforce past advantage; that is, more goes to those countries that are already more capable. Project developers presumably seek out host countries offering the lowest cost-mitigation opportunities; the underlying logic of the CDM is efficiency, not necessarily equity. A properly operating CDM cannot be expected to lead to an equitable distribution of projects; nonetheless, building the capacity of smaller, poorer developing countries to attract CDM investment can help.

Fairness may be well and good, but is it not correct that scarce mitigation resources be allocated as effectively and efficiently as possible? Estimates are that Kyoto Protocol parties and private sector companies will have a compliance demand of about 2.4 billion metric tons of $CO_2$-equivalent units, to be met from the units of the three flexible mechanisms. Theoretically, credits generated by the CDM could supply two-thirds of this demand, at a relatively low abatement cost.[124] Nonetheless, the overall contribution to mitigation is decidedly modest.[125] One answer is that making resources available directly to developing countries, with a view to putting them on a low-carbon development path, may be a better use of resources. Another is to ask whether the CDM has met its other objective, namely, promoting sustainable development in the host countries. In this respect, it remains to be seen whether the CDM can deliver broader sustainable development benefits for host countries, for instance, with respect to the transfer of clean technology.[126] An analysis of the *development dividend* – the social, economic, and environmental benefits – for CDM host countries found that projects giving rise to the highest number of CERs received very low scores.[127] Given that the CDM transfers technology in only 39 percent of projects, another study noted the room for improvement, while also

---

[124] *See* CAPOOR & AMBROSI, *supra* note 105, at 50–51. *Cf.* UNDP, *supra* note 123, at 13–14 (estimate CDM could meet 15 to 20 percent of demand for Kyoto units).

[125] It is estimated that by 2012, total $CO_2$-equivalent emissions ($CO_{2\text{-eq}}$) abated under the CDM could eventually reach 1.6 billion tons, with a range of 1.4–2.2 billion. *See* CAPOOR & AMBROSI, *supra* note 105, at 18. According to the IPCC, from 2000 to 2005, annual worldwide emissions of $CO_2$ from fossil fuels and land use are estimated to have been about 32 billion annually. The total reductions achieved under the CDM are thus equivalent to approximately 4.8 percent of annual $CO_2$ emissions.

[126] *See* HELEEN C. DE CONINCK ET AL., TECHNOLOGY TRANSFER IN THE CLEAN DEVELOPMENT MECHANISM, ECN-E-07-009, Energy Research Centre of the Netherlands (2007); Katrin Millock, *Technology Transfers in the Clean Development Mechanism: An Incentives Issue*, 7 ENVIRONMENT AND DEVELOPMENT ECONOMICS 449 (2002).

[127] AARON COSBEY, MAKING DEVELOPMENT WORK IN THE CDM: PHASE 2 OF THE DEVELOPMENT DIVIDEND REPORT, IISD (2007), http://www.iisd.org/climate/global/dividend.asp.

finding that transfer is distributed unevenly across technologies and countries.[128] Finally, CDM ought to be evaluated against the backdrop of the climate regime as a whole, particularly the obligations of developed countries to transfer environmentally sound technologies and provide financial assistance to fund the mitigation in developing countries. On fairness and policy grounds, the CDM cannot be a substitute for those commitments.

The CDM is at the intersection of international and domestic law: established under a treaty, the Kyoto Protocol is overseen by an international body exercising administrative functions, the EB, in accordance with rules adopted by the COP. Project developers and investors – the key private entities in the system – are subject to both the provisions of the Protocol and the international rules adopted by the COP, decisions of the EB, and domestic rules of the host country, for instance, with respect to environmental impact assessments and taxation. While some have criticized this governance structure as unwieldy and bureaucratic, a more balanced perspective view might hold that progress in establishing an innovative and unusual set of institutions has been quite successful thus far. Uncertainty concerning the post-2012 climate framework and the future prospects of an international carbon market is the most important factor influencing the outlook for the CDM.

### 3.2.3.3. International Emissions Trading.

Under Article 17, Annex I parties to the Protocol may engage in emissions trading for the purposes of fulfilling their commitments. The Protocol provides that each Annex I party has a number of AAUs corresponding to its individual emission allowance inscribed in Annex B of the Protocol.[129] The emission targets in Annex B to the Kyoto Protocol are expressed as a percentage relative to 1990 emissions; the AAUs simply express this as units of $CO_2$-equivalent emissions.

The concept of international emissions trading was introduced in the negotiations by the United States, winning the support of the other members of the JUSSCANNZ coalition, but opposed initially by the EU, and rejected by developing countries. In the knowledge that significant domestic emissions cuts would be politically difficult to obtain, the United States regarded trading as critical to meeting any target it might assume. The

---

[128] Malte Schneider et al., *Understanding the CDM's Contribution to Technology Transfer*, 36 ENERGY POLICY 2933 (2008).
[129] Protocol, Art. 3(7).

EU, skeptical at first, came to accept the concept but argued that trading should remain supplementary to domestic action. The most serious opposition came from the developing countries, which argued that trading would allow the United States, the largest emitter of GHGs, to avoid meaningful domestic action.[130] This, in turn, threatened the position of countries such as China and India, which, at times, advocated the position that over time, the per capita emissions of industrialized countries should contract, eventually converging at equal per capita levels with those of developing countries. Finally, developing countries were aware that under trading, the Russian Federation potentially stood to gain from trading with its large number of surplus AAUs, with an attendant transfer of wealth.[131] Flooding the market with AAUs would also have the effect of depressing the price of CERs generated by CDM projects in developing countries.

**3.2.3.4. Compliance Mechanism.** January 1, 2008, marked the formal start of the compliance period of the Kyoto Protocol. Article 18 requires the COP to "approve appropriate and effective procedures and mechanisms to determine and to address cases of non-compliance with the Provisions of the Protocol." This rather basic provision, while specifying that the procedure should include an "indicative list of consequences," left a great deal to be fleshed out in the post-Kyoto negotiations in the COP.[132] Objections to the proposal for binding penalties were overcome with the insertion of the final sentence of the article, providing that "any procedures or mechanisms ... entailing binding consequences shall be adopted by means of an amendment."[133] The compliance mechanism of the Kyoto Protocol has been hailed as unique to international law.[134] Together with market-based flexibility mechanisms, it comprises the innovative features of the Protocol. This section starts with a brief outline of approaches to compliance in

---

[130] *See* GRUBB ET AL., GUIDE AND ASSESSMENT, at 94–95.
[131] With the withdrawal of the United States from the Kyoto Protocol, the market for credits from Russia and other EITs is much smaller. In any event, it is thought that buyers will be reluctant to purchase "hot air" or windfall allowances. Various options have been explored to "green" such allowances. *See* VÄYRYNEN & LECOQ, *supra* note 95, at 155.
[132] For details, *see* WERKSMAN, *supra* note 32; Jacob Werksman, *The Negotiation of a Kyoto Compliance System*, *in* IMPLEMENTING THE CLIMATE REGIME: INTERNATIONAL COMPLIANCE 17 (Olaf Schramm Stokke et al. eds., 2005).
[133] *See* OBERTHÜR & OTT, INTERNATIONAL CLIMATE POLICY, at 216–18.
[134] WERKSMAN, *supra* note 131, at 19.

international environmental law. This scene setting is followed by a description of the compliance mechanism itself.[135]

Classically, breach of an obligation under international law entitles the wronged party to reparation or compensation – such as in the seminal *Trail Smelter* arbitration[136] – with the parties arguing their case before an independent third party. In truth, this third-party dispute resolution is quite uncommon in international law, and even more so in international environmental law.[137] For one thing, states tend to avoid the confrontational (and unpredictable) approach entailed by formal dispute settlement, generally preferring negotiations. More important, traditional dispute settlement – akin to domestic tort action – is simply not appropriate for harms involving a range of actors, diffuse causation, and long timescales.[138] In such circumstances, a process resting on monitoring, supervision, and management is a preferred means of achieving the objectives of the instrument concerned. Accordingly, some scholars view noncompliance procedures, whether formal or informal, as a natural extension of existing information-gathering, monitoring, and supervision activities that are normally carried out by the conferences of the parties of many treaties.[139] This view is strongly represented by the so-called managerial school, which holds that although many international regimes invest little in explicit enforcement, the degree of compliance is quite good.[140] This position is supported by a number of

---

[135] See also, on the compliance mechanism, Geir Ulfstein & Jacob Werksman, *The Kyoto Compliance System: Towards Hard Enforcement*, in IMPLEMENTING THE CLIMATE REGIME: INTERNATIONAL COMPLIANCE, supra note 133, at 39; Farhana Yamin, *The International Rules on the Kyoto Mechanisms*, in CLIMATE CHANGE AND CARBON MARKETS, supra note 80, at 61–66; Andries Nentjes & Ger Klaassen, *On the Quality of Compliance Mechanisms of the Kyoto Protocol*, 32(4) ENERGY POLICY 531, 534 (2004); CHRISTIAN HOLTWISCH, DAS NICHTEINHALTUNGSVERFAHREN DES KYOTO-PROTOKOLLS: ENSTEHUNG-GESTALT-WIRKUNG (2006).

[136] *Trail Smelter Arbitration (United States v. Canada)*, 33 AJIL 182 (1939) and 35 AJIL 684 (1941).

[137] A notable exception is the *Gabcikovo-Nagymaros Dam Case* (Hungary v. Slovakia), ICJ Rep. (1997).

[138] PATRICIA BIRNIE & ALAN BOYLE, INTERNATIONAL LAW AND THE ENVIRONMENT, 2ND ED. 180 (2002). But see also Hari M. Osofsky, *Is Climate Change "International"? Litigation's Diagonal Regulatory Role*, 49(3) VIRGINIA JOURNAL OF INTERNATIONAL LAW 587 (2009), contending that climate change regulation necessitates "multiscalar legal approaches – that is, ones which simultaneously engage more than one level of governance."

[139] See id.

[140] ABRAM CHAYES & ANTONIA HANDLER CHAYES, THE NEW SOVEREIGNTY: COMPLIANCE WITH TREATIES IN INTERNATIONAL REGULATORY REGIMES (1995).

## 3.2. The Kyoto Protocol

empirical studies.[141] A conclusion drawn from this line of thought is that compliance does not derive predominantly from deterrent effects or consequences. Another group of scholars, however, regard enforcement and the calculations underlying compliance and participation as central to the design of effective international regimes.[142] Faced with evidence of relatively widespread compliance, advocates of this position ask whether states choose to participate only in treaties in which compliance imposes little or no cost. Finally, it has also been noted that the perceived legitimacy[143] and fairness[144] of a particular rule will influence parties' compliance with its terms.

The process of drawing up the rules for a compliance mechanism began at the first conference after the adoption of the Protocol. The Buenos Aires Programme of Work on Adaptation and Response Measures, adopted at COP-4 in 1998, established the Joint Working Group on Compliance, which was mandated to articulate procedures by which "compliance with the obligations under the Kyoto Protocol should be addressed."[145] At the resumed COP-6 at Bonn, agreement was reached, among other things, on the objectives of the mechanism, the consequences of enforcement, the scope of the enforcement, and the conditions for lodging appeals.[146] At COP-7 in Marrakech, parties agreed that the compliance mechanism would consist of a Compliance Committee, with two functioning branches: a Facilitative Branch and an Enforcement Branch.[147] The committee consists of 20 members, with 10 elected to serve in each respective branch. Members, who serve

---

[141] *See* ENGAGING COUNTRIES: STRENGTHENING COMPLIANCE WITH INTERNATIONAL ENVIRONMENTAL ACCORDS (Edith Brown Weiss & Harold K. Jacobson eds., 1998).

[142] *See* SCOTT BARRETT, ENVIRONMENT AND STATECRAFT (2003); Scott Barrett & Robert Stavins, *Increasing Participation and Compliance in International Climate Change Agreements*, 3 INTERNATIONAL ENVIRONMENTAL AGREEMENTS: POLITICS, LAW AND ECONOMICS 349–76 (2003).

[143] THOMAS M. FRANCK, THE POWER OF LEGITIMACY AMONG NATIONS (1990).

[144] THOMAS M. FRANCK, FAIRNESS IN INTERNATIONAL LAW AND INSTITUTIONS (1995).

[145] Decision 8/CP.4, in REPORT OF THE CONFERENCE OF THE PARTIES ON ITS FOURTH SESSION, ADDENDUM, PART II: ACTION TAKEN BY THE CONFERENCE OF THE PARTIES, annex 2, FCCC/CP/1998/16/Add.1 (1999).

[146] Decision 27/CMP.1, in REPORT OF THE CONFERENCE OF THE PARTIES SERVING AS THE MEETING OF THE PARTIES, ADDENDUM, PART II: ACTION TAKEN BY THE CONFERENCE OF THE PARTIES SERVING AS THE MEETING OF THE PARTIES, FCCC/KP/CMP/2005/8/Add.3 (2006).

[147] Decision 24/CP.7, in REPORT OF THE CONFERENCE OF THE PARTIES, ADDENDUM, PART II: ACTION TAKEN BY THE CONFERENCE OF THE PARTIES, vol. III, annex, FCCC/CP/2001/13/Add.3 (2002).

in their individual capacities, must have recognized "competence relating to climate change and in relevant fields such as the scientific, technical, socio-economic or legal fields."[148] Membership in each branch is composed as follows: one member from each of the five regional groups of the UN,[149] one member from the small island developing states, two members from parties included in Annex I, and two members from non–Annex I parties. This means that developing countries have a majority representation on both branches. The committee is required to make "every effort to reach agreement on any decision by consensus."[150] Where this fails, decisions shall be adopted by a majority of three-fourths of the members present and voting. However, as Annex I parties were unwilling to permit developing country members to have the final say in the Enforcement Branch, a double majority provision applies – decisions also require a three-fourths majority of members of Annex I parties.

Expert review teams (ERTs) are responsible for reviewing Annex I parties' performance of their technical reporting requirements, for example, with respect to inventories of GHG sources. ERTs form a crucial part of the compliance system. As independent and technical experts, they are not meant to make judgments on compliance, but instead to raise "questions of implementation." ERTs are drawn up by the Secretariat of the Convention, from a list nominated by the parties. Action by the committee can be triggered in the following ways: questions of implementation raised in reports submitted by the ERTs, by a party with respect to itself, or by a party with respect to another party.[151] After allocation to one or the other branch by the bureau of the committee, the relevant branch carries out an initial screening, including weeding out de minimis submissions.

The mandate of the Facilitative Branch consists of providing advice and facilitation to the parties in implementing the Protocol and promoting compliance by parties with their obligations, "taking into account the principle of common but differentiated responsibilities and respective capacities."[152] With respect to matters falling outside the mandate of the

---

[148] *See id.* at annex, section II.
[149] They are African Group, Latin American and Caribbean, Asian Group, Eastern European, and Western Europe and Other.
[150] Decision 24/CP.7, in REPORT OF THE CONFERENCE OF THE PARTIES, *supra* note 146, at annex, section II.
[151] *See id.* at annex, section VI.
[152] *See id.* at annex, section IV.

Enforcement Branch, the Facilitative Branch is responsible for addressing *questions of implementation* – the technical term for matters brought before the committee – concerning steps taken by industrialized countries to minimize the adverse effects of climate change response measures on developing countries, and information provided by Annex I countries on the extent to which use of the flexibility mechanisms is supplementary to domestic mitigation efforts.[153] In addition, as a means of "providing for early warning of potential non-compliance," the Facilitative Branch is responsible for providing parties with advice and facilitation on a number of issues, prior to the first commitment period.[154] These provisions appear designed to allow one party to involve the Facilitative Branch in a question whether another party has, before the commitment period, established the requisite national monitoring and reporting systems.

The consequences that the Facilitative Branch is competent to apply, taking into account the principle of common but differentiated responsibilities, encompass, among other things, the facilitation of financial and technical assistance, including technology transfer and capacity building from sources other than climate funds established under the Convention and Protocol and the formulation of recommendations to the party concerned, taking into account Article 4(7) of the Convention, which states that effective implementation by developing countries of their commitments will depend on industrialized countries meeting their commitments to make available financial resources and technology.[155] It is clear from this outline of consequences as well as from the contrasting language relating to the Enforcement Branch that decisions of the Facilitative Branch are not intended to be binding. While the Facilitative Branch "shall decide" on the application of consequences, its enforcement counterpart "determine[s] that a Party is not in compliance."[156]

The Enforcement Branch is responsible for determining whether an Annex I party is not in compliance with its emissions limitation and reduction target under the Protocol; the methodological requirements for estimating emissions by sources and removals by sources and the reporting requirements; and the eligibility requirements for participation in JI,

---

[153] *See id.* at annex, section IV.
[154] *See id.*
[155] *See id.* at annex, section XIV.
[156] *See id.* at annex, section XIV and XV.

CDM, and international emissions trading.[157] At a more technical level, the Enforcement Branch is also empowered to make adjustments and corrections in the event of disagreements between a party and an expert review team regarding, respectively, inventories under Article 5(2) and databases for the accounting of AAUs.

If the Enforcement Branch determines that a party is not in compliance with the Protocol's requirements concerning the GHG monitoring and accounting systems, that party is obliged to submit to the Enforcement Branch for review and assessment a plan analyzing the causes of noncompliance, measures to remedy the noncompliance, and a timetable for doing so.[158] Where the Enforcement Branch determines that an Annex I party does not meet eligibility requirements for JI, CDM, or international emissions trading, "it shall suspend the eligibility of that Party."[159] Provision is made for reinstatement. Finally, revealing the teeth of the compliance system, where the Enforcement Branch determines that a party has exceeded its assigned amount, a deduction equal to the excess plus 30 percent (excess × 1.3) will be made from the assigned amount for the second commitment period. In addition, a noncompliant party is required to draw up a compliance action plan and is suspended from making transfers under international emissions trading, pending reinstatement.[160]

If a party believes it has been denied due process by a final decision of the Enforcement Branch, it may lodge an appeal with the COP/MOP, which may, by a three-fourths majority of parties present and voting, override an Enforcement Branch decision.[161] Aside from the appeals procedure, the relationship of the COP/MOP with respect to the Compliance Committee is explicitly limited to matters such as "providing general policy

---

[157] See id. at annex, section V.

[158] See id. at annex, section XV. On April 16–17, 2008, the Enforcement Branch confirmed a preliminary finding that Greece was not in compliance with its national system requirements, making it the first country found to be noncompliant with a Protocol obligation. See ENFORCEMENT BRANCH, REPORT OF THE FOURTH MEETING, April 16–17, 2008, CC/EB/4/2008/2. Greece subsequently submitted a revised plan pursuant to the request of the Enforcement Branch and a request to have its eligibility to participate in the market mechanisms reinstated. After considering the revised plan and most recent ERT report, the Enforcement Branch found that there was no longer a question of implementation with respect to Greece. See ENFORCEMENT BRANCH, DECISION UNDER PARAGRAPH 2 OF SECTION X, CC-2007-1-13/Greece/EB, November 13, 2008.

[159] See id.
[160] See id.
[161] See id. at annex, section XI.

## 3.2. The Kyoto Protocol

guidance," considering the reports of the committee, and adopting decisions on administrative and budgetary matters. This indicates that those countries that wished to insulate the committee from more politicized COP/MOP deliberations succeeded, at least on paper, in doing so. Equally, the potential grounds for appeal appear fairly narrow, subject, of course, to the interpretation adopted by the Enforcement Branch. Certainly the end result is closer to a process with fairly predictable consequences and limited discretion, as advocated by the United States, rather than with case-by-case review, as preferred by the EU.[162] Because decisions by the Enforcement Branch will presumably be based largely on technical questions – submitted by the ERT or another party – the scope for arguing denial of due process appears limited. Moreover, the Enforcement Branch is likely to evaluate all information carefully. The material on which the branch bases its determinations would, in practice, consist of the report of the ERT or the party having raised the question. Outside organizations, such as nongovernmental organizations (NGOs), are permitted to make submissions. The Enforcement Branch is empowered to appoint experts to assist it. Some deference by the Enforcement Branch to factual contentions by the party before it, as is found in the practice of judicial and quasi-judicial bodies with respect to findings of fact, would not be surprising.

The generally positive assessment of the compliance regime must be balanced against the critical views of some scholars. Barrett, for instance, singles out the compliance regime as one of the Protocol's grave defects.[163] Barrett points out that there is little to prevent a party determined to have exceeded its emissions quota from simply carrying its penalty from one commitment period to the next. In addition, a party found to be noncompliant will bargain for a generous allocation in a succeeding commitment period. In short, he argues that the consequences contemplated in the noncompliance procedure are simply not enforceable.

Another observer of the compliance system notes that in the course of its negotiation, the parties gradually moved away from the soft managerial compliance regime, exemplified by the Montreal Protocol, toward hard compliance.[164] In essence, it appears that the parties came to believe that it was appropriate that tougher compliance provisions should back binding

---

[162] WERKSMAN, *supra* note 131, at 24–25.
[163] BARRETT & STAVINS, *supra* note 141, at 350.
[164] WERKSMAN, *supra* note 131, at 22. *See already* WERKSMAN, *supra* note 32, at 48–66.

emissions limitation and reduction commitments. The Kyoto compliance system is also distinguished from its Montreal Protocol counterpart in that the tools of the managerial approach – technical and financial assistance – are of less relevance to the exclusively industrialized group of countries subject to binding targets under the Protocol. Finally, fairness requires a strong and impartial compliance mechanism, which fully upholds the tenets of procedural fairness. A weak mechanism, with loopholes that are easy to exploit, raises the possibility that noncompliant parties could avoid doing their fair share and, in the longer term, increase the burden on compliant parties.

### 3.3. FINALIZING THE PROTOCOL: CONSOLIDATION AND CHANGE – THE LONG ROAD TO ENTRY INTO FORCE

Its imminent demise already certified by critics, the Protocol finally entered into force on February 16, 2005.[165] The legal instrument adopted in 1997 set targets and timetables, but the technical details to bring the overall framework into operation remained to be worked out. This task, in what came to be known as the Kyoto process, fell to the COP, which, in the period before the Protocol came into force, was requested to carry out a range of tasks to ensure its prompt start.[166] This process of filling in the gaps is covered in greater detail in this section.

Like the Convention, the Protocol is also, in many respects, a framework instrument, with the drafters having left many details to subsequent negotiation. In particular, the rules for the market-based flexibility mechanisms remained to be elaborated. The same was true for other basic operational details relating to reporting and accounting for emissions, financial assistance for developing countries, and the compliance mechanism. After protracted negotiations, most of these issues were resolved at COP-7 in

---

[165] *See* DAVID VICTOR, THE COLLAPSE OF THE KYOTO PROTOCOL AND THE STRUGGLE TO SLOW GLOBAL WARMING (2001). The Russian Federation deposited its instrument of ratification with the United Nations on November 18, 2004, following a long period of uncertainty.

[166] *See* Decision 1/CP.3, in REPORT OF THE CONFERENCE OF THE PARTIES ON ITS THIRD SESSION, ADDENDUM, PART II: ACTION TAKEN BY THE CONFERENCE OF THE PARTIES, FCCC/CP/1997/7/Add.1 (1998). *See also* OBERTHÜR & OTT, INTERNATIONAL CLIMATE POLICY, at 245. In effect, the COP served as an ad hoc preparatory body for the first COP/MOP. The first session of the COP/MOP formally adopted the COP decisions taken in preparation for the entry into force of the Protocol.

## 3.3. Finalizing the Protocol

Marrakech in 2001, where the parties adopted the so-called Marrakech Accords, containing the Protocol rule book. This section traces the completion – and, to an extent, the evolution – of the Protocol through the various COPs. It concludes with a short assessment of the strengths and weaknesses of the climate regime.

### 3.3.1. Conference of the Parties (COP)-4: Attending to Unfinished Business

The Kyoto Protocol was adopted at the third COP, in 1997. COP-4, the first meeting of the parties after the adoption of the Kyoto Protocol, was an opportunity to deal with the unfinished business of those climactic negotiations.[167] The parties adopted a number of decisions – the Buenos Aires Plan of Action – that established a negotiating agenda for the coming into operation of the Protocol.[168] The Plan covered a number of issues, including the financial mechanism, the development and transfer of technology, the implementation of Convention and Protocol articles concerning adverse effects of climate change on developing countries, and the Kyoto mechanisms.

With respect to the financial mechanism, the parties agreed that the restructured GEF would serve as an entity entrusted with the operation of the financial mechanism referred to in Article 11 of the Convention and that the COP would review the performance of the GEF every four years.[169] Among other things, it was also agreed that the GEF should fund the full cost of initial and subsequent reports by developing countries on emissions and measures taken to implement the Convention (known as national communications).[170] Demonstrating the early concern of developing countries regarding adaptation and vulnerability, the GEF was also asked to implement adaptation response measures in particularly vulnerable

---

[167] GRUBB ET AL., GUIDE AND ASSESSMENT, at 248–53. For a summary of the meeting, see also Report of the Fourth Conference of the Parties to the Framework Convention on Climate Change, 12(97) EARTH NEGOTIATIONS BULLETIN (1998), available at http://www.iisd.ca/vol12/. The Earth Negotiations Bulletin (ENB) is widely regarded as a factual and authoritative source of information on international environmental and sustainable development negotiations.

[168] See Decision 1/CP.4, in REPORT OF THE CONFERENCE OF THE PARTIES ON ITS FOURTH SESSION, ADDENDUM, PART II: ACTION TAKEN BY THE CONFERENCE OF THE PARTIES, FCCC/CP/1998/16/Add.1 (1999).

[169] See id. Decision 3/CP.4.

[170] See id. See also UNFCCC Art. 4(1) and Art. 12(1).

countries such as preparations for adaptation activities and related capacity building.[171] The decision on the adverse impacts of climate change launched a work program to examine the issue, including identification and consideration of measures such as technology transfer and insurance.[172] The decision on the Kyoto (flexibility) mechanisms set a deadline of COP-6 in 2002 for the parties to make decisions on the rules to flesh out the details necessary to make these mechanisms operational.[173]

The conference highlighted once again the persistent fault line between industrialized and developing countries, which came to fore with the proposal by Argentina, to place the issue of voluntary commitments for developing countries on the agenda.[174] The proposal faced immediate and fierce resistance from G-77 and China, representing the developing countries. After the predictable rejection of the proposal, Argentine president Menem pledged that his country would assume a voluntary target at the next COP.[175] (At recent conferences, for instance, COP-12 in Nairobi in 2006, the Russian Federation has also advocated the amendment of the Protocol to allow for voluntary commitments by developing

---

[171] So-called stage II activities, where stage I consists of planning, the identification of vulnerable areas and regions, and capacity building. *See* Decision 11/CP.1, in REPORT OF THE CONFERENCE OF THE PARTIES ON ITS FIRST SESSION, ADDENDUM, PART II: ACTION TAKEN BY THE CONFERENCE OF THE PARTIES, para 4(d)(i)-(ii), UNFCCC/CP/1995/7/Add.1 (1996). The GEF has, until recently, limited its activities with respect to adaptation to planning and preparations for adaptation in the form of support for developing countries' national communications. The lack of support for actual adaptation projects has been a source of frustration for many developing countries, particularly small island developing states (SIDS). In 2004, the GEF launched the US$50 million Strategic Priority on Adaptation (SPA), which is intended to pilot an operational approach to adaptation. *See* GLOBAL ENVIRONMENT FACILITY, GEF ASSISTANCE TO ADDRESS ADAPTATION, GEF/C.23/Inf.8/Rev.1 (2004), and GLOBAL ENVIRONMENT FACILITY, JOINT SUMMARY OF THE CHAIRS, GEF COUNCIL MEETING, May 19–21, para. 26 (2004), available at http://www.gefweb.org/Documents/Council_Documents/GEF_C23/gef_c23.html#JointSummary.

[172] *See* Decision 5/CP.4, in REPORT OF THE CONFERENCE OF THE PARTIES ON ITS FOURTH SESSION, *supra* note 166. It should be noted that Protocol Art. 4 refers to "adverse effects of climate change and/or the impacts of response measures" on non-Annex I countries. The reference to the impact of response measures reflects the concern of the OPEC countries that mitigation policies will affect their economies. *See* GRUBB ET AL., GUIDE AND ASSESSMENT, *supra* note 41, at 14, 141.

[173] Decision 7/CP.4, in REPORT OF THE CONFERENCE OF THE PARTIES ON ITS FOURTH SESSION, *supra* note 166.

[174] *Report of the Fourth Conference of the Parties to the Framework Convention on Climate Change*, *supra* note 165.

[175] In the end, Argentina took no action in this regard.

countries.[176]) In legal terms – and consistent with the principle of common but differentiated responsibilities – the Protocol does not provide for the negotiation or assumption of voluntary commitments. Discussion of such commitments engenders enormous suspicion among developing countries, which regard them as a slippery slope to binding commitments, as well as undermining of the principle of common but differentiated responsibilities.

A second example of the fault line evident at COP-4, one that continues to be manifested in the negotiations, related to the review of the adequacy of commitments under the Convention.[177] While there was agreement on the inadequacy of commitments, parties could not reach agreement on the reasons, with developing countries criticizing insufficient mitigation by the industrialized countries, some of which, in turn, drew attention to the formers' lack of emissions reduction obligations. Similarly, at COP-12, in 2006, great difficulty was experienced in reaching agreement on the mandated review of the Kyoto Protocol.[178] The interests, arguments, and chief protagonists remained largely unchanged.

### 3.3.2. COP-5: Pause and Prelude

Hailed as a modest success, COP-5 was in truth largely a prelude to the more substantive decisions scheduled for COP-6.[179] The meeting adopted a number of important decisions on technical issues such as guidelines for reporting of annual inventories by Annex I countries[180] and guidelines

---

[176] The Russian Federation's insistence on this point caused the 11th COP, in December 2005, to extend into the morning hours, with the issue reportedly only resolved (temporarily) by an eleventh-hour phone call to President Putin. The proposal was once again pressed at the 12th COP in November 2006. For the text of the so-called Russian Proposal, as discussed at COP-12, see REPORT OF THE PRESIDENT ON CONSULTATIONS CONCERNING THE PROPOSAL OF THE RUSSIAN FEDERATION TO DEVELOP APPROPRIATE PROCEDURES FOR THE APPROVAL OF VOLUNTARY COMMITMENTS, FCCC/KP/CMP/2006/MISC.4 (2006), available at http://www.unfcc.int.

[177] UNFCCC, Art. 4(2)(d).

[178] Protocol, Art. 9. Essentially, parties at COP-12 sidestepped a thorough review and instead agreed to begin, in 2007, preparations for a second review of the Protocol in 2008.

[179] *Summary of the Fifth Conference of the Parties to the Framework Convention on Climate Change*, 12(123) EARTH NEGOTIATIONS BULLETIN (1999).

[180] Decisions 3/CP.5 and 4/CP.5, in REPORT OF THE CONFERENCE OF THE PARTIES ON ITS FIFTH SESSION, ADDENDUM, PART II: ACTION TAKEN BY THE CONFERENCE OF THE PARTIES, UNFCCC/CP/1999/6/Add.1.

96     *Development of the International Climate Change Regime*

for expert review of inventories submitted by Annex I countries.[181] These decisions contributed to the transparency, integrity, and comparability of emissions data – all critical qualities in the negotiations on climate change. The modalities and procedures for the flexibility mechanisms, particularly the CDM, and the design of the compliance mechanism were key topics discussed. In both cases, the COP adopted decisions requesting the relevant subsidiary bodies working on the two topics to continue their work, with a view to adopting decisions by the COP at its sixth session. With respect to the CDM, NGOs were vocal in rejecting the eligibility of nuclear energy as an option.

### 3.3.3. COP-6: Things Fall Apart

The sixth COP convened in The Hague, with the aim of completing the negotiations on the topics under the Buenos Aires Plan of Action. Despite vigorous attempts to rescue the meeting,[182] it ended in failure, with the parties unable to reach agreement on a number of issues.[183] Among the issues that derailed the negotiations were disagreements as to what extent CDM and JI should be supplemental to domestic action by Annex I countries,[184]

---

[181] Decision 5/CP.5, in REPORT OF THE CONFERENCE OF THE PARTIES ON ITS FIFTH SESSION, *supra* note 178.

[182] When difficulties surfaced, the president of the COP, Mr. Jan Pronk of the Netherlands, tried to cluster related issues for negotiation in high-level groups. *See Summary of the Sixth Conference of the Parties to the Framework Convention on Climate Change*, 12(163) EARTH NEGOTIATIONS BULLETIN (2000). When negotiations stalled, the president submitted, in his personal capacity, a note with proposals designed to achieve a breakthrough. *See* Decision 1/CP.6, in REPORT OF THE CONFERENCE OF THE PARTIES ON ITS SIXTH SESSION, ADDENDUM, PART II: ACTION TAKEN BY THE CONFERENCE OF THE PARTIES, Vol. II, annex, FCCC/CP/2000/2/Add.2 (2001).

[183] Andrew C. Revkin, *Odd Culprits in Collapse of Climate Talks*, NEW YORK TIMES, November 28, 2000. For an analysis of the meeting and its sequels, *see* SURAJE DESSAI, THE CLIMATE REGIME FROM THE HAGUE TO MARRAKECH: SAVING OR SINKING THE KYOTO PROTOCOL?, Working Paper 12, Tyndall Centre (2001), available at http://www.tyndall.ac.uk/publications/working_papers/wp12.pdf; CHRISTIAN EGENHOFER & JAN CORNILLIE, REINVENTING THE CLIMATE NEGOTIATIONS: AN ANALYSIS OF COP 6, Policy Brief 1, CEPS (2001), available at http://www.ceps.be.

[184] Art. 6(1)(d) of the Protocol provides that the acquisition of ERUs from JI projects should be "supplemental to domestic action" for the purposes of meeting emission reduction commitments. Similarly, Art. 12(3)(b) states that Annex I countries may use CERs from CDM projects "to contribute to compliance with part of their emission reduction obligations." The "supplementarity" proviso was supported by the EU and others concerned that the uncapped recourse to the flexibility mechanisms would allow Annex I countries to avoid

how much credit countries should get for the carbon dioxide absorbed by forests and grasslands,[185] and the compliance mechanism.[186] The COP suspended its sessions and requested that the president "seek advice on the desirability of resuming that session in May/June 2001 in order to complete work."[187] Overall, aside from the divergence regarding specific issues, observers identified the sheer scale of the agenda and the lack of trust and understanding among parties as reasons for failure.[188]

### 3.3.4. COP-6bis: Compromise and Concessions

After the meltdown at The Hague, the resumed sixth session of the COP, COP-6 (Part II), ended with negotiators managing to reach agreement on most of the critical political issues relating to the implementation of the Kyoto Protocol. This was despite – or perhaps partly because of – unfavorable developments in the United States. Responding to a letter from a group of senators requesting clarification of his stance on the Protocol, President George W. Bush stated his opposition to the Protocol on the basis that it exempted major emitters and would harm the U.S. economy.[189] In June, President Bush confirmed the United States' rejection of the Kyoto

---

taking domestic action to reduce emissions. The exact meaning of the "supplemental" and "part of" provisions has remained contested.
[185] The technical term of art is land use, land-use change, and forestry (LULUCF). Under Art. 3(3), Annex I parties can count removals by sinks resulting from direct human-induced LULUCF activities "limited to afforestation, deforestation and reforestation since 1990." This approach entails methodological and measurement difficulties of its own, but the clear limitation in Art. 3(3) is muddied somewhat by Art. 3(4), which directs the COP to decide on rules and guidelines for counting "additional human-induced activities," such as forestry management and cropland management. The United States advocated recognition of what it claimed were extensive $CO_2$ savings from sinks through forestry management, while the EU preferred much more limited recognition of sink activities. *See* DESSAI, *supra* note 181, at 4.
[186] While the EU argued for a binding compliance mechanism, countries such as Australia, Japan, and the Russian Federation preferred a nonbinding system. The parties also disagreed over the composition of compliance bodies, with the Annex I countries unwilling to accept equal regional representation as advanced by the G-77 group. *See Summary of the Sixth Conference of the Parties*, *supra* note 181.
[187] Decision 1/CP.6, in REPORT OF THE CONFERENCE OF THE PARTIES ON ITS SIXTH SESSION, *supra* note 180, at para. 2.
[188] DESSAI, *supra* note 181, at 4–5; Michael Grubb & Farhana Yamin, *Climatic Collapse at The Hague: What Happened, Why and Where Do We Go from Here?*, 7 INTERNATIONAL AFFAIRS 261–76 (2001).
[189] President G. W. Bush, Text of letter to Senators Helms, Craig, Hagel, and Roberts, March 13, 2001, available at http://www.whitehouse.gov/news/releases/2001/03/20010314.html.

Protocol and unveiled the administration's climate change program, with a focus on research and technology.[190] The U.S. opposition to the Protocol opened a rift in transatlantic relations.[191] At the same time, the supporters of the Protocol, in the first place, the EU, were aware that if they could not clinch a deal on the key outstanding issues, there would probably not be another opportunity to resuscitate the treaty.

Progress was made in Bonn regarding four main areas: the rules for emissions trading and the flexibility mechanisms; the eligibility of forestry projects under the CDM and rules on the counting of forestry management; funding and capacity building for developing countries to combat climate change; and key aspects of the compliance mechanism. At the beginning of the second week of negotiations, the parties agreed to adopt a political statement – the Bonn Agreement – proposed by the president, which encapsulated agreement on the outstanding issues, with the understanding that negotiations would continue on individual decisions.[192] The Bonn Agreement settled certain issues that had bedeviled COP-6 in The Hague, among them that the flexibility mechanisms "shall be supplemental to domestic action, and that domestic action shall thus constitute a significant element" of the effort made by Annex I parties to meet their emission reduction commitments.[193] It also stated that Annex I parties "are to refrain from" using JI and CDM credits from nuclear facilities to meet their commitments, thus effectively ensuring that nuclear energy projects would not be eligible under these mechanisms.[194] The parties also agreed that forestry projects could be included in the CDM, but that (1) these would be limited to afforestation and reforestation in the first commitment period, with the detailed technical procedures and methodologies governing such projects to be drawn up by one of the subsidiary bodies, and (2) credits from such

---

[190] See President G. W. Bush, *President Bush Discusses Global Climate Change*, Office of the Press Secretary, White House, June 11, 2001, available at http://www.whitehouse.gov/news/releases/2001/06/20010611-2.html.

[191] See, e.g., Frank Bruni, *Deep U.S.-Europe Split Casts Long Shadow on Bush Tour*, NEW YORK TIMES, June 15, 2001. A discussion of the various diplomatic efforts to bring the administration back to the table is summarized by DESSAI, *supra* note 181, at 5–8.

[192] See REPORT OF THE CONFERENCE OF THE PARTIES ON THE SECOND PART OF ITS SIXTH SESSION, PART I: PROCEEDINGS, paras. 34–38, 45–50, FCCC/CP/2001/5 (2001). *See also Summary of the Resumed Sixth Session of the Conference of the Parties to the UN Framework Convention on Climate Change*, 12(176) EARTH NEGOTIATIONS BULLETIN 4 (2001).

[193] *Report of the Conference of the Parties*, *supra* note 190, at 41.

[194] *See id.* at 43.

## 3.3. Finalizing the Protocol

forestry projects could constitute no more than 1 percent of a party's assigned amount in the first commitment period.[195] With respect to forestry management and other additional land use, land-use change, and forestry activities, under Article 3.4, the contribution of these sinks was subject to individual country caps, set out in an appendix.[196] Agreement was reached on many aspects of the compliance system, including such contentious issues as membership,[197] decision-making procedures,[198] and consequences of noncompliance.[199] Consensus could not be achieved, however, on whether the consequences of noncompliance should be binding.[200]

The issues on which the parties reached detailed agreement essentially related to developing country concerns.[201] Most important, the parties created three new funds: two under the Convention – the Special Climate Change Fund (SCCF) and the Least Developed Countries Fund (LDCF)[202] – and one, the Adaptation Fund,[203] under the Kyoto Protocol. In something of

---

[195] *Id.* at 43.
[196] *Id.* at 46–47. E.g., Canada is permitted to count removals of 12 million tonnes of $CO_2$ (Mt/$CO_2$) per year in the commitment period, Japan 12 Mt/$CO_2$, and the Russian Federation 17.63 Mt/$CO_2$. Some observers maintain that these allowances undermine the environmental integrity of the Protocol. It is interesting, too, that a footnote at 46 states that "consideration was also given to national circumstances (including the degree of effort needed to meet Kyoto commitments and the forest management measures implemented)."
[197] A total of 10 members, with the selection formula resulting in six representatives from non-Annex I countries and four from Annex I. *Report of the Conference of the Parties, supra* note 190, at 49.
[198] *See id.* at 49. Decisions are to be made by consensus, failing which a three-quarters majority prevails. For the Enforcement Branch, Annex I parties insisted on a double majority voting procedure so as to avoid the possibility of non-Annex I countries colluding against them.
[199] *See id.* at 48. The consequences include subtraction of excess emissions times 1.3 from the assigned amount of first commitment period, added to the assigned amount in the next commitment period.
[200] *See Summary of the Resumed Sixth Session, supra* note 190, at 8.
[201] At COP-6bis, the parties converted the political Bonn Agreement into one set of decisions forwarded to COP-7 for adoption and another requiring further elaboration and completion. *See* REPORT OF THE CONFERENCE OF THE PARTIES ON THE SECOND PART OF ITS SIXTH SESSION, respectively, Addendum, Part III, decisions on which the COP noted that negotiations were completed and consensus reached at the second part of the sixth session and which the Conference decided to forward to its seventh session for adoption, FCCC/CP/2001/5/Add.1 (2002), and Addendum, Part IV, Draft decisions on which progress was noted by the COP at the second part of its sixth session and which the COP decided to forward to its seventh session for elaboration, completion, and adoption, FCCC/CP/2001/5/Add.2 (2002).
[202] *See* REPORT OF THE CONFERENCE OF THE PARTIES ON THE SECOND PART OF ITS SIXTH SESSION, ADDENDUM PART III, *supra* note 199, at 44–45.
[203] *See id.* at 54.

an innovation, parties decided that the Adaptation Fund would be financed from a 2 percent share of proceeds from CDM projects. In a victory for developing countries, agreement was also reached on the creation of an Expert Group on Technology Transfer.[204] A decision under Protocol Article 3.14, strongly supported by OPEC countries, requested Annex I parties to report annually on the steps taken to minimize the adverse effects of their response measures on developing countries.[205]

### 3.3.5. COP-7: The Marrakech Accords – Hard Bargaining

COP-7, in Marrakech, succeeded in the task of translating the political Bonn Agreement into a legal text.[206] Decisions were prepared with respect to nuts-and-bolts issues such as the rules and procedures applicable to systems and inventories relating to GHG emissions and removals by sinks[207]; the compliance regime[208]; guidelines and procedures for the implementation of the flexibility mechanisms[209]; and land-use and forestry as sinks for the removal of GHGs.[210] The more than two hundred pages of text comprising the Marrakech Accords are also known as the "Kyoto rule-book."

After Marrakech, the Protocol might perhaps have been compared to a new house that – while still requiring a few touch-ups here and there – was essentially ready to be occupied. The cost in environmental integrity of "getting the job done" in Bonn and Marrakech was judged by some as

---

[204] See id. at 21.
[205] See id. at 50. Countries with economies dependent on oil exports, particularly some OPEC members, are concerned that mitigation measures under the Protocol may harm their markets.
[206] For a summary and overview, see Summary of the Seventh Conference of the Parties to the UN Convention on Climate Change, 12(189) EARTH NEGOTIATIONS BULLETIN (2001).
[207] Decisions 20/CP.7, 21/CP.7, 22/CP.7, and 23/CP.7, in REPORT OF THE CONFERENCE OF THE PARTIES ON ITS SEVENTH SESSION, ADDENDUM, PART II: ACTION TAKEN BY THE CONFERENCE OF THE PARTIES, Vol. III, FCCC/CP/2001/13/Add.3 (2002).
[208] Decision 24/CP.7, in REPORT OF THE CONFERENCE OF THE PARTIES ON ITS SEVENTH SESSION, supra note 205.
[209] See Decisions 15/CP.7, 16/CP.7, 17/CP.7, 18/COP.7, and 19/CP.7, in REPORT OF THE CONFERENCE OF THE PARTIES ON ITS SEVENTH SESSION, ADDENDUM, PART II: ACTION TAKEN BY THE CONFERENCE OF THE PARTIES, Vol. II, FCCC/CP/2001/13/Add.2 (2002).
[210] See Decisions 11/CP.7 and 12/CP.7, in REPORT OF THE CONFERENCE OF THE PARTIES ON ITS SEVENTH SESSION, ADDENDUM, PART II: ACTION TAKEN BY THE CONFERENCE OF THE PARTIES, FCCC/CP/2001/13/Add.1 (2002).

too high.[211] The main count in this indictment relates to the role played by sinks, particularly the fact that the verification of GHGs through forestry management and other land-use measures is very loose.[212] With the United States having pulled out, another group of countries – Canada, Japan, and the Russian Federation – assumed considerable sway with respect to the final details of the Marrakech negotiations, and they were able to extract a number of concessions from the EU.[213]

The combination of fungibility[214] of allowances and credits under the Protocol and so-called banking[215] has the potential to water down the environmental integrity of the Protocol.[216] (Parties with surplus allowances and credits in the first commitment period may bank them for subsequent commitment periods.) Particularly problematic may the units derived from sinks projects in Annex I countries under Protocol Article 3(3)–(4). Although these removal units (RMUs) cannot themselves be banked or carried over, their interchangeability or fungibility with other Kyoto units means that an Annex I party could simply surrender RMUs for compliance purposes in the first commitment period, retaining surplus AAUs, CERs, and ERUs to carry over into the next commitment period.[217]

---

[211] See analysis of "Kyoto loopholes" by BILL HARE & MALTE MEINSHAUSEN, GREENPEACE INTERNATIONAL, BACKGROUND INFORMATION ON POTENTIAL LOOPHOLES IN THE KYOTO PROTOCOL, UPDATE FOR COP-6 (PART TWO), BONN, (2001).

[212] E.g., while parties must demonstrate that removals from cropland management, forestry management, and similar activities are human induced, there is no requirement for the submission of annual inventories, as there is for sources of GHG emissions and removals by sinks in the case of afforestation and deforestation. This potentially undermines the rigor and environmental integrity of the exercise. See Decision 11/CP.7, annex, para. 8. And while sinks from forestry management are capped by country, no such limit applies to the other land-use measures mentioned previously. With respect to rewards of hard bargaining, the concession obtained by the Russian Federation is particularly striking – it was able to double the amount of removals from forestry management it could count toward its target, up from 17 Mt/$CO_2$ to 33 Mt/$CO_2$ per year times five.

[213] See Summary of the Seventh Conference of the Parties, supra note 204, at 15–16. See also DESSAI, supra note 181, at 14–17.

[214] See Decision 18/CP.7, in REPORT OF THE CONFERENCE OF THE PARTIES ON ITS SEVENTH SESSION, supra note 207, annex, paras. 11–12.

[215] Banking refers to the possibility of retaining unused AAUs from one commitment period for use in a subsequent commitment period. See id. annex, paras. 15–16.

[216] There is no limit on the number of AAUs that may be banked or carried over. For CERs and ERUs, respectively, a party may not bank an amount greater than 2.5 percent of its initial assigned amount under Art. 3(7)–(8) of the Protocol.

[217] In theory, banking introduces flexibility and improves the economic efficiency of a cap-and-trade mechanism, helping to overcome the limitations of fixed and rather short

Careless engagement in international emissions trading, and, to a lesser extent, JI projects, raised the possibility that Annex I parties could find themselves short of allowances at the end of the commitment period. To mitigate the risk of overselling by Annex I parties, it was decided that they would be required to maintain a commitment period reserve, which is an amount equal to 90 percent of a party's initial assigned amount, or five times its most recently reviewed emissions inventory, whichever is lowest.[218]

### 3.3.6. COP-8: Focus on Adaptation in New Delhi

With the technical details of the Kyoto flexibility mechanism in place, COP-8, held in New Delhi, saw the concerns of developing countries take center stage.[219] Prominent among them was adaptation – of immediate concern to developing countries, but an issue that has generally played second fiddle to mitigation in the climate negotiations.[220] The parties adopted the Delhi Declaration on Climate Change and Sustainable Development, which reaffirms that development and poverty eradication are the overwhelming priorities of developing countries.[221] It emphasizes that climate change should be addressed while meeting the requirements of sustainable development and the need to integrate measures to combat climate change into national development programs. It stresses the importance of adaptation to the impacts of climate change for all countries, noting that developing countries are particularly vulnerable, and calls on industrialized countries to further implement their commitments relating to financing, capacity building, and technology transfer. With COP-8 taking place little more than a month after the World Summit on Sustainable Development, it is unsurprising that the declaration

---

commitment periods. However, with the potential of large numbers of forestry and land-use RMUs entering the system, allowing Annex I countries to bank AAUs, it is possible that newcomers in a second commitment period will be disadvantaged. Under a tighter cap, new entrants will not have the buffer of the easily acquired, banked credits of some Annex I parties.

[218] See Decision 18/CP.7, in REPORT OF THE CONFERENCE OF THE PARTIES ON ITS SEVENTH SESSION, supra note 207, annex, para. 6.

[219] For an account of the negotiations, see Summary of the Eighth Conference of the Parties to the UN Convention on Climate Change, 23 October to 1 November 2002, 12(209) EARTH NEGOTIATIONS BULLETIN (2002).

[220] Andrew C. Revkin, Climate Talks Shift Focus to How to Deal with Changes, NEW YORK TIMES, November 3, 2002.

[221] REPORT OF THE CONFERENCE OF THE PARTIES ON ITS EIGHTH SESSION, ADDENDUM, PART II: ACTION TAKEN BY THE CONFERENCE OF THE PARTIES, 3, FCCC/CP/2002/7/Add.1 (2002).

borrows language from the Plan of Implementation, calling for diversifying energy supplies as well as actions to substantially increase the global share of renewable energy sources.[222]

### 3.3.7. COP-9: Milan

The uncertain fate of the Kyoto Protocol hung over the discussions at COP-9, held in Milan in December 2003.[223] Entry into force was conditional on the ratification of the Russian Federation, which sent mixed but largely negative signals on this point.[224] Nevertheless, the parties adopted an important decision operationalizing the SCCF. The decision provides that adaptation will enjoy priority in allocation of resources and that technology transfer and associated capacity building will also be covered.[225] Supported adaptation activities will fall in a range of areas such as water resources management, agriculture, integrated coastal zone management, monitoring of vector-borne diseases, and coping with disasters caused by extreme weather events. A sticking point in the negotiations was how funds under the SCCF would be used to support the economic diversification of countries with economies dependent on oil exports,[226] which was an issue because the initial decision establishing the fund provided that such diversification activities would be covered.[227] Supported by provisions in the Convention and the Kyoto

---

[222] See Plan of Implementation of the World Summit on Sustainable Development, in REPORT OF THE WORLD SUMMIT ON SUSTAINABLE DEVELOPMENT, UN Doc. A/Conf./199/20, para. 20(e). The Plan of Implementation is accessible at http://www.un.org/esa/sustdev/documents/docs_key_conferences.htm.

[223] For an account of the negotiations, see Summary of the Ninth Conference of the Parties to the UN Convention on Climate Change, 1 to 12 December 2003, 12(233) EARTH NEGOTIATIONS BULLETIN (2003). See also SURAJE DESSAI ET AL., CHALLENGES AND OUTCOMES AT COP-9, Briefing Note No. 11, Tyndall Centre (2004).

[224] Steven Lee Myers & Andrew C. Revkin, Russia to Reject Pact on Climate Putin Aide Says, NEW YORK TIMES, December 3, 2003.

[225] Decision 5/CP.9, in REPORT OF THE CONFERENCE OF THE PARTIES ON ITS NINTH SESSION, ADDENDUM, PART II: ACTION TAKEN BY THE CONFERENCE OF THE PARTIES, Vol. I, 11–12, FCCC/CP/2003/6/Add.1 (2004).

[226] EU countries argued that the inclusion of diversification for oil exporters would preclude them making substantial contributions to the fund. The issue was deferred for further consideration at COP-10, following input by the parties. See DESSAI ET AL., supra note 221.

[227] See Decision 7/CP.7, in REPORT OF THE CONFERENCE OF THE PARTIES ON ITS SEVENTH SESSION, ADDENDUM, PART II: ACTION TAKEN BY THE CONFERENCE OF THE PARTIES, Vol. I, para. 2(d), FCCC/CP/2001/13/Add.1 (2002). This provision represented a considerable victory for the OPEC countries, building on Protocol Art. 4(8)(h), which situates the

Protocol referring to the adverse impact of response (mitigation) measures, oil-producing developing countries have advocated for assistance to enable their economies to diversify beyond hydrocarbon exports.[228] In this context, oil-producing countries emphasize the potential adverse impacts resulting from carbon taxes and similar mitigation measures aimed at fossil fuels.

The parties also adopted guidelines for the operation of the LDCF, which is designed to provide assistance to LDCs.[229] In the first instance, the fund would be tapped to support the preparation of national adaptation programs of action, identifying immediate and urgent adaptation needs. Finally, in adopting the technical rules for afforestation and deforestation projects under the CDM, the Milan meeting completed the last item on the Buenos Aires Plan of Action.[230]

### 3.3.8. COP-10: Buenos Aires

The Russian Federation's decision to ratify the Protocol,[231] made shortly before COP-10, reinvigorated the negotiations. A major outcome of this meeting was the adoption of the Buenos Aires Programme of Work on Adaptation and Response Measures. It covers the following areas: adverse effects of climate change, impact of the implementation of response measures, and a request to the SBSTA to develop a structured, five-year program of work on the scientific, technical, and socioeconomic aspects of impacts, vulnerability, and adaptation to climate change.[232]

---

potential negative economic impacts of mitigation measures with the adverse impacts of climate change on developing countries.

[228] See UNFCCC Art. 4(8)(h) and Protocol Art. 2(3) and Art. 3(14).

[229] Decision 6/CP.9, in REPORT OF THE CONFERENCE OF THE PARTIES ON ITS NINTH SESSION, PART II: ACTION TAKEN BY THE CONFERENCE OF THE PARTIES, supra note 223, at 13.

[230] Decision 19/CP.9, in REPORT OF THE CONFERENCE OF THE PARTIES ON ITS NINTH SESSION, ADDENDUM, PART II: ACTION TAKEN BY THE CONFERENCE OF THE PARTIES, Vol. II, 13, FCCC/CP/2003/6/Add.2 (2004). The decision addresses complex issues relating to the permanence of sinks by providing for two types of CERs: a temporary CER (tCER), which expires five years after its issue, and a long-term CER (lCER), which expires at the end of the crediting period of the project activity.

[231] Seth Mydans & Andrew C. Revkin, With Russia's Nod, Treaty in Emissions Clears Last Hurdle, NEW YORK TIMES, October 1, 2004.

[232] Decision 1/CP.10, in REPORT OF THE CONFERENCE OF THE PARTIES ON ITS TENTH SESSION, ADDENDUM, PART II: ACTION TAKEN BY THE CONFERENCE OF THE PARTIES, Vol. I, FCCC/CP/2004/10/Add.1 (2005).

## 3.3. Finalizing the Protocol

The discussions on support for adaptation activities were again complicated by the coupling of impacts from climate change with the impacts of response measures because under this agenda item, certain oil-producing states argued that assistance under the GEF should be made available for activities such as economic diversification.[233] Donor countries resisted this linkage and equivalence. The EU announced that donors had pledged over US$30 million for the SCCF.[234] During discussions on additional guidelines for the SCCF and LDCF, developing countries reiterated their complaints concerning their difficulty in accessing funds under the GEF, which had been designated as the entity to manage both these funds.

Other decisions made by the parties concerned the adoption of simplified modalities and procedures for small-scale afforestation and reforestation CDM projects,[235] seen as facilitating community-level CDM projects in developing countries,[236] as well as further guidelines for quality assurance of the international transactions log (ITL), the software and technical backbone of international emissions trading under the Protocol.[237] The ITL is designed to verify that transactions involving allowances and other units are consistent with rules agreed on under the Kyoto Protocol.

With the Protocol's entry into force assured, negotiators also turned some of their attention to the issue of the future direction of the climate regime, bearing in mind the expiry in 2012 of the first commitment period under the Protocol. A proposal by the EU to hold two seminars was rebuffed, and it was only at the last minute that agreement was reached on one seminar.[238]

---

[233] Hermann E. Ott et al., *It Takes Two to Tango – Climate Policy at COP 10 in Buenos Aires and Beyond*, JOURNAL OF EUROPEAN ENVIRONMENTAL & PLANNING LAW 84, 86 (2005).

[234] *Summary of the Tenth Conference of the Parties to the UN Convention on Climate Change, 6–18 December 2004*, 12(260) EARTH NEGOTIATIONS BULLETIN 9 (2004).

[235] Decision 3/CP.10, in REPORT OF THE CONFERENCE OF THE PARTIES ON ITS TENTH SESSION, ADDENDUM, PART II: ACTION TAKEN BY THE CONFERENCE OF THE PARTIES, Vol. II, FCCC/CP/2004/10/Add.2 (2005).

[236] E.g., the BioCarbon Fund of the World Bank, http://carbonfinance.org/Router.cfm?Page=BioCF&ItemID=9708&FID=9708.

[237] Decision 16/CP.10, in REPORT OF THE CONFERENCE OF THE PARTIES ON ITS TENTH SESSION, *supra* note 233.

[238] As expected, this discussion proved difficult and the results were meager, with the parties only able to agree on a seminar for an informal exchange of views, subject to the express condition that it would not "open any negotiations leading to new commitments." *See* REPORT OF THE CONFERENCE OF THE PARTIES ON ITS TENTH SESSION, PART I: PROCEEDINGS, 37, FCCC/CP/2004/10 (2005). Strong opposition came from the United States. *See* Larry Rohter, *U.S. Waters Down Global Commitment to Curb Greenhouse Gases*, NEW YORK TIMES, December 19, 2004. For analysis, *see also* OTT ET AL., *supra* note 231, at 85.

### 3.3.9. COP-11: Breakthrough in Montreal

Since the Protocol had entered into force in February 2006, COP-11 was held together with COP/MOP-1 to the Kyoto Protocol.[239] The Montreal meeting was historic on several counts. The first meeting of the supreme body of the Kyoto Protocol, the COP/MOP, formally adopted the draft decisions that constituted the rule book agreed on in the Marrakech Accords and subsequent COPs.[240] The meeting also launched two parallel processes, or tracks, addressing the next stage in the climate regime. Under the Protocol, parties initiated the mandated review of the commitments of Annex I parties by establishing the Ad Hoc Working Group (AWG) to negotiate industrialized parties' commitments for the post-2012 period. Under the Convention, parties agreed to establish a non-negotiating "dialogue on long-term cooperative action" to address climate change.[241]

The review of Annex I commitments was triggered by Article 3.9 of the Protocol, which requires that the COP/MOP shall initiate the consideration of Annex I commitments at least seven years before the end of the first commitment period, in other words, by 2005. The mandate of this review covered only industrialized (Annex I) parties. Developing countries proposed that negotiations on the second commitment period should conclude in 2008 and argued that it was incumbent on industrialized countries to demonstrate leadership on mitigation. For their part, Annex I parties – now excluding the United States, which, as a nonparty, was relegated to an observer role – resisted the establishment of a timeline. Eventually, parties settled on less specific language stating that the negotiations of the AWG on Annex I commitments should be completed in time to ensure that there is no gap between the first and second commitment periods.[242] Some

---

[239] For an analysis of the meeting, see Hermann E. Ott et al., *The Montreal Climate Summit: Starting the Kyoto Business and Preparing for Post-2012*, JOURNAL OF EUROPEAN ENVIRONMENTAL & PLANNING LAW 90 (2006).

[240] A total of nineteen draft decisions were recommended for adoption by the COP/MOP at its first session, as contained in the reports of COP-7, COP-8, COP-9, and COP-10. See COMPENDIUM OF DRAFT DECISIONS FORWARDED FOR ADOPTION BY THE CONFERENCE OF THE PARTIES SERVING AS THE MEETING OF THE PARTIES TO THE KYOTO PROTOCOL AT ITS FIRST SESSION: NOTE BY THE SECRETARIAT, para. 2, FCCC/KP/CMP/2005/3.

[241] Decision 1/CP.11, in REPORT OF THE CONFERENCE OF THE PARTIES ON ITS ELEVENTH SESSION, ADDENDUM, Part II: ACTION TAKEN BY THE CONFERENCE OF THE PARTIES, 3, FCCC/CP/2005/5/Add.1 (2006).

[242] Given the time required to complete the requisite ratifications, an agreement would probably need to be reached by the end of 2009.

## 3.3. Finalizing the Protocol

industrialized country parties attempted to link the preceding process with the broader review of the Protocol provided for under Article 9.[243] This review of the adequacy of the Protocol would also apply to developing countries. Article 9 states that the parties "shall periodically review this Protocol in the light of the best scientific information and assessments on climate change and its impacts," with the first review required at COP-12/MOP-2 in 2006. As a negotiating tactic, establishing a link between the two processes presented an opportunity to bring pressure to bear on certain developing countries; however, in legal terms, the Article 9 review is intended to be a separate process, based on a thorough review of the latest science as well as technical and economic information.

As noted earlier, the second track begun in Montreal consisted of a dialogue under the Convention. What it lacked in ambition, it partially compensated for in terms of inclusiveness, both in relation to the issues (adaptation and mitigation) and with respect to parties. For those taking the longer view, the dialogue could be regarded as the first tenuous toehold in a process leading toward greater involvement of developing countries and those developed countries then outside the Kyoto process, Australia, and the United States. However, the latter maintained that any new process – in fact, carefully labeled as a "dialogue" – should in no way lead to new commitments.[244] Thus the parties explicitly resolved that the dialogue would consist of an "open and non-binding exchange of views" and would "not open any negotiations leading to new commitments."[245]

Among other things, the decision on the dialogue on long-term cooperative action to address climate change reaffirms that development and poverty eradication are the first and overriding priorities of developing country parties, recognizes the diversity of approaches to address climate change, and emphasizes the essential role of technology in addressing climate change.[246] The parties agreed that the dialogue would be structured as four workshops covering the following topics: advancing development

---

[243] OTT ET AL., *supra* note 237, at 91.
[244] *See id.* at 92. *See also Summary of the Eleventh Conference of the Parties to the UN Convention on Climate Change, 28 November–10 December 2005*, 12(291) EARTH NEGOTIATIONS BULLETIN 14 (2005).
[245] *See supra* note 241, at 3.
[246] REPORT OF THE CONFERENCE OF THE PARTIES ON ITS ELEVENTH SESSION, ADDENDUM, PART II: ACTION TAKEN BY THE CONFERENCE OF THE PARTIES, 3–4, FCCC/CP/2005/5/Add.1 (2006).

goals in a sustainable way, addressing action on adaptation, realizing the full potential of technology, and realizing the full potential of market-based opportunities.

The adoption of the decision on the compliance mechanism gave rise to considerable discussion.[247] Article 18 of the Protocol states that "any procedures and mechanisms under this Article entailing binding consequences shall be adopted by means of an amendment to this Protocol." In the Marrakech Accords, the legal status of the compliance mechanism as well as its consequences were left open, and the accords referred to COP/MOP in the following terms: "it is the prerogative of the Conference of the Parties serving as the Meeting of the Parties to the Kyoto Protocol to decide on the legal form of the procedures and mechanisms relating to compliance."[248] At the risk of some uncertainty about its exact legal status, both developing and industrialized countries preferred adopting the compliance regime in the form of a decision of the COP/MOP.[249] Opting for an amendment to the Protocol raised the possibility of two categories of parties to the Protocol, namely, those who had ratified the amendment and those who had not, with associated legal uncertainty.[250]

While the climate negotiations have, from their inception, attracted attention from the business community and environmental negotiations, the Montreal conference will be remembered for the manner in which one part of the business lobby pressed for a clear signal on the future of the climate regime. The representatives of the carbon finance industry – consultants, investors, lawyers, project developers – now had a great deal at stake in the continuation of the Kyoto flexibility mechanisms. It became clear that this interest group would represent a significant new private sector voice in the evolution and development of the climate regime.

---

[247] OTT ET AL., *supra* note 237, at 94.
[248] Decision 24/CP.7, in REPORT OF THE CONFERENCE OF THE PARTIES ON ITS SEVENTH SESSION, ADDENDUM, PART II: ACTION TAKEN BY THE CONFERENCE OF THE PARTIES, Vol. III, FCCC/CP/2001/13/Add.3 (2002).
[249] The implications are analyzed by ULFSTEIN & WERKSMAN, *supra* note 134, at 58.
[250] *Summary of the Eleventh Conference of the Parties to the UN Convention on Climate Change, 28 November–10 December 2005*, 12(291) EARTH NEGOTIATIONS BULLETIN 14 (2005). Saudi Arabia proposed an amendment. *See* PROPOSAL FROM SAUDI ARABIA TO AMEND THE PROTOCOL: NOTE BY THE SECRETARIAT, FCCC/KP/CMP/2005/2 (2005).

### 3.3.10. COP-12: Nairobi – The African Adaptation COP

This section summarizes the discussions and main outcomes of the twelfth COP and the second COP/MOP.[251] As the first COP to be held in sub-Saharan Africa, the Nairobi conference was naturally expected to advance the adaptation agenda. As it turned out, progress was made on the establishment of the Adaptation Fund and the work program of the SBSTA on impacts, vulnerability, and adaptation.

The AWG on Annex I commitments held its second session at COP-12, agreeing that future work would proceed under three headings: analysis of mitigation potential and ranges of emission reduction objectives, analysis of possible means to achieve mitigation objectives, and consideration of further commitments. The first review of the Protocol, mandated by Article 9(2), proved to be a contentious issue that kept negotiators occupied quite late into the final days of the meeting. Developing countries, particularly the African group and China, advocated concluding the review at the meeting, while the EU wanted to launch a review process. Developing countries also supported scheduling the second review in four to five years.[252] Not coincidentally, perhaps, the second review would then take place safely after the date – generally assumed to be 2009 – by when targets for the second Kyoto commitment period would have had to be agreed on. In the end, developing countries obtained language that the review would not lead to new commitments, while in return, industrialized countries prevailed on the timing of the second review, which was set for COP-14 in 2008.[253] The Russian proposal to amend the Protocol to allow for voluntary commitments by non–Annex I parties again kept negotiators busy until the final hours of the conference.[254] The proposal as it stands was not readily compatible

---

[251] The author attended the second week of the meeting (November 15–17, 2006) in an observer capacity. For an account of discussions and decisions at the Nairobi conference, see *Summary of the Twelfth Conference of the Parties to the UN Convention on Climate Change and Second Meeting of the Parties to the Kyoto Protocol, 6–17 November*, 12(318) EARTH NEGOTIATIONS BULLETIN (2006).

[252] *See id.* at 7.

[253] Decision 7/CMP.2, in REPORT OF THE CONFERENCE OF THE PARTIES SERVING AS THE MEETING OF THE PARTIES ON ITS SECOND SESSION, ADDENDUM, PART II: ACTION TAKEN BY THE CONFERENCE OF THE PARTIES SERVING AS THE MEETING OF THE PARTIES, FCCC/KP/CMP/2006/10/Add.1 (2007).

[254] As a compromise, parties requested the president of the COP to hold a workshop in May 2007 to explore the scope and implications of the proposal. *See* REPORT OF THE

with the structure of the Protocol. It would, for instance, enable those developing countries assuming voluntary commitments to participate in all the Protocol's flexibility mechanisms, including international emissions trading, the latter, of course, being predicated on emission limitation and reduction targets. In short, the mechanisms designed to assist Annex I parties in meeting their binding targets would be extended to other parties assuming voluntary commitments.[255] Finally, under the Convention track, the second workshop of the Convention dialogue on long-term cooperative action addressed the topics of advancing development goals in a sustainable way and realizing the full potential of market-based opportunities.[256]

The COP/MOP took an important step forward by defining the principles and modalities governing the administration of the Adaptation Fund.[257] Notably, the governing body will have a majority of members from developing countries (non–Annex I) and follow a one-country-one-vote rule, differentiating it from the double majority of the other funds under the GEF voting system.[258] The Adaptation Fund is unique in a number of respects. First, unlike the other funds, it is solely the creature of the parties to the Protocol, outside the direct influence of United States, with negotiations led by the EU.[259] Second, unlike the other funds – which are financed from voluntary contributions and hence dependent on solidarity – revenue for the AF will be derived from a 2 percent levy on emissions credits under

---

CONFERENCE OF THE PARTIES SERVING AS THE MEETING OF THE PARTIES ON ITS SECOND SESSION, PART I: PROCEEDINGS, paras. 134–36, FCCC/KP/CMP/2006/10 (2007).

[255] REPORT OF THE PRESIDENT ON CONSULTATIONS CONCERNING THE PROPOSAL OF THE RUSSIAN FEDERATION TO DEVELOP APPROPRIATE PROCEDURES FOR THE APPROVAL OF VOLUNTARY COMMITMENTS: SUBMISSION FROM A PARTY, 9, FCCC/KP/CMP/2006/MISC.4 (2006).

[256] Copies of presentations are available on the UNFCCC secretariat Web site at http://unfccc.int/meetings/dialogue/items/3759.php.

[257] Decision 5/CMP.2, in REPORT OF THE CONFERENCE OF THE PARTIES SERVING AS THE MEETING OF THE PARTIES ON ITS SECOND SESSION, supra note 251.

[258] Legal questions were raised concerning how the voting procedure for the fund would operate within the GEF's governance system. The GEF maintained that the hybrid formula of the GEF was flexible enough to accommodate the unique features of the fund, including the fact that CERs, which will finance the fund, originate from projects in developing countries. Additionally, a legal opinion from the World Bank, which is the trustee of the GEF funds, indicated that the unique aspects of the Adaptation Fund would be compatible with GEF procedures. See GEF, GOVERNANCE OF THE GLOBAL CLIMATE CHANGE FUNDS, GEF/C.29/5, para. 11 (2006).

[259] BENITO MÜLLER, NAIROBI 2006: TRUST AND THE FUTURE OF ADAPTATION FUNDING 3 (2007), available at http://www.oxfordenergy.org/.

the CDM.[260] By one estimate, the levy is projected to generate up to $950 million for the fund, considerably more than the $278 million that had been deposited or pledged for the LDCF and SCCF by the end of 2008.[261] Third, the parties also decided that the Adaptation Fund "should operate under the authority and guidance of and be accountable" to COP/MOP, which will decide on its overall policies. It is legally and politically significant that the AF will operate not only under the guidance of the COP/MOP, but also under its authority. The reason is that with respect to the other climate change funds operated by the GEF, the COP provides "guidance"; effective authority rests with the GEF council, in practice dominated by donor countries. For developing countries, many of which have chafed under what they view as the excessively bureaucratic and onerous procedures of the GEF, the decision on the Adaptation Fund, particularly the voting procedure, was rightly hailed as a major victory.

The SBSTA failed to make progress in reviewing the mandate of the Expert Group on Technology Transfer (EGTT), which was established at COP-7, with the objective of enhancing technology transfer under the Convention. Developing country parties had long been of the view that the highly industrialized (Annex II) parties were not fulfilling their commitment under Article 4(5) of the Convention to take "all practicable steps to promote, facilitate and finance, as appropriate, the transfer of, or access to, environmentally sound technologies and know-how to other Parties, particularly developing country Parties." While the EGTT fulfilled a useful role, there was a sense that the issue of technology transfer required a more ambitious mandate. On a more positive note, the SBSTA adopted decisions concerning its "five year program of work on impacts, vulnerability and adaptation to climate change," which consists of activities (workshops, technical papers, submissions, etc.) to help countries make informed decisions on practical actions and measures.[262] The G-77 and China focused on a learning-by-doing approach and actual projects, while the United States led the argument for an approach based on assessment and

---

[260] Decision 17/CP.7, in REPORT OF THE CONFERENCE OF THE PARTIES ON ITS SEVENTH SESSION, *supra* note 117, at para. 15(a)-(b). CDM projects in least developed countries are exempt from the levy.
[261] MÜLLER, *supra* note 257, at 3.
[262] REPORT OF THE SUBSIDIARY BODY FOR SCIENTIFIC AND TECHNOLOGICAL ADVICE ON ITS TWENTY-FIFTH SESSION, paras. 11–71, FCCC/SBSTA/2006/11 (2007).

research.[263] The adoption by the COP of the work program marked the achievement of one concrete goal established by the Buenos Aires Programme of Work on Adaptation and Response Measures, adopted in 2004 at COP-10. The COP also gave guidance to the GEF for the operation of the SCCF under the Convention.[264] Under the Protocol, parties adopted guidance to the EB of the CDM, where disagreement surfaced among the parties with respect to the eligibility of carbon dioxide capture and storage projects,[265] and adopted the rules of procedure for the body responsible for supervising certain JI projects.[266] On the issue of emissions from deforestation, Brazil submitted a proposal for an international fund to finance activities to reduce the rate of deforestation in developing countries.[267] This came after Papua New Guinea, supported by other tropical rainforest nations, had placed the issue of incentives for avoided deforestation on the Convention agenda at COP-11 in Montreal.[268]

In sum, COP-12 did not deliver any breakthroughs, nor was it expected to do so. This was not necessarily the view taken by the media, which perhaps found it difficult to reconcile the self-contained negotiating process – its set

---

[263] *Summary of the Twelfth Conference of the Parties to the UN Convention on Climate Change and Second Meeting of the Parties to the Kyoto Protocol, 6–17 November*, 12(318) EARTH NEGOTIATIONS BULLETIN 7 (2006).

[264] Decision 1/CP.12, in REPORT OF THE CONFERENCE OF THE PARTIES ON ITS TWELFTH SESSION, ADDENDUM, PART II: ACTION TAKEN BY THE CONFERENCE OF THE PARTIES, FCCC/CP/2006/5/Add.1 (2007).

[265] *See* Decision 1/CMP.2, in REPORT OF THE CONFERENCE OF THE PARTIES SERVING AS THE MEETING OF THE PARTIES ON ITS SECOND SESSION, *supra* note 251. The decision requests that the CDM Executive Board continue consideration of new carbon capture and storage (CCS) methodologies under the CDM, but with approval subject to further guidance from the COP/MOP, with a decision to be made at COP/MOP-4 in 2008. As the (extended) registration date for CDM projects was March 31, 2007, CCS projects will not be included under the CDM in the first commitment period.

[266] Decision 2/CMP.2, in REPORT OF THE CONFERENCE OF THE PARTIES SERVING AS THE MEETING OF THE PARTIES ON ITS SECOND SESSION, *supra* note 251.

[267] Brazil's proposal envisages "positive incentives" for a net reduction of emissions from deforestation, with funding to come from industrialized countries. *See* POSITIVE INCENTIVES FOR VOLUNTARY ACTION IN DEVELOPING COUNTRIES TO ADDRESS CLIMATE CHANGE: BRAZILIAN PERSPECTIVE ON REDUCING EMISSIONS FROM DEFORESTATION, Submission from Brazil, Dialogue Working Paper 21, available at http://unfccc.int/files/meetings/dialogue/application/pdf/wp_21_braz.pdf. The proposal stops well short of embracing the concept of avoided deforestation as such; rather, the proposal is aimed at the *reduction of emissions* from deforestation.

[268] *See* REDUCING EMISSIONS FROM DEFORESTATION IN DEVELOPING COUNTRIES: APPROACHES TO STIMULATE ACTION: SUBMISSIONS FROM PARTIES, FCCC/CP/2005/MISC.1 (2005).

timelines and stylized group positions – with the greater urgency of climate change in the public debate.

### 3.3.11. COP-13: Down to the Wire in Bali

In the year leading up to the Bali conference, a number of meetings contributed to setting a tone of urgency with respect to climate change. In April, the Security Council, under the rotating presidency of the United Kingdom, convened its first ever debate on climate change.[269] In June, under the German presidency, the G-8 countries adopted a summit document pledging to "seriously consider" deep cuts in emissions in their developing countries, but only after prolonged opposition by the United States.[270] At the UN, the General Assembly convened a thematic debate on climate change, which saw an almost exhaustive list of countries address the topic.[271] At this meeting, as before, the EU reiterated its position of a 20 percent cut by 2020, to be deepened to 30 percent, if other major actors committed to serious mitigation action. Likewise, the statements of certain developing countries, such as Brazil and South Africa, hinted that they would approach Bali with a mandate to begin negotiations. In early September, the Asia Pacific Cooperation Summit (APEC) countries, hosted by Australia, adopted a final declaration pledging to work constructively toward a successful meeting in Bali, and they also agreed to "work to achieve a common understanding on a long-term aspirational global emissions reduction goal to pave the way for an effective post-2012 international arrangement."[272]

On September 24, the UN secretary-general convened a one-day, high-level event on climate change, which was organized around the four themes of adaptation, mitigation, technology, and finance, and which drew the participation of almost 80 heads of state or government.[273] Although a forum for discussion, not negotiation, the meeting did generate momentum going

---

[269] See Reuters, *U.N. Council Hits Impasse over Climate Change*, NEW YORK TIMES, April 17, 2007. UN SC, 5663rd mtg., UN Doc. S/PV.5663 and S/PV.5663 (Resumption 1) (2007).

[270] See GROWTH AND RESPONSIBILITY IN THE WORLD ECONOMY, Summit Declaration, June 7, para. 49, adopted at the G-8 Summit, Heiligendamm, available at http://www.g-8.de/Webs/G8/EN/G8Summit/SummitDocuments/summit-documents.html.

[271] See, for details of speakers and statements, http://www.un.org/ga/president/61/followup/thematic-climate.shtml.

[272] See http://www.apec.org/apec/leaders__declarations/2007/aelm_climatechange.html.

[273] Warren Hoge, *U.N. Chief Urges Fast Action on Climate Change*, NEW YORK TIMES, September 25, 2007.

forward to Bali, with participants highlighting the need for action on climate change.[274] Later that same week, the United States convened its first meeting in a planned series of meetings of major economies on energy security and climate change, which brought together 18 major economies as well as the EU and the UN.[275] The stated aim of this initiative, quickly dubbed the "major emitters" meeting, is to arrive at a long-term (nonbinding) goal among the major economies and establish nationally defined goals and programs for improving energy security and reducing GHG emissions.[276]

The Bali conference – COP-13 and COP/MOP-3 – saw governments make progress on several important agenda items, but the dominant issue was the expectation that the meeting would launch negotiations on a future agreement. The release of the IPCC's Fourth Assessment Report had strengthened the scientific case for action, and media and public interest in climate change reached a new level with the joint award of the Nobel Peace Prize to Albert Gore and the IPCC. A full day after the scheduled close, and after high-profile pleas for flexibility from the UN secretary-general and the president of Indonesia, the Bali conference concluded with agreement on launching negotiations on future actions to mitigate GHG emissions.[277] At the heart

---

[274] See http://www.un.org/climatechange/2007highlevel/summary.shtml.

[275] *Invitation to Meeting of Major Economies on Energy Security and Climate Change*, letter from President George W. Bush, August 2, 2007, available at http://www.whitehouse.gov/news/releases/2007/08/20070803-7.html. See also details on the initiative at http://www.state.gov/g/oes/;climate/mem/.

[276] John M. Broder, *At Climate Meeting, Bush Does Not Specify Goals*, NEW YORK TIMES, September 29, 2007.

[277] *Some Like It Cool*, THE ECONOMIST, December 22, 2007, at 10; Thomas Fuller & Andrew Revkin, *Climate Plan Looks beyond Bush's Tenure*, NEW YORK TIMES, December 16, 2007. For accounts of the negotiations and summaries of key outcomes, see *Summary of the Thirteenth Conference of the Parties to the UN Convention on Climate Change and Third Meeting of the Parties to the Kyoto Protocol, 3–15 December*, 12(354) EARTH NEGOTIATIONS BULLETIN (2007); Pew Center on Global Climate Change, *Summary of the Thirteenth Conference of the Parties to the UN Convention on Climate Change and Third Meeting of the Parties to the Kyoto Protocol, 3–15 December* (undated), available at http://www.pewclimate.org/docUploads/Pew%20Center_COP%2013%20Summary.pdf; Robert N. Stavins & Joseph Aldy, BALI CLIMATE CHANGE CONFERENCE: KEY TAKEAWAYS, Harvard Project on International Climate Agreements, December 18, 2007, available at http://belfercenter.ksg.harvard.edu/publication/17781/bali_climate_change_conference.html; Daniel Bodansky, *Bali High?*, in OPINIO JURIS, weblog, entry posted December 19, 2007, available at http://www.opiniojuris.org/posts/1198075277.shtml; BENITO MÜLLER, OXFORD INSTITUTE FOR ENERGY STUDIES, BALI 2007: ON THE ROAD AGAIN (2007), available at http://www.oxfordclimatepolicy.org/publications/mueller.html; Rie Watanabe et al., *The Bali Roadmap for Global Climate Policy – New Horizons and Old Pitfalls*, 5(2) JOURNAL OF EUROPEAN ENVIRONMENTAL & PLANNING LAW 139 (2008).

## 3.3. Finalizing the Protocol

of the so-called Bali road map – in fact, a collection of decisions – is the much expected and politically crucial agreement to launch a new process for negotiations on "long-term cooperative action" beyond 2012. As noted in section 3.3.9, at the Montreal conference in 2005, parties launched two parallel processes – or tracks – to begin addressing the post-2012 action. The first, the AWG, was established under Article 3.9 of the Protocol, with the aim of elaborating for Annex I countries only, for the second, post-2012 commitment period. The second track, the dialogue on long-term cooperative action – explicitly not a forum for negotiations – concluded with its last workshop in August 2007. In their report to the Bali conference, the cofacilitators of the dialogue outlined four options for the future, ranging from an extension of the dialogue to a fully integrated negotiating process under both the UNFCCC and the Kyoto Protocol. The key outcome was the Bali Action Plan, launching a negotiating process, the Ad Hoc Group on Long-Term Cooperative Action (AWG-LCA), which would proceed in parallel with the Kyoto negotiations, with the expectation that the two tracks would converge, resulting in a comprehensive post-2012 agreement, in 2009.

The two critical issues in the negotiations on the Bali Action Plan were whether to reference an IPCC scenario under which developed country emissions would fall 20 to 40 percent below 1990 levels by 2020, and the degree to which the paragraphs on developed and developing countries resembled each other in terms of level of implied mitigation effort.[278] The figures, especially language relating to cuts proposed by 2020, were strongly opposed by a number of developed countries, which argued that settling on numbers at the outset of the meeting amounted to prejudging the outcome of the process.[279] The paragraphs of the mandate relating to developed and developing countries are worth quoting in full, to illustrate the nuances[280]:

(b) Enhanced national/international action on mitigation of climate change, including, inter alia, consideration of:
(i) Measurable, reportable and verifiable nationally appropriate mitigation commitments or actions, including quantified emission limitation and reduction objectives, by all developed country

---
[278] BODANSKY, *supra* note 275.
[279] PEW CENTER ON GLOBAL CLIMATE CHANGE, *supra* note 275, at 3.
[280] Decision 1/CP.13, in REPORT OF THE CONFERENCE OF THE PARTIES ON ITS THIRTEENTH SESSION, ADDENDUM, PART II: ACTION TAKEN BY THE CONFERENCE OF THE PARTIES, FCCC/CP/2007/6/Add.1 (2008).

Parties, while ensuring the comparability of efforts among them, taking into account differences in their national circumstances;
(ii) Nationally appropriate mitigation actions by developing country Parties in the context of sustainable development, supported and enabled by technology, financing and capacity-building, in a measurable, reportable and verifiable manner.

The mandate retains, but softens, the differentiation between developed ("mitigation commitments or actions") and developing countries ("actions") and, for this reason, marks an important step. In contrast, the Berlin Mandate, which, in 1995, launched the negotiations leading to the Kyoto Protocol, explicitly ruled out any commitments for developing countries. Even a cursory reading, however, reveals that the negotiators managed to introduce considerable leeway and flexibility. To begin, the chapeau calls for enhanced "national/international" action – satisfying the interests of parties, such as the United States, that preferred national actions over internationally mandated targets. Second, the chapeau calls for "consideration," not negotiation, of the commitments and actions referenced in paragraphs (b)(i) and (b)(ii). It is worth noting that the developed country paragraph – paragraph (b)(i) – lists actions as an alternative to commitments, and emission targets are referred to as "objectives," rather than "commitments," as in an earlier draft.[281] Further scope for differentiation is introduced by the words "nationally appropriate" as a qualifier for "actions and commitments."

The concept of "measurable, reportable and verifiable" is a very significant aspect of the Bali Action Plan, as it requires quantification of mitigation, whether pursuant to commitments in developed countries or in the form of nationally appropriate action in developing countries.[282] In a major shift, developing countries moved from the qualitative commitments under Article 4(1) of the Convention to potentially quantifiable "nationally appropriate mitigation actions" that are "measurable, reportable and verifiable," or MRV.[283] But the Bali Action Plan is consistent with principles of fairness

---

[281] BODANSKY, *supra* note 275.
[282] *See* Harald Winkler, *Measurable, Reportable and Verifiable: The Keys to Mitigation in the Copenhagen Deal*, 8 CLIMATE POLICY 534, 535 (2008); CLARE BREIDENREICH & DANIEL BODANSKY, MEASUREMENT, REPORTING AND VERIFICATION IN A POST-2012 CLIMATE AGREEMENT, PEW CENTER ON GLOBAL CLIMATE CHANGE (2009).
[283] *Id.*

## 3.3. Finalizing the Protocol

and common but differentiated responsibilities because the flow of technological and financial assistance from developed countries must also be MRV. (The result of a last-minute amendment proposed by India, it enables developing countries to insist on the contingency of MRV mitigation action on support, financial and technological, from developed countries.) This also marks a departure from the past, when voluntary contributions were the rule and there existed no provision for measuring assistance flows. The balances between and within the two paragraphs "reaffirm a core balance in the Convention, in its agreement that the extent of developing country-country action is dependent on the provision of finance and technology by developed countries (Art. 4.7)."[284] In short, principles of fairness relating to the sharing of mitigation costs remain integral to progress in the climate regime.

A final point worth mentioning is that the Bali Action Plan eschews the usual Annex I and non–Annex I language – categories codified in the Convention – in favor of "developed" and "developing" countries. This opens up the possibility of the negotiations introducing some differentiation with respect to mitigation effort among developing countries, recognizing the reality that this category contains economically ascendant emerging economies as well as far in less developed nations.

In Bali, the parties also agreed on the scope of the second Article 9 review of the Protocol, which provides that the parties are required to periodically review the Protocol in light of the best available scientific information. To satisfy the terms of the Protocol, a perfunctory first review took place at COP-12, and it was agreed that a more far-reaching effort would be carried out in 2008. The review is contentious because industrialized countries, pointing to scientific findings on the future global mitigation effort, tend to argue that effectiveness demands that developing countries also shoulder some of the responsibility for reducing GHGs. The parties agreed that the second review would focus on issues such as the scope and effectiveness of the Kyoto Protocol's flexibility mechanisms and progress by developed countries in meeting their commitments on finance and technology for developing countries.[285] It was reiterated that the second review would not lead to new commitments for any party.

---

[284] *Id.* at 536.
[285] Decision 4/CMP.3, in REPORT OF THE CONFERENCE OF THE PARTIES SERVING AS THE MEETING OF THE PARTIES TO THE KYOTO PROTOCOL ON ITS THIRD SESSION, ADDENDUM

In a long-awaited decision, the parties agreed on the governance structure of the Adaptation Fund, paving the way for this institution to become operational. As noted earlier, the issue dividing the developing and developed countries centered around who should manage and operate the fund – the GEF, an perceived to be institution dominated by donor countries, or another body, with greater decision-making powers for developing countries. In Nairobi, developing countries had won agreement on the point that decision making should be according to majority rule. In Bali, the parties agreed to establish the Adaptation Fund Board as the operating entity to "supervise and manage the Adaptation Fund, under the authority and guidance of the Conference of the Parties serving as the Meeting of the Parties to the Kyoto Protocol."[286] Unlike the other climate change funds, therefore, the Adaptation Fund is not subject to the Council of the GEF; rather, it is the Adaptation Fund Board that will assume the function of drawing up operational guidelines and policies as well as making decisions on projects and the allocation of funds. The decision provides that the board will be composed of 16 members representing parties to the Protocol, with two representatives from each of the five UN regional groups, one from small island developing states, one from the LDCs, two from non–Annex I parties, and two from Annex I parties. Decision making is on the basis of consensus, failing which, by two-thirds majority. Because the developed countries have 6 representatives and developing countries 10, the latter have a majority.

The decision designated the GEF as the fund's secretariat, and the World Bank as its trustee, on an interim basis, with a review schedule to be held in three years. Overall, the decision means that developing countries have secured a key objective – control over the fund – and, at the same time, benefit from the experience and technical resources of the GEF as the secretariat supporting the fund on a day-to-day basis. It remains to be seen whether the board will be in a position to exercise real supervision and management, or whether the secretariat will exert effective control, and in this respect, the interim nature of the arrangement is almost certainly intended to have a moderating influence. Finally, although the available

---

PART II: ACTION TAKEN BY THE CONFERENCE OF THE PARTIES SERVING AS THE MEETING OF THE PARTIES TO THE KYOTO PROTOCOL, FCCC/KP/CMP/2007/9/Add.1 (2008).

[286] Decision 1/CMP.3, in REPORT OF THE CONFERENCE OF THE PARTIES SERVING AS THE MEETING OF THE PARTIES TO THE KYOTO PROTOCOL ON ITS THIRD SESSION, *supra* note 283.

## 3.3. Finalizing the Protocol

resources are a welcome increase over the trickle thus far made available for adaptation, they come nowhere near matching the need so that allocation and priority setting are destined to be difficult and contentious.

Despite the fact that deforestation in developing countries accounts for an estimated 20 percent of global carbon dioxide emissions, projects designed to avoid deforestation – as opposed to reforestation – are not eligible for credits under the CDM.[287] At Bali, progress was made in recognizing efforts aimed what has become known as reducing emissions from deforestation and degradation (REDD) in developing countries. Papua New Guinea, as the head of a coalition of 15 rainforest countries, placed the issue of crediting efforts to avoid deforestation on the agenda at COP-11 in Montreal. At COP-12, Brazil, which had thus far been skeptical of international discussions of avoided deforestation, unveiled an alternative proposal under which countries reducing their deforestation rates would be eligible for payments from an international fund established by donors, as opposed to emission credits under a market mechanism.

Moving in the direction of recognizing REDD efforts, the parties adopted a decision that, in carefully chosen language, encourages developing countries to explore a range of actions, including demonstration activities, to address deforestation and forest degradation.[288] The decision also encourages work on methodological issues such as the critical question of baselines against which reductions can be measured. In this respect, the decision states that countries may have recourse to the "indicative guidance" provided in an annex to the decision, as an aid in undertaking and evaluating demonstration activities. Not addressed in the decision is whether the incentives to reduce deforestation would flow from a market-based mechanism or donors. The issue of "policy approaches for and incentives" for REDD is singled out in the Bali Action Plan as one of the items for discussion by the AWG-LCA.

The issue of incentives for reducing deforestation is methodologically complex because deforestation is the result of diverse social and economic factors. Extending credits for REDD would be a boon to countries that have so far been left out of the CDM market; however, the beneficiaries under the current CDM arrangements are wary of a flood of cheap REDD

---

[287] WORLD RESOURCES INSTITUTE, NAVIGATING THE NUMBERS 92 (2005).
[288] Decision 2/CP.13, in REPORT OF THE CONFERENCE OF THE PARTIES ON ITS THIRTEENTH SESSION, *supra* note 278.

credits. Nonetheless, the issue has gained momentum, with the World Bank announcing a US$300 million Forest Carbon Partnership Facility with the dual aim of building capacity to undertake projects and demonstrating the methodologies that could be scaled up for a full-scale market.[289]

In the climate negotiations, when industrialized countries exert pressure on developing countries with respect to mitigation action, the latter push back with demands for access to clean technology and greater financial support. In the opening days of the Bali conference, developing countries tried very hard to turn the attention to technology transfer and what they argued were the unfulfilled commitments made by industrialized countries.[290] Their emphasis on technology transfer reflected a concern that the emphasis on new mitigation commitments, including possibly for developing countries, should not come at the expense of agenda items reflecting their interests. In the end, the parties agreed on a decision requesting the GEF to establish a strategic program to scale up technology transfer.[291] This request had its roots in a more ambitious proposal by the G-77 and China to establish a fund under the Convention dedicated to technology transfer.[292] At the institutional level, the parties decided to reconstitute the EGTT for a period of five years, with a number of tasks, including the development of a set of performance indicators, for use by the Subsidiary Body on Implementation to evaluate technology transfer activities.[293] Politically, an undoubted coup for the G-77 and China is the language of the Bali Action Plan, which very tightly links "mitigation action by developing countries" with technology and financing "in a measurable, reportable and verifiable manner."[294] Opening the door to "mitigation actions" is significant, but the decision now spells out one of the conditions for progress: increased financial support and access to technology for developing countries. Attempts by industrialized countries to defect from the more stringent targets-and-timetables approach

---

[289] *Forest Carbon Partnership Facility Takes Aim at Deforestation*, World Bank, December 11, 2007, available at http://go.worldbank.org/1ELJCN2F60.

[290] *COP-13 and COP/MOP-3 Highlights: Tuesday, December 4*, 12(345) EARTH NEGOTIATIONS BULLETIN (2007), available at http://www.iisd.ca/download/pdf/enb12345e.pdf.

[291] Decision 4/CP.13, in REPORT OF THE CONFERENCE OF THE PARTIES ON ITS THIRTEENTH SESSION, *supra* note 278, at para. 3.

[292] *Summary of the Thirteenth Conference of the Parties to the UN Convention on Climate Change and Third Meeting of the Parties to the Kyoto Protocol*, *supra* note 275, at 5.

[293] Decision 3/CP.13 and Decision 4/CP.13, in REPORT OF THE CONFERENCE OF THE PARTIES ON ITS THIRTEENTH SESSION, *supra* note 278.

[294] Bali Action Plan, *supra* note 278, at para. 1(b)(ii).

of the Kyoto track to the Convention process could fatally undermine the willingness of developing countries to define their mitigation actions. The negotiating process must thus balance commitments and actions under the Kyoto and Convention tracks. Given the variety of mitigation approaches likely to be considered, the ability to demonstrate comparability of effort across different policy options assumes great importance.

### 3.3.12. COP-14: Poznań, Poland

COP-14 and COP/MOP-4 opened against the backdrop of an ever deepening, worldwide financial crisis.[295] Coming after the dramatic events in Bali, the Poznań meeting was not expected to deliver any breakthroughs, but instead maintain a sense of forward momentum on key issues, while carrying out the day-to-day business of the COP.

After the Bali conference, it was clear that technology transfer and finance would be key issues in the runup to COP-15 in Copenhagen. At a climate talk held in August 2008, developing countries tabled a proposal that included a Multilateral Climate Technology Fund, by which Annex I governments would use finances from environmental and energy taxes and auctioning of pollution rights to fund technology transfer. They would also use public financing to promote public-private partnerships, including enterprises as well as research and development institutions. The aim of this mechanism is to address cooperation on technology research as well as development, diffusion, and transfer. Meanwhile, the World Bank, in 2008, established the Clean Investment Funds (CIFs), which are a collaborative effort among the multilateral development banks and some donor countries to bridge the financing and learning gap until a post-2012 global climate change agreement comes into effect.[296] The CIFs consist of two funds: one aimed at large-scale investments in developing countries, with the aim of contributing to the demonstration, deployment, and transfer of low-carbon

---

[295] For reports on Poznań, see *Fourteenth Conference of the Parties to the UN Convention on Climate Change and Fourth Meeting of the Parties to the Kyoto Protocol*, summary prepared by the Pew Center on Global Climate Change (undated); *Summary of the Fourteenth Conference of the Parties to the UN Convention on Climate Change and Fourth Meeting of the Parties to the Kyoto Protocol, 1–12 December*, 12(395) EARTH NEGOTIATIONS BULLETIN (2008).
[296] *World Bank Board Approves Climate Investment Funds*, World Bank, press release, July 1, 2008.

technologies, and a second that will identify and promote targeted programs for scaling up efforts and relate capacity-building assistance. These CIFs do not fall under the Convention, a point of contention for developing countries. Responding to a request made at COP-13 in Bali, the GEF in Poznań presented a program on technology transfer, which was adopted as the Poznań strategic program on technology transfer.[297] The program will consist of three funding windows to support technology transfer activities: (1) preparation of technology needs assessments, (2) piloting priority technology projects linked to technology needs assessments, and (3) the dissemination of GEF experience and successfully demonstrated environmentally sound technologies.[298] The initial funding for the program was set at a modest US$50 million.

On REDD, a draft conclusion of the technical body, the SBSTA, made progress on methodological issues relating to the estimation of baselines and the need for robust monitoring frameworks. While some countries wanted to broaden the scope of carbon sequestering activities, in the form of conservation and sustainable forest management, others preferred a narrower focus on avoided deforestation. A proposal to refer to the UN Declaration on the Rights of Indigenous Peoples was rejected by several developed countries, but the draft did recognize "the need to promote the full and effective participation of indigenous people and local communities."[299] Overall, there appeared to be an increasing acceptance that CDM-style offset and fund-based mechanisms would have a role to play.

Although there was broad agreement on the need for the Adaptation Fund to become operational as soon as possible in 2009, extensive discussions took place on the question of enabling direct access of parties to the fund.[300] In Bali, it was decided that parties could access the fund in three ways: directly, that is, without any intermediary agency or body; through existing implementing entities, that is, UN agencies and programs; and through accredited executing entities at the national level. Direct access would have

---

[297] Development and transfer of technologies, FCCC/SBI/2008/L.28/Add.1 (2008).
[298] REPORT OF THE GLOBAL ENVIRONMENT FACILITY ON THE ELABORATION OF A STRATEGIC PROGRAMME TO SCALE UP THE LEVEL OF INVESTMENT IN THE TRANSFER OF ENVIRONMENTALLY SOUND TECHNOLOGIES: NOTE BY THE SECRETARIAT, FCCC/SBI/2008/16 (2008).
[299] REDUCING EMISSIONS FROM DEFORESTATION IN DEVELOPING COUNTRIES: APPROACHES TO STIMULATE ACTION, FCCC/SBSTA/2008/L.23 (2008).
[300] *Summary of the Fourteenth Conference of the Parties to the UN Convention on Climate Change and Fourth Meeting of the Parties to the Kyoto Protocol, supra* note 293.

## 3.3. Finalizing the Protocol

the effect that funds could be disbursed directly by the Adaptation Fund Board, rather than by the GEF, which had been designated as secretariat to the board on an interim basis. At the insistence of developing countries, the COP/MOP decided to confer on the board the necessary legal capacity to enable direct access by parties to the fund.[301] Parties also carried out the periodic review of the Kyoto Protocol mandated by its Article 9, which was dominated by discussions of the CDM and the means of augmenting adaptation financing. As noted earlier, the Adaptation Fund is supported by a 2 percent levy on the credits generated by CDM projects. In an attempt to boost the flow of funds to the Adaptation Fund, developing countries called for extending the levy to the other Kyoto flexible mechanisms: JI and international emissions trading. This proposal was resisted by developed countries, on the basis that this issue should be considered as part of a comprehensive agreement in Copenhagen.[302]

In Poznań, the chair of the AWG-LCA presented a compilation document of submissions from parties on the five core elements of the Bali Action Plan.[303] The AWG-LCA resolved to "shift into full negotiating mode in 2009" and, to this end, adopted a work program authorizing the chair to prepare two documents to advance its work.[304] The first would describe "areas of convergence" and explore "options for dealing with areas of divergence." The second document would be a draft negotiating text, prepared for the AWG-LCA's second session in June 2009.

Observers noted that the prospect of the incoming U.S. administration created anticipation in Poznań.[305] Also, while the conference was in full swing, the leaders of the EU were meeting to adopt their climate and energy package, with any sign of wavering auguring badly for the future. As it turned out, the EU confirmed its target of a 20 percent cut by 2020, but not after concerns from countries heavily reliant on coal had been addressed. The package, covering the period from 2013 to 2020, establishes the rules for the third phase of the EU ETS, details individual emission targets for

---

[301] REPORT OF THE ADAPTATION FUND BOARD, FCCC/KP/CMP/2008/L.7 (2008).
[302] PEW CENTER, *supra* note 293.
[303] IDEAS AND PROPOSALS ON PARAGRAPH 1 OF THE BALI ACTION PLAN: REVISED NOTE BY THE CHAIR, FCCC/AWGLCA/2008/16/Rev.1 (2008).
[304] REPORT OF THE AD HOC WORKING GROUP ON LONG-TERM COOPERATIVE ACTION UNDER THE CONVENTION TO THE CONFERENCE OF THE PARTIES AT ITS FOURTEENTH SESSION, FCCC/AWGLCA/2008/L.11 (2008).
[305] PEW CENTER, *supra* note 293.

EU member states in sectors not covered by the EU ETS, and contains a 20 percent target for renewable energy, a 10 percent target for biofuels, and a 20 percent target for increasing energy efficiency by 2020. In the runup to the Copenhagen conference, Brazil, Mexico, and South Africa announced mitigation plans in Poznań. Brazil pledged to cut the deforestation rate in the Amazon by more than half within a decade,[306] while Mexico stated that it would cut emissions by 50 percent by 2050, relative to 2000 emissions.[307] South Africa announced a strategy to arrest emissions growth by 2020–2025, level off for up to 10 years, and then decline in absolute terms.[308]

It is in the nature of negotiations for parties not to tip their hats and instead to wait for the end game. At the close of the Poznań conference, many key issues remained unclear, including concrete proposals from industrialized countries to implement the Bali Action Plan language on finance and technology transfer and even the final status – whether ratifiable or not – of the agreement to be reached in Copenhagen.

### 3.3.13. International Developments outside the Convention Process

Climate change was one of the key topics addressed at Gleneagles G-8 Summit, held under the presidency of the United Kingdom. In the summit communiqué, countries agreed to launch a Dialogue on Climate Change, Clean Energy, and Sustainable Development and asked the International Energy Agency (IEA) and World Bank, respectively, to develop alternative, clean energy scenarios and a new framework for clean energy financing and investment.[309] Forming part of the communiqué was a short plan of action setting out specific actions taken and planned with respect to climate change. A number of dialogue meetings were convened under the G-8 plus 5 format,[310] and their size and composition (outside the environment

---

[306] Joshua Partlow, *Brazil's Decision on Deforestation Draws Praise*, WASHINGTON POST, December 6, 2008, at A09.

[307] Gerard Wynn, *Mexico Says to Set Climate Targets, Cap and Trade*, REUTERS, December 11, 2008, available at http://www.reuters.com/article/environmentNews/idUSTRE4-BA55T20081211?feedType=RSS&feedName=environmentNews.

[308] Statement delivered at the UN Climate Change Conference in Poznań by Marthinus van Schalkwyk, Minister of Environmental Affairs and Tourism, South Africa, December 11, 2008, available at http://www.deat.gov.za//NewsMedia/MedStat/2008Dec11/statement11122008.pdf.

[309] The Gleneagles Communiqué, available at http://www.fco.gov.uk/Files/kfile/PostG8_Gleneagles_CCChapeau.pdf.

[310] The five are Brazil, China, India, Mexico, and South Africa.

## 3.3. Finalizing the Protocol

portfolio) had the potential to turn them into forums for meaningful discussion. Given the generally private nature of these discussions, not much is known of the conclusions reached, and it is difficult to assess to what extent the G-8 dialogue has contributed to progress in international climate change negotiations. For their part, both the IEA and the World Bank prepared a number of studies and reports pursuant to their Gleneagles mandates, with the Bank's work putting some hard numbers to the financing challenge for clean energy and adaptation to the adverse effects of climate change.[311] At the G-8 Summit in Heiligendamm in 2007, under the German presidency, climate change was prominently on the agenda, but leaders could only agree to seriously consider at least a halving of global emissions by 2050.[312] The statement issued at the Hokkaido Toyako Summit, under the presidency of Japan, in 2008, expressed their willingness to pursue the 50 percent reduction goal within the UNFCCC, on the basis of contributions from all major economies and consistent with the principle of common but differentiated responsibilities and respective capabilities.[313] The statement did not address the question of the base year against which the 50 percent reductions would be measured.

Governments, NGOs, and the business community have joined together in partnerships at local, national, regional, and international levels. A few examples provide an indication of the scope and variety of partnerships and cooperative ventures that have arisen, some with international political and legal significance, others not. In January 2006, the United States and Australia – the two industrialized countries that had rejected the Kyoto Protocol and its approach of binding targets – launched the Asia-Pacific Partnership on Clean Development and Climate, dubbed APP.[314] (Australia

---

[311] *See* WORLD BANK, CLEAN ENERGY AND DEVELOPMENT: TOWARDS AN INVESTMENT FRAMEWORK (2006); CLEAN ENERGY AND DEVELOPMENT: A PROGRESS REPORT (2006); and CLEAN ENERGY FOR DEVELOPMENT: THE WORLD BANK ACTION PLAN (2007), available at http://web.worldbank.org/WBSITE/EXTERNAL/TOPICS/EXTENERGY/0,menuPK:336812~pagePK:149018~piPK:149093~theSitePK:336806,00.html.

[312] Chair's Summary, Heiligendamm, June 8, 2007, available at http://www.g-8.de/Webs/G8/EN/G8Summit/SummitDocuments/summit-documents.html.

[313] Chair's Summary, Hokkaido, Toyako, July 9, 2008, available at http://www.mofa.go.jp/policy/economy/summit/2008/doc/doc080709_09_en.html.

[314] *See* http://www.asiapacificpartnership.org/. For perhaps the only legal analysis of the Asia-Pacific Partnership, *see* Christoph Holtwisch, *Asiatisch-pazifische Partnerschaft für umweltverträgliche Entwicklung und Klima – Blockade oder Antrieb für das internationale Klimaregime?*, master's thesis, June 2007, copy on file with the author.

of course later went on to ratify the Protocol.) Other founding members – all Kyoto parties – are China, India, Japan, and the Republic of Korea, with Canada joining in 2007. The APP aims to accelerate the deployment of clean energy technologies through focused cooperation between member countries, working closely with industry. The APP established a policy and implementation committee to guide its work and oversee the activities of the eight public-private task forces addressing eight focal areas ranging from energy-intensive sectors (e.g., aluminum) to renewable energy. In ambition and institutional structure, the APP stands head and shoulders above other partnerships in the energy and climate field; continued engagement of key members and the commitment of financial resources are likely to determine whether it makes a real contribution with respect to clean technology or, as many skeptics suspected, merely served as a diversion by countries opposed to the Kyoto Protocol. Certainly the deployment of clean energy technology has been insufficiently addressed under the current climate regime, and an initiative such as the APP – perhaps expanded to include membership from the EU and with closer links to the UNFCCC – could go some way toward remedying this deficiency.

The Carbon Sequestration Leadership Forum (CLSF) is an example of a technology partnership with participation, including from the United States, Germany, Japan, China, and India. The aim of the CLSF is to develop and make available cost-effective technologies for carbon dioxide capture and storage.[315] Methane is a powerful GHG emitted from landfills, mines, and oil and gas installations. Bringing together 20 governments and well over 100 corporations, the Methane to Markets Partnership is an international initiative aimed at advancing cost-effective, near-term methane recovery and use as a clean energy source.[316] Other partnerships have been formed in specific industry sectors, for instance, the cement industry, which is responsible for about 5 percent of global carbon dioxide emissions from human activities. An example of practical cooperative action to address emissions from this vital economic sector is the Cement Sustainability Initiative, formed by leading cement producers under the umbrella of the World Business Council on Sustainable Development.[317]

---

[315] *See* http://www.cslforum.org/about.htm.
[316] *See* http://www.methanetomarkets.org/.
[317] *See* http://www.wbcsdcement.org/.

## 3.4. CONCLUSION AND THE ROAD AHEAD

Drawing together the material covered in this chapter, this section briefly assesses the climate change regime to date. Challenges for the way forward are also outlined. As outlined in this chapter, states have steadily (albeit slowly) built a climate change regime through successive COPs. Beginning with the historic UNFCCC, which established the goal of preventing dangerous interference with the climate system, states have established an impressive and intricate multilateral regime. While management and further development by COPs are now regarded as a feature of modern multilateral environmental agreements (MEAs), the Convention and the Protocol have set a new mark for the development of rules by such treaty bodies. The multifaceted nature and technical complexity of many of the issues dealt with are quite staggering. At the same time, deep policy differences and weighty economic interests underlie many supposedly technical issues. This is true, for instance, of the somewhat arcane rules relating to emissions credits for land-use change and forestry. The political dimension stems from a number of sources. First, nominally, the Convention and the Protocol are environmental treaties; in reality, they have profound social and economic implications. The future division of the mitigation burden between industrialized and developing countries cuts to the core of disagreements on global development and fairness in the relations between states. This chapter has touched on how industrialized countries have attempted to extend binding commitments to developing countries, which, in turn, have invoked the principle of common but differentiated responsibilities, underlining the historical responsibility of developed countries. This aspect is explored in greater depth elsewhere.[318] Second, and more narrowly, the binding nature of Annex I parties' targets under the Kyoto Protocol endows otherwise technical matters, for instance, guidelines and standards for reporting and maintenance of emissions inventories, with greater significance. Failure to maintain adequate accounting standards for GHG emissions and removals can lead to suspension of eligibility to use the emissions trading mechanisms.

The process of regular COPs, backed by the preparatory work of the subsidiary bodies, has proved capable of sustaining and further developing

---

[318] *See* Chapter 4.

the climate regime. In drafting the Convention, the parties went as far as they could at that time in addressing climate change; some, like the states of the EU, would have preferred going further. (In fairness, it should be recalled that the IPCC's First Assessment Report, issued in 1990, concluded that the evidence as to whether warming was attributable to human or natural causes was evenly balanced.[319]) The need to supplement the Convention with an instrument containing emission limitation and reduction targets was quickly recognized, leading to the launch of the negotiations for the Protocol.

The Convention and Protocol have established a number of important institutions and mechanisms. The Protocol's compliance system, while borrowing from the experience of the Montreal Protocol, is, in the view of many observers, the most sophisticated mechanism of its kind in any MEA. The three flexibility mechanisms, particularly the CDM, exist at the intersection of public international law and domestic laws. The Protocol has led to the establishment of an international carbon market, in the process giving rise to a private sector constituency with a direct pecuniary interest in the continuation of emission controls. An international body, the CDM EB, guided in its work by the COP, regulates the activities of private sector entities involved with project activities in host countries. Host countries, in turn, set the criteria for approving projects and apply domestic laws as they would to any other investment activity. Putting this edifice in place has been the painstaking task of the parties in the years after the adoption of the Protocol in 1997 and the agreement on the Marrakech Accords in 2001. The next few years were spent tying up remaining loose ends. The Protocol also became caught in a debilitating waiting game concerning its entry into force. Only with COP-11 in Montreal, in 2005, did negotiators turn to the next phase, that is, what would come after 2012 when the first Kyoto commitment period expires.

It is perhaps not entirely unfair to say that the climate change regime has been a victim of its own success. After all, few other environmental regimes would be criticized for the level of productivity and range of issues considered under the Convention and Protocol. However, one problem may be that *success* is increasingly defined within the parameter of climate

---

[319] INTERGOVERNMENTAL PANEL ON CLIMATE CHANGE, SCIENTIFIC ASSESSMENT OF CLIMATE CHANGE – REPORT OF WORKING GROUP 1 (John Houghton et al. eds., 1990).

## 3.4. Conclusion and the Road Ahead

negotiations themselves, so that it means incremental (and admittedly necessary) advances, but no breakthrough on the central issues dividing industrialized and developing countries.

As summarized in this chapter, and posited by scholars,[320] regular and institutionalized procedures – such as those typified by COPs – contribute to a situation where states with diverse interests can nonetheless agree on, and steadily develop, institutions and rules to respond to a complex global problem. In short, the existence of a regular forum for discussion and generating agreement and coordination on core issues, such monitoring and reporting of emissions, has value, which is admitted by those who believe a decentralized approach is more practicable.[321] Nevertheless, it is possible that the facilitating embrace of the rules and institutions of the climate regime may have become a straitjacket, insulating the process from new ideas and permitting elaboration and refinement to substitute for action and innovation. The climate regime, as summarized in this chapter, demonstrates a number of other disadvantages and weaknesses. First, the approach taken in the Protocol emphasized binding targets to be met over a relatively short time frame (2008–2012). Assuming full compliance by all countries, the cuts under the Protocol would have had a minor effect on global emissions and overall a negligible impact on climate change; nonetheless, several countries are having difficulty meeting their individual targets. The combination of very modest environmental impact and the fact that some Annex I parties are not on track to meet their targets may appear to give credence to critics' arguments. This situation, coupled with uncertainties about compliance costs, naturally increased the incentive to exploit available loopholes. The overview of COP-6 (Part II) and COP-7 showed how the rules concerning the counting of sinks (forestry) were (re-) defined. This leads some scholars to conclude that agreements like the Kyoto Protocol are essentially unenforceable because some parties will always find and exploit loopholes, and enforcement with real teeth is a nonstarter in an international system based on voluntary agreement.[322]

---

[320] Stephen D. Krasner, *Structural Causes and Regime Consequences: Regimes as Intervening Variables*, 36(2) INTERNATIONAL ORGANIZATION 185 (1982).
[321] David Victor, *Fragmented Carbon Markets and Reluctant Nations: Implications for the Design of Effective Architectures*, in ARCHITECTURES FOR AGREEMENT: ADDRESSING GLOBAL CLIMATE ON THE POST-KYOTO WORLD 133 (Joseph E. Aldy & Robert N. Stavins eds., 2007).
[322] Scott Barrett, *A Multitrack Climate Treaty System*, in ARCHITECTURES FOR AGREEMENT: ADDRESSING GLOBAL CLIMATE ON THE POST-KYOTO WORLD, *supra* note 319, at 237.

Second, the sheer size of the annual COPs (drawing anywhere from 6,000 to 10,000 people) and the number of interest groups represented (environmental NGOs, business NGOs of various stripes) lends them an overwhelming quality. The sheer number of issues and their complexity elevated the transaction costs of effective participation in the negotiations. Only large and well-resourced delegations can participate meaningfully as national actors. This raises concerns about procedural fairness. Recent COPs seem to suggest that these mega-meetings may not lend themselves to creative solutions among the key players in developed and developing countries. Third, while groups have always been a feature of the climate negotiations, lack of trust among key players means that negotiations are sometimes trapped in unproductive dynamics. Fourth, while the multilateral process has almost universal participation,[323] the reality is that a relatively small group of some 15 large emitters are responsible for over three-quarters of global emissions.[324] By and large, they will also be responsible for much of the emissions growth in the coming decades. Theory suggests that a meaningful agreement among members of a group such as this could have a major impact on global emissions. The G-8 plus 5 and the Major Economies Meeting process, spearheaded by the U.S. administration from 2007 to 2008, were initiatives intended to find common ground among large emitters. The experience with these initiatives suggests that although the existence of extra forums for the exchange of ideas and proposals is valuable, the Convention process is imbued with considerable legitimacy and remains the focus of the international climate change regime. However, if the Convention and Protocol multilateral negotiations do not deliver on the mandate agreed at Bali, key parties may well consider that more is to be gained outside the existing process.

What are some fairness implications of a core of major emitters reaching a deal? If such an agreement were substantially arrived at outside the Convention process, it would undermine the basic notion of equality and participation that has so far been a feature of the climate change regime.

[323] As of August 22, the Convention had 192 members. *See* LIST OF SIGNATORIES AND RATIFICATION OF THE CONVENTION, available at http://unfccc.int/essential_background/convention/status_of_ratification/items/2631.php. As of January 14, 2009, the Protocol had 183 countries and one regional integration organization (the EEC). *See* STATUS OF RATIFICATION, available at http://unfccc.int/kyoto_protocol/background/status_of_ratification/items/2613.php.
[324] WORLD RESOURCES INSTITUTE, *supra* note 285.

An agreement reached in the absence of so many of the affected parties would probably not be considered fair, bearing in mind the importance of an open and legitimate process. In particular, meaningful participation of all countries in the process of setting a long-term target is crucial because of their shared interest. (This underlines the importance of the "shared vision" mentioned in the Bali Action Plan.) In fact, vulnerable groups of countries, like small island states, have a great deal at stake in charting the long-term mitigation path. Fairness entails that countries particularly vulnerable to climate impacts should have their concerns fully considered. Assuming an acceptable long-term target, it is somewhat more difficult to see why a smaller group of the most responsible countries should not take the lead in working out a deal to allocate the mitigation burden. For LDCs and other poor countries, a fairness concern would be whether an agreement leaves them enough growth space; in this context, access to low-carbon technologies will be of great importance for them to realize development objectives in a carbon-constrained future. Countries also have a key interest in the design of institutions, for instance, a potential successor to the CDM. As new instruments, such as REDD in developing countries, are introduced, new tensions and fairness concerns may arise. Deforestation and other forms of land-use change, mainly in developing countries, cause some 20 percent of global $CO_2$ emissions. A mechanism to slow the rate of deforestation therefore makes sense. And REDD potentially offers revenue streams for tropical countries that have not benefited from the carbon market, but also raises the possibility of a tide of cheap credits that could depress the price of carbon, lessening the incentive for clean energy development and deployment. If one considers that the crux of the climate problem is the world's entrenched, carbon-intensive way of life, then excessive developed country reliance on market-based REDD may well serve as a distraction from tackling the more challenging, but also enduring, mitigation tasks.[325] In accordance with the principle of sovereignty over natural resources, developing countries are quite entitled to trade the rights to the sink capacity of their forests. But here context is important. Do tropical developing countries have a real choice between (1) additional assistance and funding to help manage and preserve forests for both domestic and global benefit and (2) participation in a

---

[325] Sunita Narain, *2009 Is Full of Promise*, editorial, CSE Equitywatch, January 1, 2009, available at http://www.cseindia.org/equitywatch/editorial20090115.htm.

trading scheme, where preservation of forest tracts offsets equivalent emissions in developed countries? Specific fairness concerns relate to the people that live in, or derive benefits from, forests – will their interests be adequately safeguarded? Thus mechanisms should be put in place for communities and local governments to be beneficiaries and stakeholders of REDD. It should also be remembered that forests deliver a range of benefits, in addition to carbon storage, including water storage, soil conservation, nutrient flows, and biodiversity.

The Bali Action Plan makes it plain that developing countries regard mitigation actions on their part as contingent on access to technology and financial support from industrialized countries. Thus far, the climate regime has, despite promises embedded in the text of the Convention, delivered little in the way of credible incentives for developing countries. Given the complicated nature of the climate change regime, and the widely diverging interests of parties, it may be optimistic to assume that one down-to-the-wire negotiation will resolve all the outstanding issues. Certainly the widely appreciated need to begin implementing some adaptation and mitigation policies now militates against a "Kyoto 2," on which years are spent fleshing out the rules, without initiating actual policy changes. At the same time, the number and complexity of the issues facing negotiators suggests that a progress will likely come in the form of general agreements, with details filled in. There is increasing understanding that future commitments should establish a stable, long-term framework, providing certainty for the carbon market and incentives for technological innovation. A graduated phasing in of policies would ensure that economic costs are minimized, thereby avoiding the premature retirement of expensive infrastructure. Targets would be tightened over time.

The conclusion has drawn out a number of challenges facing the next phase of the climate regime. At this point, the direction and shape of that next phase remain to be determined.

# 4

## Theoretical Aspects of Fairness

### 4.1. INTRODUCTION

Claims about fairness and justice stand at the center of debates about our collective response to climate change. But what does *fairness* mean? Clearly it is a deeply contested concept, one that reasonable persons can understand in inconsistent and even incompatible ways. As fairness assumes greater currency and salience in climate policy, it is worthwhile to outline briefly the main approaches that lead to some of the arguments put forward in the climate regime. Fairness and justice can be analyzed at quite abstract levels, but the problem of climate change quickly directs the enquiry to the practical, real-world questions. Thus the chief aim of this chapter is to identify a number of principles that could shape different conceptions of fairness in the context of climate change – principles around which one can construct a rough, working consensus of values influencing the debate on the question of sharing the burdens and benefits of combating climate change. Yet caution is advised in plucking conceptions of fairness and justice developed in particular theoretical frameworks and attempting to apply them, in a somewhat pell-mell fashion, to the problem of climate change. The potential for error is large, but fairness in climate change should also be carried at a level that mixes ethics and morals, science and interests.

A question that may quickly be asked is, fairness to whom? Since nation-states are the main (and most visible) international actors, it is often assumed that we are dealing with fairness between nations, in other words, international justice. This raises at least two issues. First, fairness issues also penetrate within the borders of a state. Different communities within a particular state may have very different levels of exposure to the impacts of climate change, and similarly, different groups may be differentially affected by mitigation measures, that is, in the form of higher taxes and fuel prices. At the national and local levels, resources for adaptation activities – sea walls and dykes are one quintessential example – are likely to be limited, which raises the question of how they are to be allocated. Second, important from a theoretical perspective, there is the question whether conceptions of fairness and justice conceived and justified in the context of the nation-state can – or should – be extended to the international level. In modern nation-states, citizens are bearers of rights (voting, freedom of association, freedom of speech, rule of law) and responsibilities or duties (taxes). The institutions sustaining these rights and obligations exist at the national level and barely at all internationally, perhaps with the exception of regional developments in the European Union[1]; philosophical justifications of rights and state power (taxation, deprivation of liberty) are predominantly articulated within the context of nation-states.[2] This implies that fairness claims may not be valid outside the context of community or state. There may be obstacles in directly translating principles of fairness and justice, from the national to the international level, but this has not prevented prominent efforts to do so.[3] The philosopher John Rawls, the author of the very influential *A Theory of Justice*, did not, in a later work, extend his famous difference principle of distributive fairness to the international level.[4] In addressing the question of justice at the international level, Rawls substituted for the difference principle a much weaker duty to "assist other peoples living under unfavorable conditions that prevent their having a just or decent political and social regime."[5] Supporters of a global or cosmopolitan conception of distributive justice have argued that his theory of justice is applicable not

---

[1] *See* Dino Kritsiotis, *Imagining the International Community*, 13 EUROPEAN JOURNAL OF INTERNATIONAL LAW 961 (2002).
[2] JOHN RAWLS, THE LAW OF PEOPLES (1999); WILL KYMLICKA, CONTEMPORARY POLITICAL PHILOSOPHY: AN INTRODUCTION 255 (2002); Thomas Nagel, *The Problem of Global Justice*, 33(2) PHILOSOPHY & PUBLIC AFFAIRS 113 (2005). But *cf.* THOMAS POGGE, WORLD POVERTY AND HUMAN RIGHTS (2nd ed. 2008).
[3] THOMAS M. FRANCK, FAIRNESS IN INTERNATIONAL LAW AND INSTITUTIONS (1995) (hereinafter referred to as FRANCK, FAIRNESS).
[4] JOHN RAWLS, A THEORY OF JUSTICE (1971). The difference principle holds that inequality in the distribution of society's resources is only permissible if it benefits those who have lesser shares. *See id.* 302–3 and KYMLICKA, *supra* note 2, at 56–57.
[5] RAWLS, *supra* note 2.

only nationally, but internationally also.[6] Importantly, cosmopolitanism does not imply a commitment to any particular conception of justice – liberal, libertarian, utilitarian – only that the preferred conception applies across national borders, to any person anywhere.

Liberal theories of justice seek to ensure that morally arbitrary circumstances of birth (race, sex, class) do not determine life chances – circumstances should not be destiny. This finds expression in the well-known concept of equality of opportunity. At the individual level, there are a range of views on what is necessary to attain equal opportunities: outlawing discrimination on the basis of gender and race, or going further to adopt measures such as affirmative action to truly level the playing field. Do these animating ideas make sense outside the domestic context? The argument could be advanced that persons in affected countries should not suffer disadvantage simply due to morally arbitrary factors such as geography (low-lying areas) or history (legacy of underdevelopment). In any theory of justice, bald indifference to international injustice seems a rather unsatisfactory state of affairs. Efforts to conceive conceptions of global justice are therefore necessary. At the same time, the absence of a meaningful international community – at least in the sense that approximates the core functions of a state – means that it is difficult to conceive of processes that could establish basic fairness norms and then ensure implementation that is consistent with these distributive principles.

Questions such as those touched on in the preceding discussion go to the heart of political philosophy, and the intention here is simply to note the existence of disagreement on this point. In broad terms, the enquiry here focuses less on the justification of a particular conception of justice – a major aim of political philosophy – and more on the identification and application of principles of fairness that can be, and are being, applied, by various parties, to understand and evaluate international climate law and policy.

At the legal level, has international law reached a stage where it makes sense to analyze whether it is fair or not? Thomas Franck has answered this question in the affirmative. Yet it remains easy to point to examples reinforcing the conception that in a system of nation-states, international

---

[6] KYMLICKA, *supra* note 2, at 269. *See also* THOMAS POGGE, REALIZING RAWLS (1989); BRIAN BARRY, DEMOCRACY, POWER, AND JUSTICE: ESSAYS IN POLITICAL THEORY (1989).

law remains dominated by interstate bargaining and ad hoc development, based on consent. At the same time, international lawmaking in the area of climate change has gone well beyond once-off treaty making, expanding into a shifting and flexible process of review and rule making, covering initiation and acceptance of scientific assessments (e.g., by the Intergovernmental Panel on Climate Change [IPCC]) and the development of complex rules for the implementation of the mechanisms of the Kyoto Protocol. This treaty making and the associated international regulations are intended to deal with one of the most pressing problems facing all nations of the world. Climate change intersects with other leading international preoccupations, especially the social and economic development of the poorer countries of the world. On those terms, this area of international law deserves to be analyzed on fairness grounds. International climate law may be many things, but it arguably does not aspire simply to set the rules of the game, demarcate minimum standards, or express the raw reality of power politics.

Following Shue, key questions relating to distributive justice in the case of climate change are, at least, the following[7]:

1. What is a fair allocation of the costs of preventing the climate change that is still avoidable?
2. What is a fair allocation of the costs of adapting to climate change impacts that will, in fact, not be avoided?
3. What is a fair allocation of scarce resources available for adaptation measures?
4. What background allocation of wealth would allow international bargaining – about issues like points 1, 2, and 3 – to be a fair process?
5. What is a fair allocation of emissions of greenhouse gases (GHGs) (1) over the long term and (2) during the transition to long-term allocation?

These questions usefully frame the discussion of distributive fairness in the context of climate change. This chapter and this book are concerned with distributive fairness in the context of climate change, primarily with respect to principles that could be used to analyze proposals for allocating

---

[7] *See* Henry Shue, *Subsistence Emissions and Luxury Emissions*, 15 LAW & POLICY 40 (1993). The wording has been slightly altered, and I have added question 3.

## 4.1. Introduction

the mitigation burden between countries, that is, the preceding point 5. Yet it is also necessary to remain cognizant of point 4.

Issues of fairness generally relate to at least one of two dimensions: either fairness of general background conditions or fairness specific to the problem at hand.[8] The former leads to the question, what conditions are sufficient for the parties to be considered in a position to bargain for a so-called fair outcome? If the parties are in grossly unequal positions, this undercuts the legitimacy of the process and the eventual outcome. For instance, it could be argued that relations between states are not structured in a neutral fashion, and there does exist a "global basic structure" of economic and political rules and relationships, which has distributional effects on states inter se as well as on individuals within states.[9] Some have argued that this structure is revealed in the unequal relations between states, with key aspects of the international system skewed in favor of affluent and powerful states.[10] The negotiations about the allocation of costs and emission entitlements in the future take place in the context of radical inequality among participating states. Billions still lack adequate access to the rudiments of a decent life: clean water, sanitation, energy services, health care, and education. In an era of economic globalization, some regions, such as sub-Saharan Africa, barely register on the map of world trade.

Thus it is legitimate to ask whether the background conditions of the international system are such that they would permit fair bargaining between states about the allocation of burdens and benefits in combating climate change. There can be no easy answer to questions such as this; however, the backdrop of social and economic inequality is one reason why the broader development issue is so intertwined with the ostensibly narrower allocation questions of the climate change regime. Simply put, in the eyes of many developing countries, the climate regime cannot be separated from the perceived unfairness of the international system and at once presents the risk of deepening and further perpetuating that unfairness, and simultaneously

---

[8] Henry Shue, *Environmental Change and Varieties of Justice*, in EARTHLY GOODS: ENVIRONMENTAL CHANGE AND SOCIAL JUSTICE 9, 13 (Fen Osler Hampson & Judith Reppy eds., 1996).

[9] Allen Buchanan, *Rawls's Law of Peoples: Rules for a Vanished Westphalian World*, 110(4) ETHICS 697, 705–6 (2000); John Tasioulas, *International Law and the Limits of Fairness*, 13 EUROPEAN JOURNAL OF INTERNATIONAL LAW 993, 1009 (2003).

[10] TASIOULAS, *supra* note 9, at 1006, quoting Thomas Pogge, *Priorities of Global Justice*, 32 METAPHILOSOPHY 9, 16–17 (2001).

the prospect of winning a fairer share of global economic and social opportunities. In general, the approach to fairness adopted here will focus on the narrower question of principles guiding allocation of responsibility for combating climate change, rather than analyzing the deeper inequalities of the international system. Nonetheless, in pursuing the former, it is necessary to bear in mind the implications of the broader context in which parties make fairness claims.

### 4.1.1. The Role of Interests

An examination of the role of fairness must also acknowledge the role of interests in negotiations and formation of agreements. A discussion of fairness needs to bear in mind the importance of national interest in the positions taken by states in the climate arena. Even if cogent grounds of fairness support a given outcome, few countries would accept the outcome if it goes against the national interest, for instance, by imposing economic costs on important domestic constituencies without tangible (political) benefits. In negotiations and the articulation of policy positions, the parties will naturally attempt to cast their positions in the most favorable and persuasive light. Sometimes references to fairness may therefore simply be disguised arguments concerning interests.

Realists focus on the primacy of interests in determining the conduct of states.[11] In analyzing a possible treaty outcome, a realist analysis might focus on the willingness to pay of the various actors, rather than on conceptions of equity or fairness.[12] Realism developed as a reaction against Wilsonian liberal internationalism, and the so-called political realists of the period after World War II articulated a theory of relations between states based on their respective national interests.[13] Politics was struggle for power, with no place for law as a constraining force.[14] Over time, the political realism of the postwar period was redefined into what came to be known as

---

[11] See, for the classic exposition, HANS J. MORGENTHAU, POLITICS AMONG NATIONS: THE STRUGGLE FOR POWER AND PEACE (4th ed. 1967).

[12] See David Victor, The Regulation of Greenhouse Gases: Does Fairness Matter?, in FAIR WEATHER? EQUITY CONCERNS IN CLIMATE CHANGE 193 (Ferenc L. Tóth ed., 1999).

[13] See MORGENTHAU, supra note 11; GEORGE KENNAN, AMERICAN DIPLOMACY, 1900–1950 (1951)

[14] Anne-Marie Slaughter Burley, International Law and International Relations Theory: A Dual Agenda, 87 AMERICAN JOURNAL OF INTERNATIONAL LAW 205, 207–9 (1993).

4.1. Introduction 139

*neorealism*.[15] A full description of neorealism is beyond the scope of this chapter; however, it holds as a key tenet that the basic laws of the international system flow from the relative distribution of capabilities (power) across the system.[16] Under neorealism's structural conception of international politics, there is almost no role for international law. A basic assumption of realism is that states are rational actors, which, against the background of an anarchic international system, seek to further their interests with ultimately little regard for international law. Realists are skeptical of the idea that states can cooperate in international institutions to advance their common interests.

The second broad school of international relations is *neoliberal institutionalism* or *regime theory*.[17] This school places less emphasis on power differentials between states, drawing attention instead to the role of international regimes and institutions in assisting states to realize their common interests. Neoliberal institutionalism shares realism's commitment to a theory of rational, self-interested actors, but it argues that regimes and institutions help states coordinate their behavior and achieve mutually beneficial outcomes.[18] The standard definition of regimes is from Krasner: "regimes are sets of implicit or explicit principles, norms, rules, and decision-making procedures around which actors' expectations converge in a given area of international relations."[19] The neoliberal institutionalist approach, in recognizing the role that regimes and institutions can play in empowering

---

[15] *See* SLAUGHTER BURLEY, *supra* note 14, at 214–17. The architect of this development in international relations theory was Kenneth Waltz, and the classic exposition of his systemic theory is KENNETH N. WALTZ, THEORY OF INTERNATIONAL POLITICS (1979). According to Waltz, it is structural factors, particularly the relative distribution of power in the international system, that determine world politics. He differs from political realism in that power is regarded not as an end, but as a means to secure survival or security.

[16] WALTZ, *supra* note 15, at 66.

[17] A key text is ROBERT KEOHANE, AFTER HEGEMONY: COOPERATION AND DISCORD IN THE WORLD POLITICAL ECONOMY (1984).

[18] ANDREAS HASENCLEVER ET AL., THEORIES OF INTERNATIONAL REGIMES 23–24 (1997).

[19] Stephen D. Krasner, *Structural Causes and Regime Consequences: Regimes as Intervening Variables*, 36(2) INTERNATIONAL ORGANIZATION 185 (1982). International institutions are regarded as having a potentially positive effect on compliance with the rules because they expand or shrink the options available to rational state actors, which are constantly attempting to maximize their respective self-interests. It is important to note that in general, neoliberal institutionalism assumes, in common with realism, that states' interests tend to be fairly stable over time and that interests shape interaction or cooperation and not vice versa. *See* also HASENCLEVER ET AL., *supra* note 18, at 23–24.

states, rather than acting as constraints, at least conceives a facilitative role for international law.[20]

An analysis based on a hard-nosed calculation of interests may appear more rigorous and useful than engagement with the more amorphous concept of fairness. It is, however, worth considering realism in more detail. First, in complex climate negotiations, actually determining *the* national interest on a particular issue is far less obvious than a casual consideration of realism suggests. Does the national interest lie in minimizing short-term costs, at the risk of a flawed outcome, leading to the probability of more severe climate impacts in the future? At a time when climate change is seen as potentially contributing to population migrations and conflicts over natural resources, there may be some degree of convergence with traditional national security interests. In sum, one can rightly question whether the national interest is readily definable and not highly dependent on context. Second, the interests of a state, and its willingness to pay for outcomes, are hardly monolithic – positions can, and do, change over time. If the interests of states are neither monolithic nor static, then how exactly do they change, and why? It is suggested that there exists a dynamic interplay between interests and concepts such as fairness and equity. Confronted by the strongly held views of allies concerning the fairness of a certain issue, a state may decide it is in its interests, after all, to concede the point (and bear the cost).

While realist analysis appears to provide a sharp, rigorous counterpoint to the seemingly fuzzier normative analysis that is advocated here, realism generally takes interests (or willingness to pay) as given and cannot account adequately for their formation and change over time. In the bargaining context of climate negotiations, ethical and moral enquiry can help to frame positions and function as a standard for evaluating policy options. In short, it is suggested that in understanding climate change policy, interests-based analysis and normative enquiries both have a place.

## 4.2. PHILOSOPHICAL ROOTS

According to Hart, fairness is primarily of relevance in two situations: in the distribution of a burden or benefit among a class of persons, and where

---

[20] SLAUGHTER BURLEY, *supra* note 14, at 219–20. She concludes that institutionalism has led to a convergence between international relations and international law, with the former arriving at a new appreciation of the latter.

## 4.2. Philosophical Roots

compensation or redress is claimed for an injury or wrong.[21] It is thus common to refer to distributive fairness and corrective fairness or justice. Also central to the notion of fairness or justice is the injunction to treat like cases alike, which can be traced to Aristotle.[22] This principle emphasizes impartiality and consistency, and has characteristics of fairness and justice, but is purely formal in nature, as it does not prescribe when cases are alike or unalike. Applying this principle thus requires reference to a substantive theory of justice that determines which differences are relevant (e.g., merit) and which are not (race). The content of such substantive theories is further explored subsequently.

Equity is closely linked to fairness, and the two terms are often used synonymously.[23] Thus it has been observed that in common usage, *equity* means "the quality of being fair or impartial," or "something that is fair and just."[24] In addition to notions of distributive justice, equity also encompasses the sense of rendering individualized justice.[25] Thus Aristotle describes equity as mitigating the excesses implied by law's absoluteness and thus facilitating the application of the law to a concrete case.[26] In this view, equity serves as a corrective to the harshness or injustice that may result from the inflexible application of a rule. This sense is reflected in expressions such as "equitable principles." Equity prevents or ameliorates injustice – it promotes fairness. The choice has been made to use the term *fairness* throughout this book, but in general, the conception of equity reflected in international environmental law, especially the climate change regime, is practically identical.

When poor countries vulnerable to the impacts of climate change claim resources for adaptation measures, this corresponds, in part, to the corrective dimension of fairness. This argument relies on the historical and

---

[21] HLA Hart, The Concept of Law 154 (1961).
[22] Aristotle, Nicomachean Ethics book 5, chap. 9 (W. D. Ross trans.), available at http://www.ilt.columbia.edu/publications/artistotle.html.
[23] Henry Shue, *Global Environment and International Inequality*, 75(3) International Affairs 531 (1999) ("What diplomats and lawyers call equity incorporates important aspects of what ordinary people everywhere call fairness").
[24] Tariq Banuri et al., *Equity and Social Considerations, in* Climate Change 1995: Economic and Social Dimensions of Climate Change. Contribution of Working Group III to the Second Assessment Report of the Intergovernmental Panel on Climate Change 85 (James P. Bruce et al. eds., 1996).
[25] Dinah Shelton, *Equity, in* The Oxford Handbook of International Environmental Law 639, 640 (Daniel Bodansky et al. eds., 2007).
[26] Aristotle, *supra* 22, book 5, chap. 10.

continuing responsibility of developed countries for the bulk of cumulative GHG emissions and thus for the impacts presently being experienced, especially sea-level rise. Whether or not such claims are founded on the responsibility of the polluters or the need of the vulnerable, questions of distributive justice also arise in the context of adaptation. Adaptation needs will certainly outstrip available resources. According to which criteria, then, should resources be distributed at the international and domestic levels? Take the Adaptation Fund, established under the Kyoto Protocol to support concrete adaptation projects in developing countries; adaptation needs are estimated at billions of dollars per year, but the fund is likely to have tens of millions available initially, possibly rising to a few hundred million later. One can imagine requests for assistance that appeal to different notions of need and value. Island country A, with a small population, appeals for assistance to design a sea wall to defend against the remote but catastrophic threat of a storm surge. State B, more populous, poorer, and drought wracked, applies for funding to design a water management system that would allow it to sustain its agricultural sector, in the face of regional climate that is projected to become even drier. The cost of the support requested is identical. Does one prioritize action against catastrophic, but statistically less probable scenarios, affecting a relatively small number of persons? Or does one concentrate on measures that build resilience to climate impacts, with positive consequences for a large number of persons? In general, financing and other support mechanisms of all kinds raise important questions of procedural and distributive fairness. Procedural fairness is an issue in provisions for accessing resources – overly complex procedures may serve as a barrier and may also obscure the real basis for decision making, creating the impression that allocation decisions are arbitrary. Openness, transparency, accountability, and consistency are hallmarks of fair procedures. Some consideration of distributive fairness, whether explicit or implicit, is unavoidable, and it is likely to find its expression in criteria giving substance to notions of need, vulnerability, and risk.[27] Thus, inasmuch as adaptation to climate change involves the allocation of scarce resources, distributive fairness will be a consideration.

[27] Marco Grosso, *A Normative Ethical Framework in Climate Change*, 81(3–4) CLIMATIC CHANGE 223 (2007). Grosso applies Sen's "capability approach" in deciding how to distribute what he refers to as compensation for damages caused by climate change. AMARTYA K. SEN, DEVELOPMENT AS FREEDOM (1999).

## 4.2. Philosophical Roots

The next section briefly examines two broad – and opposing – approaches to justice, which are relevant to understanding the character of fairness claims in the climate change context. Thereafter, the analysis considers specific examples of fairness principles in the context of the climate change regime. The remainder of this chapter considers the intersection between economic analysis of climate change and fairness claims and presents selected examples of fairness in international environmental law.

### 4.2.1. Utilitarianism

At its most basic, utilitarianism holds that the morally right act or policy is the one that leads to the greatest happiness or utility for members of society.[28] Thus the attraction of utilitarianism is that it evaluates the merits of an action, not according to an abstract standard of right or wrong – religious texts or other system of morals – but in terms of its consequences.[29] It stands in contrast to moral theories based on rules or rights, which require conformity with the relevant standards, without giving primacy to consequences.[30] Variants of utilitarianism are widespread, and utilitarian thinking is an aspect of everyday commonsense reasoning.

Because of the way utilitarianism calculates overall utility – by adding individual preferences – it has been criticized for not accommodating the notion of just or fair shares.[31] For example, if, in a community where all possess an equal (fair) share of land, the majority nonetheless prefer to use part of my land as a public park, that would be an acceptable outcome under utilitarianism because it maximizes the utility of the community.[32] Utilitarianism thus justifies policies that maximize the collective good (aggregate utility) but is not sensitive to the distribution of burdens and benefits across individuals (or countries). It serves as the basis for the traditional economic approach to resource allocation and thus underpins debates on the costs

---

[28] KYMLICKA, *supra* note 2, at 10.
[29] *Id.* at 11.
[30] Moral theories based on rules are generally known as *deontological theories*.
[31] KYMLICKA, *supra* note 2, at 41–45. For defenses of utilitarianism, *see* DAVID LYONS, FORMS AND LIMITS OF UTILITARIANISM (1965), and R. M. HARE, MORAL THINKING (1981). For an attempt to apply utilitarianism to a range of global problems, including climate change, *see* PETER SINGER, ONE WORLD: THE ETHICS OF GLOBALIZATION (2002).
[32] KYMLICKA, *supra* 2, at 41.

and benefits of various proposals to combat climate change.[33] Other aspects of the climate change issue, however, appeal, not to utilitarianism, but to its opposite, namely, moral theories based on rules and rights. Thus inhabitants of small, low-lying island nations appeal for the equal consideration of their claim to continue their way of life; conservationists argue for the protection of species and ecosystems independent of their economic value and for the right of future generations to enjoy the earth in a comparable state as present generations.[34]

### 4.2.2. Rule-Based Theories of Justice

Although it may be easy to see the importance of fairness – whether at the level of interpersonal relationships or in the conduct of states – it is difficult to agree on a common, accepted understanding of what fairness means in practice. Society is simply too pluralistic for a settled consensus to exist with regard to fairness or similarly contested concepts. Because of the difficulty in defining fairness from first principles, theories of fairness or justice have therefore shifted toward process-based models. Thus one enormously influential theory of justice has been that of John Rawls, who famously posited a "veil of ignorance" so that people would not know what place they would occupy in society. Ignorant of their race, sex, class, health, economic status, and so forth, what kind of framework would they choose for their society?[35] According to Rawls, they would select two basic principles of justice: (1) every individual in a just society has an equal right to a fully adequate scheme of equal basic liberties consistent with a similar scheme for everyone and (2) social and economic inequalities must satisfy two conditions, that, first, such inequalities must be attached to offices and positions open to all under conditions of fair equality of opportunity, and second, they must be to the greatest benefit of the least advantaged members of society.[36] The latter is the famous *difference principle*, according

---

[33] INTERGOVERNMENTAL PANEL ON CLIMATE CHANGE, CLIMATE CHANGE 2007: MITIGATION. CONTRIBUTION OF WORKING GROUP III TO THE FOURTH ASSESSMENT REPORT OF THE INTERGOVERNMENTAL PANEL ON CLIMATE CHANGE 144 (Bert Metz et al. eds., 2007).
[34] EDITH BROWN WEISS, IN FAIRNESS TO FUTURE GENERATIONS (1989).
[35] RAWLS, *supra* note 4.
[36] Maimon Schwarzschild, *Constitutional Law and Equality*, *in* A COMPANION TO PHILOSOPHY OF LAW AND LEGAL THEORY 156, 165 (Dennis Patterson ed., 1999).

to which the aim is not to eradicate all inequality, but instead to permit only those inequalities that benefit everyone in society by promoting socially useful talent and initiatives.[37] Importantly, this principle disallows unequal distributive outcomes that would be quite compatible with principles of equality of opportunity, itself a foundational belief concerning justice.[38]

Libertarian theories of justice stand in sharp contrast to liberal theories of distributive justice. Rather than judging a distribution against a principle of justice, Robert Nozick, a prominent libertarian, holds that a distribution is just if everyone is entitled to the goods they currently possess.[39] Under this *entitlement theory*, a just distribution simply follows from the free exchange of goods originally acquired and then successively transferred by legitimate means. In cases where goods are unjustly acquired or transferred, a principle of rectification of these violations operates. Only a moment's reflection is required to realize that this line of reasoning is strongly represented in the climate change regime, as seen when countries maintain that current emission levels constitute a continuing entitlement that cannot easily be disturbed. This finds expression in grandfathering, that is, the free allocation to emitters of emission entitlements or allowances. In broad terms, the argument would be that countries have legitimately acquired a share of the atmosphere's capacity to serve as a sink for GHGs. Naturally, this leads to the question whether – or up to what point in time – continued acquisition of the sink properties of the atmosphere could be considered legitimate or just. Here it seems that one is drawn back to notions of substantive fair shares – perhaps conditioned on reasonable scientific evidence of the link between GHG emissions and climate change – of precisely the kind libertarians reject. Just acquisition under Nozick's theory is quite complicated and not relevant for the purposes of this discussion.[40] Nonetheless, two observations may be relevant in the present context. First, the argument proceeds

---

[37] KYMLICKA, *supra* note 2, at 55.
[38] KYMLICKA, *supra* note 2, at 57. Imagine that the two equally hard-working individuals earn, respectively, $20,000 and $80,000. In the absence of discrimination and other barriers, the inequality of $60,000 in earnings would be consistent with an equality of opportunity approach. For Rawls, the inequality would only be justifiable if it benefits the least disadvantaged in society, e.g., by fostering special skills that are of benefit to all, but perhaps, in particular, to the poor.
[39] ROBERT NOZICK, ANARCHY, STATE, AND UTOPIA 150–51 (1974). *See also* KYMLICKA, *supra* note 2, at 103–4.
[40] *See* KYMLICKA, *supra* note 2, at 111–21

from the assumption that the world is initially unowned, but a case could be made that the atmosphere was and is subject to some form of common ownership.[41] The notion of the atmospheric sink as a *terra nullius*, there for the taking, is not self-evident, at least not since the advent of international environmental law in the latter part of the twentieth century. Second, Nozick accepts that an unjust acquisition (e.g., by force) taints title and is subject to rectification.[42] The *principle of rectification* that he tentatively proposes is essentially Rawls's difference principle.

### 4.2.2.1. Thomas Franck: A Detailed Account of Fairness.

Rawls's theory has been adapted and applied at the international level by Thomas Franck in *Fairness in International Law and Institutions*.[43] Franck asserts that international law has entered a "post-ontological" age – it has entered an era in which it is no longer necessary to defend the status of international law as law, but where a vital task is to analyze its fairness.[44] According to Franck, fairness consists of two elements: "right process," or procedural fairness, and substantive fairness, or the fairness of outcomes.[45] We have an intuitive

---

[41] KYMLICKA, *supra* note 2, at 121 (raising the possibility of a world jointly owned and not subject to unilateral privatization). But *cf.* Richard Starkey, *Allocating Emission Rights: Are Equal Shares, Fair Shares?*, Working Paper 118, Tyndall Centre (2008).

[42] NOZICK, *supra* note 39, 230–31.

[43] *See* Harold Koh, *Review Essay: Why Do Nations Obey International Law?* 106 YALE LAW JOURNAL 2599 (1997) (reviewing ABRAM CHAYES AND ANTONIA HANDLER CHAYES, THE NEW SOVEREIGNTY: COMPLIANCE WITH INTERNATIONAL REGULATORY AGREEMENTS (1998); FRANCK, FAIRNESS); Phillip R. Trimble, *Globalization, International Institutions, and the Erosion of National Sovereignty and Democracy*, 95 MICHIGAN LAW REVIEW 1944 (1996–97) (review of FRANCK, FAIRNESS); Gerry J. Simpson, *Is International Law Fair?* 17 MICHIGAN JOURNAL OF INTERNATIONAL LAW 615 (1996–97) (review essay); *Symposium on Thomas M. Franck's Fairness in International Law and Institutions*, 13(4) EUROPEAN JOURNAL OF INTERNATIONAL LAW 901–1030 (2002); Christopher Ward, *Book Review*, 48 INTERNATIONAL & COMPARATIVE LAW QUARTERLY 237 (1999); Elisabeth Zoller, *Book Review*, 36 VIRGINIA JOURNAL OF INTERNATIONAL LAW 1079 (1996).

[44] FRANCK, FAIRNESS, at 6.

[45] *Id.* at 7. The two elements of fairness are independent in that a law viewed as substantively unjust can be applied in a procedurally fair manner – one need only think of the ruling of the U.S. Supreme Court on the separate but equal question in *Plessy v. Ferguson*, 163 US 537 (1896). A well-known work taking the procedural element further to develop a procedural morality of law is LON L. FULLER, THE MORALITY OF LAW (1964). *Cf.* criticism by Hart and others that an unjust law could meet the requirements of Fuller's inner morality. In the same way, a rule that is considered just could be adopted or applied in a manner that violates the tenets of right process. Tension may arise between the two aspects of fairness because the one, substantive justice, privileges change, while the other, right process, tends toward stability and order.

## 4.2. Philosophical Roots

understanding of what constitutes right process, which is the rules of the game, as reflected in concepts familiar to lawyers such as the principles of natural justice.[46] Franck ties right process to legitimacy – decisions or allocations are legitimate where they are the outcome of a fair process.[47] When it is said that a rule or its application is legitimate, this implies that the rule was made or applied in accordance with right process *and* that, as a consequence, it is deserving of voluntary compliance.[48] Franck goes on to state that "any analysis of fairness must include consideration of the consequential effects of a law: its distributive justice."[49] In theory and in practice, it is the second aspect of fairness that proves particularly nettlesome, for how are we to settle on a common understanding of what is fair or just? Like the belief that a law is legitimate, the belief that it is distributively fair will promote voluntary compliance, "primarily because most people think it is *right* to act justly."[50]

Franck regards the "growing awareness of irrefutable interdependence" and its effects as mounting evidence of the emergence of global community, or as we might term it, the *international community*.[51] Having set the stage, Franck turns to the question of common values or conceptions of justice in the international community. While a range of allocation formulas can be applied, such as "to each according to capacity" or "to each according to just desserts," arriving at a shared perception of fairness is much more difficult.[52] He concludes that there is no one conception of fairness, but rather that fairness "is a product of social context and history" that "captures in one word a *process of discourse, reasoning and negotiation*."[53] He thus aligns himself with liberal thinking on justice, more particularly, with the very influential work of John Rawls.[54] For the fairness discourse,

---

[46] Two principal rules of natural justice are expressed in the following Latin phrases: *audi alteram partem* (hear the other side) and *nemo judex in sua causa* (no person can judge a case in which he or she is a party).
[47] *See* Thomas Franck, The Power of Legitimacy among Nations (1990).
[48] Franck, Fairness, at 26.
[49] *Id.* at 8.
[50] *Id.* (emphasis in original).
[51] However, he states that global community should not be seen as an alternative to the state, which remains the basis unit, and he does not advocate abandoning the concept of state sovereignty. *Id.* at 12–13.
[52] *Id.* at 13.
[53] *Id.* at 14 (emphasis in original).
[54] *See* Rawls, *supra* note 4.

Franck postulates two minimum assumptions that serve as prerequisites for participation in the discourse.[55]

Since Franck has consciously adopted an approach drawn from the liberal tradition, his conception of fairness attracts some familiar criticisms. Developed and developing countries disagree radically about the responsibility for climate change and the allocation of burdens to combat it. Against this backdrop, some have questioned whether Franck's fairness discourse amounts to foisting one particular conception of fairness on the international community.[56] Another criticism of Franck's approach is that fairness is too narrow to serve as a standard for an ethical evaluation of international law.[57] Values other than legitimacy and distributive justice that play a role in the international system, such as peace, compassion (exemplified in humanitarian law), prosperity, and species survival, risk being excluded.[58] The emphasis on distributive justice could result in the neglect of retributive and corrective justice, which are both strands firmly entwined in the discourse of justice in the international community.[59] Last, Franck's adoption of distributive justice as the primary value against which to evaluate environmental law supposedly "implicates him in an anthropocentric perspective that regards the natural world as simply made up of so many 'resources' that are to be apportioned among humans in order to realize their interests."[60]

---

[55] FRANCK, FAIRNESS, at 18. Franck puts forward two such gatekeepers: the first is the no trumping rule and the second is the maximin principle. The former holds that no participant may raise a principle – whether religious, philosophical, or ideological – that is nonnegotiable. Instead, everything must be subject to discussion. The maximin principle holds that "unequal distribution is justifiable only if it narrows, or does not widen, the existing inequality of persons' and/or states' entitlements." Franck provides the following example: a scheme that allocates $100 to every person who already has $100 but only $50 to persons with $10 proportionately narrows the gap between them and is therefore not axiomatically excluded from fairness discourse.

[56] This could be termed the *ethnocentric* critique. See TASIOULAS, *supra* note 9, at 994; TRIMBLE, *supra* note 43, at 1952–54. Because Franck relies on a process-based approach, buttressed by his two gatekeeper principles, this, in theory, should allay some of the fears regarding ethnocentrism. However, on closer examination, his no trumping principle would effectively exclude parties holding strong core beliefs. These points parallel those who criticize liberal approaches to diversity and multiculturalism for misunderstanding the nature of deeply held worldviews or religious faith.

[57] TASIOULAS, *supra* note 9, at 1000. He provides a more closely argued criticism of the primacy Franck assigns to the maximin principle, pointing out that in Rawls's account, it is subordinate to a first principle of the equal right to liberty.

[58] *Id.* at 1001.

[59] The former is reflected in the tribunals established for Rwanda and the former Yugoslavia and the International Criminal Court, while the latter finds expression in the calls for assistance in adapting to the effects of climate change.

[60] TASIOULAS, *supra* note 9, at 1002.

Franck adopts and adapts concepts from legal theory and political philosophy and applies them to the international community. It is an open question whether these theories can validly be applied at the interstate level.[61] Franck's conception of fairness draws heavily on the work of John Rawls, who himself saw his original work as applying only within a liberal democratic society, not between states.[62]

The next section turns briefly to procedural justice before presenting a detailed analysis of distributive fairness in the context of climate change.

### 4.3. DISTRIBUTIVE JUSTICE: FROM ABSTRACTION TO BURDEN-SHARING PRINCIPLES

Fairness in climate change is of prominent concern in the context of allocating the costs of mitigation among countries. Distinct, but related, dimensions of fairness in the climate change context are procedural fairness and fairness in the context of adaptation to the adverse effects of climate change. Procedural justice within climate negotiations was briefly touched on earlier.

---

[61] The existence of a real and meaningful "global community" is open to question, or at the very least, it is a nascent and fragile community. For an analysis of the notion of community in FRANCK, FAIRNESS, see KRITSIOTIS, supra note 1. Technological advances and greater interdependence may not necessarily lead to a convergence in values, but may, in fact, prove compatible with fragmentation and the spread of extremist ideologies of all stripes. For example, seen from the early twenty-first century, the vision triumph of liberal values articulated by FRANCIS FUKUYAMA, THE END OF HISTORY (1992), appears somewhat premature. It can also be questioned whether principles or process-oriented explanations developed against the backdrop of a (liberal) state can be employed in the realm of relations between states, which lacks the constitutional structure and order of domestic systems and is characterized, to a greater extent, by the exercise of power. The extreme view is that interests determine states' behavior; reference to principles is a distraction. The competing approaches to international law, including the realist conception, are considered elsewhere and cannot be treated in greater detail here.

[62] See RAWLS, supra note 5. In this later work, he addresses the question of justice at the international level. Rawls dispenses with a distributive principle, substituting for it a much weaker principle to "assist other peoples living under unfavourable conditions that prevent their having a just or decent political and social regime." Id. at 37. This principle of assistance is founded, not on principles of distributive justice, but on humanitarian grounds, with the aim of helping societies that are not liberal or decent achieve this status. The reason Rawls opts not to extend the difference principle to the global level is revealed in the following passage: "I would conjecture that there is no society anywhere in the world – except marginal cases – with resources so scarce that it could not, were it reasonably and rationally organized and governed, become well-ordered." Id. at 108. Franck faults two elements that he identifies in this argument: that underdevelopment or being burdened is largely the result of societies' value choices and that no distributive obligations exist in the absence of a meaningful global community. FRANCK, FAIRNESS, at 18–19.

Some of the ethical questions relating to adaptation are common to the analysis pursued in this book, although mitigation, more than adaptation, is the focus of this enquiry.[63] Climate change also has important implications for the sharing of burdens and benefits within countries, but a detailed consideration of the intranational equity issue falls outside the scope of this book.

As noted earlier, fairness considerations can be applied to the general background conditions, that is, the conditions under which distributions are made, as well as the fairness of the allocation itself. Procedural fairness can be understood as belonging to the general background conditions under which bargaining takes place. It encompasses rules on participation, access to information, the exclusion of coercive tactics, and the general ability of parties to bargain on roughly equal terms. As recognized in principle 10 of the Rio Declaration, access to information, public participation, and access to justice are important domestic procedural rights. These protections have been further developed in the Aarhus Convention on Access to Information, Public Participation in Decision-Making, and Access to Justice in Environmental Matters, which establishes comprehensive and binding standards in each of the three procedural areas of its title.[64] Although the Aarhus Convention has a regional (European) basis, it has been suggested that it contains standards that could be usefully drawn on at the international level.[65] Basic and formal elements of procedural fairness flow from the sovereign equality of states so that countries are entitled to participate equally in the intergovernmental negotiations. As in other contexts, such formal equality is substantially reduced by the inequalities among states, reflected in developed countries' generally superior ability to design and analyze policy proposals, availability of technical expertise, and negotiating experience. The negotiating structure and bargaining process can be structured to incorporate aspects of procedural justice, for instance, by

---

[63] *See* Fairness in Adaptation to Climate Change (W. Neil Adger et al. eds., 2006).
[64] Convention on Access to Information, Public Participation in Decision-Making, and Access to Justice in Environmental Matters, June 25, 1998, 2161 UNTS 447.
[65] International Council on Human Rights Policy, Climate Change and Human Rights: A Rough Guide 49 (2008). The study points out that Article 3(7) of the Aarhus Convention states that "each Party shall promote the application of the principles of this Convention in international environmental decision-making processes and within the framework of international organizations in matters relating to the environment." The suggestion is that this constitutes an affirmative duty applicable to Aarhus Convention parties in the context of the UNFCCC negotiations. *See id.* at 50.

formulating a broad and inclusive agenda, choosing clear and transparent rules, and giving all parties a say in selecting procedures.[66]

Fairness in the negotiating process will become more salient as some developing countries consider mitigation actions in the context of the negotiations, may the attendant need to analyze options and make counterproposals.[67] Until recently, strength in numbers has permitted developing countries to achieve common aims – pressing for leadership on mitigation by industrialized countries, while blocking emission limitation commitments for developing countries – but the next phase of the negotiations may demand a more proactive stance, with the risks that this entails. Undoubtedly, industrialized countries possess advantages in terms of resources – size of delegations, experts, and ability to design and evaluate technical proposals – that most developing countries generally cannot match. (This is not necessarily true of larger, rapidly industrializing developing countries, which have a sophisticated capacity to analyze and formulate climate policies.) In general, developing country delegations are small, which makes it more difficult to participate meaningfully in the negotiations, which quite often take place simultaneously in small groups. Maintaining continuity is also a challenge – the loss of institutional memory and familiarity with the issues is particularly acute for small delegations. When countries are at a significant disadvantage as regards analytical expertise and capacity, this may undermine trust and the possibility of finding novel solutions. In practice, the climate change negotiations break into a number of inordinately technical and complex areas. Sheer complexity and thickets of jargon may undermine effective participation, thus having a negative effect on procedural fairness. In these cases, one could question whether meaningful and effective participation, in the sense of having access to the necessary information and the expertise to evaluate its implications, is actually possible for many parties. This point may be reached when some parties with

---

[66] Cecilia Albin, *Getting to Fairness: Negotiations over Global Public Goods, in* PROVIDING GLOBAL PUBLIC GOODS: MANAGING GLOBALIZATION 263, 270–72 (Inge Kaul et al. eds., 2003).

[67] Pamela Chasek & Lavanya Rajamani, *Steps toward Enhanced Parity: Negotiating Capacity and Strategies of Developing Countries, in* PROVIDING GLOBAL PUBLIC GOODS: MANAGING GLOBALIZATION 245 (Inge Kaul et al. eds., 2003); DEUTSCHE GESELLSCHAFT FÜR TECHNISCHE ZUSAMMENARBEIT, SOUTH-NORTH DIALOGUE ON EQUITY IN THE GREENHOUSE: A PROPOSAL FOR AN ADEQUATE AND EQUITABLE CLIMATE CHANGE AGREEMENT 2 (2004), available at http://www.wupperinst.org/en/home/.

a stake in the issue cannot reasonably assess how a given proposal would affect their interests. Compromises, deals, and trade-offs should not be so obscured by technical intricacies that the full implications only become known much later. Ideally, all countries with an interest in a particular issue should be adequately informed and equipped for full, and meaningful, participation.

To level the playing field, some observers have suggested increased capacity building for developing country negotiators and technical experts.[68] Fortunately, a great deal of relevant information is already available, disseminated by the various entities of the United Nations (UN) system and other institutions. The rise of nongovernmental organizations and think tanks that concentrate on climate change has also vastly increased the variety of freely available, open source analysis. It also bears repeating that the periodic reports of the IPCC represent an enormous resource; even nonspecialists could benefit from selectively referring to the full reports, rather than only the widely read summaries for policy makers. What may be missing is information and analysis that extends to the regional and national scales so that more regional-level studies and analyses may be useful. Especially with respect to adaptation, poor and vulnerable countries need to have access to reliable data to formulate policies and then seek international assistance to support implementation. In the end, acceptance of negotiating processes and outcomes will be affected by participants' sense of ownership and mutual adherence to procedures. Violations of fairness in the negotiating process undermine trust and could ultimately influence the stability of the agreement (compliance). The international climate change regime is a long-term, iterative project, not a once-off deal, and therefore trust and fairness of procedures assume added significance.

A satisfactory definition of fairness is destined to remain elusive. Therefore the chosen approach is to identify and briefly discuss a number of – by no means all – fairness principles. In particular, the objective of this section is to articulate a number of fairness principles that could potentially constitute the basis for a rough, working consensus in the climate change regime. The following representative fairness principles have been selected and are analyzed in turn: egalitarian, need-based, responsibility- or

---

[68] CHASEK & RAJAMANI, *supra* note 67.

contribution-based, and capability-based principles. Naturally, these various principles interact and overlap in the climate change discourse.

### 4.3.1. Egalitarian Principles

Equality exerts a powerful pull in ethical as well as legal arguments, and it is often presumed to be the default standard for allocation so that the burden of proof falls on those advocating differential treatment.[69] Egalitarian principles recognize the equal entitlement of persons to some good, condition (happiness), opportunity, and so forth. In the context of climate change, egalitarian principles would hold that all humans have an equal right in the protective qualities of the atmosphere. More specifically, this might translate to an equal share in total atmospheric capacity to safely absorb GHG emissions. But the formal rule of equal treatment or equal shares alone is insufficient because very much depends on the substantive rule by which one is entitled to equal treatment and in what circumstances.[70] While the commitment to equal treatment is important, in the climate change context, it is also important to determine on what basis countries are considered alike because weather, location, and level of social and economic development may constitute relevance differences. For example, to be habitable, some regions of the world require space heating in winter, resulting in higher GHG emissions per capita than temperate regions.[71] Is an equal allocation fair in these circumstances? Failure to account for relevant differences risks engendering injustice. Because both the costs and gains from addressing climate will vary across countries, a strict per capita allocation may give the appearance, but not the reality, of fairness. Thus the operation of equality in practice needs to be informed and guided by substantive principles of fairness or justice, and it is these principles that determine which differences justify differential treatment.[72] One possibility is to interpret equality

---

[69] DONALD BROWN ET AL., WHITE PAPER ON THE ETHICAL DIMENSIONS OF CLIMATE CHANGE 21 (undated), available at http://rockethics.psu.edu/climate/index.htm.

[70] For the argument that equality lacks independent force, see Peter Westen, *The Empty Idea of Equality*, 95 HARVARD LAW REVIEW 537 (1982). But *cf.* Erwin Chemerinsky, *In Defense of Equality: A Reply to Professor Westen*, 81 MICHIGAN LAW REVIEW 575 (1982–83).

[71] For an exploration of related philosophical questions, see STARKEY, *supra* note 41.

[72] Distributive justice, remedial aims, participation, and dignity are all values that may shape substantive conceptions of equality. See SANDRA FREDMAN, INTRODUCTION TO DISCRIMINATION LAW 17–23 (2002).

as equality of opportunity, thus giving all persons an equal possibility of benefiting from the absorptive (sink) capacity of the biosphere. Such a conception moves away from an insistence on equal shares toward a definition of a share of the atmosphere that is commensurate with setting a fair starting point. This line of thought might acknowledge that addressing the unequal access to the atmospheric sink is one factor influencing whether countries have a fair opportunity to develop and prosper.[73]

Variants of equality that hold that differences are intrinsically wrong – that is, regardless of how they came about – can result in unacceptable outcomes when pushed to the limit. For example, strict adherence to intrinsic equality would hold in a situation where one group lives just above subsistence levels and another at subsistence levels: the just outcome would be for both groups to be "equal" and live at the subsistence level. Thus adherence to equality as an overriding standard may lead to what is termed the *leveling down effect*.[74] In addition, if the social and economic development of the countries most in need is a primary concern, per capita allocation schemes do a poor job for sparsely populated, poor countries. Relative to more populated, wealthy countries, they have less to gain, although they may also be more vulnerable to climate impacts.

Equality principles would favor both preventative and compensatory transfers, particularly as climate change is likely to exacerbate the inequality of developing countries. Egalitarian approaches might also support stronger mitigation action in the present, so as to secure the interest of future generations, and at the same time, a redistribution to equalize the position of states.

### 4.3.2. Need-Based Principles

Another line of equity and fairness thinking emphasizes that a distribution of benefits and burdens should accord priority to the poorest or most at risk. In accordance with Rawls's difference principle, an unequal distribution would be permissible only to the extent that it benefits the most disadvantaged. Unlike egalitarianism, the priority approach is unconcerned with the

---

[73] *Cf.* Eric A. Posner & Cass Sunstein, *Climate Change Justice*, 96 GEORGETOWN LAW JOURNAL 1565, 1583–86 (2008) (arguing that if redistribution and improved welfare are the aim, direct transfers are preferable to emission entitlements).

[74] EDWARD A. PAGE, CLIMATE CHANGE, JUSTICE AND FUTURE GENERATIONS 80–81 (2006).

4.3. *Distributive Justice*

comparative properties of distributive outcomes but holds that it is morally relevant that some persons are disadvantaged as such.[75] This position is insensitive to the origin of the unfair distribution; it is not concerned with making good inequality resulting from some wrong. In practical terms, an approach emphasizing needs might assign priority to achieving the Millennium Development Goals, which cover basic global development objectives such as the eradication of extreme poverty and hunger and provision of basic education and access to health care.[76] The argument would be that all people have the right to emit *at least* the amount of GHG emissions associated with the services to secure these basic human needs. An argument from needs may also imply a greater share of resources for adaptation in the most vulnerable countries. Thus it has been argued that priority should be given to the poorest populations now, rather than devoting the bulk of scarce resources to expensive mitigation efforts.[77] A fair climate regime should, at a minimum, help, not hinder, the efforts of the poorest countries to meet the basic needs of their citizens.[78]

### 4.3.3. *Responsibility-Based Principles*

In 2004, the 20 percent of the global population living in developed countries accounted for 46 percent of GHG emissions; the 80 percent living in developing countries accounted for only 54 percent.[79] Industrialized countries' responsibility for the largest share (about 76 percent) of the accumulated stock of carbon dioxide emissions is also frequently cited in the climate negotiations.[80] Responsibility as an ethical principle has an intuitive appeal; it is a commonly held notion that those who have caused a problem, for example, emitted a pollutant into the environment, should also be the ones to rectify the situation. It is reflected in the polluter pays principle of

---

[75] Edward A. Page, *Justice between Generations: Investigating a Sufficientarian Approach*, 3(1) JOURNAL OF GLOBAL ETHICS 3, 7 (2007).
[76] For the eight goals and related information, *see* http://www.un.org/millenniumgoals/.
[77] *See* Alan Manne & Robert Mendelsohn, *Climate Change Alternative Approaches*, *in* GLOBAL CRISES, GLOBAL SOLUTIONS 44, 49 (Bjørn Lomborg ed., 2004).
[78] JOHN ASHTON & XUEMAN WANG, EQUITY AND CLIMATE: IN PRINCIPLE AND PRACTICE 5 (Pew Center on Global Climate Change ed., 2003).
[79] INTERGOVERNMENTAL PANEL ON CLIMATE CHANGE, *supra* note 33, at 30.
[80] WORLD RESOURCES INSTITUTE, NAVIGATING THE NUMBERS 32 (2005).

domestic and international environmental law.[81] However, the contribution or responsibility principle has been criticized on a number of grounds.[82]

One criticism relates to the notion of responsibility across generations. Among philosophers, fairness with respect to future generations encounters several theoretical hurdles, among them the nonidentity problem, which holds that policies or actions that are likely to diminish welfare in the future will harm few members of future generations because those very same policies are the necessary conditions for those people to come into existence.[83] In the context of climate change, the statement of the problem holds that "the emissions that contributed to the emergence of climate change as a global problem originated in acts and policies that have affected the size and composition of subsequent generations, such that very few members of the present generation can plausibly argue that they have been harmed, or made worse off, by the historical greenhouse gas emissions associated with industrialization."[84] In short, individuals of a future generation cannot argue that climate change has harmed them because without it, they (that particular group of persons) would not have been born. Although the nonidentity problem may seem fit to remain confined to the philosophy seminar room, the effect of this line of argument is to severely weaken the theoretical underpinnings of arguments for intergenerational equity, particularly where it is founded on responsibility. The problem is most acute for theories that focus on harm to individuals, as opposed to nonanthropocentric accounts of environmental ethics, which concern not primarily future generations of humans, but instead, the integrity of the biosphere. Furthermore, the argument has also been made that the harm posed by rising sea levels to distinct groups or collectivities, such as inhabitants of small islands, avoids the nonidentity problem.[85] The nonidentity problem

---

[81] PATRICIA BIRNIE & ALAN BOYLE, INTERNATIONAL LAW AND THE ENVIRONMENT 92–95 (2002).

[82] For a list of criticisms and defenses, see id. 92–95. For a list of criticisms and rebuttals, see Eric Neumayer, *In Defence of Historical Accountability for Greenhouse Gas Emissions*, 33(2) ECOLOGICAL ECONOMICS 185 (2000). See also Simon Caney, *Cosmopolitan Justice, Responsibility and Global Climate Change*, 18 LEIDEN JOURNAL OF INTERNATIONAL LAW 747 (2005).

[83] PAGE, supra note 74, at 132. On the problem in a context of ethics and philosophy, see DEREK PARFIT, REASONS AND PERSONS 351–59 (1984).

[84] PAGE, supra note 74, at 170.

[85] Edward Page, *Intergenerational Justice and Climate Change*, 47(1) POLITICAL STUDIES 61–63 (1999).

bars the argument that any particular individuals would either suffer harm from, or benefit under, particular climate policies. But when one considers the impact of alternative climate policies on a collective or group (which can be expected to exist irrespective of whether emissions are reduced or not), the thrust of the nonidentity problem is avoided.

A second criticism holds that arguments from responsibility are undermined if the conduct that caused the harm was not recognized as wrongful at the time that it occurred.[86] Is it fair to assign responsibility for consequences of actions that were not considered harmful at the time they took place? Moreover, states could hardly be faulted for pursuing social and economic development, which was and remains the driver of GHG emissions. Is it correct that ignorance invalidates arguments from responsibility? Two responses can be put forward. First, it has been suggested that one ought to distinguish between responsibility, arising from moral culpability, and accountability for the consequences of one's actions.[87] Ignorance alone does not rule out accountability for remedial action. Consider a corporation that developed a new pesticide that provided genuine benefits and proved enormously profitable, but later turned out to have serious but unanticipated side effects. Assuming no negligence on the corporation's part, it would still be an odd ethical and moral universe in which the firm did not owe innocent victims any remedial duties whatsoever. Consider then that the so-called safe absorptive capacity of the atmosphere is finite, climate change is in many respects irreversible, the possibility of catastrophic impacts cannot be ruled out, and at least some nations face an existential threat. Denial of any accountability does not seem satisfactory in ethical terms. Second, ignorance of harmful effects does not address a fundamental question of responsibility for choices. While social and economic development could not reasonably have occurred without burning fossil fuels, there is considerable divergence in energy use among developed countries that have attained similar income

---

[86] Page explains that arguments from responsibility depend on what he terms *historical principles*, which evaluate the distribution of benefits and burdens in terms of how they came about; if their origins involved no wrongdoing they are just, but if wrongdoing occurred, then a redistribution is allowed to reestablish justice. *Id.* 169. This means answering the question whether the actions that led to the GHG emissions were wrongful. One of the most well known exponents of an approach tracing justice based on initial distributions is NOZICK, *supra* note 39.

[87] NEUMAYER, *supra* note 82, at 188, 189 note 4. *See* also Henry Shue, *supra* note 23, at 535–36 (1999).

levels. On the face of it, then, this suggests that some countries chose development paths built on higher than average energy consumption.[88] Why, then, should newcomers be made to subsidize, in effect, the consumption choices made by at least some developing countries?

It is questionable whether the bulk of past emissions can be considered unlawful under existing international law.[89] Under the prevailing view in international law, an action must have been wrongful or unlawful in that it violated a duty of care or breached a rule of international law to establish responsibility.[90] In law, foreseeability is usually considered as a prerequisite for liability. Ignorance of the reality and consequences of climate change – at what point this ceased to be the case is open to debate – could negate, or at least mitigate, the wrongfulness of industrialized countries' past emissions. It has been suggested that 1990 serves as the date after which emitters could no longer claim ignorance.[91] Arguably, prior ignorance of the effects of GHG emissions was not culpable, as the emitters could not have been expected to know with reasonable certainty the harmful effects of burning fossil fuels.[92] Again, this argument can be advanced only so far; historical GHG emissions did not take place in a vacuum, but were at the heart of the broader framework of production and consumption patterns in the developed world, where warning signals of resource depletion were cause for concern well before climate change was recognized as a problem.

---

[88] Equalizing for some involuntary factors, such as extra heating in cold climates and transportation needs in larger countries, with more dispersed settlement patterns.

[89] But for a detailed attempt to construct a basis for liability, see RODA VERHEYEN, CLIMATE CHANGE AND INTERNATIONAL LAW: PREVENTION DUTIES AND STATE RESPONSIBILITY (2005). See also Richard S. J. Tol & Roda Verheyen, *State Responsibility and Compensation for Climate Change Damages – A Legal and Economic Analysis*, 32 ENERGY POLICY 1109 (2004).

[90] See the Draft Articles on State Responsibility prepared by the International Law Commission. Art. 1 states, "Every internationally wrongful act of a State entails the international responsibility of that State." Art. 2 provides that "there is an internationally wrongful act of a State when conduct consisting of an action or omission: (*a*) Is attributable to the State under international law; and (*b*) *Constitutes a breach of an international obligation of the State*" (italics added). REPORT OF THE INTERNATIONAL LAW COMMISSION ON ITS 53RD SESSION, UN GAOR, 56th Sess., Suppl. 10, UN Doc. A/56/10. The Draft Articles are available at http://www.un.org/law/ilc/. The approach taken in the Draft Articles does not encompass strict or direct liability. For an overview of the Draft Articles, see VERHEYEN, *supra* note 89, at 229–48.

[91] PETER SINGER, ONE WORLD: THE ETHICS OF GLOBALIZATION 34 (2002).

[92] CANEY, *supra* note 82, at 761.

## 4.3. Distributive Justice

A related argument is that those responsible for much of the accumulated atmospheric stock of GHGs are now dead, and that it would be unfair to shoulder the present generation with the burden of responsibility.[93] In short, those alive now should not be made to pay for actions over which they had no say. Holding present generations accountable for harm that occurred in the past may be generally undesirable, but it is not necessarily an *unjustifiable* infringement; there are a number of historical examples of collective responsibility for historical injustices. The line of argument that present generations should not be held responsible for the acts of dead wrongdoers emphasizes the rights of individuals alive today and takes a dim view of collective responsibility. As defensible as this view may be – after all, children are rarely held accountable for the misdeeds of their parents – it does not translate automatically to the realm of relations between nation-states. Consider a government that, through profligate spending and imprudent management of its economy, runs up large debts to a variety of international creditors. As a consequence, the succeeding generation is saddled with the onerous debt-servicing and repayment obligations. Although the consequences of the previous generation's actions are clearly visited (unfairly) on the current generation, would one necessarily deem that this an unjustifiable form of collective responsibility? (The argument might go that protecting creditors' contractual rights – and generally upholding the principle of *pacta sunt servanda* – justifies holding the present generation accountable, but that in the climate change example, there is perhaps no justification of equal weight for imposing responsibility.) Holding present generations accountable for harms caused by previous generations may be morally undesirable but not necessarily unjustifiable; ascribing responsibility may depend on the nature of the harm and the surrounding circumstances. At a minimum, one might conclude that forms of collective accountability are consistent with the existing pattern of relations between states. Last, viewing the problem from the perspective of individuals in developed countries means that lesser consideration is given to the potential claims of individuals in developing countries, which could presumably be pursued by countries on their behalf.

---

[93] Eric A. Posner & Cass Sunstein, *Climate Change Justice*, 96 GEORGETOWN LAW JOURNAL 1565, 1593–94 (2008); CANEY, *supra* note 82, at 76.

The argument has been made that the responsibility approach is incomplete because it requires a background theory of justice that provides an account of entitlements, that is, of fair shares.[94] Ascribing responsibility only makes sense if the emissions in question exceeded some notional fair share.[95] Responsibility is contingent on some commission or omission; the wrong in question consists of exceeding the fair share, determined with reference to anterior principles of fairness or justice. On the face of it, the cumulative emissions of developed countries are not in accordance with basic notions of fair and equitable shares. However, a more precise determination of fair shares must wait for the establishment of a global GHG budget, that is, a decision on the safe level GHG concentration. That point has not yet been reached.

Discussions concerning fairness in climate change tend to neglect distinctions between distributive and corrective justice.[96] Corrective justice is backward looking, focused on compensation or reparation for wrongs that occurred in the past. Strictly speaking, arguments concerning historical responsibility for climate change are, in the first instance, claims about corrective, not distributive, justice.[97] Yet the technical philosophical concept of corrective justice does not fit comfortably with the multifaceted climate change problem, which cuts across time and space. In practice, claims about historical responsibility are tightly interwoven with arguments about fair distributions of emission entitlements.

### 4.3.4. Capability-Based Principles

Another strand of equity and fairness thinking considers capability as the relevant criterion for distributing the burden of mitigation and adaptation support costs. This notion is reflected in the UN Framework Convention on Climate Change's (UNFCCC) invocation that developed countries should take the lead in mitigation activities. In securing the provision of a global public good, countries that are most able, in terms of technological, financial, and human capacities, should contribute more than countries that are

---

[94] CANEY, *supra* note 82, at 765.
[95] *See* NEUMAYER, *supra* note 82, at 186 (equal per capita emissions, adjusted for historical emissions).
[96] POSNER & SUNSTEIN, *supra* note 93, at 1567.
[97] *See* Matthew D. Adler, *Corrective Justice and Liability for Global Warming*, 155 UNIVERSITY OF PENNSYLVANIA LAW REVIEW 1859 (2007).

## 4.3. Distributive Justice

less able. A combination of need and capability provides the ethically relevant grounds on which to justify differential treatment.[98] Climate change will have differential impacts, and countries expecting to suffer little under moderate warming may need to assume quite expensive mitigation commitments. In this scenario, one might ask whether capability to contribute is sufficient grounds for an affirmative duty, as opposed to charity or altruism. Page asks us to consider a situation in which climate change was an entirely natural phenomenon, but the distribution of impacts remained the same as under the current scenario.[99] Would a duty to assist seem equally compelling under such circumstances? It may be that there is an implicit assumption that those who have the capability to address global environmental problems are also the ones that caused them.

A commonly cited yardstick of capability is income per capita, or gross domestic product (GDP); other indices seek also to reflect social equity and development such as the UN Development Programme Human Development Index.[100] Scholars have sought to widen the understanding of development beyond economic goods and services to also include health and education, enjoyment of economic and social security, and the freedom to engage in economic interchange and social decision making.[101] Capability, understood as the freedom or opportunity to achieve valued aims, depends on an interlocking and wide-ranging set of social and economic factors. How might this be interpreted in the context of climate change policy? Here one could consider the principle of equality, expressed as an equal per capita emission entitlement. The capability approach would point out that because an equal allocation is not sensitive to differences in capabilities, it will have different consequences across individuals and countries. An equal per capita allocation is not sensitive to the cost of mitigation, nor the capacity to mitigate. In the climate change context, the capability approach illustrates the social and institutional dimension of development – applied to the climate change problem, it may yield useful insights. After all, climate impacts can be measured in dollar amounts, but in the first place, they will affect and test the resilience of health services, disaster management, and

---

[98] BROWN ET AL., *supra* note 69, at 21.
[99] PAGE, *supra* note 74, at 172–73.
[100] *See* UN DEVELOPMENT PROGRAMME, HUMAN DEVELOPMENT REPORT 2007/2008, FIGHTING CLIMATE CHANGE: HUMAN SOLIDARITY IN A DIVIDED WORLD (2007).
[101] *See* AMARTYA K. SEN, DEVELOPMENT AS FREEDOM (1999).

other institutions. Countries with similar levels of per capita income may vary significantly with respect to the individual and societal capability to cope with climate impacts. With respect to mitigation, income levels would not fully reflect the capability of a country's institutions to formulate and implement effective policies as well as develop or adapt and deploy climate-friendly technologies. Understanding differences in relevant capabilities can contribute to more effective policy making, while also promoting fairness.

### 4.3.5. Principles for a Working Consensus

The objective of the preceding discussion was not to select a winner, but instead to identify several principles that might plausibly contribute to a rough, working consensus on the critical fairness dimensions of climate change. There are, of course, other fairness principles as well as different formulations. Although not included with the principles discussed in this section, reference was made earlier in this chapter to the entitlement conception of distributive fairness. This approach is, of course, well represented in the climate regime, which, in the grandfathering provisions of the Kyoto Protocol, essentially treated the emissions of developed countries as acquired rights. Eschewing any commitment to substantive principles for evaluating the fairness of distributive outcomes, the entitlement conception strongly supports the status quo. The notion of sufficiency, a quite different conception of distributive justice, is also worth mentioning. According to this conception, what matters is not having some roughly equal share, but each person having enough to pursue the aims and aspirations that matter.[102] It is argued that once a certain threshold of well-being has been reached, attaining what individuals care about no longer depends on increasing welfare. Accordingly, there is no entitlement to an allocation over and above this sufficiency level. From an empirical perspective, Smil, plotting per capita energy consumption in various countries against key indicators, for example, infant mortality, has found that a society can achieve a fairly decent level of well-being on the basis of a per capita energy consumption that is less than one-sixth that of the United States and less than one-third that of Germany.[103] Higher levels of energy consumption correlate with improved

[102] PAGE, *supra* note 75, 9–10.
[103] VACLAV SMIL, ENERGY AT THE CROSSROADS: GLOBAL PERSPECTIVES AND UNCERTAINTIES 103–5 (2003).

indicators of well-being, for example, lower infant mortality, but no further gains are seen at levels approaching one-third that of the per capita consumption in the United States.

The preceding discussion analyzed selected fairness principles at a very abstract level. To explore the practical implications for climate policy, it is necessary to go one step further and identify particular burden-sharing rules implied by a given set of fairness principles. Table 4.1 sets out some of the burden-sharing rules implied by the fairness principles that have been considered.[104] For instance, egalitarian approaches support a distribution of entitlements on a per capita basis. By contrast, a scheme guided by a capability approach would allocate a larger share of the mitigation costs to countries with higher per capita GDP.

The next section briefly outlines a few issues relating to the intersection between the economics of climate change and fairness.

## 4.4. ECONOMICS

Economic analysis plays an important role in the debate on climate change, and this section will briefly examine conflicts arising at the intersection of economics and principles of fairness. The objective of welfare economics, which is fundamental to much analysis of public policy, is to work out policies that maximize overall social welfare, where welfare is understood as the consumption of goods and services by individuals.[105] The ethical framework animating welfare economics is then consequentialism – what matters are the effects of an action, in this case, welfare maximization.[106] This standard approach does not incorporate ethical concerns related to procedures for decision making nor a commitment to rights, fairness, or freedom.[107]

---

[104] Adam Rose, *Equity Considerations of Tradeable Carbon Emission Entitlements*, in COMBATING GLOBAL WARMING: STUDY ON A GLOBAL SYSTEM OF TRADEABLE CARBON EMISSION ENTITLEMENTS 55 (UN CONFERENCE ON TRADE AND DEVELOPMENT ed., 1992); Lasse Ringius et al., *Burden Sharing and Fairness Principles in International Climate Policy*, 2(1) INTERNATIONAL ENVIRONMENTAL AGREEMENTS: POLITICS, LAW AND ECONOMICS 1 (2002).
[105] NICHOLAS STERN, CABINET OFFICE, HM TREASURY, THE ECONOMICS OF CLIMATE CHANGE, THE STERN REVIEW 28 (2006).
[106] STEVEN C. HACKETT, ENVIRONMENTAL AND NATURAL RESOURCE ECONOMICS: THEORY, POLICY AND THE SUSTAINABLE SOCIETY 24 (2001).
[107] STERN, *supra* note 105, at 29; Seth Baum, *Beyond the Ramsey Model for Climate Change Assessments*, 7 ETHICS IN SCIENCE & ENVIRONMENTAL POLITICS 15, 16 (2007).

TABLE 4.1. *Selected principles and related burden-sharing rules*

| Equity principle | Content | Implied burden sharing |
| --- | --- | --- |
| Egalitarian | Every individual has an equal right to pollute or to be protected from pollution | Limit emissions in proportion to population – equal per capita emissions |
| Sovereignty/acquired rights | Current level of emissions constitutes a status quo right; every country has an equal right to pollute or be protected from pollution | Limit emissions proportionally across all countries; effect is to maintain relative emissions between them – grandfathering |
| Capability | The greater the ability to pay, the greater the economic burden | Net cost of abatement is inversely correlated with per capita GDP – progressive sharing of cost burden |
| Needs | Prioritize and maximize benefits for the poorest nations | Least limitations on poorest countries; large proportion of entitlements for poorest countries |
| Responsibility | Economic burden is proportional to emissions, thus polluter pays; narrow version covers present emissions only, can be extended to include historical emissions | Abatement of costs shared across countries in proportion to present emissions or cumulative emissions – one measure is $CO_2$ per capita; contribution to temperature increase, e.g., Brazilian proposal |

*Source:* Adapted from Ringius (1999) and Rose (1992).

As noted earlier, developing countries, which have a lower economic and social resource base than industrialized countries, will be hardest hit by climate change. One effect of climate change will thus be to reinforce existing global inequalities in welfare. Recently, there has been an acknowledgment that climate change poses difficult questions for standard economic approaches to policy analysis, and that there is consequently a need to refer to a broader range of ethical perspectives and frameworks than those underpinning the orthodox approach.[108]

[108] STERN, *supra* note 105, at 28.

## 4.4. Economics

Putting a cost on the likely impacts of climate change has a number of potential ethical pitfalls, which may not be immediately apparent from the rational presentation of economic studies.[109] First, it is not clear how one should aggregate and compare impacts on different countries to arrive at a measure of global welfare. In practice, economists express the aggregate measure of well-being in terms of real income.[110] This process of arriving at an overall welfare function by (notionally) summing the well-being of different people involves value judgments about how this affects the utility of consumption for these individuals. Thus these models have to account for the fact that the same increase in consumption means more to a poor person than it does to a rich one. There are doubts whether the models meaningfully capture the utility of consumption.[111] Second, expressing well-being in terms of income raises the question of how to value impacts on the environment and health, especially human life.[112] The problem arises because in order to make cost-benefit comparisons, a monetary value must be assigned to human life, which is usually arrived at in relation to per capita GDP, yielding the result that the life of a person in a developed country is usually "worth" more than that of a person living in a developing country. In itself it may not be objectionable to value life differently in different places – a poor country simply cannot afford to spend the same amount on medical care as a richer one and must take this fact into account when making policy. Ethical questions arise, however, because climate change involves the actions of some countries impacting on others. It seems unfair that developed countries – on aggregate, responsible for the climate impacts on poor countries – should be able to dilute their responsibility on the basis of the assignment of a low value of life measure in poor countries.

This points raises the more general problem concerning the valuation of nonmarket goods: how would one value the loss of coral reefs or cultural practices associated with a way of life on small islands?[113] The available economic tools and methodologies give widely divergent answers and do

---

[109] Michael Grubb, *Seeking Fair Weather: Ethics and the International Debate on Climate Change*, 71 INTERNATIONAL AFFAIRS 463, 470 (1995). The text accompanying notes 109–116 draws on the arguments articulated by Grubb.
[110] STERN, *supra* note 105, at 30.
[111] BAUM, *supra* note 107, at 16–17.
[112] GRUBB, *supra* note 109, at 470.
[113] BROWN ET AL., *supra* note 69, at 30–31.

not appear to be adequate to the challenge.[114] At some level, attempts to bring large-scale global nonmarket goods into the ambit of economic analysis may not be possible in any coherent way. This touches on the deeper question of how, if at all, the economic system can ever be integrated with the natural system.[115] Fairness, and other moral values are critical in adequately assessing the impacts of climate change on nonmarket goods.

A third important issue in relation to economics and climate change concerns intergenerational equity. How much should current generations pay to save future generations from the impacts of climate change? Climate change will result in damages occurring in the future, but mitigation costs will be incurred from now into the future. It is therefore useful to have some method of comparing these near-term costs with the more distant benefits. In tackling this question, economics applies a discount rate to determine at what point it is socially more beneficial to spend money on, say, education, rather than increasing the share of renewable energy to avoid emissions of carbon dioxide, and therefore future damages from climate change. A low discount rate results in a higher net present value for future damages, justifying more mitigation action; a high discount rate favors allocating resources to other socially useful priorities over climate change mitigation.[116] Far from a technicality, the selection of the discount rates has far-reaching implications for equity and the assessment of policy options.[117] There has long been disagreement among economists on the choice of discount rate.[118] Those advocating a high discount rate justify this

---

[114] See GRUBB, *supra* note 109, at 472. He points out that two methods for valuing nonmarket goods, willingness to pay (WTP) and willingness to accept, almost always result in different figures. A reason may be that while people are limited in what they can pay to avoid damage, there is no limit on what they could demand as compensation to accept a loss they consider irreplaceable. It should also be obvious, then, that at a systemic level, the WTP criterion is biased against the poor: they may not be able to pay much, even to avoid the loss of their livelihood.

[115] For detailed consideration of how economics can be reconciled with its biophysical foundations, *see* the essays in VALUING THE EARTH: ECONOMICS, ECOLOGY, ETHICS (Herman E. Daly & Kenneth N. Townsend eds., 1993).

[116] Damages of US$1 million 100 years in the future have a present value of US$52,000 at an annual discount rate of 3 percent, but only US$455 at a discount rate of 8 percent. Using the latter rate, it would be worth spending only a maximum of US$455 in the present to avoid those damages.

[117] STERN, *supra* note 105, at 31; UN DEVELOPMENT PROGRAMME, *supra* note 100, at 62–63. The HUMAN DEVELOPMENT REPORT provides an excellent and accessible overview of the issues.

[118] *See* Kenneth Arrow et al., *Decision-Making Frameworks for Addressing Climate Change*, in INTERGOVERNMENTAL PANEL ON CLIMATE CHANGE, CLIMATE CHANGE 1995: ECONOMIC

choice with reference to actual market behavior, in other words, long-term interest rates. From an ethical perspective, it is questionable why trade-offs made by people living now with respect to *their* present and future benefits should be extended to trading off future benefits to others. In other words, while individuals may prefer consumption to saving for retirement, it is hardly obvious why this logic should determine societal choices for future generations. An influential recent study of the economics of climate change, which opted for a low discount rate on equity grounds, has served to reopen the debate.[119] Decisions about what we owe future generations – or what they may rightly expect from us – clearly concern fairness and equity. The same is true for the policy and economic analyses that influence and shape decision making on this question.

Finally, there are good reasons to believe that standard economic modeling of the socially optimal level of abatement action does not account adequately for uncertainty.[120] Specifically, events with a low probability of occurring, but severe impacts are not properly captured in standard cost-benefit analysis of climate change, which is based on the central estimates of warming. The upshot of considering the deep uncertainty inherent in climate change uncertainty is to strip away the probably false sense of precision conveyed by standard cost-benefit analysis.[121] Standard economic models have been criticized for assuming that natural capital is perfectly substitutable for various forms of capital, such as buildings and technology.[122] In other words, the question may be whether in the long run it is correct to hold that ever-rising economic prosperity can compensate for the environmental impact of climate change.

AND SOCIAL DIMENSIONS OF CLIMATE CHANGE. CONTRIBUTION OF WG III (James P. Bruce et al. eds., 1996), summarizing the two sides in the debate as those favoring a descriptive discount rate, which is based on observations of the financial system (in the range of 6 percent), and those who take a prescriptive approach, preferring a lower discount rate in relation to environmental damages, including climate change. Due to the uncertainties related to climate change, there is support for lower discount rates. *See* RICHARD NEWELL & WILLIAM PIZER, DISCOUNTING THE BENEFITS OF CLIMATE CHANGE MITIGATION: HOW MUCH DO UNCERTAIN RATES INCREASE VALUATIONS? (2001) (Pew Center on Global Climate Change ed., 2001).
[119] STERN, *supra* note 105, at 31. But *cf.* William Nordhaus, *A Review of the Stern Review of the Economics of Global Warming*, 45 JOURNAL OF ECONOMIC LITERATURE 686 (2007).
[120] Martin Weitzman, *On Modeling and Interpreting the Economics of Catastrophic Climate Change*, 91(1) THE REVIEW OF ECONOMICS AND STATISTICS 1 (1999).
[121] *Ibid.* at 18.
[122] Eric Neumayer, *Discounting Is Not the Issue, But Substitutability Is*, 27 ENERGY POLICY 33 (1999).

Economic analyses of climate change policies assist decision makers in understanding the cost-effectiveness of policies and their overall economic impact, including trade-offs against other goals. However, the application of cost-benefit analysis to climate change policy options may give rise to ethical concerns, as has been recognized in recent economic studies. Acknowledging the relevance of ethical concerns in policy analysis could strengthen analytical outcomes and enhance the acceptance of policy recommendations.

## 4.5. FAIRNESS IN INTERNATIONAL ENVIRONMENTAL LAW

The fairness principles considered previously are not legal in nature; they do not possess normative character, that is, point to legal obligations. Nonetheless, responsibility, equality, and other fairness principles are quite frequently articulated in support of courses of action in international environmental negotiations. What I have termed fairness principles are also employed to interpret so-called principles of international environmental law (IEL) such as *common but differentiated responsibilities* and *equitable utilization*. These IEL principles find their place somewhere at the bottom of the hierarchy of international law, neither hard law, nor quite in the soft law category either.[123] There is considerable divergence among scholars about the legal status of many IEL principles.[124] Yet the status and role of these IEL principles are of some interest because they can be conceived of as functioning as potential conduits into the international lawmaking process for moral and ethical values. Unlike legal rules, principles have a somewhat contradictory quality – on one hand, they presume to guide action, yet on the other hand, it is unclear in what circumstances they ought to be applied. According to Dworkin, there exists a logical distinction between legal rules and legal principles.[125] Principles are standards that ought to be observed as a requirement of justice, fairness, or some other dimension of morality.[126] Although both imply legal obligations in particular circumstances, legal

---

[123] Ulrich Beyerlin, *Different Types of Norms in International Environmental Law: Policies, Principles and Rules*, in THE OXFORD HANDBOOK OF INTERNATIONAL ENVIRONMENTAL LAW 425, 426 (Daniel Bodansky et al. eds., 2007). See also Dinah Shelton, *Soft Law*, in ROUTLEDGE HANDBOOK OF INTERNATIONAL LAW (David Armstrong ed., 2008).
[124] BEYERLIN, *supra* note 123, at 429–33 (concluding that a survey "reflects utter confusion").
[125] RONALD DWORKIN, TAKING RIGHTS SERIOUSLY 24 (1977).
[126] *Id.* at 22.

rules apply in an all-or-nothing manner; they are either valid or invalid, and no conflict between rules is permitted. Principles are characterized by weight or relative strength; they must be taken into account if relevant, and while they give reasons for a decision, they are not dispositive. Dworkin uses the concept of legal principles to expose weaknesses in legal positivist theories of law, in particular, that such theories do not adequately explain what happens in the hard cases, where no existing legal rules are clearly applicable.[127] On his account, judges facing such cases are not in a legal vacuum, left to exercise their discretion, but are instead bound to consider relevant legal principles. If hard cases and an absence of positive law encourage recourse to principles, then IEL has proven to be fertile soil for the development of a range of principles. The proliferation of principles may reflect a compromise between a willingness to tackle international environmental problems and a reluctance to immediately infringe on sovereignty, as might be the case with adoption of more clear-cut rules.[128] In this sense, principles may enable states with very different interests to enter into agreements, thus recognizing a shared interest in addressing an issue and potentially opening a path to the further development of more precise and binding rules.

The question whether a particular principle has attained legal status depends on how deeply it is rooted in treaty law, customary international law, or both.[129] Where a principle of environmental law, such as the precautionary principle, finds expression in treaty law, it assumes a different legal character as compared to ethical, moral, or prudential principles, which may be enunciated in political declarations and other similar documents. There are many principles of environmental law that have not been securely anchored in treaty law. Such principles could also be considered part of international law if they are judged to have acquired the status of customary international law. According to the orthodox account, "customary international law results from a general and consistent practice of states

---

[127] Dworkin, *supra* note 125, at 17.
[128] Beyerlin, *supra* note 123, at 427–28.
[129] Article 38(1) of the Statute of the International Court of Justice provides that the sources of law to be applied by the court are international treaties (conventions) establishing rules expressly recognized by the parties; international custom, as evidence of a general practice accepted as law; and as a supplementary source, "general principles of law recognized by civilized nations." *See* The American Law Institute, Restatement of the Law, Third, Foreign Relations Law of the United States §102 (1987); Ian Brownlie, Principles of Public International Law 3–17 (4th ed., 1990).

followed by them from a sense of legal obligation."[130] The degree of generality and consistency in practice – significant regularity or uniformity – as well as demonstration of the internal element (*opinio juris*) pose problems in their application. Treaty law largely consists of obligations based on consent of sovereign states; in contrast to treaty obligations, customary law allows for the emergence of binding norms without requiring explicit consent.[131] Consequently, determination of customary international law has vexed generations of international lawyers.[132] The decentralized structure of the international system complicates the identification and validation of custom. There have been attempts to identify structural principles relevant to the formation of customary international law.[133] Scholars hewing to a restrictive approach emphasize consent and the necessity of demonstrating actual state practice, from which custom appears by means of an inductive approach.[134] Another approach proceeds in a more deductive manner, isolating customary norms primarily by reference to statements, or *opinio juris*, such as multilateral treaties and statements in international forums such as the UN General Assembly.[135] The creation of new rights and obligations by treaty can serve as evidence of emerging customary norms. In short, the manner in which norms attain the status of customary international law is a messy and contested question.

According to Shelton, "soft law is a type of social rather than legal norm... [that] usually refers to any written international instrument, other than a treaty, containing principles, norms, standards, or other statements of expected behavior."[136] This covers a wide range of instruments, including the political declarations, plans of action, and resolutions of

---

[130] RESTATEMENT, *supra* note 129, at §102.
[131] *Id.*; BROWNLIE, *supra* note 129, at 7–11.
[132] *See* Martti Koskenniemi, *Hierarchy in International Law: A Sketch*, 8(4) EUROPEAN JOURNAL OF INTERNATIONAL LAW 566 (1997).
[133] Michael Byers, *Custom, Power, and the Power of Rules: Customary International Law from an Interdisciplinary Perspective*, 17 MICHIGAN JOURNAL OF INTERNATIONAL LAW 109 (1995). Byers considers how the principles of jurisdiction, personality, reciprocity, and legitimate expectation qualify the application of state power in the process of customary international law.
[134] For a forceful statement of this position, *see* J. Shand Wilson, *State Consent and the Sources of International Law*, 86 AMERICAN SOCIETY OF INTERNATIONAL LAW PROCEEDINGS 108 (1992).
[135] *See* Anthea Elizabeth Roberts, *Traditional and Modern Approaches to Customary International Law: A Reconciliation*, 95 AMERICAN JOURNAL OF INTERNATIONAL LAW 757, 758 (2001).
[136] SHELTON, *supra* note 123.

## 4.5. Fairness in International Environmental Law

intergovernmental bodies that are often cited as sources for IEL principles. Excessive focus on efforts to delineate the precise legal status of environmental law norms may obscure the valuable role that so-called soft law actually plays. According to Bodansky, while few principles of IEL qualify as customary law in the strict sense, they nonetheless reflect the "evaluative standards used by states to justify their actions and to criticize the actions of others."[137] In other words, the principles of IEL and other norms constitute the language of the interstate discourse on environmental law.[138] The point here is not to enter into a discussion on the hierarchical standing of IEL norms, but to emphasize functions that exist independent of their legal status. Bodansky locates the primary effect of international environmental norms in the context of negotiations[139]: "in this second-party control process, international environmental norms can play a significant role by setting the terms for the debate, providing evaluative standards, serving as a basis to criticize other states' actions, and establishing a framework of principles within which negotiations may take place to develop more specific norms, usually in treaties." (By emphasizing the negotiating context, this view reveals to what extent thinking about IEL norms is conditioned on [implicit] assumptions about the centrality of judicial dispute resolution, which remains rare in IEL.[140]) In the climate change context, the IEL principle of common but differentiated responsibilities has, in fact, functioned in much this way, especially in setting a framework in which to structure respective mitigation actions by developed and developing countries.[141]

---

[137] Daniel Bodansky, *Symposium: Customary (and Not So Customary) International Environmental Law*, 3 INDIANA JOURNAL OF GLOBAL LEGAL STUDIES 105, 109–15 (1995).

[138] For an analysis of factors leading international actors to select different legal forms to solve problems, *see* Kenneth W. Abbott and Duncan Snidal, *Hard and Soft Law in International Governance*, 54(3) INTERNATIONAL ORGANIZATION 421 (2000). On the topic of soft law, *see* COMMITMENT AND COMPLIANCE: THE ROLE OF NON-BINDING NORMS IN THE INTERNATIONAL LEGAL SYSTEM (Dinah Shelton ed., 2000).

[139] BODANSKY, *supra* note 137, at 119.

[140] But *cf. Gabcikovo-Nagymaros Dam Case* (Hungary v. Slovakia) ICJ Rep. (1997) and the International Tribunal for the Law of the Sea (ITLOS): *MOX Plant Case (Ireland v. United Kingdom) – Order Related to Request for Provisional Measures*, No. 10 (December 3, 2001). However, compared to international criminal law, or trade law, environmental law lacks jurisprudence. In general, the scholarship on compliance has taken a turn away from judicial modes of resolution and enforcement. *See* CHAYES & CHAYES, *supra* note 43; Jake Werksman, *The Negotiation of a Kyoto Compliance System*, in IMPLEMENTING THE CLIMATE CHANGE REGIME: INTERNATIONAL COMPLIANCE 17 (O. Stokke et al. eds., 2005).

[141] The principle of common but differentiated responsibilities is discussed in detail in Chapter 5.

International lawyers have no ready definition of fairness or justice.[142] Instead, there is reference to equity under the heading of general principles of law, discussed previously as one of the supplementary sources of international law. The understanding is likewise of equity in the sense of fairness and reasonableness to supplement the more settled rules of law, to permit their sensible application.[143] Akehurst, in his article on equity and general principles of law, distinguishes three ways in which an international judge might apply equity: equity within the law (*infra legem*), equity as a gap filler (*praeter legem*), and equity against the law.[144] While the former application of equity, as a rule of interpretation, is not controversial, the other two applications are much more controversial. Thus, in the Continental Shelf Case, the International Court of Justice held that in those cases in which the court can choose between two possible interpretations, it is bound to opt for the interpretation that appears "to be closest to the requirements of justice."[145] Equity and equitable principles have found their primary application in the continental shelf delimitation cases.[146] Equitable utilization is also of relevance in other instances concerning shared natural resources, namely, watercourses and fish stocks.[147] The principles of unjust enrichment, estoppel (good faith), and acquiescence may also incorporate equity.[148]

The next section provides an overview of equity and fairness principles in selected areas of IEL.

### 4.5.1. Stockholm, the United Nations Conference on Environment and Development, the Johannesburg Plan of Implementation, and the Commission on Sustainable Development

The political processes of the UN in the area of environment and sustainable development have made a lasting impact with respect to the introduction of

---

[142] Frank Biermann, *Justice in the Greenhouse: Perspectives from International Law*, in FAIR WEATHER? EQUITY CONCERNS IN CLIMATE CHANGE 160 (Ferenc L. Tóth ed., 1999).
[143] BROWNLIE, *supra* note 129, at 26.
[144] Michael Akehurst, *Equity and General Principles of Law*, 25 INTERNATIONAL AND COMPARATIVE LAW QUARTERLY 801 (1976).
[145] *Continental Shelf Case (Tunisia v. Libyan Arab Jamahiriya)* (Judgment) 1982 ICJ Rep. 60 (para. 71).
[146] *North Sea Continental Shelf Case* (ICJ Rep. 1969). *See also* Franck's extensive comment on this case. FRANCK, FAIRNESS, at 61–65.
[147] SHELTON, *supra* note 25, at 647.
[148] FRANCK, FAIRNESS, at 50–54.

fairness principles into the global debate. The UN Conference on the Human Environment in Stockholm heightened awareness of global environmental concerns, underlining the fundamental principle of regulating the use of the planet's resources, while maintaining developmental opportunities.[149] Principle 5 of the Stockholm Declaration calls for the sharing among all humankind of the benefits of the use of nonrenewable resources. Principle 12 provides for capacity building and financial assistance for developing countries.

Twenty years later, at the UN Conference on Environment and Development (UNCED), the concept of sustainable development, earlier advanced in the Brundtland report, came to prominence as the core principle for reconciling protection of the natural environment and economic and social development.[150] Overall, the UNCED marked a clear turn toward concerns about development. The meaning of sustainable development is difficult to pin down, which may be one reason for its wide acceptance. It has been suggested that sustainable development emphasizes "the fundamental importance of equity within the economic system."[151] This interpretation is supported by principles 3 to 9 of the Rio Declaration, in which principle 3, for instance, states that "the right to development must be fulfilled so as to equitably meet developmental and environmental needs of present and future generations."[152] Principle 6 calls for giving special priority to the situation and needs of developing countries, particularly the least developed and most vulnerable. There is thus a clear articulation of need as a basis for distributive justice. In turn, principle 7, which articulates the "common but differentiated responsibilities" of developed and developing counties, introduces notions of responsibility and capability.

The 2002 World Summit on Sustainable Development adopted two instruments, the Johannesburg Declaration on Sustainable Development and the Johannesburg Plan of Implementation (JPOI). Together, these two documents reaffirm the key principles adopted at UNCED 10 years earlier. The JPOI recognized the understanding that economic development, social equity, and environmental protection constitute the three pillars of

---

[149] BIRNIE & BOYLE, *supra* note 81, at 38.
[150] REPORT OF THE WORLD COMMISSION ON ENVIRONMENT AND DEVELOPMENT: OUR COMMON FUTURE, UN Doc. A/42/427, annex (1987).
[151] *Id.* at 45.
[152] REPORT OF THE UNITED NATIONS CONFERENCE ON ENVIRONMENT AND DEVELOPMENT, Annex 1, UN Doc. A/CONF.151/26 of August 12, 1992.

sustainable development, while also accentuating poverty eradication.[153] Energy was one of the most important issues debated at the summit, and among other things, there was agreement to increase the use of renewable energy, ensure more efficient use of energy, and promote greater reliance on advanced and cleaner fossil fuel technologies.

Agenda 21 contains the program of action to promote the implementation of sustainable development. The follow-up and review of the implementation of Agenda 21 was entrusted to the Commission on Sustainable Development (CSD), which is a functional commission of the UN Economic and Social Council.[154] Institutionally, the CSD disappointed some with respect to its function as a review mechanism – examining progress made in attaining sustainable development goals – and providing policy guidance for future action.[155] However, unfavorable comparisons with the former UN Human Rights Commission are unfair, particularly given the criticism of that body.[156] In fact, the CSD is among the more active and innovative of the various functional commissions, especially with respect to securing meaningful participation from governments and to giving civil society a voice. It provides a unique forum for discussing issues in an integrated manner, especially topics, such as energy, that would otherwise not be properly considered within the system of UN agencies, programs, and multilateral environmental agreements.[157] Although states are rightly wary of duplicating consideration of the climate change issue, the CSD process can be used to map the interlinkages between climate change issues falling within its mandate, such as agriculture, small island developing states, and water.

### 4.5.2. *International Water Law*

The principles relating to international watercourses have been codified in the UN Convention on the Law of Non-navigational Uses of International

---

[153] MARIE CORDONIER SEGGER & ASHFAQ KHALFAN, SUSTAINABLE DEVELOPMENT LAW: PRINCIPLES, PRACTICES & PROSPECTS 28–29 (2004).
[154] GA Res. 191, December 22, 1992, UN Doc. A/RES/47/191.
[155] Stine Madland Kaasa, *The UN Commission on Sustainable Development: Which Mechanisms Explain its Accomplishments?* 7(3) GLOBAL ENVIRONMENTAL POLITICS 107 (2007).
[156] *See* BIRNIE & BOYLE, *supra* note 81, at 52. The United Nations Human Rights Council replaced the Human Rights Commission in 2006. *See* GA Res. 251, March 15, 2006, UN Doc. A/RES/60/251.
[157] COMMISSION ON SUSTAINABLE DEVELOPMENT, REPORT ON THE 9TH SESSION, UN Doc. E/2001/29, E/CN.17/2001/19 (2001).

## 4.5. Fairness in International Environmental Law

Watercourses.[158] The Convention is the product of 20 years of work, and in the view of one of its most authoritative commentators, several of the Convention's key provisions reflect customary international law.[159] McCaffrey writes that on the basis of state practice, the following three general principles incorporated in the Convention correspond to customary norms: the obligation to use an international watercourse in an equitable and reasonable manner, to use such a watercourse in a manner not to cause significant harm to other riparian states, and to notify potentially affected riparian states of planned measures on an international watercourse.[160] States are enjoined to utilize an international watercourse in an equitable and reasonable manner in their own territories, and states "shall participate in the use, development and protection of an international watercourse in an equitable and reasonable manner," where such participation includes the right to utilize the watercourse and the duty to cooperate to protect and develop it.[161] The Convention sets out a nonexhaustive list of factors and circumstances relevant to equitable and reasonable utilization of a river, including "the social and economic needs of the watercourse States concerned" and "the effects of the use or uses of the watercourses in one watercourse State on other watercourse States."[162]

### 4.5.3. Law of the Sea

Franck details how the law of the sea negotiations moved away from the principle of equidistance in maritime delimitations to embrace equity.[163]

---

[158] *See* GA Res. 229, May 21, 1997, annex, UN Doc. A/RES/51/229; reprinted in 36 ILM 700 (1997).
[159] Stephen McCaffrey, *The Contribution of the UN Convention on the Law of the Non-navigable Uses of International Watercourses*, 1 INTERNATIONAL GLOBAL ENVIRONMENTAL ISSUES 250 (2001).
[160] *Id.* at 260.
[161] Art. 5.
[162] Art. 6(b) and 6(d).
[163] FRANCK, FAIRNESS, at 66–68. *See* Geneva Convention on the Continental Shelf, April 29, 1958, Art. 6, 499 UNTS 311, 315, defining the principle of equidistance as follows: "where the same continental shelf is adjacent to the territories of two or more States whose coasts are opposite each other, the boundary of the continental shelf appertaining to such States shall be determined by agreement between them. In the absence of agreement, and unless another boundary line is justified by special circumstances, the boundary is the median line, every point of which is equidistant from the nearest points of the baselines from which the breadth of the territorial sea of each State is measured."

Article 83(1) of the UN Convention on the Law of the Sea (UNCLOS) states[164] that "the delimitation of the continental shelf between States with opposite or adjacent coasts shall be effected by agreement on the basis of international law, as referred to in Article 38 of the Statute of the International Court of Justice, in order to achieve an equitable solution."

UNCLOS provisions concerning transfer of technology[165] to developing countries, provisions concerning access and freedom of transit for land-locked states,[166] and those relating to the resources of the seabed[167] also reflect equity and fairness principles. The question of fairness in the distribution of benefits was a major issue in discussions concerning the resources of the seabed.[168] The 1995 Agreement on Straddling Fish Stocks and Highly Migratory Fish Stocks requires that recognition be given to the special requirements of developing states in relation to conservation and management of fish stocks, inter alia, by ensuring that such measures do not result in a disproportionate burden of conservation action for developing countries and that developing states, in particular, the least developed among them and small island developing states, obtain assistance to enable them to participate in high-seas fisheries.[169]

### 4.5.4. Montreal Protocol

In the course of the Montreal Protocol negotiations, developing nations, pointing to the fact that industrialized countries had been responsible for the overwhelming share of ozone-depleting chlorofluorocarbons (CFCs), took the position that they should not be subject to the same controls as wealthier countries.[170] Consequently, the Protocol makes specific provision for the circumstances of developing countries in the form of an

---

[164] United Nations Convention on the Law of the Sea, December 10, 1982, 21 ILM 1261, 1286, 1833 UNTS 3.
[165] Arts. 266–78.
[166] Arts. 124–32.
[167] Arts. 133–49.
[168] SHELTON, *supra* note 25, at 649.
[169] AGREEMENT FOR THE IMPLEMENTATION OF THE PROVISIONS OF THE UNITED NATIONS CONVENTION ON THE LAW OF THE SEA OF DECEMBER 10, 1982, RELATING TO THE CONSERVATION AND MANAGEMENT OF STRADDLING FISH STOCKS AND HIGHLY MIGRATORY FISH STOCKS, Arts. 24–25, 2167 UNTS 3, UN Doc. A/CONF.164/37.
[170] CASS R. SUNSTEIN, MONTREAL VERSUS KYOTO: A TALE OF TWO PROTOCOLS, Working Paper 06-17, AEI-Brookings Joint Center for Regulatory Studies 15 (2006).

exemption, technology of transfer, and a fund to meet the incremental cost of switching to non-CFC substitutes.[171] For instance, under Article 5, developing parties are permitted to meet "basic domestic needs" by delaying the implementation of control measures. The Multilateral Fund established under the Protocol provides financial resources for the closure or conversion of facilities producing ozone-depleting substances (ODS), technical assistance, information dissemination, and capacity building aimed at phasing out ODS use in a broad range of sectors.[172] Over the period from 1991 to 2007, donors have pledged US$2.2 billion.[173] These provisions contributed to a negotiated agreement in which fairness played an openly acknowledged part.[174]

## 4.6. CONCLUSION

Equity and fairness concerns are reflected in the UNFCCC itself. Equity is considered explicitly in many of the proposals for a post-Kyoto climate agreement.[175] This chapter examined the relevance of selected conceptions of fairness to the problem of climate change. The aim has been to identify principles that could form the basis for a rough, working consensus for engaging in a discourse about distributing the burdens and benefits of combating climate change. The objective is to identify principles that can be applied in the evaluation, on fairness grounds, of actual proposals for a post-2012 climate agreement. The core principles identified and discussed were egalitarian, responsibility, need, and capability. The approach adopted here does not deny the role of perceived self-interests in determining the actions of states in international climate negotiations. In the view of many, international law and the international community lack key attributes of a system in which it makes sense to speak of fairness. Nonetheless, IEL is predicated, to a significant degree, on common responsibility for the protection of the

---

[171] Montreal Protocol on Substances That Deplete the Ozone Layer, September 16, 1987, 26 ILM 1541, 1522 UNTS 3. The text of the Montreal Protocol as amended is available on the Web site of the Ozone Secretariat at http://www.unep.org/ozone/pdfs/Montreal-Protocol2000.pdf.
[172] Art. 10.
[173] See the Web site of the Ozone Secretariat, http://www.multilateralfund.org/about_the_multilateral_fund.htm, last visited February 2, 2008.
[174] FRANCK, FAIRNESS, at 386.
[175] Perhaps most prominently, the Contraction and Convergence proposal, put forward by the Global Commons Institute; see http://www.gci.org.uk/contconv/cc.html.

global environment as well as a nascent sense of community. Furthermore, not only is there an overt fairness discourse in this area of law, but in fact, various elements of fairness have been concretized in legal principles.[176] The analysis of fairness principles in the climate change regime is the subject of the next chapter.

[176] Lasse Ringius et al., *Burden Sharing and Fairness Principles in International Climate Policy*, 2(1) INTERNATIONAL ENVIRONMENTAL AGREEMENTS: POLITICS, LAW AND ECONOMICS 1 (2002).

# 5

# Fairness in the Climate Change Regime

## 5.1. INTRODUCTION

The preamble of the United Nations Framework Convention on Climate Change (UNFCCC) is striking for the prominence it gives to issues of fairness. It states, "*Noting* that the largest share of historical and current global emissions of greenhouse gases has originated in developed countries, that per capita emissions in developing countries are still relatively low and that the share of global emissions originating in developing countries will grow to meet their social and developmental needs."[1] Prominent reference is made to the principle of common but differentiated responsibilities.[2] The special vulnerability to the impacts of climate change of low-lying, small island developing countries and other developing countries is recognized.[3] It is also recognized that to achieve sustainable social and economic development, the energy consumption of developing countries will have to grow.[4] Although the language of the preamble is aspirational, it forms part of the context in which the terms of the Convention can be interpreted.[5]

---

[1] United Nations Framework Convention on Climate Change, adopted on May 9, 1992, preamble para. 3, 1771 UNTS 164, Article 3(1) (hereinafter referred to as UNFCCC).
[2] *Id.* preamble, paras. 6, 23.
[3] *Id.* preamble, para. 24. Also mentioned, in paras. 25–26, is the vulnerability of countries "whose economies are particularly dependent on fossil fuel production," that is, the Organization of Petroleum Exporting Countries (OPEC) states. This is a reflection of the negotiating dynamics and the kinds of compromise extracted to reach agreement.
[4] *Id.* preamble, para. 27.
[5] Vienna Convention on the Law of Treaties, May 23, 1969, Art. 31, 1155 UNTS, 331. It states, "1. A treaty shall be interpreted in good faith in accordance with the ordinary meaning to be given to the terms of the treaty in their context and in the light of its object and purpose.

Sovereign equality of states is the formal hallmark of international law. In reality, of course, states vary widely with respect to their military power, economic might, and strength of their institutions. Nonetheless, the ground rule is that states are bound as equals when international agreements are struck – weak or strong, poor or rich, parties assume undifferentiated obligations. The law of the climate change regime is an exception to this rule, providing the impetus for new norms intended to promote collective responses by states with widely diverging interests and capabilities. This chapter consists of a closer analysis of the Convention and the Protocol, with a view to identifying provisions of these instruments that have a bearing on fairness. The chapter begins with a brief overview of differentiation under international environmental law, in particular, the principle of common but differentiated responsibilities, as manifested in the Convention. The conceptual underpinning of the principle and its relationship with equity and fairness are examined. The transfer of cleaner technology and financial assistance are identified as examples of fairness in sharing the burden of environmental protection under international environmental law. The implementation of relevant provisions in the Convention and its Protocol is discussed in more detail.

## 5.2. DIFFERENTIATION: ENTRY POINT FOR FAIRNESS OR INSTRUMENT OF EXPEDIENCY?

The emergence of differential treatment must be seen against the broader context in which such treatment arose. A historical impetus for the development of differential treatment in international law was the expansion in membership of the state system with the process of decolonization after the Second World War.[6] In parallel, the world has experienced a greater degree of interdependence through growth in trade, investment, and changes in technology. Many developing countries contend that the changes occurring under the rubric of economic globalization have brought them limited

---

2. The context for the purpose of the interpretation of a treaty shall comprise, in addition to the text, including its preamble and annexes...."

[6] Philippe Cullet, *Differential Treatment in International Law: Towards a New Paradigm of Inter-state Relations*, 10 EUROPEAN JOURNAL OF INTERNATIONAL LAW 549, 564 (1999).

benefits, or even contributed to a further decline in their economic prospects.[7] Many developing countries are not closing the gap with developed countries, let alone attaining basic indicators of social and economic development. In this context, the Millennium Development Goals aim for the achievement of eight development-related goals by 2015, including halving the number of people whose daily income is less than US$1 per day, achieving universal primary education, and ensuring environmental sustainability.[8] While progress has been notched up in Asia, it appears unlikely that sub-Saharan Africa will meet key goals relating to poverty and the number of people suffering from hunger.[9] For instance, although over the period 1990 to 2000, the percentage of people in sub-Saharan Africa living in absolute poverty declined marginally, the absolute number of those in extreme poverty rose by 140 million. And although flows of development assistance have recovered from the decline of the 1990s, they still fall short of targets adopted by the international community.[10]

---

[7] E.g., Africa's declining share of world trade stands at only 1.5 percent, and while recent years have seen economic growth, this has been driven by commodities (minerals, hydrocarbons) exports. E.g., oil and other fuels accounted for almost 60 percent of Africa's exports in 2005. See ORGANISATION FOR ECONOMIC CO-OPERATION AND DEVELOPMENT, AFRICAN ECONOMIC OUTLOOK 2007 (2007). Changes in the world trading system, particularly the phasing out of market access preferences, are impacting negatively on a number of small island developing states that have achieved a degree of prosperity, e.g., Antigua and Barbuda (sugar industry) and Mauritius (textiles).

[8] See http://www.un.org/millenniumgoals/. The MDGs were derived from the Millennium Declaration, adopted by the UN in GA Res. 2 of September 8, 2000, UN Doc A/RES/55/2.

[9] See UNITED NATIONS, MILLENNIUM DEVELOPMENT GOALS REPORT 2007 4 (2007), available at http://www.un.org/millenniumgoals/pdf/mdg2007.pdf.

[10] According to the Development Assistance Committee (DAC) of the OECD, its 22 member countries, the world's major donors, provided US$103.9 billion in aid in 2006, down by 5.1 percent from 2005. This represents a significant increase over the low recorded in 1997. Nonetheless, the DAC points out that aid to sub-Saharan Africa, excluding debt relief, was static in 2006, leaving a challenge to meet the Gleneagles G-8 summit commitment to double aid to Africa by 2010. See ORGANISATION FOR ECONOMIC CO-OPERATION AND DEVELOPMENT, FINAL AID FLOWS IN 2006, DCD/DAC/RD(2007)15/RD2 (2007). See MONTERREY CONSENSUS OF THE INTERNATIONAL CONFERENCE ON FINANCING FOR DEVELOPMENT, REPORT OF THE INTERNATIONAL CONFERENCE ON FINANCING FOR DEVELOPMENT, UN DOC. A/CONF.198/11 (2002). Para. 42 of the Monterey Consensus statement urged developed countries to "take concrete steps towards the target of 0.7 per cent of Gross National Product (GNP)" in aid for developing countries.

Early examples of differentiation in international law existed in the trade law,[11] the United Nations Law of the Sea Convention,[12] and the movement to establish a New International Economic Order.[13] The 1972 Stockholm Declaration emphasized the need to consider "the applicability of standards which are valid for the most advanced countries but which may be inappropriate

---

[11] General Agreement of Tariffs and Trade, October 30, 1947, 55 UNTS 187. Part IV recognized the disadvantaged position of less developed countries, stating in Art. XXXVI, sub-para. 8, that "the developed contracting parties do not expect reciprocity for commitments made by them in trade negotiations to reduce or remove tariffs and other barriers to the trade of less-developed contracting parties." This provision was, in essence, more an exhortation to "good practice" and lacked binding force. See ALEXANDER KECK & PATRICK LOW, SPECIAL AND DIFFERENTIAL TREATMENT IN THE WTO: WHY, WHEN AND HOW?, Staff Working Paper ERSD-2004-03, World Trade Organization 4 (2004), available at http://www.wto.org/english/res_e/reser_e/ersd200403_e.htm. The *Decision on Differential and More Favourable Treatment, Reciprocity and Fuller Participation of Developing Countries* of November 28, 1979 (L/4903), provides for certain aspects of regional or global preferential agreements among developing countries, provides for special treatment for least-developed countries, and restates the principle of nonreciprocity (available at http://www.wto.org/english/docs_e/legal_e/prewto_legal_e.htm). The Doha Declaration calls for a review of all special and differentiation provisions "with a view to strengthening them and making them more precise, effective and operational," para. 44. See Ministerial Declaration, adopted on November 14, 2001, WT/MIN(01)/DEC/1, available at http://www.wto.org/english/thewto_e/minist_e/min01_e/mindecl_e.htm. More specifically, the decision on implementation-related issues and concerns calls for members "to consider the legal and practical implications for developed and developing Members of converting special and differential treatment measures into mandatory provisions, to identify those that Members consider should be made mandatory," para. 12(i). See IMPLEMENTATION-RELATED ISSUES AND CONCERNS, decision of November 14, 2001, WT/MIN(01)/17, available at http://www.wto.org/english/thewto_e/minist_e/min01_e/mindecl_implementation_e.htm. However, little action has been taken to advance the Doha agenda in this respect. It is difficult to avoid the conclusion that under the General Agreement on Tariffs and Trade/World Trade Organization, there has been a move toward the elimination of differentiation, with provision for procedural differentiation, such as longer time periods for the phasing in of rules, as well as technical assistance. Renewed efforts to secure special treatment – exemplified by the Doha agenda – seem bogged down.

[12] See UN Convention on the Law of the Sea, December 10, 1982, Part XI, 1833 UNTS 3, 21 ILM 1261. But *cf.* agreement relating to the implementation of Part XI of the UN Convention on the Law of the Sea of December 10, GA Res. 263, 48th Sess., UN Doc. A/RES/48/263, Annex. The text of the agreement is available at http://www.un.org/Depts/los/convention_agreements/convention_overview_part_xi.htm.

[13] The New International Economic Order (NIEO) constituted an attempt by the developing countries to bring about changes in the international economic and legal system, with an emphasis on control of developing countries over their natural resources. See MOHAMMED BEDJAOUI, TOWARDS A NEW INTERNATIONAL ECONOMIC ORDER (1979). The calls for the establishment of the NIEO faded away by the end of the 1980s. See CULLET, *supra* note 6, at 568.

## 5.2. Differentiation

and of unwarranted social cost for the developing countries."[14] But it was the Rio Conference in 1992 that was conspicuous for its endorsement of the differentiated responsibilities between developed and developing countries.[15] Special concern for the needs of developing countries and differentiation was articulated in Principles 6 and 7 of the Rio Declaration, which state that[16]

> The special situation and needs of developing countries, particularly the least developed and those most environmentally vulnerable, shall be given priority. (Principle 6)
>
> States shall cooperate in the spirit of global partnership to conserve, protect and restore the health and integrity of the Earth's ecosystem. In the view of the different contributions to global environmental degradation, States have common but differentiated responsibilities. The developed countries acknowledge the responsibility that they bear in the international pursuit of sustainable development in view of the pressures their societies place on the global environment and of the technologies and financial resources they command. (Principle 7)

According to Rajamani, differential treatment in international environmental agreements can be divided into three broad categories, as follows: (1) provisions that differentiate between developed and developing countries with respect to the central obligation of the instrument in question; (2) differentiation with respect to implementation, for instance, phased-in compliance and delayed reporting schedules; and (3) the granting of assistance in the form of capacity building, financial resources, and transfer of technology.[17] As regards provisions establishing differentiation concerning the central obligations, prime examples are Article 4(2) of the UNFCCC,

---

[14] REPORT OF THE UNITED NATIONS CONFERENCE ON THE HUMAN ENVIRONMENT, UN Conference on the Human Environment, 26th Sess., princ. 23, UN Doc. A/CONF. 48/14 (1972); 11 ILM 1416, 142.

[15] Duncan French, *Developing States and International Environmental Law: The Importance of Differentiated Responsibilities*, 49 INTERNATIONAL & COMPARATIVE LAW QUARTERLY 35 (2000).

[16] DECLARATION OF THE UNITED NATIONS CONFERENCE ON ENVIRONMENT AND DEVELOPMENT, UN Doc. A/CONF.151/26(Vol. I), annex.

[17] LAVANYA RAJAMANI, DIFFERENTIAL TREATMENT IN INTERNATIONAL ENVIRONMENTAL LAW 93–94 (2006). *See also* FRENCH, *supra* note 15, at 39–41 (identifying two broad categories, namely, applying a standard for developing countries that takes account of their special needs as well as provisions relating to financial assistance and access to technology); Dinah Shelton, *Equity, in* THE OXFORD HANDBOOK OF INTERNATIONAL ENVIRONMENTAL LAW 639, 650 (Daniel Bodansky et al. eds., 2007).

which sets out the commitments of developed countries, and the Kyoto Protocol, which establishes emission limitation and reduction commitments for the countries contained in its Annex B.[18] Provisions that differentiate between developed and developed countries with respect to implementation are far more common than those falling under the first category. For instance, the UNFCCC,[19] the Convention on Biological Diversity,[20] the Desertification Convention,[21] the 1994 International Tropical Timber Agreement,[22] and the 1995 Agreement on Straddling Fish Stocks[23] are provisions that recognize the special needs and circumstances of developing countries. The Montreal Protocol is a well-known example of delayed, or phased-in, compliance, with its requirement to cease the production and use of ozone-depleting substances. Provisions relating to financial assistance

---

[18] Kyoto Protocol to the UNFCCC, December 11, 1997, 2303 UNTS 148, 37 ILM 22, text available from the Web site of the UNFCCC Secretariat, at http://unfccc.int/kyoto_protocol/items/2830.php.

[19] See, e.g., Art. 3(1): "the developed country parties should take the lead in combating climate change and the adverse effects thereof."

[20] CONVENTION ON BIOLOGICAL DIVERSITY, June 5, 1992, 1760 UNTS 79. See preamble, para. 16: "acknowledging further that special provision is required to meet the needs of developing countries." In relation to research and training, Art. 12 provides that the contracting parties shall take into account the "special needs of developing countries."

[21] UN CONVENTION TO COMBAT DESERTIFICATION IN THOSE COUNTRIES EXPERIENCING SERIOUS DROUGHT AND/OR DESERTIFICATION, PARTICULARLY IN AFRICA, October 14, 1994, 1954 UNTS 3, 33 ILM 1238. Compare preamble para. 4, asserting that "desertification and drought are problems of global dimension in that they affect all regions of the world and that joint action of the international community is needed to combat desertification," and preamble para. 5, noting the particular impact of drought and desertification on developing countries, particularly in Africa. See also references to needs of developing countries in Arts. 3(d), 4(2)(b), 5, and 6. Art. 7 introduces further differentiation, stating that in implementing the Convention, parties shall give priority to African countries.

[22] INTERNATIONAL TROPICAL TIMBER AGREEMENT, January 26, 1994, 1955 UNTS 81, 33 ILM 1016. Under Art. 34 on special measures, providing the developing country parties can apply for "appropriate differential and remedial measures."

[23] AGREEMENT FOR THE IMPLEMENTATION OF THE PROVISIONS OF THE UNITED NATIONS CONVENTION ON THE LAW OF THE SEA OF 10 DECEMBER 1982 RELATING TO THE CONSERVATION AND MANAGEMENT OF STRADDLING FISH STOCKS AND HIGHLY MIGRATORY FISH STOCKS, 2167 UNTS 3, UN Doc. A/CONF.164/37. See preamble para. 8, recognizing the need for specific assistance to developing countries to permit them to participate fully in the conservation, management, and so forth, of fish stocks. In particular, the "special requirements of developing countries in relation to the conservation and management" of fish stocks, including "the need to ensure that such measures do not result in transferring, directly or indirectly, a disproportionate burden of conservation action onto developing States," Art. 24(1) and 24(2)(c). Also, Art. 26, providing for special assistance to developing countries in the implementation of the Agreement.

in the UNFCCC,[24] the Convention on Biodiversity,[25] and the Stockholm Convention on Persistent Organic Pollutants[26] are put into operation through the Global Environmental Facility (GEF). Examples of provisions concerning access to, or transfer of, technology on favorable terms are found in the UNFCCC and the Convention to Combat Desertification.[27] Statements endorsing differentiation are also found in the nonbinding instruments adopted at the Rio Conference: Agenda 21,[28] the Rio Declaration of Principles,[29] and the Statement on Forests.[30]

### 5.2.1. Conceptual Framework of the Principle of Common but Differentiated Responsibility

The conceptual framework for differentiation in international environmental law has been approached from a number of angles. In general, differentiation can be regarded, at its most positive, as a manifestation of resolve to tackle common problems, motivated by partnership and cooperation.[31]

---

[24] UNFCCC, Art. 11.
[25] CONVENTION ON BIOLOGICAL DIVERSITY, *supra* note 20, Art. 21.
[26] Stockholm Convention on persistent organic pollutants, May 22, 2001, Art. 13, text available on the Web site of the Secretariat, at http://www.pops.int/.
[27] *See* Arts. 4 and 18, respectively.
[28] UN Doc. A/CONF.151/26/(Vol. I), Annex 3, Agenda 21. *See*, e.g., chapter 9, "Protection of the Atmosphere," stating that activities undertaken in pursuit of the objectives of the chapter should take into account "the legitimate priority needs of developing countries for the achievement of sustained economic growth and the eradication of poverty" (para. 9.3). A general reference to differentiation is found in para. 39.3(d), noting that in drawing up international standards, states should "take into account the different situations and capabilities of countries."
[29] DECLARATION OF THE UNITED NATIONS CONFERENCE ON ENVIRONMENT AND DEVELOPMENT, *supra* note 16.
[30] NON-LEGALLY BINDING AUTHORITATIVE STATEMENT OF PRINCIPLES FOR A GLOBAL CONSENSUS ON THE MANAGEMENT, CONSERVATION AND SUSTAINABLE DEVELOPMENT OF ALL TYPES OF FORESTS, UN Doc. A/CONF.151/26(Vol. III), Annex 3. Developed countries are to take the lead in greening and afforestation (principle 8[a]) efforts by developing countries, and countries with economies in transition making efforts to strengthen sustainable forest management should be supported (principle 9[a]). On December 17, 2007, the UN General Assembly adopted the NON-LEGALLY BINDING INSTRUMENT ON ALL TYPES OF FORESTS, *see* GA Res. 89, 62nd Sess., UN Doc. A/RES/62/98. The Instrument references the principle of common but differentiated responsibilities and calls attention to the need for financial and technical assistance for forest conservation and management in developing countries.
[31] But *cf.* the analysis of Christopher D. Stone, *Common but Differentiated Responsibilities in International Law*, 98 AMERICAN JOURNAL OF INTERNATIONAL LAW 276 (2004).

Differentiation of responsibilities is thus identified as one aspect of an emerging "shared compact" between developed and developing countries, with the latter conditioning their participation in global environmental agreements on assistance from the former.[32] Scholars argue that differentiation does the following in international law: first, it promotes the achievement of substantive equality among states by recognizing the different needs and circumstances of developing countries; second, it fosters partnership and cooperation among states; and third, it promotes effective implementation of agreements.[33] The above grounds for differentiation, it is contended, have gained in currency as compared to reasoning based on the historical responsibility of the developed world for the bulk of global environmental problems as well as its capacity (in contrast to the developing nations) to remedy them.[34] Certainly in the climate change context, it would be incorrect to maintain that ascriptions of responsibility based on past conduct have been superseded as a dominant strain of argument. Nonetheless, an approach based on partnership and cooperation was heralded in Agenda 21 and, in more hedged fashion, the major legal instruments adopted at the Rio Conference. The impasse around climate change signals that the earlier vision and optimism have frayed. The same authors who discern partnership and cooperation as one of the grounds for differentiation are also clear-eyed in noting that while differentiation arguably rests on concerns of fairness, it could also be characterized as expediency in ensuring that developing countries act on what are – for the time being – largely northern concerns.[35]

As appears from the formulation of Principle 7 of the Rio Declaration, the differentiated responsibility is ostensibly grounded in the different contributions to global environmental degradation, on one hand, and on the other, greater financial resources and capacities of the developed

---

[32] *See* Mark A. Drumbl, *Poverty, Wealth, and Obligation in International Law*, 76 TULANE LAW REVIEW 843 (2002).
[33] *See* CULLET, *supra* note 6, at 550; FRENCH, *supra* note 15, at 35, 46.
[34] FRENCH, *supra* note 15, at 35, 46.
[35] *Id.* at 35. FRENCH, *supra* note 15, at 57; CULLET, *supra* note 6, at 574; and DRUMBL, *supra* note 32, at 930–32, conclude that developed countries have been most accommodating to southern demands for differentiation and financial support in areas where they perceive their interests to lie, e.g., climate change. By contrast, the UN Convention to Combat Desertification, which covers an issue primarily of concern to developing countries, contains softer language on differentiation and has, in general, received less prominence than the UNFCCC and the CBD. *See* DRUMBL, *supra* note 32, at 932–33.

nations.[36] The two grounds for responsibility also neatly reflect the divide between the camps – developing countries favor the first, as it could conceivably give rise to legal obligations; developed countries naturally favor the second ground, perceived as weaker because resting on moral and political grounds is essentially akin to charity.[37] A more positive perspective on the argument from relative capacities could hold that developing countries should be granted the opportunity to achieve economic and social development before assuming the full burden of environmental protection obligations in question.[38] The relative wealth and historical contribution of states to the problem can be regarded as a salient reason to permit differential treatment.

The principle of common but differentiated responsibilities gives effect to conceptions of equity and fairness in international environmental law and policy making. It does so first as a normative principle, for example, as articulated in Rio Principle 7 and subsequently reaffirmed in documents such as the Johannesburg Plan of Implementation, adopted at the World Summit on Sustainable Development in 2002. Second, it gives effect to conceptions of fairness in concrete provisions, for instance, in the differentiated emission limitation and reduction commitments of the Kyoto Protocol. The philosophical roots of common but differentiated responsibilities have been traced to notions of equality and of restoring equality[39] as well as to the concept of intergenerational equity.[40] Scholars have also identified the justifications for the principle, primarily the dichotomous responsibility

---

[36] RAJAMANI, *supra* note 17, at 137–50. *See also* Yoshiro Matsui, *Some Aspects of the Principle of "Common but Differentiated Responsibilities,"* 2 INTERNATIONAL ENVIRONMENTAL AGREEMENTS: POLITICS, LAW AND ECONOMICS 151, 155 (2002). As Matsui notes, this position is shared by most writers on the topic. *See*, e.g., CULLET, *supra* note 6, at 577; FRENCH, *supra* note 15, at 46–52. *See also* Ileana M. Porras, *The Rio Declaration: A New Basis for International Cooperation*, *in* GREENING INTERNATIONAL LAW 25, 29 (Philippe Sands ed., 1993).

[37] Illustrative of the perceived power of norms – even the soft-law variety – the United States issued an interpretative statement to the effect that Principle 7 merely acknowledged the "special leadership role of developed countries" due to their "wealth, technical expertise and capabilities" and that the principle does not "imply a recognition... of any international obligations... or any diminution in the responsibility of developing countries." Cited by FRENCH, *supra* note 15, at 37. *See* UN Doc. A/CONF.151/26 (Vol. IV) 20 (1992).

[38] *Cf.* INTERNATIONAL LAW ASSOCIATION, REPORT OF THE SIXTY-SIXTH CONFERENCE 116 (1995), rejecting this ground and arguing for responsibility on the basis of "different contributions to global environmental degradation."

[39] RAJAMANI, *supra* note 17, at 150–51, 154–55.

[40] CULLET, *supra* note 6, at 571.

and capacity/capability grounds,[41] and extended it to include taking into account the special needs and circumstances of developing countries and a "global partnership" featuring more equitable forms of cooperation.[42]

It is suggested that this approach is correct but does not go far enough. In fact, common but differentiated responsibilities can be better understood by going one step further to explicitly identify the notions of equity and fairness that underpin the principle. These are the interlinked aspects of fairness that were discussed in Chapter 4: egalitarian, responsibility, needs, and capability. It is no coincidence that these aspects of fairness also correspond to the various – at times, competing – characterizations of common but differentiated responsibilities. In a very broad sense, equality demands that "like cases be treated alike," but this begs the question, what criteria determine similarity and dissimilarity in a given case? In this respect, a more substantive and contextualized understanding of equality proves useful. As opposed to formal equality, which stresses neutrality, the promotion of substantive equality entails enquiring into which factors count in determining whether cases ought to be treated in a like manner.[43] In the context of climate change, equality in tackling the burden of combating climate change is contextualized and supported by the notion of responsibility. Equal sharing of the mitigation burden between developed and developing countries is unfair and inequitable when the respective responsibilities for atmospheric greenhouse gas (GHG) concentrations are accounted for. Nonetheless, as noted in the analysis of the responsibility aspect of fairness, industrialized countries' historical contribution to the "bad" of climate change should also be seen in the light of the global public goods such as advances in science and technology that flowed from the process of industrialization.[44] The principle's different underpinnings – differential contributions to environmental degradation, greater capabilities on the part of the developed

---

[41] STONE, *supra* note 31, at 291–94.
[42] FRENCH, *supra* note 15, at 53, 55.
[43] Even in the environmental arena, notions of formal equality have a strong hold. *See* PROTOCOL TO THE 1979 CONVENTION ON LONG-RANGE TRANSBOUNDARY AIR POLLUTION ON LONG-TERM FINANCING OF THE CO-OPERATIVE PROGRAMME FOR MONITORING AND EVALUATION OF THE LONG-RANGE TRANSMISSION OF AIR POLLUTANTS IN EUROPE, September 24, 1984, 1491 UNTS 167, where a uniform reduction was accepted, even though it was much more burdensome for the former Soviet and Eastern European states.
[44] STONE, *supra* note 31, at 300, noting the difficulty holding current generations in industrialized countries responsible for the actions of their forebears as well as the "ironic argument of adverse possession and prescription."

countries, and commitment to solidarity and partnership – are all consistent with a broad understanding of what is fair or equitable. Thus it could be considered unfair if those who have contributed the most to the problem do not contribute more to the solution than those whose contribution is much smaller. Similarly, in the face of a problem demanding a collective solution, it would be unfair to expect those with the least resources to commit a higher share to the solution of the problem.

As the preceding discussion has revealed, the terms, grounds, and justifications put forward for differentiated responsibilities in favor of developing countries emanate from considerations of fairness.[45] The language of sharing responsibilities for collective problems, of taking account of the relative position and capacities of developing and developed countries in the establishment and implementation of international regimes, is the idiom of fairness in relations between states.

Growing evidence of state practice supports the view that the principle of common but differentiated responsibility is a principle of international environmental law. This is apparent from its prominent expression in the Convention[46] as well as from a large number of nonbinding instruments, decisions, and resolutions of UN organs dealing with sustainable development.[47] Given that some developed countries have resisted the

---

[45] *See* Philippe Sands, *The "Greening" of International Law: Emerging Principles and Rules*, 1 INDIANA JOURNAL OF GLOBAL LEGAL STUDIES 293, 307 (1994) (differentiated responsibility results from the application of the broader principle of equity in general international law as well as recognition that the special needs of developing countries must be taken into account in international environmental law); *see also* MATSUI, *supra* note 36, at 155, citing Henry Shue, *Global Environment and International Equity*, 75 INTERNATIONAL AFFAIRS 533–40 (1999).

[46] The principle is also referred to in the decisions of the COP, including in the decisions to implement the Kyoto Protocol. *See*, e.g., Decision 24/CP.7 (procedures and mechanisms relating to compliance), in REPORT OF THE CONFERENCE OF THE PARTIES ON ITS SEVENTH SESSION, ADDENDUM, PART II: ACTION TAKEN BY THE PARTIES, vol. III, FCCC/CP/2001/13/Add.3.

[47] REPORT OF THE GLOBAL CONFERENCE ON THE SUSTAINABLE DEVELOPMENT OF SMALL ISLAND DEVELOPING STATES, chap. 2, "Programme of Action for the Sustainable Development of Small Island Developing States," UN Doc. A/CONF./167/9, May 6, 1994. Para. 14 refers to Principle 7 of the Rio Declaration in the context of addressing global environmental degradation. REPORT OF THE NINTH SESSION OF THE COMMISSION ON SUSTAINABLE DEVELOPMENT, 1, Decision 9/1, Energy for Sustainable Development, at paras. 5, 7; at 15, Decision 9/2, Protection of the Atmosphere, para. 1. REPORT OF THE WORLD SUMMIT ON SUSTAINABLE DEVELOPMENT, UN Doc. A/Conf./199/20, chap. 1, 6, Johannesburg Plan of Implementation. E.g., the principle of common but differentiated responsibilities as set out in Principle 7 of the Rio Declaration is referred to in paras. 14 (production and

interpretation that the practice is determined by a legal obligation (*opinio iuris*), this casts doubt on whether it has attained the status of general customary international law.[48] Most legal scholars are reluctant to characterize precisely the principle's legal status, but stop short of maintaining that it has become customary international law.[49] The establishment of new obligations under international environmental law, or the deepening of existing ones, would prove difficult – and be perceived as inequitable – without taking the principle into account. Therein lies its true significance.

### 5.2.2. Common but Differentiated Responsibilities in the UNFCCC

The principles in Articles 3 of the Climate Change Convention consist of a particularly clear elaboration of the principle of common but differentiated

> consumption), 20 (energy for sustainable development), 38 (climate change), 39 (air pollution), and 81 (implementation). Mauritius Strategy for the Further Implementation of the Programme of Action for the Sustainable Development of Small Island Developing States, REPORT OF THE INTERNATIONAL MEETING TO REVIEW THE PROGRAMME OF ACTION FOR THE SUSTAINABLE DEVELOPMENT OF SMALL ISLAND DEVELOPING STATES, UN DOC. A/Conf./207/11, January 14, 2005, chap. 1, at 10. Para. 18(2)(b), where the Mauritius Strategy provides that the international community should "continue to take, in accordance with the Convention and the Kyoto Protocol, as applicable, steps to address climate change, including through: adaptation and mitigation in accordance with the principle of common but differentiated responsibilities and respective capabilities." Principle 7 of the Rio Declaration is referred to elsewhere in the text, at para. 3 (specific expression of the principle required for small island developing states) and 83 (implementation). See NON-LEGALLY BINDING INSTRUMENT ON ALL TYPES OF FORESTS, preamble para. 4, reaffirming commitment to Rio Principle 7, *supra* note 30. The principle has also been recalled in successive General Assembly resolutions in the context of climate change. See, e.g., GA Res. 54/222 of December 22, 1999, UN Doc. A/RES/54/222, para. 2, and Decision 55/443 of December 20, 2000, GAOR., Supp. 49. See also GA Res. 55/443 of 56/199 of December 21, 2001, UN Doc. 56/199, para. 2 (calling on "all States parties to continue to take effective steps to implement their commitments under the Convention, in accordance with the principle of common but differentiated responsibilities"); 57/257 of December 20, 2002, UN Doc. A/RES/57/257, preamble para. 3; 58/243 of December 23, 2003, UN Doc. A/RES/58/243, preamble para. 2; 59/234 of December 22, 2004, UN Doc. A/RES/59/234, preamble para. 2.
> 
> [48] Vito De Lucia, *Common but Differentiated Responsibility*, in ENCYCLOPEDIA OF EARTH (Cutler J. Cleveland ed., 2007), available at http://www.eoearth.org/article/Common_but_differentiated_responsibility. De Lucia points out that the United States adopted an interpretive statement relating to Rio Principle 7, proving that "the United States does not accept any interpretation of principle 7 that would imply a recognition or acceptance by the United States of any international obligations or liabilities, or any diminution in the responsibilities of developing countries."
> 
> [49] See CULLET, *supra* note 6, at 578–79; MATSUI, *supra* note 36, at 167; RAJAMANI, *supra* note 17, at 158–60; SHELTON, *supra* note 17, at 657. *Cf.* STONE, *supra* note 31, at 300 (denying that a new normative principle is in play).

## 5.2. Differentiation

responsibilities and the special needs of developing countries, particularly on account of their vulnerability to the adverse effects of climate change:

1. The Parties should protect the climate system for the benefit of present and future generations of humankind, on the basis of equity and in accordance with their common but differentiated responsibilities and respective capabilities. Accordingly, the developed country Parties should take the lead in combating climate change and the adverse impacts thereof.

2. The specific needs and special circumstances of developing country Parties, especially those that are particularly vulnerable to the adverse effects of climate change, and of those parties, especially developing country Parties, that would have to bear a disproportionate or abnormal burden under the Convention, should be given full consideration.

The close proximity of the provisions on the special needs of developed countries and the principle of differentiation points to the connection between them. The phrasing of the principle as one intended to guide the parties as well as use of the word *should* rather than *shall* indicate that the obligation to protect the climate system should not be understood in binding legal terms. At the time of drafting, developed countries had argued that developing countries should assume the lead in combating climate change because they – through their high per capita energy consumption – historically bear the main responsibility for the rising concentrations of GHGs.[50] The attempt to include language to this effect was unsuccessful, and the reference to "respective capabilities" was inserted to underline that capabilities – rather than the differential contribution to global emissions – are the reason for developed countries taking the lead in combating climate change.[51] (Language referencing the responsibility of developed countries is found in paragraph three of the preamble, which states "that the largest share of historical and current global emissions of greenhouse gases has originated in developed countries.") The phrase "take the lead in combating climate change" now refers directly to "respective capabilities," not the historically unequal share of GHG emissions, which serves to undermine the responsibility element.

---

[50] Daniel Bodansky, *The United Nations Framework Convention on Climate Change: A Commentary*, 18 YALE JOURNAL OF INTERNATIONAL LAW 451, 498 (1993).
[51] *Id.* at 503. He notes that developing countries wanted developed countries to take the lead because they bear the main responsibility for climate change.

The principle of common but differentiated responsibilities finds concrete application in a number of the Convention's provisions. Thus the commitments enumerated under Article 4 are qualified in that parties are to take into account "their common but differentiated responsibilities." Furthermore, under Article 4(2), only the industrialized countries (Annex I) committed themselves to the "aim of returning... to their 1990 levels" of emissions of GHGs.[52] Similarly, it is the Annex I countries that "shall adopt national policies and take corresponding measures on the mitigation of climate change, by limiting [their] anthropogenic emissions of greenhouse gases."[53] Reporting requirements are differentiated, with Annex I parties also required to report more frequently.[54] Special consideration for the needs of developing countries recurs in a number of articles.[55] Article 4(7) represents an attempt to condition the fulfillment by developing countries of their obligations on financial and technology support by the developed countries.[56] It provides that "the extent to which developing country Parties will effectively implement their commitments under the Convention will depend on the effective implementation by developed country Parties of their commitments under the Convention related to financial resources and transfer of technology and will take fully into account that economic and social development and poverty eradication are the first and overriding priorities of the developing country Parties."

As noted in Chapter 3, differentiation was the key in launching several negotiating processes under the Convention. First, the exclusion from the so-called Berlin Mandate of targets for developing countries was critical in launching the negotiations on what became the Kyoto

---

[52] UNFCCC, Art. 4(2)(b).
[53] *Id.* Art. 4(2)(a).
[54] Under Art. 12, non–Annex I parties have three years to submit their initial communication, or upon the availability of financial resources, sufficient to cover the full cost of reporting, from developed country parties. Least developed country parties may report at their discretion. Annex I parties are required to submit reports on a yearly basis.
[55] *See* Art. 4, sub-paras. 4 (assistance of developing countries particularly vulnerable to adverse effects of climate change), 8 (full consideration of actions necessary to meet the specific needs of developing countries), and 9 (specific needs of least developed countries in relation to funding and technology transfer).
[56] *See* DRUMBL, *supra* note 32. He analyses this and similar provisions in terms of "shared compact" between developed and developing countries. Similar provisions exist in a number of MEAs; *see*, e.g., Art. 20(4) of the Convention on Biological Diversity, which replicates the language of Art. 4(7) of the UNFCCC.

Protocol.[57] Second, the Bali Action Plan of 2007 reiterates the principles and fleshes out their application, providing for mitigation commitments by developed countries and mitigation actions by developing countries, enabled by financial support and technology transfer.[58]

The next two sections of this chapter examine the distributive fairness dimension of common but differentiated responsibilities in the form of technology transfer and financial assistance under the Convention and its Kyoto Protocol.

### 5.3. TECHNOLOGY TRANSFER

The question of technology transfer relates in a number of ways to international environmental law and the principle of common but differentiated responsibilities. First, it is clear that to manage the global environment, it is critical that developing countries are able to develop in a fashion that is less wasteful, resource-intensive, and polluting than the path followed by the industrialized countries. In particular, in the context of climate change, anything like an equalization of per capita GHG emissions at current developed country levels would be disastrous for the global climate. Second, it would be profoundly unfair and inequitable if the peoples of the developing world were to be permanently consigned to a much lower level of economic activity than the rich. The economies – and the emissions – of developing countries will grow, as is fair and equitable. Sustainable development, by integrating social, economic, and environmental concerns, ought to point to a way out of this conundrum. A differentiated approach to obligations considers the relative capacities of the parties as well as their contribution to the problem at hand and guides the assumption of responsibilities for action on this basis. Technology transfer is intended to assist developing countries in achieving the national imperatives of growth and poverty eradication, while also assuming responsibility for combating global environmental degradation.[59] Success in combating climate change will require

---

[57] Decision 1/CP.1, REPORT OF THE PARTIES TO THE CONVENTION ON ITS FIRST SESSION, ADDENDUM, PART II: ACTION TAKEN BY THE PARTIES, FCCC/CP/1995/7/Add.1 (1995).
[58] Decision 1/CP.13, REPORT OF THE CONFERENCE OF THE PARTIES ON ITS THIRTEENTH SESSION, ADDENDUM, PART II: ACTION TAKEN BY THE CONFERENCE OF THE PARTIES, FCCC/CP/2007/6/Add.1 (2008).
[59] Colin M. Alberts, *Technology Transfer and Its Role in International Law: A Structural Dilemma*, 6 HARVARD JOURNAL OF LAW & TECHNOLOGY 63, 65 (1992).

both technological innovation and the rapid and widespread transfer and implementation of environmentally sound technologies (ESTs) for mitigating the effects of GHG emissions and for adapting to climate change.[60]

### 5.3.1. Technology Transfer in Multilateral Environmental Agreements

Provisions relating to the transfer of environmentally sound technology are a staple of multilateral environmental agreements (MEAs) and other instruments. For instance, technology transfer is referred to in Principle 20 of the Stockholm Declaration and Principle 9 of the Rio Declaration. Chapter 34 of Agenda 21 also pertains to technology transfer. The commitments are generally cast in terms of a commitment by developed countries to promote, facilitate, or finance the transfer of environmentally sound technology to developing countries.[61] It appears that generally, the commitments have seldom gone beyond the rhetorical to real transfer and uptake of technologies.[62] Technology transfer was an element of the defunct quest to establish a New International Economic Order.[63] The UN Convention on the Law of the Sea of 1982 also contains far-reaching technology transfer provisions, which can be regarded as the high-water mark in this regard.[64] Important provisions also are contained in the major MEAs adopted at Rio and afterward.[65] The reemergence of technology transfer in the context of MEAs has been traced to the recognition by developed countries that global environmental

---

[60] INTERGOVERNMENTAL PANEL ON CLIMATE CHANGE, SPECIAL REPORT: METHODOLOGICAL AND TECHNOLOGICAL ISSUES IN TECHNOLOGY TRANSFER (Bert Metz et al. eds., 2000).

[61] Gaetan Verhoosel, *Beyond the Unsustainable Rhetoric of Sustainable Development: Transferring Environmentally Sound Technologies*, 11 GEORGETOWN INTERNATIONAL & ENVIRONMENTAL LAW REVIEW 49 (1998).

[62] *Id.* at 49–51.

[63] On the NIEO, *see supra* note 13.

[64] UN Convention on the Law of the Sea, *supra* note 12. The Law of the Sea Convention provides for technology transfer in the context of the protection and preservation of the marine environment, Part XII (Arts. 202–3), and the development and transfer of marine technology, Part XIV (Arts. 266–74). The objective of Part XIV is to enable developing countries to share in the exploration and exploitation of marine resources, particularly with respect to deep seabed mining. The Agreement on the Implementation of Part XI of the Convention modified the scheme with respect to deep seabed mining so that technology transfer is on a commercial, not mandatory, basis, and provides for the protection of intellectual property rights. *Supra* note 12. *See also* D. H. Anderson, *Legal Implications of the Entry into Force of the U. N. Convention on the Law of the Sea*, 44 INTERNATIONAL COMPARATIVE LAW QUARTERLY 313, 318 (1995).

[65] *See*, e.g., Convention on Biological Diversity, *supra* note 20, Art. 16; UNFCCC, Art. 4(5); and Convention to Combat Desertification and Drought, *supra* note 21, Art. 6(e) and 18.

problems require a collective response, which could be facilitated by offering technology transfer to developing countries.[66] With the London and Copenhagen Amendments to the Montreal Protocol, parties were required to take steps to ensure that the "best available, environmentally safe substitutes and related technologies are expeditiously transferred to" (Article 10A) developing-country parties and that those transfers occur under fair and the most favorable conditions. This was coupled with recourse to the Multilateral Fund to meet the incremental costs of compliance in adopting substitutes to ozone-depleting substances.

The Convention contains a number of provisions relating to technology transfer. Article 4(5) provides that

> The developed country Parties... shall take all practicable steps to promote, facilitate and finance, as appropriate, the transfer of, or access to, environmentally sound technologies and know-how to other parties, particularly developing country Parties, to enable them to implement the provisions of the Convention. In this process, the developed country parties shall support the development and enhancement of endogenous capacities and technologies of developing country parties.

A few points may be made in relation to this provision. First, it does not mandate the transfer of technology, but rather requires parties to take "all practicable" steps, and the obligation may consist of facilitating access to EST – not necessarily a very strong or binding duty. Second, the provision applies to transfer from developed to developing countries (vertical transfer) as well as transfer between developed countries (horizontal transfer). Third, it recognizes the need to build capacity in (recipient) developing countries because technology transfer is not limited to the installation of hardware, but includes also the "software," or the knowledge and skills needed to employ the technology.[67]

The commitment to technology transfer in Article 4(5) of the Convention (echoed in Article 10[c] of the Protocol) is cast in general terms and lacks procedures for implementation. It is therefore not surprising that the Conference of the Parties (COP) to the Convention has adopted a series

---

[66] VERHOOSEL, *supra* note 61, at 53–54. *See also* ALBERTS, *supra* note 59, at 65.
[67] *See* CAPACITY-BUILDING IN THE DEVELOPMENT AND TRANSFER OF TECHNOLOGIES, UNFCCC Technical Paper, para. 10, UN Doc. FCCC/TP/2003/1 (2003). *See also* E7 TECHNOLOGY DIFFUSION WORKING GROUP, RENEWABLE ENERGY DIFFUSION: FINAL REPORT para. 2.4 (2003), available at http://www.e7.org/PDFs/e7_Renewable_Energy_Technology_Diffusion_Final_Report.pdf.

of decisions on technology transfer.[68] For instance, the COP has tasked the Subsidiary Body for Scientific and Technological Advice with carrying out a "consultative process" on technology transfer, with the aim of making recommendations to enhance the implementation of Article 4(5).[69] At the request of the COP, the Secretariat of the Convention has carried out a number of activities to promote technology transfer, including the compilation and synthesis of information on financial resources and technology transfer activities and the development of a Web-based technology information system.[70] At Marrakech, the COP also adopted a "framework for meaningful and effective actions to enhance the implementation of article 4(5)" and requested that the GEF provide funding to implement the framework.[71] The COP also established an expert group on technology transfer to analyze and report on means to facilitate technology transfer.[72]

5.3.2. *Technology Transfer in Action*

Technology transfer is best understood as a broad set of processes covering the flows of know-how, experience, and equipment for mitigating and adapting to climate change among different stakeholders such as governments, private sector entities, financial institutions, nongovernmental organizations, and research/education institutions.[73] The terms *diffusion of technologies* and *technology cooperation* are also sometimes used synonymously with *transfer* and connote a "pull" model that is closer to reality than the "push" element associated with transfer as a concept.[74] Importantly, the definition should extend to understanding, utilizing, and even replicating

---

[68] *See*, e.g., Decision 11/CP.1, in Report of the Conference of the Parties on its First Session, Addendum, Part II: Action Taken by the Conference of the Parties, FCCC/CP/1995/7/Add.1 (1995).

[69] Decision 4/CP.4, in Report of the Conference of the Parties on its Fourth Session, Addendum, Part II: Action Taken by the Conference of the Parties, FCCC/CP/1998/16/Add.1 (1999).

[70] Web site of the UNFCCC Secretariat, http://unfccc.int/cooperation_and_support/technology/items/3031.php.

[71] Decision 4/CP.7, in Report of the Conference of the Parties on its Seventh Session, Addendum, Part II: Action Taken by the Conference of the Parties, vol. I, FCCC/CP/2001/13/Add.1.

[72] *Id.*

[73] Intergovernmental Panel on Climate Change, *supra* note 60.

[74] Industry and the private sector are certainly more comfortable with a more decentralized, voluntary, and market-based understanding of diffusion. *See supra* note 67.

## 5.3. Technology Transfer

the technology, including adapting it to local conditions and integrating it with indigenous technologies.[75]

Practically, technology transfer encompasses all of the following: direct purchases, licensing, franchising, foreign direct investment, sale of turnkey plants, joint ventures, subcontracting, cooperative research arrangements, exchange of scientific and technical personnel, science and technology conferences/trade shows/exhibits, open literature, information exchange mechanisms, and official development assistance (ODA).[76] Successful technology transfer is generally viewed as requiring a number of steps, including agreement and establishment of partnerships between stakeholders; technology transfer needs assessment; implementation of technology transfer, including policy measures and capacity building to remove barriers; evaluation and refinement; and replication.[77]

The debate over technology transfer has tended to be entangled in the opposing views of developed countries, which view it as a private sector matter, and developing countries, which assign greater responsibility to the developed-country governments, and to the public sector in general.[78] There has recently been a shift toward a position that recognizes that the greatest potential for technology transfer resides with multinational corporations (MNCs), resulting in more focus on how to create an "enabling environment" for transfer by the private sector.[79] Much, if not most, environmentally sound technology is owned by the private sector, which is also

---

[75] INTERGOVERNMENTAL PANEL ON CLIMATE CHANGE, supra note 60, at 1.

[76] The UNFCCC Secretariat has established a Web-based technology clearinghouse with the aim of improving the flow of, access to, and quality of the information relating to the development and transfer of environmentally sound technologies. The site is available at http://ttclear.unfccc.int/ttclear/jsp/.

[77] CLIMATE TECHNOLOGY INITIATIVE, METHODS FOR CLIMATE CHANGE TECHNOLOGY NEEDS ASSESSMENTS AND IMPLEMENTING ACTIVITIES: DEVELOPING AND TRANSITION COUNTRY APPROACHES AND EXPERIENCES 4 (2002), available at http://ttclear.unfccc.int/ttclear/pdf/TNA/CTI/Tech%20Transfer%20Guidelines-12%20_final_.pdf; TECHNICAL PAPER ON TERMS OF TECHNOLOGY TRANSFER AND KNOW-HOW: BARRIER AND OPPORTUNITIES RELATED TO THE TRANSFER OF TECHNOLOGY, FCCC/TP/1998/1 5 (1998).

[78] VERHOOSEL, supra note 61, at 66.

[79] Id. at 66. See also COMMISSION ON SUSTAINABLE DEVELOPMENT, REPORT OF THE SIXTH SESSION, E/CN.17/1998/20, chap. I, Decision 6/3, repeating the stalemate language of "access to and transfer of environmentally sound technologies ... on favourable terms, including on concessional and preferential terms, as mutually agreed, taking into account the need to protect intellectual property rights" at para. 2(g), but also stating that "governments should try to facilitate the transfer of environmentally sound technologies by creating a policy environment that is conducive to technology-related private sector investments and long-term sustainable development objectives," para. 2(e)(i).

a major innovator, responsible for some 80 percent of research and development spending[80]; in the eyes of developing countries, intellectual property rights present a barrier to technology transfer. In this respect, trade rules also have important implications for technology transfer. The Agreement on Trade-Related Aspects of Intellectual Property Rights (TRIPS) sets out the standards of protection for a comprehensive list of intellectual property rights, including patents and industrial designs. The TRIPS Agreement also includes several provisions on technology transfer, including an obligation of developed countries' governments to provide incentives for their companies to transfer technology to least developed countries (LDCs) (Article 66.2).[81]

Foreign direct investment (FDI) can serve to diffuse and transfer technology, as it not only introduces technologically advanced capital goods, but also so-called technology spillover to national firms through the turnover of skilled personnel, imitation, and more rigorous standards for local suppliers.[82] However, a World Trade Organization study concluded that the impact of trade on technology transfer is mixed, with some goods (machinery and equipment) associated with greater diffusions of technology.[83] With fears that older, dirty technology could be dumped in developing countries, it is worth examining the effect of FDI on the environment. The analysis of the relationship between FDI and the environment breaks down into a number of strands, one focusing on the effect of competition for FDI (the *pollution haven* thesis) and the other investigating the effect on the environment of increased FDI flows.[84] A recent review of the literature suggests that no general conclusion can be drawn concerning the effect of FDI on the

---

[80] UN CONFERENCE ON TRADE AND DEVELOPMENT, INVESTMENT AND TECHNOLOGY POLICIES FOR COMPETITIVENESS: REVIEW OF SUCCESSFUL COUNTRY EXPERIENCES, UNCTAD/ITE/IPC/2003/2 10 (2003).

[81] Due to unhappiness on the part of least developed countries with the implementation of Art. 66(2), it was agreed that a mechanism would be put into place to ensure the monitoring and implementation of the obligation. *See* IMPLEMENTATION-RELATED ISSUES AND CONCERNS, Ministerial Decision, WT/MIN(01)/17, para. 12.2, November 14, 2001.

[82] WORLD TRADE ORGANIZATION SECRETARIAT, TRADE AND TRANSFER OF TECHNOLOGY, WT/WGTTT/W/1 16 (2002) (background note by the Secretariat); ORGANISATION FOR ECONOMIC CO-OPERATION AND DEVELOPMENT, WORKING PARTY ON GLOBAL AND STRUCTURAL POLICIES, ENVIRONMENTAL BENEFITS OF FOREIGN DIRECT INVESTMENT: A LITERATURE REVIEW, ENV/EPOC/GSP(2001)10/FINAL (2002).

[83] WORLD TRADE ORGANIZATION SECRETARIAT, *supra* note 82, at 13–14.

[84] ORGANISATION FOR ECONOMIC CO-OPERATION AND DEVELOPMENT, *supra* note 82, at 6.

environment – the answer is context-dependent.[85] A well-supported conclusion is that host country environmental policies are important in improving the environmental performance of FDI.[86] In addition to the enforcement of national environmental standards, the spread of good practice at the firm level by MNCs may also lead to improved environmental performance at local affiliates, based on home country practices.[87]

At present, there appears to be a dearth of detailed data on the scale of technology transfer in relation to technologies relevant to ESTs in general, and to climate change in particular.[88] The extent of investment in climate-relevant sectors and technology is poorly documented.[89] Nonetheless, an idea of the volume of investment and its trends can be gleaned from the financing provided by the World Bank, GEF, and export credit agencies.

5.3.2.1. **International Institutions and Donors.** The World Bank Group[90] has been criticized for its support of extractive and GHG-intensive industries, including loans for the development of oil and gas reserves. Although the total volume of bank commitments for oil and gas is relatively low, for instance, totaling about US$480 million in 2003, bank investment often serves as a precondition for the participation of private sector lenders, with the result that bank approval can be decisive for a project's financial viability. The *Extractive Industries Review* – a multistakeholder, bank-initiated review of the World Bank Group's activities in the mining, oil, and gas sectors – issued a wide-ranging series of recommendations to improve the Bank's performance with respect to sustainable development and human

---

[85] *Id.* at 7.
[86] JANE ELLIS ET AL., TAKING STOCK OF PROGRESS UNDER THE CLEAN DEVELOPMENT MECHANISM (CDM), COM/ENV/EPOC/IEA/SLT(2004)4/FINAL, OECD 17 (2004).
[87] *See* MANAGING THE ENVIRONMENT ACROSS BORDERS: A STUDY OF TNC AFFILIATES' ENVIRONMENTAL PRACTICES IN CHINA, MALAYSIA AND INDIA (Michael W. Hansen ed., 2002). Key findings are summarized in UN CONFERENCE ON TRADE AND DEVELOPMENT, MANAGING THE ENVIRONMENT ACROSS BORDERS, UNCTAD/ITE/IPC/MISC.12 (2002).
[88] INTERGOVERNMENTAL PANEL ON CLIMATE CHANGE, *supra* note 60. The Intergovernmental Panel on Climate Change's study provides aggregate data for technology transfer by source, but not climate-specific data.
[89] TRENDS OF FINANCIAL FLOWS AND TERMS AND CONDITIONS EMPLOYED BY THE MULTILATERAL LENDING INSTITUTIONS, FCCC/TP/1997/1 10 (1997).
[90] Consisting of the International Development Association, the International Bank for Reconstruction and Development, the International Finance Corporation, and the Multilateral Investment Guarantee Association.

rights criteria.[91] Noting that renewable energy made up only 6 percent of the bank's energy portfolio, the *Review* recommended that the Bank phase out investments in oil production by 2008 and devote its resources to investments in renewable energy resource development, clean energy technology, and energy efficiency projects.[92] During the period 1990 to 2005, total World Bank Group commitments in the energy sector totaled $56 billion, of which US$2.5 billion was for new renewables, US$4.3 billion was for large hydropower, and US$2.2 billion was for energy efficiency.[93] In other words, commitments for new renewables, that is, excluding large hydropower, constituted about 4.5 percent of energy sector commitments.

Although the Bank declined to implement the recommendation of the *Review* to phase out investment in the hydrocarbons sector, it pledged, in 2004, to increase its commitments for energy efficiency and new renewable energy – defined as biomass, solar, wind, geothermal, and hydro with a capacity of less than 10 MW – by 20 percent per year between 2005 and 2009.[94] From a commitment of US$459 million in 2004, the investment in new renewable and energy efficiency rose to almost US$1.7 billion in 2008.[95] The share of renewable energy (including large hydro) and energy efficiency constituted 35 percent of the bank's energy lending in 2007.

There are considerable difficulties in arriving at numbers for climate change-related ODA. This stems from a general lack of available data, as well as problems defining what expenditures should be considered as climate-related. A study of the allocation of ODA for mitigation-related projects finds a significant increase in such financing, from around US$1 billion per year

---

[91] *See* EXTRACTIVE INDUSTRIES REVIEW, STRIKING A BETTER BALANCE – THE WORLD BANK GROUP AND EXTRACTIVE INDUSTRIES: STRIKING A BETTER BALANCE, Vol. 1 (2004). *See also* WORLD BANK MANAGEMENT RESPONSE TO THE EXTRACTIVE INDUSTRIES REVIEW, September 17, 2004. The response suggests that the World Bank Group (WBG) agrees with a number of the recommendations. However, the WBG vowed to remain engaged in oil and coal, while agreeing to increase investment in "new" renewable (including hydro 10 MW or smaller) energy and energy efficiency by 20 percent for five years.

[92] EXTRACTIVE INDUSTRIES REVIEW, *supra* note 91, at 65–66.

[93] WORLD BANK, CLEAN ENERGY AND DEVELOPMENT: TOWARDS AN INVESTMENT FRAMEWORK 110–11 (2006).

[94] *See* WORLD BANK, *supra* note 91.

[95] *World Bank Group Renewable Energy & Energy Efficiency Funding Rises 87 Percent*, press release, World Bank, October 2, 2008. The World Bank uses a baseline commitment of US$209 million (equal to the average of the previous three years) for calculating its 20 percent target. The reason given for selecting this baseline methodology is to permit a meaningful interpretation of investment trends that would balance the "lumpy" nature of investments in the energy sector.

in the early 2000s to US$10 billion by 2006, with hydropower accounting for a large share.[96] The database tracking ODA provided by the donor countries of the Organisation for Economic Co-operation and Development (OECD) suggests that the amount flowing to all climate change-related activities, that is, adaptation and mitigation, totaled about US$7.2 billion between 2005 and 2007.[97]

The GEF is an important channel for multilateral assistance for global environmental problems. Since its inception in 1991 until 2007, the GEF has generated US$17 billion in assistance for climate change projects, consisting of $2.4 billion in GEF investment and $14.6 billion in cofinancing from the World Bank, regional development banks, and bilateral funds.[98] About half the amount has been allocated to renewable energy, with a significant share also for energy efficiency projects. The GEF climate change portfolio is organized into four areas: removing barriers to energy efficiency and energy conservation, promoting the adoption of renewable energy by removing barriers and reducing implementation costs, reducing the long-term costs of low-GHG-emitting energy technologies, and supporting the development of sustainable transport. Given the limited funds at its disposal, the GEF approach to climate change is, in large part, devoted to technology diffusion – removing barriers to the adoption of energy efficiency and renewable energy technology, reducing implementation costs for renewable energy, and reducing long-term technology costs by accelerating technological development and increasing the market share of low-GHG-emitting technologies.[99]

[96] ROBERT HICKS ET AL., GREENING AID? EXPLAINING ENVIRONMENTAL FOREIGN ASSISTANCE (2008).
[97] Author's own calculation using the online OECD.Stat Creditor Reporting Service, retrieving data for the "climate change" marker. Available at http://stats.oecd.org/WBOS/Index.aspx?DatasetCode=CRSNEW. An earlier report prepared by the Development Assistance Committee of the OECD put the amount committed to bilateral ODA for climate change–related activities at US$8.1 billion for the period 1998–2000, or 7.2 percent of total bilateral ODA. See OECD/DAC, AID TARGETING THE OBJECTIVES OF THE RIO CONVENTIONS: A CONTRIBUTION BY THE DAC SECRETARIAT FOR THE INFORMATION OF PARTICIPANTS AT THE WORLD SUMMIT ON SUSTAINABLE DEVELOPMENT, Johannesburg, August 2002.
[98] GLOBAL ENVIRONMENT FACILITY, INVESTING IN OUR PLANET: GEF ANNUAL REPORT 2006–2007 31 (2008)
[99] GEF, TRANSFER OF ENVIRONMENTALLY SOUND TECHNOLOGIES: THE GEF EXPERIENCE (2008). See also ERIC MARTINOT & OMAR MCDOOM, GLOBAL ENVIRONMENT FACILITY, PROMOTING ENERGY EFFICIENCY AND RENEWABLE ENERGY: GEF CLIMATE CHANGE PROJECTS AND IMPACTS (2000). Martinot and McDoom, at 35, conclude that "overall,

The export credit agencies of the OECD countries have, on average, provided around US$90 billion in loans, credit guarantees, and investment insurance per year to developing countries.[100] These entities are also significant actors in financing energy technologies. For instance, from 2000 to 2004, the percentage exposure (loan guarantees and loans) of the U.S. Ex-Im Bank has been around 10 to 14 percent for power projects – largely made up of gas turbine equipment, with no wind, solar, or other nonhydro renewables listed – and 10 percent for oil and gas during the same period.[101]

5.3.2.2. Clean Development Mechanism. The Clean Development Mechanism (CDM) has been hailed as an innovative instrument to bring private capital into the technology transfer process.[102] As stated in Article 12(2) of the Kyoto Protocol, the twin purposes of the CDM are to "assist Parties not included in Annex I in achieving sustainable development" and to assist Annex I parties in achieving their emission limitation and reduction commitments. Technology transfer is a necessary ingredient for sustainable development. With respect to the determination of what constitutes sustainable development, the Marrakech Accords provide that "it is the host Party's prerogative to confirm whether a Clean Development Mechanism project activity assists it in achieving sustainable development."[103] Host countries could consider transfer of technology as one possible criterion of technology transfer. Some countries have identified preferred areas for CDM projects in an attempt to promote investment in projects with multiple benefits.[104]

---

prospects for sustainability and replication of GEF climate change projects are still mixed and uncertain."

[100] CÉDRIC PHILIBERT, OECD ENVIRONMENT DIRECTORATE/INTERNATIONAL ENERGY AGENCY, INTERNATIONAL ENERGY TECHNOLOGY COLLABORATION AND CLIMATE CHANGE MITIGATION, COM/ENV/EPOC/IEA/SLT(2004)1 16 (2004).

[101] EXPORT-IMPORT BANK, 2004 FINANCIAL REPORT (2004). The financial reports for the years 2000–2004 provide a breakdown of items covered by country and show no listing for renewable energy, excluding hydro, which may have been reported under headings for generators. In its 2000 financial report, the bank stated that its environmental portfolio amounted to over US$2 billion, out of a total of over US$61 billion. A similar breakdown is not presented in subsequent reports. Reports are available at http://www.exim.gov.

[102] VERHOOSEL, supra note 61, at 70.

[103] Decision 16/CP/7, in REPORT OF THE CONFERENCE OF THE PARTIES ON ITS SEVENTH SESSION, ADDENDUM, PART II: ACTION TAKEN BY THE CONFERENCE OF THE PARTIES, vol. II, FCCC/CP/2001/13/Add.2 (2002).

[104] E.g., the rules applicable to CDM projects provide that "priority areas for CDM projects in China are energy efficiency improvement, development and utilization of

## 5.3. Technology Transfer

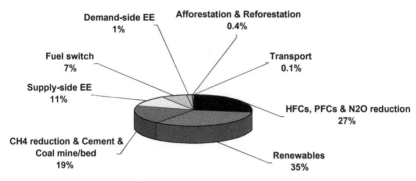

FIGURE 5.1. CDM portfolio: Projected share of total CERs in 2012 by project type. *Source:* CDM Pipeline, Jørgen Fenhann, UNEP Risøe Centre (2008).

The value of CDM credits traded in 2007 amounted to US$8.2 billion.[105] And since CDM finance makes up an estimated one-sixth to one-eighth of total project cost, the amount of investment stimulated by CDM could be roughly in the range of US$48 billion to US$64 billion.[106] As these figures show, the market for credits from CDM is quite substantial. After a slow start, energy efficiency and renewable energy projects are now emerging as the most common type of CDM projects and are also projected to account for the largest share of CDM credits, known as certified emission reductions (CERs). Volumes transacted from clean energy projects (renewable energy, fuel switching, and energy efficiency) achieved 64 percent market share, compared to just 33 percent in 2006 and 14 percent in 2005 (Figure 5.1 provides 2012 projections).[107] However, energy efficiency projects at large industrial facilities accounted for the lion's share of these emission reduction transactions.

This development is encouraging, as projects with limited technology transfer potential had earlier dominated the market. These projects – such

---

new and renewable energy, and methane recovery and utilization." *See* Art. 4, Measures for the Operation and Management of Clean Development Mechanism Projects in China, National Development and Reform Commission, November 21, 2005, available at http://cdm.ccchina.gov.cn/english/main.asp?ColumnId=27. More concretely, the rules also provide for very different government shares of the proceeds of the credits – taxation – for different types of project. Thus, according to Art. 24 of the rules, the government share from HFC and PFC projects is 65 percent, while for projects falling into the preferred category, it is only 2 percent.

[105] KARAN CAPOOR & PHILIPPE AMBROSI, WORLD BANK, STATE AND TRENDS OF THE CARBON MARKET 2008 1 (2008).
[106] The estimate on the CDM share of project financing is from ELLIS ET AL., *supra* note 86, at 18.
[107] KAPOOR & AMBROSI, *supra* note 105, at 28.

as methane capture from landfills or the destruction of HFC-23, an industrial waste gas – are outside the energy sector and do not offer significant benefits in terms of technology transfer.[108] HFC-23 is a waste gas created in the production of HCFC-22, a gas used in air-conditioners and itself a potent ozone-depleting substance. This gave rise to a perverse incentive – a CDM project at a new HCFC plant offered potentially hundreds of millions of dollars in credits but at the same time worked at cross purposes with the effort to cut down on substances that deplete the ozone layer.[109]

High transaction costs, partly the result of the complicated approval process, have dogged the CDM. The impact of transaction costs on a given project is largely determined by its size.[110] For large projects, which generate many CERs, the ratio of transaction costs to total costs will be small and will thus not be a major determinant of project feasibility. However, for small, community-scale projects that may yield local sustainable development benefits, transaction costs constitute a more important barrier. Among the solutions to accommodate small-scale projects within the CDM framework are simplified rules as well as bundling of smaller projects, which consists of aggregating several activities under one CDM project.[111] Bundling is also permissible for large-scale projects, and "project activities under a programme of activities can be registered" as a single project.[112] However,

---

[108] These projects are profitable due to the very high greenhouse warming potential (GWP) of the gases involved, yielding very high carbon-equivalent reductions for very low cost. For more details on GWP, see Chapter 1. $N_2O$-reduction projects, related to adipic acid production, also attracted attention on the grounds of the high GWP of $N_2O$ and low costs. With the introduction of control technologies, nitrous oxide emissions from adipic acid production have fallen significantly in developed countries. See INTERGOVERNMENTAL PANEL ON CLIMATE CHANGE, CLIMATE CHANGE 2001: MITIGATION, CONTRIBUTION OF WG III TO THE THIRD ASSESSMENT REPORT 213 (Ogunlade Davidson & Bert Metz eds., 2001).

[109] The situation is made worse in that substitutes for HCFC, which is used in home air conditioners, are not cheap. This comes at a time when sales of air conditioners are soaring in China and other developing countries. See Keith Bradsher, Moving Faster on Refrigerants, NEW YORK TIMES, March 15, 2007.

[110] AXEL MICHAELOWA & MARCUS STRONZIK, TRANSACTION COSTS OF THE KYOTO MECHANISMS, Discussion Paper, Hamburg Institute of International Economics 175 (2002).

[111] See Decision 17/CP.7, supra note 103, and Decision 21/CP.8, in REPORT OF THE CONFERENCE OF THE PARTIES ON ITS EIGHTH SESSION, ADDENDUM, PART II: ACTION TAKEN BY THE PARTIES, vol. III, FCCC/CP/2002/7/Add.3.

[112] Decision 7/CMP.1, in REPORT OF THE CONFERENCE OF THE PARTIES SERVING AS THE MEETING OF THE PARTIES TO THE KYOTO PROTOCOL AT ITS FIRST SESSION, ADDENDUM, PART II: ACTION TAKEN BY THE CONFERENCE OF THE PARTIES SERVING AS THE MEETING OF THE PARTIES TO THE KYOTO PROTOCOL, paras. 20–21, FCCC/KP/CMP/2005/8/Add.1.

national or regional policies or standards do not qualify as CDM projects.[113] The implementation of an air-conditioner efficiency standard, or a similar measure, in a developing country is thus not eligible under the CDM.

Every CDM project must be based on a project-specific baseline methodology approved by the Executive Board. A baseline is needed because the CERs generated by a project are calculated by comparing the emissions of the CDM project with the emissions under a business-as-usual scenario.[114] In other words, for a wind farm project that feeds electricity to the grid, the emissions intensity of power supplied from the grid is the baseline against which credits for the project are calculated. The baseline calculation basically involves a counterfactual analysis to establish the situation that would have obtained in the absence of the project activity. Deciding what should be the baseline is not necessarily straightforward. If it is set too low, assuming little or no technological advance, the project developer will reap an unjustified advantage. If the baseline standard is too stringent – mandating "best available technology" when the prevailing standard is less advanced technology – it would hinder, rather than promote, the transfer of cleaner technology to developing countries.[115] The three alternative approaches prescribed for establishing a baseline methodology are strict but not overly stringent.[116] Methodologies are quite specific, for example, "landfill gas capture and electricity generation projects where landfill gas

---

For an examination of what could fall under the "programmatic CDM," see JANE ELLIS, ISSUES RELATING TO IMPLEMENTING "PROGRAMMATIC CDM," available at http://www.oecd.org/dataoecd/42/31/36278652.pdf.

[113] Decision 7/CMP.1, supra note 112, at para. 20.

[114] Axel Michaelowa, Determination of Baselines and Additionality for the CDM: A Crucial Element of the Credibility of the Climate Regime, in CLIMATE CHANGE AND CARBON MARKETS: A HANDBOOK OF EMISSIONS REDUCTIONS MECHANISMS 287, 290–92 (Farhana Yamin ed., 2005).

[115] Michael A. Toman, Establishing and Operating the Clean Development Mechanism, in CLIMATE CHANGE ECONOMICS AND POLICY: AN RFF ANTHOLOGY 216, 220 (Michael A. Toman ed., 2001).

[116] Decision 17/CP.7, supra note 118, annex, para. 48(c): "The average emissions of similar project activities undertaken in the previous five years, in social, economic, environmental and technological circumstances, and whose performance is among the top 20 per cent of their category." See also elaboration in REPORT OF THE EIGHTH MEETING OF THE CDM EXECUTIVE BOARD, Annex 1 (clarifications on issues relating to baseline and monitoring methodologies), March 19–20, 2003, available at http://cdm.unfccc.int/EB/Meetings/008/repan1.pdf. Further guidance is provided in REPORT OF THE TENTH MEETING OF THE CDM EXECUTIVE BOARD, Annex 1 (further clarification on methodological issues), available at http://cdm.unfccc.int/EB/Meetings/010/eb10repan1.pdf.

capture is not mandated by law."[117] A project developer wishing to establish a project under slightly different circumstances would need to draw up a new methodology, and submit it for approval to the Executive Board. This entails added expense, because once approved methodologies are publicly available, others can use them, but without sharing in the cost of their development, which may act as a disincentive. Sequestration projects – afforestation and reforestation are permitted under the CDM – are among the limited opportunities available in LDCs, which lack the industrial infrastructure for emission mitigation projects. Although such projects may yield a range of benefits, direct technology transfer is not among them.

To safeguard the environmental integrity of the Protocol, CDM projects must result in real, measurable GHG reductions that are "additional to any that would occur in the absence of the certified project activity."[118] The interpretation of this requirement has given rise to some uncertainty,[119] but the responsible subsidiary organ has issued a step-by-step guideline that makes clear that a rigorous approach to additionality will be applied.[120] Pursuant to demonstrating additionality, a significant number of CDM projects submitted for approval have referred to low penetration rates, or barriers to deployment, of the technology in question.[121] Thus, if a developer can show that the proposed technology has not previously been deployed

---

[117] See "Approved Baseline Methodology AM0010," available at http://cdm.unfccc.int/ UserManagement/FileStorage/CDMWF_AM_675903718.

[118] See Kyoto Protocol, supra note 18, Art. 12(5)(c). See also Decision 17/CP.7, REPORT OF THE CONFERENCE OF THE PARTIES ON ITS SEVENTH SESSION, ADDENDUM, PART II: ACTION TAKEN BY THE CONFERENCE OF THE PARTIES, vol. II, annex, para. 43, FCCC/CP/2001/13/Add.2, which provides that "a CDM project activity is additional if the anthropogenic emissions of greenhouse gases by sources are reduced below those that would have occurred in the absence of the... CDM project activity."

[119] Under the stricter standard recommended by the Methodology Panel, the additionality assessment must show that the proposed CDM project would not have occurred in the absence of the CDM. See REPORT OF THE SIXTH MEETING OF THE METHODOLOGIES PANEL, July 7–8, available at http://cdm.unfccc.int/Panels/meth/Report_06_rev.pdf. For a discussion of additionality and the work of the subsidiary organs protocol, see JANE ELLIS, EVALUATING EXPERIENCE WITH ELECTRICITY-GENERATING GHG MITIGATION PROJECTS, COM/ENV/EPOC/IEA/SLT(2003)8 12–16 (2003). For a critical view of the approach to additionality, see Editor's Note, CDM: Birth or Abortion, 9(2) JOINT IMPLEMENTATION QUARTERLY (2003), available at http://jiq.wiwo.nl/2-2003.pdf.

[120] REPORT OF THE SIXTEENTH MEETING OF THE CDM EXECUTIVE BOARD, ANNEX 1, 21–22 OCTOBER 2004, available at http://cdm.unfccc.int/EB/Meetings. One of the steps that may be used in demonstrating additionality is a barrier analysis, including whether the proposed project faces technological barriers or is a "first of its kind" in the host country.

[121] See ELLIS, supra note 119, at 18–19, setting out projects and additionality assessments.

in a similar market in similar circumstances, this can help the project clear the "additionality" hurdle.

CDM investment holds considerable potential with respect to the transfer of low- and no-GHG-emitting technology, particularly to the extent that it can stimulate or augment private sector inflows.[122] The analysis of the methodological aspects of the CDM has shown how technology considerations are central to its implementation. However, the very rigor of the methodologies has served to constrain – if for good reason – the application of the CDM. Being predicated on efficiency, it has also meant that investors have sought out those projects offering the highest volume of CERs at the lowest cost, but not necessarily providing broader sustainable development benefits. If these projects capture the market, the twin promise of the CDM – GHG mitigation at low cost and sustainable development in the host countries – will have been only partially fulfilled. This has implications for questions of equity. In addition, the private sector orientation of the CDM has also meant that investment has flowed to those countries that are already beneficiaries of FDI and have in place the required enabling environment. For instance, in 2007, Africa accounted for only 5 percent of credits transacted, a figure that is not set to change substantially by the end of the Kyoto first commitment period in 2012.[123] The CDM is, of course, concerned with mitigation, but it points to a broader concern – the focus on mitigation technology at the expense of adaptation technology. This also raises fairness questions because the adaptive capacity of developing countries is generally much weaker than that of developed countries, yet they are projected to bear the brunt of climate change impacts. There exists a need to better understand adaptation technology and to promote transfer and access to it.

## 5.4. SHARING THE BURDEN: THE GLOBAL ENVIRONMENT FACILITY AND THE CLIMATE CHANGE FUNDS

This section examines the assistance provided to developing countries by the GEF and the climate change funds established under the Convention and the Kyoto Protocol, namely, the Special Climate Change Fund (SCCF), the Least Developed Countries Fund (LDCF), and the Adaptation Fund

---

[122] ELLIS ET AL., *supra* note 86, at 7; Malte Schneider et al., *Understanding the CDM's Contribution to Technology Transfer* 36 ENERGY POLICY 2930 (2008).

[123] KAPOOR & AMBROSI, *supra* note 105, at 25.

(AF). The establishment of clean technology funds under the umbrella of the World Bank is also discussed.

The GEF stands out as a unique experiment in the international environmental arena, not only as a only source of funding dedicated to global environmental problems, but also in its governance structure.[124] It supports projects to achieve agreed global environmental benefits in the field of climate change, biodiversity, international waters, protection of the ozone layer, land degradation, and persistent organic pollutants.[125] Since its inception in 1991 until 2007, the GEF has made US$7.4 billion in grants and generated US$28 billion in cofinancing for projects in developing countries and countries with economies in transition.[126] The GEF stands as a hybrid – combining in its structure and decision-making procedures elements typical of UN entities and those associated with the Bretton Woods institutions.

---

[124] A good overview of the establishment and key institutional features of the GEF can be found in LAURENCE BOISSON DE CHAZOURNES, THE GLOBAL ENVIRONMENT FACILITY AS A PIONEERING INSTITUTION: LESSONS LEARNED AND LOOKING AHEAD, Working Paper 19, GEF (2003). Rich and comprehensive accounts of establishment and restructuring of the GEF are contained in two working papers prepared by HELEN SJÖBERG, RESTRUCTURING THE GEF, Working Paper 13 (1999) (hereinafter referred to as SJÖBERG, RESTRUCTURING) and HELEN SJÖBERG, FROM IDEA TO REALITY: THE CREATION OF THE GLOBAL ENVIRONMENT FACILITY, Working Paper 10 (1994) (hereinafter referred to as SJÖBERG, CREATION), both of which are available on the GEF Web site. *See also* Jacob Werksman, *Consolidating Governance of the Global Commons: Insights from the Global Environment Facility*, 6 YEARBOOK OF INTERNATIONAL ENVIRONMENTAL LAW 27–63 (1995); Alan S. Miller, *The Global Environment Facility and the Search for Financial Strategies to Foster Sustainable Development*, 24 VERMONT LAW REVIEW 1229 (2000); and Andrew Jordan, *Paying the Incremental Costs of Global Environmental Protection: The Evolving Role of GEF*, ENVIRONMENT, July 1994, at 12.

[125] INSTRUMENT FOR THE ESTABLISHMENT OF THE RESTRUCTURED GLOBAL ENVIRONMENT FACILITY, as amended by the Second GEF Assembly, Beijing 2002, Art. 1(2), available at http://thegef.org/GEF_Instrument3.pdf.

[126] *See supra* note 98. In the pilot phase, the thematic areas were confined to four: climate change, biodiversity, international waters, and ozone depletion. Calls to include desertification were resisted by the developed countries, which feared that this would introduce a broader agenda, to the detriment of the four thematic areas. *See* SJÖBERG, RESTRUCTURING, at 19–20. The compromise solution, reflected in the 1994 restructuring, provided that the GEF would cover "the agreed incremental costs of activities concerning land degradation, primarily desertification and deforestation, as they relate to the four focal areas that shall be eligible for funding." Amendments adopted by the Second GEF Assembly in 2002 extended land degradation and persistent organic pollutants. *See* Second Assembly of the GEF, Beijing, China, October 16–18, 2002, PROPOSED AMENDMENTS TO THE INSTRUMENT, GEF/A.2/9, available at http://www.thegef.org/participants/Assembly/2nd_Assembly/2nd_assembly.html. *See also* Stockholm Convention on Persistent Organic Pollutants, May 22, 2001, Art. 13(6), concerning the financial mechanism for the Convention.

Its serves to secure "global public goods" by seeking to protect those features of the planet in which there is a collective interest.[127] It also forms a key link in the bargaining between developed and developing countries relating to the combating of global environmental problems. Thus one chronicler of the GEF has stated that[128]

> the main purpose of the GEF from a developing country perspective is to provide the financial means to incorporate measures for the global environment as part of other plans and activities. It enables developing countries to go beyond being part of rule-making at the international level, to become active participants in multilateral efforts to protect the global environment. And in those global environmental areas covered by a convention, GEF funding enables developing country signatories to fulfill their obligations.

The genesis for the GEF is usually traced back to a 1989 French proposal, backed by a substantial financial commitment, to establish a fund of voluntary grants dedicated to the global environment.[129] In its pilot phase, from 1991 to 1994, the GEF was characterized by a loose institutional structure, heavily influenced by the World Bank and the donor countries, with limited participation from developing countries.[130] It has been noted that donor countries also saw in the GEF a means to forestall a proliferation of funds as well as discussions on alternative funding in the runup to the UN Conference on Environment and Development (UNCED).[131] Some saw the pilot phase as the first step in the direction of a more ambitious institution, while others were adamant that it should only be temporary, filling the gap until the World Bank integrated environmental matters into its activities.[132] Observers have stressed that whatever its shortcomings, the pilot phase saw the establishment of the GEF in record time, despite the different and conflicting views with respect to formal structure and future of the entity.[133] During the pilot phase, and as it has continued to do, the Bank acted as

---

[127] BOISSON DE CHAZOURNES, *supra* note 124, at 1; SJÖBERG, RESTRUCTURING, at 52.
[128] SJÖBERG, RESTRUCTURING, at 52.
[129] BOISSON DE CHAZOURNES, *supra* note 124, at 5.
[130] The GEF was legally established by World Bank resolution 91-5 of March 1991, and the bank controlled the trust fund, which put it in a very strong position. *See* BOISSON DE CHAZOURNES, *supra* note 124, at 8.
[131] *See* SJÖBERG, RESTRUCTURING, at 7, and also JORDAN, *supra* note 124, at 12, 19.
[132] *See* SJÖBERG, CREATION, at 28–29. *See also* BOISSON DE CHAZOURNES, *supra* note 124, at 6, and SJÖBERG, RESTRUCTURING, at 7.
[133] BOISSON DE CHAZOURNES, *supra* note 124, at 6.

trustee for the GEF and, with the UN Development Programme (UNDP) and the UN Environment Programme (UNEP), was also one of the implementing agencies responsible for drawing up proposals and implementing projects.

With the preparations for UNCED, and then its outcome, the dynamics around the GEF changed considerably. From a loose, collaborative structure between the bank, UNDP, and UNEP, the GEF was tossed into the thick of environmental politics between industrialized and developing countries, which wanted a greater say in how the fund was run. With disenchantment over the failure to match the lofty goals in Agenda 21 with new and additional resources, as well as the rejection by the donor countries of new funds for the conventions then being negotiated, developing countries underlined that the GEF would have to be restructured.[134] In particular, they stressed that if the GEF was to serve as the financial mechanism for the Framework Convention, it would be required to "have an equitable and balanced representation of all Parties within a transparent system of governance."[135]

The arguments of the developing countries concerning balanced representation and accountability were designed to shift an institution characterized by the World Bank formula of one dollar, one vote toward the more universal decision-making process associated with the UN. Framed in political terms, developing countries wished to have an equal say and employed the language of accountability, transparency, and equitable representation; donor nations naturally wished to retain control over the resources they provided and, to this end, fell back on arguments of efficiency and effectiveness. An example for more balanced representation already existed in the form of the Montreal Protocol Multilateral Fund, established in 1991, whose executive committee is evenly divided among developed and developing countries.[136] After a two-year negotiating process, which concluded in March 1994, there was agreement on a restructured institution that retained elements of the pilot phase, yet moved decisively in the direction of universal participation, but without adopting the UN model. Participation in the GEF is open to any state member of the UN or any of its specialized

---

[134] *Id.* at 8.
[135] *See* UNFCCC, Arts. 11(2) and 21(3).
[136] Details of procedures and voting at http://www.multilateralfund.org/executive_committee.htm. *See also* UNEP/OzL.Pro.2/3.

## 5.4. Sharing the Burden

agencies.[137] The incoming chairman of the GEF, Mr. Mohamed T. El-Ashry, concluded that "the revised institutional framework represents a change from old-style assistance to new-style cooperation."[138]

The restructured GEF was not established as an international organization under treaty, but rather, on a special legal basis, where the states concerned gave their political assent to the Instrument for the Establishment of the Restructured Global Environment Facility, which in turn was adopted by the governing bodies of the three implementing agencies, with the latter step serving to establish the new GEF.[139] Of the bodies established by the Instrument, the most important is the Council, which serves as the main executive organ of the GEF.[140] Its composition proved contentious, with donor countries and developing countries vying for control. The 32 seats on the Council are split between developed countries (14) and developing countries (16) and countries with economies in transition (2), that is to say, nations of Eastern and Central Europe and the former Soviet Union.[141] Decisions are to be made on the basis of consensus,[142] failing which a formal vote may be held, in which case a double-weighted majority is necessary, consisting of "an affirmative vote representing both a 60 percent majority of the total number of Participants and a 60 percent majority of the total contributions."[143] The restructuring also saw the formalization of the legal relationship between the GEF, the COP, and the Biodiversity Convention, provided for in the conventions and the Instrument.[144]

---

[137] *See* INSTRUMENT FOR THE ESTABLISHMENT OF THE RESTRUCTURED GLOBAL ENVIRONMENT FACILITY, *supra* note 125, para. 7.
[138] Mohamed T. El-Ashry, *The New GEF*, ENVIRONMENT, July 1994, at 36.
[139] BOISSON DE CHAZOURNES, *supra* note 124, at 10.
[140] Provision is also made for an assembly, consisting of representatives of all participating states, which meets every four years with the broad mandate to review the general policies and operations of the GEF; a Scientific and Technical Advisory Panel (STAP); and a "functionally independent" Secretariat. This latter development saw the Secretariat remain housed in the World Bank for administrative purposes, but not controled by it. *See* BOISSON DE CHAZOURNES, *supra* note 124, at 12.
[141] INSTRUMENT FOR THE ESTABLISHMENT OF THE RESTRUCTURED GLOBAL ENVIRONMENT FACILITY, *supra* note 125, at para. 16.
[142] *Id.* at para. 25(b).
[143] *Id.* at para. 25(c)(i).
[144] *See* UNFCCC, Art. 11(3); Convention on Biological Diversity, *supra* note 20, Art. 21(1); and INSTRUMENT FOR THE ESTABLISHMENT OF THE RESTRUCTURED GLOBAL ENVIRONMENT FACILITY, *supra* note 125, at para. 20(g). For an overview process and legal issues involved in formalizing the relationship between the GEF and the COPs, *see* BOISSON DE CHAZOURNES, *supra* note 124, at 21. A legal opinion prepared by the UN Legal Counsel, dated August

Paragraph 9 of the GEF Instrument states that where the GEF serves as the financial mechanisms of, respectively, the Framework Convention, the Biodiversity Convention, and the Stockholm Convention, "the Council shall act in conformity with the policies, program priorities and eligibility criteria decided by the Conference of the Parties for the purposes of the convention concerned."[145] The Memorandum of Understanding between the COP and the Council of the GEF, which gives effect to the respective roles and responsibilities of the two bodies, provides that the COP decides on "the policies, programme priorities and eligibility criteria related to the Convention for the financial mechanism which shall function under the guidance of and be accountable to the COP."[146] It also states that "the Council will ensure the effective operation of the GEF as a source of funding activities for the purposes of the Convention *in conformity with the guidance of the COP.*"[147] In practice, the COP issues so-called guidance, while the GEF establishes operational procedures and detailed project eligibility rules for resource allocation. Accountability of the GEF to the COP takes the form of regular reporting on activities and resource programming proposals. Overall, while developing countries may use their clout in the COPs to draw up fairly expansive guidance, in the GEF, it is the donor countries that set the agenda in the interpretation of COP guidance and its translation into concrete policies. In particular, groups of countries, such as small

23, 1994, noted that the GEF's parent institutions (the World Bank, UNDP, and UNEP) had not bestowed on it the legal capacity of entering into legally binding arrangements or agreements, with the consequence that any such agreements approved by the GEF Council would have to be formalized by the World Bank. *See* UN Doc. A/AC.237/74, annex, paras. 19–19. *See also* Robin R. Churchill & Geir Ulfstein, *Autonomous Institutional Arrangements in Multilateral Environmental Agreements: A Little-Noticed Phenomenon in International Law,* 94 AMERICAN JOURNAL OF INTERNATIONAL LAW 623, 650–51 (2000).

[145] Similarly, para. 20(h) of the INSTRUMENT FOR THE ESTABLISHMENT OF THE RESTRUCTURED GLOBAL ENVIRONMENT FACILITY, *supra* note 125, states that the Council shall "ensure that GEF-financed activities relating to the conventions ... conform with the policies, program priorities and eligibility criteria decided by the Conference of the Parties for the purposes of the convention concerned." The same language is echoed in para. 26, which provides that the "Council shall ensure the effective operation of the GEF as a source of funding activities.... The use of the GEF resources for purposes of such conventions shall be in conformity with the policies, program priorities and eligibility criteria decided by the Conference of the Parties of each of those conventions."

[146] Decision 12/CP.2, in REPORT OF THE CONFERENCE OF THE PARTIES ON ITS SECOND SESSION, ADDENDUM, PART II: ACTION TAKEN BY THE CONFERENCE OF THE PARTIES, *Memorandum of Understanding between the Conference of the Parties and the Council of the Global Environment Facility,* para. 2, FCCC/CP/1996/15/Add.1 (2002).

[147] *Id.* at para. 4 (emphasis added).

## 5.4. Sharing the Burden

island and African states, criticize the GEF for not adhering more closely to the COP guidance. In legal terms, it is clear that the GEF Instrument and the Memorandum of Understanding (MOU) envisage the GEF being subject to the guidance of the COP, but not to function under its authority. This is an important distinction, and the provision that the GEF must act "in conformity" with such guidance does not alter the relationship much. The word *guidance* connotes something of a broader and policy-oriented character, contrasting, for instance, with *decisions, conclusions*, or *resolutions*.

The GEF exists to fund only the *incremental cost* of projects to achieve global environmental benefits.[148] The incremental cost is understood as that portion of the costs of a project conferring global benefits but which would not normally be in the interest of the host country to fund.[149] While relatively straightforward in the abstract, it is more difficult to apply the concept in practice, and doing so has proved controversial. Arriving at a baseline, on the basis of which the incremental amount is assessed, may involve subjective judgments.[150] For instance, how does one assess what is in a country's national interest, or what course of action a country would have pursued? Critics have also questioned the feasibility, in physical and biological terms, of differentiating between national and global benefits.[151] To this the response is "that this is a conceptual distinction, or analytic tool, for the purpose of decisions on funding. It does not mean that in practice implementation of GEF projects is to be separate from other activities."[152]

The basic objective of the GEF – helping developing countries contribute to the achievement of global environmental benefits – is an expression of the principle of common but differentiated responsibilities. As such, it is linked with, and buttressed by, concerns of international fairness. Yet to the extent that donors control the institution, it mirrors the traditional model of aid as charity or enlightened self-interest, rather than a partnership. However,

---

[148] INSTRUMENT FOR THE ESTABLISHMENT OF THE RESTRUCTURED GLOBAL ENVIRONMENT FACILITY, *supra* note 125, Art. 2.
[149] *Incremental cost* is defined as "a measure of the future economic burden on the country that would result from its choosing the GEF supported activity in preference to one that would have been sufficient in the national interest." See GEF, INCREMENTAL COSTS, GEF/C.7/Inf.5 (paper prepared for the April 1996 Meeting of the GEF Council), available at http://www.gefweb.org/council/council7/c7inf5.htm.
[150] SJÖBERG, RESTRUCTURING, at 52.
[151] JORDAN, *supra* note 124, at 31.
[152] SJÖBERG, RESTRUCTURING, at 51–52.

with the advent of more equitable representation, the institution gained greater legitimacy.

### 5.4.1. Convention and Kyoto Protocol Climate Change Funds

The preceding section has set out the genesis and basic operation of the GEF, while aspects of its operations relating to disbursement of resources were covered in section 5.3. As outlined previously, the GEF acts as a financial mechanism for the Convention, and it functions under, and is accountable to, the COP. At COP-7, in 2001, the parties established three new, dedicated climate change funds, each with its own mandate, with two being managed by the GEF. Two funds, the SCCF and the LDCF, were established under the Convention.[153] They are operated by the GEF, with the same relationship vis-à-vis the COP with respect to the existing institutional arrangements.[154] The AF, established under the Protocol,[155] marks a break with these arrangements because the Conference of the Parties serving as the Meeting of the Parties (COP/MOP) has decided that the AF should "operate under *the authority and guidance of and be accountable to*" the COP/MOP.[156] The lion's share of the resources in all three funds will be dedicated to activities designed to assist countries adapt to climate change. In this respect, the GEF itself has also established a financing window for adaptation, known as the Special Priority on Adaptation, to pilot adaptation activities.

The current and potential future funding from the climate change funds must be put into perspective against estimated adaptation financing needs. The costs of adaptation in developing countries remain highly uncertain, but an influential study on the economics of climate change estimated the

---

[153] Decision 7/CP.7, in REPORT OF THE CONFERENCE OF THE PARTIES ON ITS SEVENTH SESSION, ADDENDUM, PART II: ACTION TAKEN BY THE CONFERENCE OF THE PARTIES, vol. I, FCCC/CP/2001/13/Add.1 (2002) (establishing the Special Climate Change Fund and the Least Developed Countries Fund).

[154] *Id.* Decision 7/CP.7 provides that the two funds will be operated by the GEF "under the guidance of the COP."

[155] Decision 10/CP.7, in REPORT OF THE CONFERENCE OF THE PARTIES ON ITS SEVENTH SESSION, ADDENDUM, PART II: ACTION TAKEN BY THE CONFERENCE OF THE PARTIES, vol. I, FCCC/CP/2001/13/Add.1 (2002) (establishing the Adaptation Fund).

[156] Decision 5/CMP.2, in REPORT OF THE CONFERENCE OF THE PARTIES SERVING AS THE MEETING OF THE PARTIES TO THE KYOTO PROTOCOL ON ITS SECOND SESSION, ADDENDUM, PART II: ACTION TAKEN BY THE CONFERENCE OF THE PARTIES, para. 1(e), FCCC/KP/CMP/2006/10/Add.1 (2007) (emphasis added).

TABLE 5.1. *Funding status: GEF and multilateral climate change funds*

| Fund | Amount (US$ million) |
|---|---|
| GEF — Strategic Priority on Adaptation | 50.0 |
| LDCF | 172.0 |
| SCCF* | 106.0 |
| AF | Figure unknown (range 350–950) |
| TOTAL | 328.0 |

*Source:* Compiled from GEF documents (2008); *incl. approx. $16 million for mitigation/technology transfer.

costs of adapting investments to climate risk at US$40 billion, with a range of US$10 billion to US$100 billion.[157] Another study, which analyzed the additional investments and financial flows for adaptation in 2030, concluded that an estimated US$28 billion to US$67 billion could be required in developing countries.[158]

5.4.1.1. *Special Climate Change Fund.* The SCCF finances activities, complementary to regular GEF climate change programs, under the following four windows, provided for in paragraph 2 of Decision 7/CP.7: (1) adaptation; (2) transfer of technologies; (3) energy, transport, industry, agriculture, forestry, and waste management; and (4) activities to assist oil-exporting developing countries in diversifying their economies.[159] This last window is intended to give effect to Article 4(8)(h) of the Convention, which concerns the adverse impact of mitigation measures on developing countries whose economies rely on fossil fuel exports.

At COP-9, in 2003, the parties decided to assign priority to adaptation activities, while also agreeing that technology transfer and related capacity building activities were also essential.[160] That decision elaborates several adaptation activities that should be supported under the SCCF, including

---

[157] NICHOLAS STERN, THE ECONOMICS OF CLIMATE CHANGE, THE STERN REVIEW, Cabinet Office, HM Treasury 442 (2006). *See also* WORLD BANK, CLEAN ENERGY AND DEVELOPMENT: TOWARDS AN INVESTMENT FRAMEWORK (2006).
[158] UNFCCC, para. 26.
[159] Decision 7/CP.7, *supra* note 153, para. 2.
[160] Decision 5/CP.9, REPORT OF THE MEETING OF THE PARTIES ON ITS NINTH SESSION, ADDENDUM, PART II: ACTION TAKEN BY THE CONFERENCE OF THE PARTIES, vol. I, para. 1(c)-(d), FCCC/CP/2003/6/Add.1 (2004).

TABLE 5.2. *SCCF: Proposed sliding scale for cofinancing*

| Total project cost (US$ million) | Share covered by fund |
|---|---|
| <1 | Up to 50% |
| <1.5 | Up to 33% |
| >5 | Up to 25% |

*Source:* GEF.

water resource management, infrastructure development, fragile ecosystems, improving the monitoring of disease vectors, supporting capacity building for preventive measures, and strengthening national and regional centers and information networks for rapid response to extreme weather events. Based on guidance from the COP, the GEF developed a proposal for programming under the SCCF, which provides that the fund "be available to finance the additional costs of achieving sustainable development imposed on vulnerable countries by the impacts of climate change."[161] Thus the SCCF is complementary to the GEF Trust Fund because it may support adaptation activities that generate primarily local benefits, as opposed to the latter, which may be used to support adaptation activities primarily linked to producing global environmental benefits, for instance, in the area of biodiversity. To expedite the processing of financing, the GEF also proposed the adoption of a presumptive cofinancing sliding proportional scale, set out in Table 5.2. The share of funds that can be accessed under SCCF depends on the overall scale of the project. Where projects fall within the ambit of the sliding scale, they can be approved without project-by-project negotiations to determine the additional costs of adaptation.

The GEF programming document sought to address donor concerns about the open-ended nature of financing under windows 3 and 4 by addressing only adaptation and technology transfer, which were highlighted in Decision 5/CP.9. Furthermore, the document provides that while there is one fund, contributions will be pledged and contributed to a specific program – for example, adaptation – and separate financial records and accounts will be maintained for each program.[162] Thus, although Decision 7/CP.7 provides that the SCCF will support activities in all four areas, the

---

[161] GLOBAL ENVIRONMENT FACILITY, PROGRAMMING TO IMPLEMENT THE GUIDANCE FOR THE SPECIAL CLIMATE CHANGE FUND, GEF/C.24/12, para. 55 (2004).
[162] *Id.* at para. 37.

## 5.4. Sharing the Burden

establishment of distinct programs and dedicated administrative arrangements permits donors to fund only those parts of the COP decision that they wish to support.[163] Concerns were raised by some developing countries that the cofinancing required under the sliding scale would effectively bar them from accessing the fund and that elements of the GEF programming document introduced new conditionalities that strayed into the mandate of the COP to set policies and priorities.[164] In Decision 1/CP.12, adopted in 2006, the COP notes "the concerns expressed by most Parties not included in Annex I to the Convention with regard to the operational criteria and policies to be followed in financing activities under the Special Climate Change Fund during an initial five-year period," as set out in the programming document endorsed by the GEF Council.[165] In that decision, the COP decided that the SCCF will be used to fund activities under paragraphs 2(d) and 2(e) of Decision 7/CP.7, that is, mitigation projects in areas such energy efficiency, as well as assisting oil-exporting countries with economic diversification.[166]

5.4.1.2. **Least Developed Countries Fund.** The LDCF is primarily charged with assisting LDCs in preparing and implementing national adaptation programs of action (NAPAs).[167] These consist of a process designed to enable LDCs to identify priority activities responding to their urgent and immediate adaptation needs.[168] The category of LDCs consists of 50 countries with

---

[163] *See* M. J. Mace, *Funding for Adaptation to Climate Change: UNFCCC and GEF Developments Since COP-7*, 14(3) REVIEW OF EUROPEAN COMMUNITY AND INTERNATIONAL ENVIRONMENTAL LAW 225, 237 (2005). At the end of 2008, donors had pledged/contributed US$16 million for the program on technology transfer and US$90 million for adaptation. *See* GLOBAL ENVIRONMENT FACILITY, STATUS REPORT ON CLIMATE CHANGE FUNDS AS OF OCTOBER 2, 2007, GEF/LDCF.SCCF.5/Inf.2 (2008).
[164] MACE, *supra* note 163, at 238.
[165] Decision 1/CP.12, in REPORT OF THE MEETING OF THE PARTIES ON ITS TWELFTH SESSION, ADDENDUM, PART II: ACTION TAKEN BY THE CONFERENCE OF THE PARTIES, vol. I, FCCC/CP/2006/5/Add.1 (2007).
[166] *Id.* decision 1/CP.12, paras. 1 and 2.
[167] Decision 5/CP.7, in REPORT OF THE MEETING OF THE PARTIES ON ITS SEVENTH SESSION, ADDENDUM, PART II: ACTION TAKEN BY THE CONFERENCE OF THE PARTIES, vol. I, para. 12, FCCC/CP/2001/13/Add.1 (2002). *See also* MACE, *supra* note 163, at 238–40.
[168] The COP has set out detailed guidelines for the preparation of national adaptation programs of action. *See* Decision 28/CP.7, in REPORT OF THE MEETING OF THE PARTIES ON ITS SEVENTH SESSION, ADDENDUM, PART II: ACTION TAKEN BY THE CONFERENCE OF THE PARTIES, vol. IV, FCCC/CP/2001/13/Add.4 (2002).

low capital and human resources, and which therefore have limited ability to adapt to the adverse impacts of climate change.

Although managed by the GEF, modifications have been made so that certain of that institution's normal procedures are not applicable to the LDCF.[169] One of these is the concept of *incremental costs* – additional costs associated with transforming a project with national benefits into one with global environmental benefits – that guides GEF financing under its main Trust Fund.[170] In practice, the concept is contentious, and more important, adaptation activities by definition deliver local, not global, benefits. The LDCF will support the "additional costs" arising from meeting the extra adaptation needs imposed on LDCs by the effects of climate change.[171] In a situation where a community is planning to construct a water supply system, the additional costs covered by the fund would consist only of the added expense of ensuring that the infrastructure can cope with the expected increase in flooding and droughts from climate change. The underlying cost of the water supply system – before climate-proofing – falls to the community and is not covered by the fund. The portion supported by the fund is thus the difference between the baseline scenario and the adaptation scenario. In short, in practice, the additional costs requirement seems very close to the concept of incremental costs. It is not clear where the formula of additional costs leaves projects that might not be necessary at all in the absence of climate change, for instance, planning for and implementing coastal defense measures.

---

[169] GLOBAL ENVIRONMENT FACILITY, PROGRAMMING PAPER FOR FUNDING THE IMPLEMENTATION OF NAPAs UNDER THE LDC TRUST FUND, GEF/C.28/18, para. 5 (2006). Thus the principle of financing incremental costs for global benefits and the Resource Allocation Framework are not applicable to the LDCF or the SCCF. However, the double-majority voting procedure is applicable.

[170] *See* GLOBAL ENVIRONMENT FACILITY, INCREMENTAL COST POLICY PAPER (1996), available at http://www.gefweb.org/council/council7/c7inf5.htm.

[171] GLOBAL ENVIRONMENT FACILITY, PROGRAMMING PAPER FOR FUNDING, *supra* note 169, at paras. 18–20. In Decision 6/CP.9, *supra* note 160, at para. 3(c), the COP requested the GEF to consider "criteria for supporting activities on an agreed full-cost basis," which is a somewhat confusing formulation. However, in Decision 3/CP.11, in REPORT OF THE MEETING OF THE PARTIES ON ITS ELEVENTH SESSION, ADDENDUM, PART II: ACTION TAKEN BY THE CONFERENCE OF THE PARTIES, para. 2, FCCC/CP/2005/5/Add.1, the COP stated that "full-cost funding shall be provided by the Least Developed Countries Fund to meet the additional costs of activities to adapt to the adverse impacts of climate change." A footnote provides that for "this decision 'additional costs' means the costs imposed on vulnerable countries to meet their immediate adaptation needs."

5.4. Sharing the Burden 219

TABLE 5.3. *LDCF: Proposed sliding scale for cofinancing*

| Total project cost (US$) | Share covered by fund |
|---|---|
| <300,000 | Up to 100% |
| <500,000 | Up to 75% or max. of $375,000 |
| <6 million | Up to 50% or max. of $3 million |
| <18 million | Up to 33% or max. of $6 million |
| >18 million | Up to 25% or max. determined by overall LDCF funding availability |

*Source:* GEF.

To simplify the operation of the additional cost criterion in practice, the GEF has proposed an optional sliding scale for determining the portion of financing eligible under the LCDF. Recognizing the particular vulnerability of LDCs, the sliding scale for use under the fund requires less cofinancing for smaller projects than the scale proposed for the SCCF.[172] Smaller projects focusing on capacity-building activities are almost certain to be additional – without climate change, there would be no need for them. Accordingly, for such projects, the sliding scale provides that the fund will cover the full, or almost the full, cost of the activity. The proposed sliding scale, set out in Table 5.3, requires considerably less cofinancing than an earlier GEF proposal that was subject to criticism from small islands and African countries at COP-10.[173]

The majority of LDCs have submitted their NAPAs, which outline vulnerabilities and contain priority projects.[174] The full cost of projects identified in all NAPAs is likely to be well in excess of US$1 billion.[175] If the LCDF ends up covering one-third of the project cost, that is, only the additional

---

[172] GLOBAL ENVIRONMENT FACILITY, PROGRAMMING PAPER FOR FUNDING THE IMPLEMENTATION OF NAPAS UNDER THE LDC TRUST FUND, GEF/C.28/18 para. 29 (2006).

[173] MACE, *supra* note 163, at 239. The proposed sliding scale is set out in GEF, ELEMENTS TO BE TAKEN INTO ACCOUNT IN FUNDING THE IMPLEMENTATION OF NAPAS UNDER THE LDC FUND, GEF/C.24/Inf.7, para. 22 (2004). For projects up to US$250,000, it was proposed to cover a maximum of half the cost, and for projects between US$2 million and US$5 million, one-third of the cost.

[174] As of October 2008, 39 of the 49 LDCs had submitted their NAPAs. Details of NAPAs can be found on the UNFCC Web site at http://unfccc.int/adaptation/napas/items/2679.php.

[175] STERN, *supra* note 157, at 502, estimates US$1.3 billion for all NAPAs. The figure is based on an average of US$25 million per country. The author's calculation, based on 38 NAPAs submitted as of October 2008, is US$1.5 billion, but this includes a project costing US$700 million, which is unusually high when compared to other proposals. Overall, funding needs of US$1 billion represent a conservative figure.

costs, this suggests that the required contribution will be upward of US$300 million.[176] (In comparison, the ratio of GEF resources to cofinancing in the overall GEF Trust Fund stands at about 1 to 4.[177]) It must also be borne in mind that the NAPAs are intended to identify only the most immediate and pressing adaptation needs; the full extent of adaptation funding required is much higher. Support for NAPAs corresponds squarely to the fairness principle of need, giving priority to the most vulnerable countries. At the end of 2008, the fund had received transfers and pledges of US$172 million.[178] Thus, if the fund is to meaningfully fulfill its purpose, donors will have to substantially increase the level of contributions. The success of the LCDF will be one measure of whether the climate regime will fairly address the needs of countries likely to be hardest hit by climate change and that possess the lowest adaptive capacity.

**5.4.1.3. Adaptation Fund.** The AF was established at COP-7 in 2001, pursuant to Article 12(8) of the Kyoto Protocol, which provides that the COP/MOP "shall ensure that a share of the proceeds from" CDM projects is used "to assist developing countries that are particularly vulnerable to the adverse effects of climate change to meet the costs of adaptation." The AF is intended to finance concrete adaptation projects and programs in developing countries that are parties to the Protocol, which will include activities in the areas of natural resources management, improving the monitoring of diseases and vectors affected by climate change, and supporting capacity building for preventive measures and preparedness for disasters relating to climate change.[179] Pursuant to Article 12(9) of the Protocol, the fund is financed by a 2 percent share of the proceeds from CDM projects, with the exception of projects situated in LDCs.[180] In addition to the share of

---

[176] At the end of 2008, LDCs had submitted 24 implementation projects amounting to over US$220 million, with the Fund covering US$77 million, roughly one-third of the total project costs.

[177] Every US$1 of GEF financing leverages almost US$4 in cofinancing. *See* GLOBAL ENVIRONMENT FACILITY, ANNUAL REPORT 2005 3 (2006).

[178] GLOBAL ENVIRONMENT FACILITY, PROGRESS REPORT ON LCDF AND SCCF, GEF/LDCF.SCCF.5/INF.3 (2008).

[179] *See* Decisions 5/CP.7 and 10/CP.7, *supra* note 167.

[180] *See* Decision 10/CP.7, in REPORT OF THE MEETING OF THE PARTIES ON ITS SEVENTH SESSION, ADDENDUM, PART II: ACTION TAKEN BY THE CONFERENCE OF THE PARTIES, vol. I, para. 2, FCCC/CP/2001/13/Add.1 (2002), and Decision 17/CP.7, in REPORT OF THE

## 5.4. Sharing the Burden

proceeds, the AF is also intended to receive contributions from Annex I parties that have ratified the Protocol.[181] The parties have decided that the AF will fund projects and programs to address the adverse effects of climate change on a "full adaptation cost basis."[182]

According to principles meant to guide the fund, in addition to the customary operation "under the guidance of and accountable to" the COP/MOP, the fund also "operate[s] under the authority" of the COP/MOP, "which shall decide on its overall policies."[183] An important feature that distinguishes the AF from the other funds is that its operating entity is not the GEF, but a new body, the Adaptation Fund Board (AFB). The AFB has a majority of members from developing countries (non–Annex I) and follows a one-country, one-vote rule, as opposed to the double majority of the other funds under the GEF voting system, which provides developed countries with an implicit veto.[184] It was also decided that the parties should have direct access to the AFB, and the involvement of the GEF and the World Bank in the administration of the AF was reduced to an interim provision of secretariat and trustee services, respectively.[185] The governance arrangements reflect developing countries' concerns about accountability and control.[186] Not only because the fund is meant to address their needs, but because its financing comes from CDM projects located on their territory, developing countries had a strong case for demanding effective control over the fund.

---

MEETING OF THE PARTIES ON ITS SEVENTH SESSION, ADDENDUM, PART II: ACTION TAKEN BY THE CONFERENCE OF THE PARTIES, vol. II, para. 15(a)–(b), FCCC/CP/2001/13/Add.2 (2002).

[181] *See* Decision 10/CP.7, *supra* note 180.
[182] Decision 5/CMP.2, *supra* note 156, at para. 1(d).
[183] *Id.* at para. 1(e).
[184] *Id. See* Chapter 3 for more details. At the Bali Conference in December 2007, the COP/MOP decided that the GEF would provide secretariat services to the Adaptation Fund Board on an interim basis. *See* Decision 1/CMP.3, in REPORT OF THE CONFERENCE OF THE PARTIES SERVING AS THE MEETING OF THE PARTIES TO THE KYOTO PROTOCOL ON ITS THIRD SESSION, ADDENDUM, PART II: ACTION TAKEN BY THE CONFERENCE OF THE PARTIES, FCCC/KP/CMP/2007/9/Add.1 (2008).
[185] BENITO MÜLLER & HARALD WINKLER, ONE STEP FORWARD AND TWO STEPS BACK? THE GOVERNANCE OF THE WORLD BANK CLIMATE INVESTMENT FUNDS, Oxford Energy and Environment Comment 4 (2008).
[186] *See* BENITO MÜLLER, NAIROBI 2006: TRUST AND THE FUTURE OF ADAPTATION FUNDING 3 (2007).

The resources available from the AF depend on the total number of CERs issued and the value obtained when they are monetized; both variables are subject to some uncertainty.[187] Suppose that the fund obtains an average price of US$10 per CER. On a conservative estimate of CERs actually issued, sale by the fund of its share would bring in US$320 million, which would rise to US$440 million if one assumes that more CERs are issued.[188] One observer estimates that the fund may generate between US$160 million and US$950 million, dwarfing cumulative contributions to the LDCF and the SCCF, which, in 2008, stood at roughly US$278 million.[189] These figures are purely indicative, as the prices the fund realizes for its CERs may well be higher. The viability of the fund depends very much on the continuation of the CDM or similar mechanism under a post-2012 climate regime.

### 5.4.2. World Bank Clean Investment Funds

In July 2008, the World Bank announced the launch of the Clean Investment Funds (CIFs), which consist of two distinct funds related to technology, the Clean Technology Fund (CTF) and the Strategic Climate Change Fund (SCF). The CTF is designed to promote scaled up demonstration, deployment, and transfer of low-carbon technologies in the power sector; transportation; and energy efficiency in buildings, industry, and agriculture.[190] The fund aims to address the shortfall in concessional development financing by making funds (combination of grants and loans) at rates lower than standard terms used by the multilateral development banks. In support of the Bali Action Plan, the objective is also to provide finance at a scale necessary to help provide incentives to developing countries to integrate nationally appropriate mitigation actions into sustainable development plans and investment decisions. The projects or programs must deliver significant potential for long-term GHG emissions reductions. The SCF is intended

---

[187] *See* AXEL MICHAELOWA, CLIMATE STRATEGIES: HOW MANY CERs WILL THE CDM PRODUCE BY 2012?, Discussion Paper CDM-2 7 (2007). He puts the projected supply of CERs spanning a range from 1.9 to 4.4 billion. The Secretariat of the UNFCCC projects a supply of more than 2.6 billion CERs by 2012, but this is a straight extrapolation that does not account for non- or underdelivery by some projects. *See* http://cdm.unfccc.int/ Statistics/index.html. Other analysts see 1.6 billion as a possible figure, with a range of 1.4–2.2 billion. *See* CAPOOR & AMBROSI, *supra* note 105, at 20.
[188] The figures are calculated based on a potential range in supply of 1.6 to 2.2 billion CERs.
[189] MÜLLER, *supra* note 186, at 3.
[190] WORLD BANK, CLEAN TECHNOLOGY FUND, June 9, 2008.

to provide financing to pilot new development approaches or to scale up activities.[191] Programs under consideration include activities to enhance climate resilience in highly vulnerable countries, support access to renewable energy technologies in low-income countries, and make investments to reduce emissions from deforestation and forest degradation. The World Bank announced that by early 2009 donors had pledged the equivalent of US$6.3 billion to the CIFs.[192]

As detailed previously, the GEF, as the financial mechanism of the Convention, has, until now, been the main avenue for channeling support to developing countries for climate change activities. In this context, it is interesting that the founding documents of both the CTF and the SCF refer to Convention Article 11, paragraph 5, which provides that "developed country Parties may also provide, and developing country Parties avail themselves of, financial resources related to the implementation of the Convention through bilateral, regional and other multilateral channels." The potential proliferation of institutions and mechanisms in the climate change regime is naturally a concern. The final shape of the finance and technology support architecture was far from settled when the CIFs were launched. In August 2008, developing countries proposed that financing and technology transfer mechanisms that would operate under the authority of the COP should have equitable and balanced representation of all parties and ensure recipient country involvement during the definition, identification, and implementation of actions. Since the CIFs were established while the Convention negotiations on financing and technology transfer were still ongoing, it could be asked whether these new initiatives would not have a preemptive effect. The CIFs thus include a sunset clause, providing that the funds will conclude their operations once a new financial architecture is in place. The design of the governance structure of the CIFs also accommodates concerns that decision making would be too donor-driven, with little meaningful scope for recipients' participation.[193]

---

[191] WORLD BANK, STRATEGIC CLIMATE CHANGE FUND, June 3, 2008.
[192] Clean Investment Funds, Financial Status as of January 26, 2009 (2009), available at http://siteresources.worldbank.org/INTCC/Resources/CIF_Financial_Status_Jan_26_2009.pdf. See also Donors Pledge over 6.1 Billion to Clean Investment Funds, press release, World Bank, September 26, 2008.
[193] See MÜLLER & WINKLER, supra note 185, criticizing an early draft of the proposed governance arrangements. In their final version, the governing trust fund committees of the CTF and SCF have an equal number of representatives from donor and recipient countries. See

This brief overview of the various climate change funds underlines the preoccupation of developing countries with adaptation, which is quite understandable given the threats they face from the adverse effects of climate change. Because adaptation activities are, by definition, local, and thus do not provide global benefits, they do not fit comfortably into a mitigation-driven paradigm. The funds can be regarded as a recognition that a fair climate regime ought to prioritize the needs of those most vulnerable to the impacts of climate change. Overall, it is evident that the financial resources committed to the funds are only a very modest first step in addressing the adaptation funding needs of developing countries. Given their recent genesis, it is difficult to assess the World Bank's CIFs. On the clean technology side, investment under the CTF has the potential to go beyond support of isolated projects and to bring about a real shift toward low-carbon alternatives. A question that faces this initiative is how it will be accommodated under the structure of the post-2012 climate regime.

## 5.5. CONCLUSION

This chapter has analyzed the principle of common but differentiated responsibilities from a theoretical perspective. Although equal application of the law, derived from the principle of the sovereign equality of states, is the norm under international law, forms of differentiation exist, particularly in the field of international environmental law. Various justifications have been advanced for differentiation: as a means to promote a "shared" compact to tackle global problems; as a way of reflecting the responsibility for environmental degradation; and to reflect the notion that on account of their greater financial and technical resources, industrialized countries ought to take the lead in combating global environmental problems. The conclusion reached in this chapter is that the principle of common but differentiated responsibilities gives effect to conceptions of equity and fairness in international environmental law and policy making. The accepted view among most scholars is that the principle has not attained the status of a customary international law. And while it is submitted that this conclusion

WORLD BANK, *supra* note 190, at 9 (CTF), and note 191, at 12 (SCF). Decision making is by consensus, which is defined as a situation when "no participant in the decision-making process blocks a proposed decision." If consensus cannot be achieved, a decision will be postponed or withdrawn. *Id.* at 10 and 13.

## 5.5. Conclusion

is correct, it should not lead one to dismiss the principle as being of no relevance to the international legal and policy discourse on climate change. The view adopted here is that the principle of common but differentiated responsibilities is a background principle straddling the divide between the legal and the political in international forums on sustainable development. On one hand, the principle reflects political realities and interests; on the other, it appears in legal instruments and is used to justify, explain, and interpret legal obligations.

The principle of common but differentiated responsibilities may risk being regarded as contributing to the lack of progress on international climate policy, perhaps leading some to claim, in exasperation, that it means no, rather than common, commitments for developing countries. Admittedly, for those desiring agreement on a climate policy that binds all major emitters to limit or cut emissions, the invocation of the principle can appear to be little more than a blocking maneuver. Yet in these circumstances, the principle of common but differentiated responsibilities provides the vital service of encouraging a consideration of context and differences in circumstances among countries facing a global threat, with widely varying resources at their disposal and with varying assessments of priorities and expectations of impacts. In such an international system, which lacks an arbiter of last resort, it is not surprising that the principle of common but differential responsibilities is something of a messy conglomerate, subject to a range of interpretations.

What are the limits to the application and interpretation of the principle? Two boundaries that have been suggested are as follows: first, the differentiation must contribute to the achievement of the common environmental goal, and second, it must cease when the relevant differences no longer exist.[194] Thus, in the context of the Convention, the principle must contribute to the achievement of its ultimate object, namely, the stabilization of GHGs in the atmosphere at a level that is not dangerous. Although historical responsibility for the accumulation of GHGs must be taken into account, the common commitment to the Convention's ultimate objective places limits on the differentiation in favor of developing countries whether measured in absolute or per capita terms. To

---

[194] RAJAMANI, *supra* note 17, at 253–54.

avoid a slide into unfairness, the second boundary suggests that differentiation should be time-bound and subject to review of whether the relevant differences continue to prevail.[195] Because countries disagree on what constitutes "relevant differences" justifying differentiation, this may be more difficult than it seems.

This chapter also covered the practical application of differentiation in the climate regime, in the form of the institutions and mechanisms that promote technology transfer and financial assistance to combat climate change. With respect to options for accelerating the transfer and diffusion of clean energy technology, it appears clear that the general trend toward market-based solutions will continue so that mechanisms, such as partnerships, joint ventures, and licensing arrangements, will continue to be of importance. The question is whether this is enough to get the job done – will developing countries be able to afford cleaner technologies and adopt them in sectors where they have the greatest impact? At the international level, investment and subsidies should shift from fossil fuels to cleaner energy, including, but not limited to, renewables, as it should be recognized that large-scale electrification simply cannot, at this stage, be carried out only with wind or solar energy. Providing access to basic energy services would have a negligible impact on global carbon dioxide emissions. Reallocating subsidies and investment would apply to the World Bank, bilateral aid agencies, and import-export banks. The design and effectiveness of the new financial architecture for the climate regime will be of particular importance. Adequacy of resources, accountability, and meaningful participation will be key issues.

In a future climate agreement, consideration should also be given to strengthening the provisions related to research, development, and deployment of cleaner technology, perhaps in the form of a clean technology protocol, which would include provisions related to technology transfer. A greater emphasis on technology should seek to achieve three things: first, consensus on significant action by a group of countries that are the greatest contributors to GHG emissions, recognizing that a different strategy of a different scale and scope is required; second, augmentation of those funds to transfer technology to the LDCs, recognizing their special needs and

---

[195] *Id.* at 254.

## 5.5. Conclusion

vulnerability; and three, a range of voluntary commitments and partnerships specifically aimed at clean and low-emission technology.

Finally, the international community is on the cusp of defining the next stage of the collective effort to combat climate change. It is not unexpected that the principle of common but differentiated responsibilities will come to the fore once more. Although the world has changed a great deal since the adoption of key milestones in the area of climate change and sustainable development – the Rio Conference and adoption of the Convention in 1992 and the Kyoto Protocol in 1997 – basic differences in wealth, perception, and outlook persist among nations. Confronting the worsening environmental outlook demands a forward-looking interpretation of the principle of common but differentiated responsibilities. In fashioning such an interpretation, the parties must creatively articulate and give effect to common responsibilities, while also accounting for the very real and relevant differences among members of the international community.

# 6

# Evaluation of Proposals for Future Climate Policy

## 6.1. INTRODUCTION

There are a number of ideas on how to design the next phase of the climate regime. While some proposals are variations on basic themes, a recent survey of approaches for advancing international climate policy counted 40 proposals.[1] This chapter outlines the features of a number of the main proposals and assesses them according to fairness principles. Accordingly, this chapter begins with an overview of the various assessment criteria for a future climate change agreement – and the burden-sharing rules they contain – which reflect general principles of fairness. Although fairness is the subject of this study, it is only one among a range of criteria by which to assess climate policy proposals. Consistency with principles of equity and fairness is of limited use if the proposal at issue is politically unacceptable and of limited feasibility in policy terms. Accordingly, this chapter also seeks to evaluate the proposals against a number of assessment criteria drawn from the literature on the subject.[2] The chapter sets out to do two things: first, it sets out a set of policy criteria for evaluating climate change proposals; second, it assesses a small but representative sample of actual proposals in light of both fairness principles and the set of policy criteria.

---

[1] DANIEL BODANSKY, INTERNATIONAL CLIMATE EFFORTS BEYOND 2012: A SURVEY OF APPROACHES (2004).
[2] The following part draws on criteria used by *id.*; AARON COSBEY ET AL., WHICH WAY FORWARD? ISSUES IN DEVELOPING AN EFFECTIVE CLIMATE REGIME AFTER 2012 (2005); JOSEPH E. ALDY ET AL., THIRTEEN PLUS ONE: A COMPARISON OF GLOBAL CLIMATE POLICY ARCHITECTURES (2003); Axel Michaelowa et al., *Issues and Options for the Post-2012 Climate Architecture – An Overview*, 5 INTERNATIONAL ENVIRONMENTAL AGREEMENTS 5, 16–18 (2005).

## 6.1. Introduction

Earlier, it was concluded that no single account of equity or fairness could satisfy the demands placed on it by parties with competing conceptions of what is fair and just and divergent material interests.[3] Instead, a promising approach is to identify different aspects or dimensions of fairness and apply them in the analysis. Accordingly, in a previous chapter, the following general fairness and equity principles were selected as representative and useful in the climate change context: egalitarian; responsibility or contribution; need; and capability. Taking one step further, it is in the analysis of equity and fairness that one can usefully distinguish (1) general principles of fairness and equity operating at a high level of generality; (2) more specific burden-sharing rules, which incorporate concrete applications of one or more general principles; and (3) operational indicators for the putting in place of burden-sharing proposals.[4] An example of a burden-sharing rule would be the Brazilian proposal to allocate mitigation targets on the basis of the impact of historical emissions on temperature increase. In this case, the operational indicators would consist of the methodologies for calculating historical emissions as well as for deriving changes in average mean surface temperature.

This part sets out a range of policy criteria for assessing climate change proposals, beginning with an overview of the manner in which targets and commitments are framed.[5] The framing of the target has implications for the perceived fairness of a proposal as well its political acceptability. The first approach is that followed in the Kyoto Protocol – fixed emission limitation and reduction targets, measured against a fixed baseline, with the default value set at 1990 emission levels. The setting of differentiated targets makes it possible to reflect equity concerns and the individual circumstances of countries. In theory, more rational methods can be applied to determine targets than the haggling that characterized the Kyoto negotiations. Because economic growth is uncertain over longer periods of time, such as the 5 to 10 years commonly mentioned, opponents point out that fixed targets have the potential to become a straitjacket. For this reason, a number of more flexible types of targets have been proposed, such as indexing the emissions

---

[3] See Chapter 4.
[4] CICERO & ECN, SHARING THE BURDEN OF GREENHOUSE GAS MITIGATION, FINAL REPORT OF THE JOINT CICERO-ECN PROJECT ON THE GLOBAL DIFFERENTIATION OF EMISSION MITIGATION TARGETS AMONG COUNTRIES 13–14 (2001).
[5] BODANSKY, supra note 1, at 10–13; CÉDRIC PHILIBERT, CLIMATE MITIGATION: APPROACHES FOR FUTURE INTERNATIONAL COOPERATION, COM/ENV/EPOC/IEA/SLT(2005)10 (2005).

commitment to a variable such as economic growth. Another variant is a greenhouse gas (GHG) intensity target, which allows absolute emissions to increase but commits a country to reducing the GHG emissions per unit of economic output. An emissions intensity target was a central plank of U.S. climate policy from 2002 to 2008.[6] Because uncertainty about economic growth and overall development is greatest for developing nations, intensity targets are often suggested as especially appropriate for this category of states. Seen more generally, such targets are regarded as a means to broaden participation in a future climate agreement, which has the beneficial effect of countering so-called leakage – the movement of industries from regions subject to controls to those that are not, with the associated competitiveness concerns – and broadening the market for emissions trading, thus lowering abatement costs. Intensity targets tend to be set so that absolute emissions continue rising, yet atmospheric stabilization of GHGs requires that emissions from industrialized countries begin to decline in absolute terms. This suggests that such targets are more suited for developing countries.[7]

Another approach that is designed to provide flexibility entails so-called no lose targets, which are nonbinding emission limitation or reduction commitments; exceeding them has no compliance implications, but if emissions are held below the target, the difference could be sold on the carbon market. By creating an incentive to mitigate without punishing shortfalls, this type of mechanism could contribute to the mitigation objective as well as promote equity and inclusivity because less developed countries could benefit from emissions trading. The targets could be applied to the country as a whole or only to specified sectors.[8] Reflecting the same rationale, but on the basis of GHG intensity, not fixed emission targets, are dual-intensity targets. A country would adopt two targets: the first a relatively weak but binding

---

[6] The National Climate Action Plan set an intensity reduction of 2 percent per year. Critics charged that the target amounted to business as usual and did not require additional effort to meet. During the period 1990 to 2006, U.S. emissions rose by 14.7 percent, while gross domestic product increased by 59 percent. ENVIRONMENT PROTECTION AGENCY, INVENTORY OF U.S. GHG EMISSIONS AND SINKS: 1990–2006 (2008), available at http://epa.gov/climatechange/emissions/usinventoryreport.html.

[7] NIKLAS HÖHNE & ESTHER LAHME, TYPES OF FUTURE COMMITMENTS UNDER THE UNFCCC AND THE KYOTO PROTOCOL POST 2012, Briefing Paper 8, World Wildlife Fund (2005).

[8] For a recent sector-based proposal, see JAKE SCHMIDT ET AL., SECTOR-BASED APPROACH TO THE POST-2012 CLIMATE CHANGE ARCHITECTURE (2006), available at http://www.ccap.org/international/future.htm.

compliance target, and the second a more stringent selling target, which, if bettered, would entitle the country to sell the surplus.[9] Other approaches modify a system of fixed emission targets through the incorporation of a safety valve, which effectively caps the price of permits by allowing parties to purchase additional allowances at a predetermined price. Knowledge of the maximum permit price could foster participation and enhance compliance, but could also reduce certainty with respect to abatement levels.

Rather than setting targets, mitigation objectives can also be pursued through laws and regulations that prescribe policies and measures. One prominent example of a potential policy is a harmonized global carbon tax. Economic theory suggests, in theory, that taxes are preferable to price instruments – emissions trading schemes – for tackling problems such as climate change.[10] In many countries, not least the United States, political reality dictates that for all their theoretical merit, carbon taxes are unlikely to be widely adopted. A number of European countries, among them Norway and Switzerland, have adopted taxes on carbon as part of their portfolio of climate policies.[11] From the perspective of developing countries, a globally harmonized carbon tax would be criticized on equity grounds as regressive. Other policies and measurements (PAM) approaches include the setting of international energy efficiency standards; the establishment of technology standards more generally; and a soft technology model that focuses financing for energy technology research and development, technology cooperation, and support for the deployment of new technologies. An interesting variation are the sustainable development (SD)-PAM proposals, in which countries pledge to carry out policies aimed at meeting a country's economic and social development objectives, but that also contribute to GHG mitigation and, in the longer term, a more climate-friendly development pathway.[12] There is interest in SD-PAMs as a bridge between

---

[9] BODANSKY, *supra* note 1, at 11.
[10] Richard G. Newell & William A. Pizer, *Regulating Stock Externalities under Uncertainty*, Discussion Paper 99-10-REV, Resources for the Future 1–2 (2000). The classic analysis on the merits of prices versus quantities is M. L. Weitzman, *Prices vs. Quantities*, 41(4) REVIEW OF ECONOMIC STUDIES 477–91 (1974).
[11] For details, see INTERNATIONAL ENERGY AGENCY, CLIMATE CHANGE MITIGATION: GREENHOUSE GAS POLICIES AND MEASURES, available at http://www.iea.org/textbase/ pm/Default.aspx?mode=cc; database searched for "taxes" under policies in force.
[12] KEVIN A. BAUMERT ET AL., GROWING IN THE GREENHOUSE: PROTECTING THE CLIMATE BY PUTTING DEVELOPMENT FIRST (2005).

countries with binding targets and those without.[13] The financial incentives for SD-PAMs are likely to be related to the degree of oversight and review of the implementation of the pledges.

### 6.2. ASSESSMENT CRITERIA

The next part of this chapter explores assessment criteria that have been proposed in the literature to evaluate international climate policy proposals. The criteria are grouped under three headings: environmental effectiveness, cost-effectiveness, and institutional design.

#### 6.2.1. *Environmental Effectiveness*

Environmental effectiveness is first on the list of assessment criteria. A proposal should be capable of achieving a particular stabilization level of greenhouse emissions that avoids dangerous climate change, in accordance with Article 2 of the Convention. The author supports the view that such a provision establishes a legal obligation on the parties to prevent dangerous interference with the climate system.[14] However, in the absence of a common understanding of what constitutes dangerous interference, various parties and interest groups have advocated different views on what constitutes an

---

[13] JANE ELLIS ET AL., SD-PAMS: WHAT, WHERE, WHEN AND HOW? 5 (2007). SD-PAMs have been extensively discussed in the climate negotiations. Interestingly, the Bali Action Plan adopted at the Thirteenth Session of the Conference of the Parties, held from December 3–14, 2007, refers to "nationally appropriate mitigation actions by developing country Parties *in the context of sustainable development* supported and enabled by technology, financing and capacity-building, in a measurable, reportable and verifiable manner" para. 1(b)(ii) (emphasis added). *See* Harald Winkler et al., *Methods for Quantifying the Benefits of Sustainable Development Policies and Measures (SD-PAMs)*, 8 CLIMATE POLICY 119–34 (2008).

[14] *See* RODA VERHEYEN, CLIMATE CHANGE AND INTERNATIONAL LAW: PREVENTION DUTIES AND STATE RESPONSIBILITY 56 (2005). But *cf.* Daniel Bodansky, *The United Nations Framework Convention: A Commentary*, 18 YALE JOURNAL OF INTERNATIONAL LAW 451, 500 (1993). Bodansky notes that Art. 2 is phrased in declarative language. He also questions whether Art. 2 falls within the category of "object and purpose" of the treaty, as provided for by Arts. 18 and 31 (1) of the Vienna Convention on the Law of Treaties. In that case, all parties would be under an obligation not to defeat the stabilization objective. Contrary to Bodansky's close reading, the practice of the parties in reiterating and reaffirming the stabilization objective in the course of climate negotiations, as well as in various soft law or political instruments such as the Johannesburg Plan of Implementation, have demonstrated the centrality of Art. 2.

adequate degree of environmental commitment.[15] Nonetheless, even absent consensus, there is, over time, likely to be considerable convergence around what constitutes a long-term goal for the climate regime. Improved understanding of the timing, impacts, and costs of climate change is likely to be an important driver. In this respect, the scientific input of the Intergovernmental Panel on Climate Change provides decision makers and the public with information on which decisions to adopt to mitigate the risks associated with climate change.

Stabilization of atmospheric concentrations of GHGs in this century at any level will necessitate a substantial departure from business-as-usual emissions. Several emission paths are possible in achieving a particular stabilization level, leading some to argue for delayed mitigation to avoid the premature retirement of capital stock.[16] An opposite view holds that early action is warranted due to the inertia and slow turnover of capital stock, such as power plants and buildings, making it especially important not to lock in old technology.[17] The International Energy Agency's estimate that the world energy system will require US$22 trillion in new energy infrastructure investments by 2030 tends to support the latter view.[18] A later peak in emissions implies that cuts must occur at a higher rate in the future – delaying the peak in emissions from 2020 to 2030 almost doubles the rate of reduction for one widely discussed stabilization target.[19] Overall, "the earlier the emissions peak and decline, the lower the stabilized concentration level, the lower the absolute level of climate change and the earlier that climate change is attenuated."[20]

Emissions from developing countries are set to overtake those of industrialized countries within the next two decades.[21] Accordingly, achievement of a stabilization target, even one at the high end, requires the participation

---

[15] E.g., the EU target of avoiding warming of more than 2 degrees Celsius above preindustrial levels.
[16] Thomas Wigley et al., *Economic and Environmental Choices in the Stabilization of Atmospheric CO₂ Concentrations*, 379 NATURE 240 (1996).
[17] Michael Grubb et al., *Influence of Socioeconomic Inertia and Uncertainty on Optimal CO₂-Emission Abatement*, 390 NATURE 270 (1997).
[18] INTERNATIONAL ENERGY AGENCY, WORLD ENERGY OUTLOOK 2007 42 (2007).
[19] NICHOLAS STERN, THE ECONOMICS OF CLIMATE CHANGE, THE STERN REVIEW, Cabinet Office, HM Treasury, 193 (2006).
[20] Jan Corfee-Morlot & Niklas Höhne, *Climate Change: Long-Term Targets and Short-Term Commitments*, 13 GLOBAL ENVIRONMENTAL CHANGE 279 (2003).
[21] INTERNATIONAL ENERGY AGENCY, *supra* note 18, at 199.

of at least the major emitters among the developing countries. There is thus a tension between environmental effectiveness and equity, as reflected in the differential treatment under the principle of common but differentiated responsibility. However, in case of a conflict, the stabilization objective enshrined in Article 2 arguably takes precedence over the principles enumerated in Article 3, including provisions concerning equity. Article 3(1) refers to the need for parties to "protect the climate system for the benefit of present and future generations of humankind, on the basis of equity and in accordance with their common but differentiated responsibilities and respective capabilities." Article 3(2) provides that the "specific needs and special circumstances of developing country Parties" and "those Parties, especially developing country Parties, that would have to bear a disproportionate or abnormal burden... should be given full consideration." The principles of equity and fairness reflected in these provisions should actively influence, guide, and possibly shape the actions and policies implemented to achieve the stabilization objective. However, these principles cannot direct or determine policies in a manner that would clash with the objective of the Convention. In other words, proposals should pass a threshold of environmental adequacy.

At the policy design level, environmental effectiveness is influenced by factors such as leakage (movement of emissions-generating activities to a region with weaker controls) and the efficacy of enforcement and compliance procedures.[22] Drawing on research analyzing the *pollution haven thesis*, some scholars suggest that economists may overstate the leakage problem, at least in the initial stages of international carbon policy.[23] Leakage can be reduced by an agreement with broad coverage and the assumption of core emission reduction and limitation commitments by all parties.

### 6.2.2. Cost-Effectiveness

The most cost-effective policy is the one that achieves the chosen goal at the least cost. *Cost-effectiveness* must be distinguished from *efficiency*. While

---

[22] BODANSKY, *supra* note 1, at 5.
[23] David G. Victor, *Fragmented Carbon Markets and Reluctant Nations: Implications for the Design of Effective Architectures*, *in* ARCHITECTURES FOR AGREEMENT: ADDRESSING GLOBAL CLIMATE CHANGE IN THE POST-KYOTO WORLD, 133, 135–36 (Joseph E. Aldy & Robert N. Stavins eds., 2007).

## 6.2. Assessment Criteria

cost-effectiveness takes the goal as given, efficiency involves the process of choosing a particular goal, in accordance with economic criteria.[24] Efficiency analysis may have the effect of displacing fairness considerations in the process of setting the goal. The distinction between cost-effectiveness and efficiency is relevant to fairness, policy analysis, and legal grounds. Economic analysis of climate policy attempts to arrive at a socially optimal amount of mitigation, taking into account other needs and using the tools of cost-benefit analysis. However, as we have seen in Chapter 4, such analysis is not without difficulties and is controversial in several respects.[25] Problems are encountered with respect to the rate used to discount future costs and benefits as well as uncertainty relating to the costs of future mitigation.[26] Article 3(3) of the Convention provides that the "Parties should take precautionary measures to anticipate, prevent or minimize the causes of climate change" and "tak[e] into account that policies and measures to deal with climate change should be cost-effective so as to ensure global benefits at the lowest possible cost." It will be noted that cost-effectiveness is not self-standing, but qualifies the reference to a precautionary approach. To conclude, in legal terms, the Convention states that the *achievement* of the stabilization objective shall be guided, among other things, by cost-effectiveness considerations.

In many, but by no means all, developing countries, the industrial and power generation sectors are less energy-efficient and use older, more polluting technologies than their industrialized country counterparts. It follows that developing countries, particularly large ones, have considerable potential for cost-effective emission reductions. Approaches that allow for flexibility with respect to where emission reductions are carried out, through emissions trading, would tend to be less costly than more rigid approaches. This is recognized in Article 3(3), which states that "policies and measures should take into account different socio-economic contexts, be comprehensive, cover all relevant sources, sinks... and comprise all economic sectors. In equity terms, the relative distribution of costs is a key factor.

---

[24] INTERGOVERNMENTAL PANEL ON CLIMATE CHANGE, CLIMATE CHANGE 2007: MITIGATION. CONTRIBUTION OF WORKING GROUP III TO THE FOURTH ASSESSMENT REPORT OF THE INTERGOVERNMENTAL PANEL ON CLIMATE CHANGE 751 (Bert Metz et al. eds., 2007).
[25] *See* Chapter 4.
[26] MICHAELOWA ET AL., *supra* note 2, at 7.

### 6.2.3. Institutional Design

Climate policies can be more or less sensitive and responsive to the realities of international climate politics. Successful policies will respond to several requirements, many applicable to policy making in general, and some of particular relevance to the climate change regime. Dynamic policy flexibility refers to commitments that can be adjusted – tightened or loosened – in response to new scientific insights and improved analysis of costs and benefits. With the many uncertainties in the timing and scope of impacts, as well as the costs and effectiveness of various responses to climate change, analysts, in particular, economists, advocate a sequential process of decision making that is able to respond to new information as it becomes available.[27] The concern is to ensure that resources are employed in the most productive manner, by, for instance, avoiding the premature retirement of expensive generation infrastructure in the quest to meet targets that are too stringent in the short term. To some degree, policy flexibility is found in the climate regime, with the Protocol having established a first commitment period of five years, with the assumption that the second will be negotiated with regard to new scientific and economic information. On fairness grounds, it can be argued that because of the unequal bargaining positions of the parties, a process built on frequent renegotiation risks entrenching inequitable foundations.[28] In this view, it is important to secure fairness principles from the outset.

In analyzing a scenario that foresees multiple instruments or approaches, complementarity of design would facilitate linkages among them.[29] For instance, a decentralized, bottom-up approach with a range of mitigation measures at national and regional levels will be more effective if the various initiatives are open and capable of benefiting from interlinkages such as linking of regional emissions trading markets.[30]

---

[27] ALDY ET AL., *supra* note 2, at 5.
[28] EDWARD A. PAGE, CLIMATE CHANGE, JUSTICE AND FUTURE GENERATIONS 177 (2006).
[29] BODANSKY, *supra* note 1, at 5.
[30] For arguments in favor of decentralized approaches, *see*, e.g., David G. Victor et al., *A Madisonian Approach to Climate Policy*, 309(5742) SCIENCE 1820 (2005); Taishi Sugiyama & Jonathan Sinton, *Orchestra of Treaties: A Future Climate Regime Scenario with Multiple Treaties among Like-Minded Countries*, 5(1) INTERNATIONAL ENVIRONMENTAL AGREEMENTS 65 (2005); Kristian Tangen & Henrik Hasselknippe, *Converging Markets*, 5(1) INTERNATIONAL ENVIRONMENTAL AGREEMENTS 47 (2005).

## 6.2. Assessment Criteria

In political terms, many countries favor continuity with the institutions and approach of the Convention and the Protocol. The parties have invested considerable time and resources into these two instruments; on the other hand, the United States will probably never join the Protocol. Nonetheless, the flexibility mechanisms and carbon trading pioneered under the Protocol are widely regarded as building blocks for a future agreement. Similarly, the procedures for reporting and accounting GHG emissions will prove of great value for any future climate policy. Vulnerable developing countries have a strong interest in retaining the mechanisms that exist to support adaptation activities under the current system, foremost the Adaptation Fund. On the downside, there exists the potential for policy lock-in – for instance, the switch from an approach based on targets to one based on policies, which could be more acceptable to developing countries, has become more difficult. Scholars with very different positions on the optimal international climate change architecture underline the importance of frameworks that can accommodate different policies – international emissions trading, sectoral policies, intensity measures, and technology-driven approaches.[31] Certainly an approach based on quantified emission targets favors industrialized countries with stable populations and sophisticated economies. Countries with growing populations and less advanced economies – or more rapid economic growth – are more likely to see the current target-based system as a threat to their socioeconomic development. In sum, quantified emission limitation and reduction commitments, the heart of the Kyoto Protocol, will probably remain unacceptable to developing countries for some time to come, so that initial commitments by this category of countries would need to take a different form. Instead, mitigation action by developing countries will, in the first instance, consist of slowing, and eventually halting, the rate at which their emissions are rising, with funding and access to technology playing an important role.[32]

---

[31] For an excellent summary of the various models by leading proponents, see ARCHITECTURES FOR AGREEMENT: ADDRESSING GLOBAL CLIMATE CHANGE IN THE POST-KYOTO WORLD (Joseph E. Aldy & Robert N. Stavins eds., 2007).

[32] See Bali Action Plan, adopted at the Thirteenth Session of the Conference of the Parties, held from December 3–15, 2007, which refers to "nationally appropriate mitigation actions by developing country Parties in the context of sustainable development *supported and enabled by technology, financing and capacity-building, in a measurable, reportable and verifiable manner*" para. 1(b)(ii) (emphasis added).

Compatibility with development goals and consideration of national circumstances will be particularly important in the next phase, which will need to broaden the circle of parties undertaking mitigation commitments. Developing countries regard poverty eradication as their primary objective,[33] with the result that they will be more likely to support climate policies that advance, rather than restrict, the goals of economic and social development, for instance, the achievement of the Millennium Development Goals.[34] This implies an approach that addresses climate change in the context of sustainable development, as opposed to viewing it predominantly as an environmental problem. Specifically, rather than adopting climate policies for their own sake, developing countries are likely adopt cleaner energy technologies because they reduce local air pollution, improve energy security by substituting for imported fuels, and reduce costs through greater efficiency. Mitigation is a cobenefit of these policies. The climate benefits are useful cobenefits but would not constitute the primary driver for the relevant policies and technologies. Some observers warn that climate change policy should not be linked too closely to efforts to solve broader development problems.[35] While it may be correct to point out that climate policy should not be held hostage to progress on international development issues, such as trade or development assistance policies, it remains true that the nature of global development – population growth, economic development, and technological change – determines long-term future emissions profiles.[36]

Adaptation to the impacts of climate change is of particular concern in the context of development. Policy proposals would also need to balance the effort and resources channeled to mitigation with those devoted to adaptation to the impacts of climate change. For instance, a decentralized, bottom-up approach, with its focus on national and regional action, may not adequately address the adaptation needs of poor and vulnerable countries.

Simplicity and predictability are important yardsticks for any international agreement. Proposals with complex formulas are more difficult to convey and understand, and for that reason, probably less likely to garner

---

[33] Delhi Ministerial Declaration on Climate Change and Sustainable Development, adopted at the Eighth Session of the Conference of the Parties, October 23 to November 1, 2002.
[34] Jiahua Pan, *Commitment to Human Development Goals with Low Emissions: An Alternative to Emissions Caps for Post-Kyoto from a Developing Country Perspective*, 5(1) INTERNATIONAL ENVIRONMENTAL AGREEMENTS 89 (2005).
[35] PHILIBERT, *supra* note 5.
[36] INTERGOVERNMENTAL PANEL ON CLIMATE CHANGE, SPECIAL REPORT: EMISSIONS SCENARIOS, SUMMARY FOR POLICYMAKERS 5 (2000).

## 6.2. Assessment Criteria

broad agreement. It is therefore possible that negotiators may prefer policies that are suboptimal in terms of cost-effectiveness or another important criterion over environmentally and economically sounder but more complex proposals. Countries can also be expected to prefer approaches that provide economic predictability with respect to the costs of implementation.[37]

A fairly widely held view is that a climate regime with broad participation delivers the most benefits.[38] The depth of parties' commitments, especially those shouldered by major emitters, however, will also determine the strength of the regime. An agreement with shallow commitments may secure broad participation and full compliance but could fall short with respect to effective mitigation. An alternative is a narrow-but-deep agreement that results in sizeable mitigation among a limited group of large emitters. Such an approach might also circumvent the cumbersome process of securing agreement among a very large number of parties. However, a broad-but-shallow agreement, with less mitigation per country but almost full participation, has the advantage of greater efficiency because, via emissions trading, it lowers overall costs.[39] In addition, such an approach also reduces the incentive for firms to relocate emissions-intensive activities from areas with emission controls to regions that are not subject to restrictions. Over time, broadening of effective controls on GHG emissions in all regions could initially be contingent on, and be driven by, a combination of incentives for mitigation measures and access to cleaner technologies.

An agreement with a long-term target could stimulate technological innovation and enhance cost-effectiveness, as firms and individuals can make decisions with greater certainty about the costs and benefits associated with investments. For instance, achieving the European Union's (EU) target of a maximum rise of 2 degrees Celsius above preindustrial temperatures can, subject to uncertainties, be roughly related to a range of GHG concentrations. This can provide an idea of the expected level of ambition in terms of mitigation action required. As the science remains uncertain on how precisely the climate system will respond to rising GHG emissions, any framework should make provision for relaxing or tightening the policy in response to new information. Overall, a long-term time horizon may allow a more comprehensive and efficient response to the climate change problem;

---

[37] BODANSKY, *supra* note 1, at 6.
[38] *See* ALDY ET AL., *supra* note 2. *See also* COSBEY ET AL., *supra* note 2, at 8. For an opposing view, *see* VICTOR, *supra* note 23, at 133.
[39] ALDY ET AL., *supra* note 2, at 6.

on the other hand, a long time frame may invite delay and procrastination. Some observers therefore argue that targets should be set over periods somewhat longer than the five-year commitment period of the Kyoto Protocol, but beginning with only moderate effort and becoming more stringent over time.[40]

Climate and energy policies should provide incentives to induce technological change. On one hand, public funding for basic and applied energy research can compensate for underinvestment by the private sector in research and development, which has been identified as a classic market failure.[41] Alarmingly, indications are that public and private sector energy research and development has been declining.[42] On the other hand, putting a price on the emission of GHGs, either by means of a cap-and-trade scheme or a carbon tax, should also drive firms to innovate in developing less carbon-intensive technologies and products. However, even a fairly high carbon price in a cap-and-trade scheme may not be sufficient to spur the necessary changes in the development of clean energy technologies.[43] This underlines the importance of complementary policy measures such as the promotion of energy efficiency and renewable energy.[44] The experience of the first phase (2005–2007) of the EU Emissions Trading Scheme suggests that it has failed to provide incentives for clean energy investment – the result, among other things, of an overallocation of allowances and free allocation (grandfathering).[45]

---

[40] Sheila M. Olmstead & Robert M. Stavins, *An International Policy Architecture for the Post-Kyoto Era*, 96(2) AMERICAN ECONOMIC REVIEW PAPERS & PROCEEDINGS 35, 36 (2006). They describe the Kyoto targets as "too little, too fast."

[41] Kenneth J. Arrow, *Economic Welfare and the Allocation of Resources for Invention*, in THE RATE AND DIRECTION OF INVENTIVE ACTIVITY: ECONOMIC AND SOCIAL FACTORS 609–25 (Richard R. Nelson ed., 1962). Because an individual firm does not reap the full reward of its investment in research and development – other firms stand to benefit, too, by adopting the new invention or process, but at little or no cost – it is economically rational to underinvest in such activities.

[42] Daniel F. Kammen & Gregory F. Nemet, *Real Numbers: Reversing the Incredible Shrinking Energy R&D Budget*, ISSUES IN SCIENCE AND TECHNOLOGY 84 (2005).

[43] MICHAELOWA ET AL., *supra* note 2, at 17. For an overview of why emissions trading may result in marginal technology adoption, but not innovation with respect to zero-emission technologies, see William Pizer, *Practical Global Climate Policy*, in ARCHITECTURES FOR AGREEMENT: ADDRESSING GLOBAL CLIMATE CHANGE IN THE POST-KYOTO WORLD 280, 292–93 (Joseph E. Aldy & Robert N. Stavins eds., 2007).

[44] Michael Northrop & David Sassoon, *Cap and Trade and More*, ENVIRONMENTAL FINANCE, June 2007, at 3.

[45] María Isabel Blancoa & Glória Rodrigues, *Can the Future EU ETS Support Wind Energy Investments?*, 36(4) ENERGY POLICY 1509 (2008).

The absence of any provisions to stimulate research and development in cleaner energy technologies and systems has been identified as a failing of the Kyoto Protocol.[46] Some of the proposals considered later in this chapter propose separate agreements on technology,[47] while others rely entirely on setting technology standards to ensure wider participation and compliance.[48] Proponents of a technology standards approach acknowledge the risks of locking in particular technologies and higher costs compared with market-based policies, but they also counter that technology standards are more likely to be successfully implemented than a cap-and-trade system.[49] In some cases, information and other barriers are significant – energy efficiency of consumer goods such as air-conditioners – and mandating standards is simply more effective than any conceivable market-based solution, which would rely on individual responses to market signals such as higher electricity prices. This realization seems to be behind the decision, in several jurisdictions, to phase out inefficient incandescent lightbulbs[50]; despite their demonstrated energy-saving potential, the market share of compact fluorescent lightbulbs has remained fairly low.

Finally, a proposal must be evaluated against prevailing political and institutional realities. Proposals must achieve a balance of environmental effectiveness, equity, and cost-effectiveness. The demands they place on the institutions at the national and international level should not exceed what is

---

[46] Daniel Sarewitz & Roger Pielke Jr., *The Steps Not Yet Taken, in* CONTROVERSIES IN SCIENCE AND TECHNOLOGY: FROM CLIMATE TO CHROMOSOMES 2 (Daniel Lee Kleinman et al. eds., 2008).

[47] *See* SUGIYAMA & SINTON, *supra* note 30, at 65. As one part of a trio of agreements, Sugiyama and Sinton propose a Zero Emission Technology Treaty designed to foster long-term technological change.

[48] SCOTT BARRETT, ENVIRONMENT AND STATECRAFT: THE STRATEGY OF ENVIRONMENTAL TREATY-MAKING (2003); Scott Barrett & Robert N. Stavins, *Increasing Participation and Compliance in International Climate Change Agreements*, 3 INTERNATIONAL ENVIRONMENTAL AGREEMENTS: POLITICS, LAW AND ECONOMICS 349, 366–69 (2003).

[49] BARRETT & STAVINS, *supra* note 48, at 369. Barrett and Stavins cite the example of the 1973 International Convention for the Prevention of Pollution from Ships, which required the adoption of segregated ballast tanks for oil tankers and proved more effective than previous efforts to limit oil pollution. It should also be noted that technology standards could be subject to regular adjustment and evaluation, in an effort to maximize cost-effectiveness.

[50] Tim Johnston, *Australia Is Seeking Nationwide Shift to Energy-Saving Light Bulbs*, NEW YORK TIMES, February 22, 2007, available at http://www.nytimes.com/2007/02/21/business/worldbusiness/21light.html. Claudia H. Deutsch, *No Joke, Bulb Change Is a Challenge for U.S.*, NEW YORK TIMES, December 22, 2007, available at http://www.nytimes.com/2007/12/22/business/22light.html. The Energy Independence and Security Act of 2007, section 322, sets standards banning the current generation of inefficient incandescent lightbulbs by 2012.

reasonable. Policies that are relatively easier to implement – for instance, do not involve the establishment of new international institutions – and that can be monitored easily will be at an advantage.

### 6.3. INTERNATIONAL CLIMATE POLICY: PROPOSALS

This section assesses a number of proposals for a future international climate policy in the light of fairness principles. Clearly some proposals track more closely than others actual developments in climate change policy; nonetheless, even those deemed remote from the mainstream represent currents present in the climate change regime.

#### 6.3.1. Contraction and Convergence

The contraction and convergence proposal developed by the Global Commons Institute notionally assigns each individual an equal entitlement to GHG emissions, based on an overall global carbon budget.[51] In practice, countries would negotiate a global carbon budget, the path to convergence, and the timing (contraction). Then targets for individual countries are determined so that per capita emission allowances converge from the countries' current levels to a level equal for all countries within the agreed period (convergence). The convergence value would be considerably below current per capita emissions of developed countries, which would have to be cut dramatically, while developing country emissions could grow for some time, allowing for economic and social development, before also falling to the convergence value. Industrialized countries would achieve the necessary cuts with the aid of trading, among themselves and with developing countries. The trading of emissions allowances between industrialized and developing countries would result in large resource transfers from the former to the latter.[52]

---

[51] The model is described on the Global Commons Institute Web site, at http://www.gci.org.uk/. For a recent application of the principles of contraction and convergence, see TOM ATHANASIOU & PAUL BAER, DEAD HEAT: GLOBAL JUSTICE AND GLOBAL WARMING (2002), esp. at 76–97.

[52] The Coase theorem holds that with the possibility of trading and absent transaction costs, the initial distribution of property rights (entitlements) does not affect the efficiency of the outcome. In other words, the possibility of trading means that an efficient outcome is always possible, no matter how the emission allowances are initially allocated. The cost

Supported by the fundamental notion of equality, the contraction and convergence proposal possesses a simplicity and intuitive appeal that is easily conveyed. Because we accept equality as a bedrock principle in other areas of human affairs – equal treatment for women and minorities, human rights – it seems plausible to apply the same logic to entitlements to atmospheric space. Overall, the application of the model accords with, but does not explicitly address, the responsibility, needs, and capability dimensions of equity and fairness.[53] Broadly speaking, contraction and convergence would allow developing countries to pursue poverty eradication and economic development, with an increasing focus on mitigation activities, as they acquire the requisite economic and technical capabilities, a process that could be assisted by access to funding and clean technologies from developed countries. Generally, under contraction and convergence, the onus to cut emissions would be on those nations that also have the largest share of cumulative emissions as well as the technological and financial resources necessary to carry out mitigation activities. However, the correlation between existing per capita emissions and capability is not perfect, with the result that many developing countries and countries of the former Soviet Union, which have high emissions and relatively low capability, would receive insufficient allowances.[54]

Critics argue that there is no compelling reason why the right to emit should be equally shared when the same does not hold true for other public goods.[55] They contend that contraction and convergence rests on "a contestable ideological choice."[56] It is true that proponents recognize – and,

---

reductions achieved through global emissions trading are well established in the literature. See John P. Weyant & Jennifer Hill, *Introduction and Overview*, THE COSTS OF THE KYOTO PROTOCOL: A MULTI-MODEL EVALUATION, SPECIAL ISSUE OF THE ENERGY JOURNAL vii (John P. Weyant ed., 1999).

[53] See Michel den Elzen et al., *Multi-stage: A Rule-Based Evolution of Future Commitments under the Climate Change Convention*, 6(1) INTERNATIONAL ENVIRONMENTAL AGREEMENTS 1, 21 (2006), citing as one of the cons of the contraction and convergence approach that it "takes no account of other equity principles (capacity, responsibility for historical emissions)."

[54] Paul Baer & Tom Athanasiou, *Frameworks & Proposals: A Brief, Adequacy and Equity-Based Evaluation of Some Prominent Climate Policy Frameworks and Proposals*, Global Issues Papers 30, Heinrich Böll Stiftung 13 (2007).

[55] John Ashton & Xueman Wang, *Equity and Climate: In Principle and Practice*, in BEYOND KYOTO: ADVANCING THE INTERNATIONAL EFFORT AGAINST CLIMATE CHANGE 61, 69 (Pew Center for Global Climate Change ed., 2003).

[56] *Id.* at 69.

in fact, advocate – the redistributive effect of contraction and convergence, which, it is argued, combats climate change and promotes fairer worldwide economic development.[57] However, it is also argued that if an ambitious mitigation goal is to be met, there is simply no longer sufficient atmospheric space available for a fair distribution, so that contraction and convergence is no longer a fair and equitable alternative for developing countries.[58] As noted in Chapter 5, the strict application of formal equality can have undesirable consequences, including leveling down and a lack of sensitivity to individual differences.[59] For instance, an equitable adjustment might be necessary to account for the specific circumstances of certain countries, for example, those situated in cold regions, where space-heating needs are higher. Such countries would be entitled to an upward adjustment in their allocation of emission allowances, commensurate with their demonstrated special circumstances. Similarly, the principle of need requires that the least developed countries be given special treatment, especially sparsely populated, poor countries that could be expected to lose out in relative terms. Reference is sometimes also made to the perverse incentive that contraction and convergence could have with respect to population growth. Given the many drivers of influencing population growth, it seems rather far-fetched that climate policy would have a significant impact. In any event, putting the model into practice would require selecting a population reference period or periods, which could be adjusted so as to account for any perverse incentive.

The contraction and convergence model does not specify a particular target; however, provided the chosen target is sufficiently stringent, the approach will provide environmental effectiveness. In addition, compared to approaches relying on multiple stages, contraction and convergence is conceptually simple and predictable. In fact, as, in essence, a guiding umbrella principle, it leaves the choice of tools to achieve emission reductions open to the parties. Once the global stabilization target was agreed, the parties could use the mechanisms of the Kyoto Protocol, especially emissions trading, as countries with low per capita emissions could sell a

---

[57] *See* ATHANASIOU & BAER, *supra* note 51.
[58] *See* BAER & ATHANASIOU, *supra* note 54, at 15. Although Baer and Athanasiou were proponents of contraction and convergence, they subsequently, together with others, developed, and now advocate, the Greenhouse Development Rights approach. *See infra* note 63.
[59] *See* Chapter 4.

portion of their excess emission allowances. In the end, the biggest obstacle to contraction and convergence is political acceptability – countries with high per capita emissions are, at present, not prepared to endorse the redistribution of resources to low per capita countries that would follow from its implementation. This is unlikely to change in the near term.[60]

One issue that may arise in the implementation of the proposal concerns the difficulty developing countries, especially the poorest, may experience in establishing the necessary institutional and technical capacity for emissions trading.[61] Moreover, there exists the possibility that governments might sell off so much of their stock of entitlements that they leave the next generation without reserves when their emissions reach or exceed the per capita convergence value. What is to stop a government selling entitlements, for short-term gain, without regard to the future? It could be argued that it makes sense to sell as many entitlements as possible early on to develop, on the basis that in decades to come, a wealthier and technologically advanced society will be capable of making the necessary emission cuts to meet the convergence target. Such decisions involve highly uncertain assumptions about future economic growth and rates of technological change. Possible responses to the potential danger of overselling could include delayed or staggered vesting procedures, the need to maintain a periodically adjusted reserve margin, and oversight by an international institution. Countries may regard some of these options as infringing on their sovereignty.

If the prospect for a straightforward implementation of contraction and convergence remains slim, it remains very likely that elements of this model will be reflected in any long-term solution. Simply put, achieving a stabilization target consistent with the scientific findings requires some convergence of per capita emissions – neither a continuation of business as usual in the developed economies nor an untrammeled rise in developing-country emissions is remotely compatible with low or middle-level stabilization levels. Given its appeal to the universal ideal of equality, the contraction and

---

[60] The German Chancellor, Angela Merkel, has proposed the long-term goal of converging emissions. See *Chancellor Angela Merkel Launches a New Climate Initiative*, English-language homepage of the chancellor, August 30, 2007, available at http://www.bundeskanzlerin.de/Content/EN/Artikel/2007/08/2007-08-30-bundeskanzlerin-in-japan__en.html. *Merkel Calls for Global Emissions Trading Agreement to Follow Kyoto*, INTERNATIONAL HERALD TRIBUNE, October 9, 2007, available at http://www.iht.com/articles/ap/2007/10/09/europe/EU-GEN-Germany-Climate-Conference.php.

[61] DEN ELZEN ET AL., *supra* note 53, at 20.

convergence proposal is uniquely qualified to remind all participants of the equity dimension of climate change.[62]

### 6.3.2. Greenhouse Development Rights

Like other approaches, the Greenhouse Development Rights (GDRs) framework selects capacity (capability) and responsibility as relevant guiding principles, but in a new and insightful manner.[63] The GDRs approach explicitly sets out to combine the realization of the right to development with an ambitious mitigation target. The right to development – not emissions, which have only instrumental importance – is the guiding principle of this approach.[64] The GDRs framework puts the right to development into operation in the form of a development threshold, which is a level of welfare that goes beyond mere basic needs. The assumed income threshold is US$7,500 per year.[65] Individuals above this threshold – whether living in developed or developing counties – are assumed to have realized their right to development. Accordingly, they will have to contribute to the emission reduction effort, irrespective of their nationality. Herein lies the novelty of the GDRs approach: it analyzes capacity in individual terms and, in the process, takes account of inequality within countries, not only between countries. To complete the picture, a country's total capacity is defined as the sum of all individual income, excluding income below the development threshold. Responsibility is defined as cumulative emissions since 1990 but is also adjusted to exclude those emissions corresponding to consumption below the development threshold.

The measures of capacity and responsibility are combined into a single indicator of obligation, the so-called Responsibility-Capacity Index (RCI). Putting it into practice as a tool for burden sharing, national emission limitation, and reduction obligations would be defined as shares of the

---

[62] ASHTON & WANG, *supra* note 55, at 69.
[63] PAUL BAER ET AL., THE GREENHOUSE DEVELOPMENT RIGHTS FRAMEWORK: THE RIGHT TO DEVELOPMENT IN A CLIMATE CONSTRAINED WORLD (rev. 2nd ed., 2008). *See also* Niklas Höhne & Sara Moltmann, *Distribution of Emission Allowances under the Greenhouse Development Right and Other Effort Sharing Approaches*, Report for the Heinrich Böll Stiftung (2008).
[64] Christian Egenhofer et al., POSITIVE INCENTIVES FOR CLIMATE ACTION, Report 5, ECP 9 (2008).
[65] BAER ET AL., *supra* note 63, at 10.

global target, which is allocated among countries in proportion to their RCIs. A look at various countries' RCIs confirms some patterns but also has a few surprises: the United States has the largest share at 33.1 percent; the EU follows with 25.7 percent; China has a rather significant 5.5 percent share, reflecting the output of GHGs as well as its growing middle class; and India, also large but much poorer, falls behind China with only by a 0.5 percent share of the global RCI.

Setting the start date for counting cumulative emissions at 1990 counters some of the criticisms associated with arguments from responsibility. First, this is a very defensible date from which countries should have been on notice with respect to the harm caused by GHG emissions. Second, with every passing year, it becomes harder to make the case that the present generation is paying for the sins of the past, which is an argument made when, for example, responsibility is attributed for cumulative emissions of the twentieth century.

The GDRs approach takes seriously the issue of development, recognizing "that the right to development adheres not to nations, but to people, that it can only be a right to sustainable development" and not affluence.[66] Does this approach signal a deeper engagement with interpersonal fairness? Although the GDRs approach is concerned with the right to development, the answer appears to be no. Intranational inequality is used for instrumental purposes, namely, to help define the burden-sharing criterion, that is, the RCI. When it comes to the domestic impact of RCI, it is admitted that it is up to each country to decide how to pass on the cost of mitigation action. Naturally this problem is not unique to GDRs, but it does have equity implications. When the RCI is calculated, those under the development threshold do not count, but there is nothing to prevent governments from, nonetheless, either shifting an unfair burden onto the poor or failing to cushion them from the consequences of mitigation policies, for example, increased fuel and energy prices. Another concern relates to the development threshold, where income stands in for the material resources deemed necessary for a decent life. There is definitely more than a hint of a sufficiency argument present, namely, that a fair distribution would promote having enough for a decent and fulfilling life, but no more. Although there is an arbitrary element involved, one might ask whether US$7,500 can be applied across

[66] *Id.* at 91.

such a diverse group of countries as a useful proxy for development. For instance, the U.S. federal poverty level for a single person in 2007 was set at US$10,590. One could plausibly make the case that in the U.S. context, this level of income, not to mention US$7,500, is not conducive or supportive of a decent life, one that enables human flourishing. Yet in a developing country, this income level would entail entry into the middle class. This suggests that it might be more equitable to weight the capacity calculation according to national income distribution. Individual and societal capacity is a function of many things – income, institutions, basic economic and political freedoms, technological sophistication – so that adopting a single, across-the-board measure may obscure relevant differences. From the perspective of giving priority to needs of the most vulnerable individuals and countries, there is an argument to be made that direct transfers could achieve this objective, without being mediated through climate policy.[67] This leads to another dimension where fairness enters the debate, namely, that the manner in which the world sets out to lower emissions and adapt to climate change – the choice of instruments, policies, and so forth – will have very different implications for equitable and sustainable development in the poorer parts of the world. Admittedly, GDRs are, in the first place, a model for thinking about the changes that need to take place, but their abstract attractiveness, in fairness terms, should not detract from the imperative to review the fairness of both ends and means.

How might this proposal fare in the real world of climate negotiations? On one hand, developing countries may be reluctant to wholeheartedly endorse an approach that, although demanding very stringent cuts of developed countries, also clearly maps out their own obligations. One effect of the RCI is to pierce the one-size-fits-all developing country veil. On the other hand, the GDRs approach is a bitter pill for developed countries – a shrinking carbon budget means that allocating extra development space for the south comes at a high cost. Some developed countries, the United States, notably, would be required to reduce emissions by 100 percent below 1990 levels; clearly meeting this so-called impossible target would require undertaking reductions in other countries.[68] From a technical standpoint, the envisaged annual emission reductions go beyond what many consider

---

[67] *See* Eric A. Posner & Cass Sunstein, *Climate Change Justice*, 96 GEORGETOWN LAW JOURNAL 1565, 1584–86, 1590 (2008).
[68] *Id.* at 21.

feasible, but admittedly there is a clear need to challenge the conventional wisdom on what is possible. The authors of the framework recognize that it is very improbable that the GDRs approach would be translated directly into climate policy; rather, it is meant to serve as a reference framework that "lays down a standard of comparison against which to gauge the efforts implied by actual proposals, as they emerge."[69] By admission, this is an approach for an emergency situation, and in emergencies, it is often permitted to derogate from established rights.

### 6.3.3. Brazilian Proposal

The proposal, originally made by Brazil in the Kyoto negotiations, is based on historical responsibility for temperature change.[70] Entitlements are assigned based on historical responsibility, calculated in accordance with a climate model agreed on by the parties.[71] The proposal was originally intended to apply only for purposes of differentiation among industrialized countries, but the methodology could be expanded to encompass all countries.[72] And while the original proposal counts responsibility for emissions from the Industrial Revolution, it is also possible to estimate historical responsibility over more recent periods, for instance, 1990, which is widely regarded as a time when human-induced climate change was recognized as a potentially grave threat. For reference, according to recent research, the average contributions to the global mean surface temperature increase in 2000 are around 40 percent from the Organisation for Economic Co-operation and Development (OECD) group of industrialized countries; 14 percent from Eastern Europe and the former Soviet Union; 24 percent from Asia; and about 6 and 16 percent, respectively, from Africa and Latin America.[73] The choice of

---

[69] *Id.* at 30.
[70] UN Doc. FCCC/AGBM/1997/MISC.1/Add.3 3. The proposal remains on the agenda of the Conference of the Parties to the Convention, whose Subsidiary Body for Technological and Scientific Advice has sponsored continued research into contributions to climate change. *See* UN Doc. FCCC/SBSTA/2002/INF.14 for a summary of the research efforts carried out by various institutions, while up-to-date information is available at http://www.matchinfo.net/.
[71] BODANSKY, *supra* note 1, at 22.
[72] Michel den Elzen & Michiel Schaeffer, *Responsibility for Past and Future Global Warming: Uncertainties on Attributing Anthropogenic Climate Change*, 54 CLIMATIC CHANGE 29 (2002).
[73] Michel den Elzen et al., *Analysing Countries' Contributions to Climate Change: Scientific and Policy-Related Choices*, 8(6) ENVIRONMENTAL SCIENCE & POLICY 614 (2005).

methodology and the GHGs covered may have considerable implications for attributed responsibility.[74] For instance, including only the fossil $CO_2$ emissions and not emissions from land-use change (deforestation) increases the contribution of the OECD group of countries by 21 percentage points and decreases the contribution of Asia by 14 percentage points.[75]

For the simple reason that climate change is a cumulative process – historical emissions are relevant as a matter of pure physics, not legal construct – it would be incorrect to regard the historical responsibility approach as giving large developing countries a free pass. The warming to date is a consequence of fossil fuels combusted over the past 100 years. Historical responsibility is a plausible and defensible – if not compelling – criterion for distributing the effort of dealing with a global problem. Moreover, as countries industrialize, their cumulative emissions, and hence their responsibility, will increase.[76]

The responsibility approach taps an intuitive sense that those who have caused harm – in this case, emitted the largest stock of GHGs – should also bear the primary responsibility for abatement.[77] It may also be loosely, if perhaps inaccurately, equated with the polluter pays principle. A responsibility approach is compatible with the need and capability principles, as the responsible parties are also the wealthiest and possess the technological capacity to spearhead the response to climate change.[78] Overall, a responsibility approach would not necessarily conflict with the application of the equality principle, as in the contraction and convergence proposal. An exception might be countries with historically high emission burdens, continued reliance on fossil fuel–intensive economies, and small populations, for instance, certain countries of the former Soviet Union.

---

[74] DEN ELZEN & SCHAEFFER, *supra* note 72, at 71–72. Of the methodological choices, $CO_2$ emissions from land-use and non-$CO_2$ gases have the greatest impact on outcomes.

[75] DEN ELZEN ET AL., *supra* note 73, at 614.

[76] From 1900 to 2005, the United States and the EU countries combined accounted for just over half of cumulative global energy-related carbon dioxide emissions; China accounted for only 8 percent and India for 2 percent. Under the IEA's reference scenario, China's share of emissions from 1900 to 2030 rises to 16 percent, approaching those of the United States at 25 percent and the EU at 18 percent. India's cumulative emissions (4 percent) approach those of Japan (4 percent). *See* INTERNATIONAL ENERGY AGENCY, *supra* note 18, at 199–201.

[77] In the same way that a polluter is assessed responsibility for the total discharge, the issue here is the responsibility for a share of the total stock over time.

[78] *See* CICERO & ECN, *supra* note 4, at 54. The study assigns the Brazilian proposal a high equity score on need, capacity, and "guilt" but a very low score on potential for operational implementation.

Measured against a number of policy assessment criteria, the responsibility approach does not fare that well. Although the basic concept is straightforward, uncertainties regarding non–fossil fuel emissions and related methodological issues mean that putting it into practice will be more complex. Environmental effectiveness would depend on the target that is set independently; the responsibility criterion comes into play in allocating the burden among the parties. This option is compatible with the approach of the Convention and the Kyoto Protocol, and because it relies on quantified emission targets, it would not accommodate alternatives such as growth (intensity) targets. Among the disadvantages of the responsibility approach are that it is not very sensitive to country-specific circumstances. Where the proposal is applied to a limited number of countries, cost-effectiveness may be an issue, unless trading can be expanded through instruments such as the clean development mechanism (CDM). Although a responsibility model can be adjusted to account for new scientific and economic information, it is less flexible than some other proposals.

### 6.3.4. Multistage, and Graduation and Deepening

The multistage proposal and the graduation and deepening proposal are two proposals for involving developing countries in a future climate change agreement.[79] They are representative of a set of top-down burden-sharing proposals, and because they share a number of common features, it is convenient to discuss them together. Under the multistage approach, developing countries assume progressively more stringent commitments, with passage from one stage to the next determined by a variety of criteria. (The very poorest countries, lacking in technical and economic capacity, would not be expected to assume targets but would benefit from technical and financial assistance designed to steer them toward a low-carbon development path.)

Several versions of the multistage proposal exist, but an up-to-date iteration sees it developing differentiated according to the following three distinct stages: stage 1, no quantitative limits and the emissions path is not subject

[79] *See* BODANSKY, *supra* note 1, at 36, 47; Michel den Elzen & Marcel Berk, *Options for Differentiation of Future Commitments in Climate Policy: How to Realize Timely Participation to Meet Stringent Climate Goals?*, 1(4) CLIMATE POLICY 465 (2001); Axel Michaelowa et al., *Graduation and Deepening: An Ambitious Post-2012 Climate Policy Scenario*, 5(1) INTERNATIONAL ENVIRONMENTAL AGREEMENTS 25 (2005).

to controls; stage 2, countries assume intensity targets or a prescribed deceleration in emissions growth; and stage 3, countries would be subject to quantified emission reduction targets.[80] All Annex I parties are assumed to be at stage 3; developing countries make the transition (graduate) to stage 2 on the basis of an index made up of per capita gross domestic product (GDP) (reflecting the capability to act) and per capita $CO_2$-equivalent emissions (reflecting responsibility for climate change). This is termed the capacity-responsibility index. Earlier versions used only a per capita income measure for differentiation.[81] The inclusion of per capita emissions results in the earlier inclusion of low-income countries, particularly those with relatively high per capita emissions, such as South Africa. Transition to stage 3 is based on a more stringent version of the capacity-responsibility index; alternatively, the threshold is calculated as a proportion of world average per capita emissions. The choice of an overall stabilization target determines the formulation of the thresholds for graduation – a more stringent global target would mean that advanced developing countries graduate more quickly to emission controls. At stage 3, the emission reduction burden sharing is in accordance with per capita emissions. Although not always explicit, the elaboration and implementation of the scheme would presumably be left to the existing international structures, in other words, the UN Framework Convention on Climate Change (UNFCCC).

The multistage proposal discussed here makes a conscious attempt to incorporate equity and fairness. The graduation criteria reflect the equity principles of need, capability, and responsibility. Equality is reflected in the choice of per capita emissions as the burden-sharing criteria in the final stage.[82] On a more practical note, this proposal is flexible and could be adjusted to differing national circumstances and is compatible with the architecture of the Convention and Kyoto Protocol. Cost-effectiveness is advanced through the use of emissions trading in the final stage as well as through continuation of the clean development mechanism, enabling countries in stage 3 to invest in emission reduction projects in countries that have not yet assumed quantified emission reduction commitments.

---

[80] DEN ELZEN ET AL., *supra* note 53, at 4–5.
[81] DEN ELZEN & BERK, *supra* note 79, at 465.
[82] DEN ELZEN ET AL., *supra* note 53, at 22.

The use of intensity targets in stage 2 may give rise to some concerns about environmental integrity.[83] Like other top-down proposals discussed so far, this one also requires the fixing of an explicit long-term target. Finally, implementation of the proposal would face a political hurdle because it implies dismantling the common front of the G-77 and China developing-country negotiating group. It appears that sufficient flexibility exists to ameliorate many concerns, for instance, by ensuring that adaptation to climate change – a major concern for island states and African countries – receives adequate resources under a new climate regime.

The graduation and deepening proposal is similar to the multistage proposal in several respects: transition for developing countries, in this case, directly to Kyoto-style quantified emission reductions, is on the basis of a graduation index (GI) consisting of GDP and emissions per capita measures.[84] In the multistage model, the graduation threshold is a function of the agreed stabilization target. In the graduation and deepening scenario, 550 ppm is assumed as the stabilization target, with agreement that emissions should peak no later than 2030. The overall stringency of the country targets – which are summarized subsequently – is based on this stabilization goal. Arguably, this approach lacks ambition – at the Thirteenth Conference of the Parties to the UNFCCC, the EU took the position that global GHG emissions should peak within the next 10 to 15 years and that Annex I countries, as a group, would need to cut their emissions by 25 to 40 percent by 2020.[85]

The chosen baseline year is 2012, and there are three levels of emission targets: a 6 percent reduction, a 3 percent reduction, and stabilization at the level of the baseline. Countries classified by the UN as least developed countries (LDCs), receiving assistance under the International Development Association arm of the World Bank, or receiving food aid are exempted from any targets. The GI of all countries is calculated. Differentiation then takes place as follows: developing countries with a GI higher than the Annex B average take on the most stringent reduction target, in other words, 6 percent.[86] In

---

[83] *Id.* at 22.
[84] MICHAELOWA ET AL., *supra* note 79, at 31–33.
[85] *Summary of the Thirteenth Conference of the Parties to the UNFCCC and the Third Meeting of the Parties of the Kyoto Protocol, 3–15 December,* 12(354) EARTH NEGOTIATIONS BULLETIN (2007), available at http://www.iisd.ca/climate/cop13/.
[86] Annex B of the Kyoto Protocol lists the countries subject to emission limitation and reduction commitments.

this list would be Singapore, which is nominally still a developing country, as well as oil-exporting countries with high per capita incomes and emissions such as Qatar and the United Arab Emirates. Second, developing countries with a GI above that of the lowest Annex II (highly industrialized) country are subject to the 3 percent reduction. Countries falling into this group include the Republic of Korea and Saudi Arabia. Third, countries with a GI above that of the lowest Annex B country assume a stabilization target. Finally, countries that do not pass the lowest threshold of the GI – among which are China, India, and Indonesia – and emit more than 50 million tons of $CO_2$ can assume a intensity target with trading or participate in a project-based measure like CDM.

The composition of the GI reflects two important equity principles: capability (GDP per capita) and responsibility (emissions per capita). Naturally, the proof of any such indexes lies in the application of the relevant thresholds, which, in this case, are reasonably easy to comprehend, leading to groupings that seem fair in differentiating the groups of countries. Managing and implementing the scheme – presumably the task of the intergovernmental climate negotiations – could prove to be altogether more difficult. The exemption of countries on the lowest rung of the development ladder – which would include most of sub-Saharan Africa – is a welcome recognition of the principle of need. The group of oil-exporting countries with relatively high incomes and very high per capita emissions would not find that this scheme takes account of their national circumstances; it may prove difficult to secure their participation, although the possibility of inexpensive emission reduction opportunities, and therefore emissions trading, could serve as a carrot. While the proposal is no more complex than comparable schemes, developing countries might consider the emission reductions arbitrary – those developing nations with the most stringent targets would argue that it would be more equitable to lower their targets, perhaps from 6 to 5 percent, with a commensurate increase for the group with lower targets. This gets to the point that each set of developing countries encompasses parties with rather different economic structures, such as Qatar and Singapore, and, presumably, varying abatement costs. The immediate imposition of an absolute emission reduction target would constitute a blunt instrument; equity and fairness point in the direction of a more gradual transition and a wider choice of instruments such as intensity or sectoral targets.

### 6.3.5. Orchestra of Treaties and Converging Markets

The orchestra of treaties and converging markets proposals are examples of decentralized, bottom-up approaches.[87] Based on the conviction that Kyoto-style targets give rise to adversarial negotiating stances, the orchestra of treaties aims for a more facilitative approach by taking account of sovereignty concerns related to energy policies; building on national interests in the areas of technology and economic development; and addressing long-term technological change, not only short-term emission cuts.[88] The proposal consists of four building blocks, three of which develop outside the ambit of the Convention. One, a group of emission markets (GEM), is developed, based on a gradual coordination of domestic emission markets, which takes place in the absence of internationally agreed targets. This scenario would feature an evolutionary, bottom-up process of coordination and linking of various domestic cap-and-trade schemes. Two, a Zero Emission Technology Treaty (ZETT), which has as its ultimate goal zero $CO_2$ emissions from the energy sector, is intended to address long-term technological change, but does so without infringing on sovereignty because it operates on the basis of a voluntary pledge and review basis. A third component would be a Climate-wise Development Treaty (CDT) to promote development, technology transfer, and adaptation. Finally, UNFCCC would serve as a political forum, an information exchange, and a funding mechanism. The ZETT and CDT would presumably be the result of centralized negotiations under the auspices of the UNFCCC. A key issue under the CDT would be the need to secure funding for technology transfer and other activities designed to assist developing countries.

The converging markets proposal is essentially an elaboration of one component – the group of emission markets – of the orchestra of treaties model. It would proceed through the integration of currently fragmented domestic trading systems. To be admitted to the core group, countries would have to assume mandatory national targets, and candidate countries could receive financial assistance to prepare them for entry into the system. There would be no central allocation, burden-sharing formulas, or formally agreed stabilization targets, but instead, national emission targets

---

[87] SUGIYAMA & SINTON, *supra* note 30, at 65; TANGEN & HASSELKNIPPE, *supra* note 30, at 47; BODANSKY, *supra* note 1, at 26, 48.
[88] SUGIYAMA & SINTON, *supra* note 30, at 65.

would be developed on a country-by-country basis. It would be possible to (re)integrate the scheme under the umbrella of the UNFCCC. Once a country has established a trading scheme with mandatory targets, the incentive to link with the larger market group comes from reduced abatement costs. The same is true for members of the group as a whole – expansion of the market will tend to lower the marginal costs of abatement. There is no conceptual reason standing in the way of linking and integration of various domestic markets, provided that certain design elements, such as permit allocation rules, are properly designed.[89] Overall, a functioning market would benefit from clear rules and some degree of harmonization. Corporations from sectors with high emissions and globe-spanning operations can be expected to be advocates of harmonization, preferring greater uniformity to a patchwork system of markets. Unlike the Kyoto Protocol, in which rules are made by the parties and implemented with the assistance of a central bureaucracy, the converging markets approach would rely on market-to-market coordination and cooperation.

Unlike the other proposals examined so far, the orchestra of treaties model does not consciously reflect any equity principles. The GEM, as further detailed in the convergence of markets variant, would expand in accordance with market logic – lowest-cost emission reductions – and on terms reflecting the bargaining power of the parties. Depending on its structure, the GEM would probably roughly reflect the principles of responsibility and capability; although major industrialized country emitters may elect not to undertake any emission reductions, or otherwise only very shallow ones. Due to both a lack of emission reduction opportunities, which are generally correlated with industrial activity, and inadequate institutional frameworks, LDCs are unlikely to benefit from emissions trading. A decentralized system is less likely to respect the principle of need; in particular, LDCs will have even less of a forum to press for inclusiveness and solidarity.

The environmental effectiveness of these more decentralized approaches is uncertain; there may not exist sufficient institutional glue to bind the blocks together into an effective response to climate change, with the result that emission cuts are inadequate. It is also possible that they may also entail higher transaction and coordination costs, as more time and resources

---

[89] *See* JANE ELLIS & DENNIS TIRPAK, LINKING GHG EMISSION TRADING SCHEMES AND MARKETS (2006).

would need to be spent on ensuring compatibility between systems with different characteristics.

### 6.3.6. Global Triptych

The global triptych is a bottom-up, sector-based, and technology-oriented proposal for differentiating commitments. The triptych approach was originally employed by the EU to allocate its Kyoto target among member states.[90] The reference to a triptych reflects the focus of the original model on $CO_2$ emissions from three sectors: power generation; energy-intensive industries such as cement and steel; and the domestic sector, encompassing the residential sector and transportation. The extended or global triptych takes the original a step further to cover the waste sector and agriculture, thus covering non-$CO_2$ gases such as methane and the other industrial gases controlled under the Kyoto Protocol.

A bottom-up technological analysis is employed to identify the emission reduction potential in these sectors. This analysis is coupled with projections of expected growth in the sector – for instance, are energy-intensive industries expected to maintain their share of the economy? – and population figures to derive national emission targets. For example, to calculate the emission allowance from the power sector for a country, assumptions are made about growth rates and per capita consumption, and requirements are imposed on how electricity may be generated, with minimum figures for renewable energy. The analysis takes account of the fact that countries' generation mix varies enormously, as does the renewable energy potential and public acceptance of nuclear energy.

The proposal is attractive in that it appears to offer a fairly objective and technical solution to the differentiation conundrum. The approach is sensitive to the individual circumstances of countries and to the principles of need and capability. Its main practical drawbacks are complexity and the reliance on production growth rates in industry and the power sector. As an essentially forward-looking approach, it is less responsive to historical responsibility, with the possible result that developing countries with low emissions and relatively efficient industry could end up with fairly

---

[90] BODANSKY, *supra* note 1, at 35; Helen Groenenberg et al., *Global Triptych: A Bottom-Up Approach for the Differentiation of Commitments under the Climate Convention*, 4(2) CLIMATE POLICY 153 (2004).

stringent targets. Given their very low level of industrial activity, and the difficulty in projecting their growth paths, it seems overly restrictive to set a target for LDCs. The principles of need and responsibility – whether historical or current emissions – constitute persuasive grounds on which to exempt LDCs. However, as its advocates acknowledge, the approach does imply value-laden choices with respect to the selection of long-term targets for the three sectors.[91] For instance, having energy efficiency decline too quickly to a low value may prejudice countries whose heavy industry rests on a legacy of inexpensive electricity.

## 6.4. CONCLUSION

The proposals for a future international response to climate change are intended as illustrations of different impulses in the climate negotiations, not as the latest or most "realistic" examples of climate policy. The overview of the proposals demonstrates that fairness concerns figure prominently in a number of them. In addition, equity principles are also present in the policy evaluation criteria that are commonly put forward – for instance, in the concern that a future agreement should be responsive to the poverty eradication and economic development objectives of developing countries and that proposals should be capable of taking country-specific circumstances into account. That some of the approaches reviewed contain an explicit engagement with equity concerns is fitting and timely because the climate regime as it stands has deferred the knottier, controversial topics. In the interests of broadening participation, the UNFCCC did not include emission targets; the Kyoto Protocol did set targets, for a rather short time frame, and only for industrialized countries, with much of the parties' energies devoted to fleshing out its provisions and bringing into operation the flexibility mechanisms. With steadily rising GHG concentrations, the trade-offs, national interests, and equity dimensions are ratcheted up. The longer the delay, the less time there is to begin taking sensible, low-cost options in the near-term, while integrating the need to move a low-carbon future into public awareness, public policy, and private investment decisions.

On the policy side, a successful future framework would ensure environmental effectiveness in line with a broadly defined and widely supported

[91] Helen Groenenberg & Jeroen van der Sluijs, *Valueloading and Uncertainty in a Sector-Based Differentiation Scheme for Emission Allowances*, 71(1–2) CLIMATIC CHANGE 75 (2005).

goal and, at the same time, would satisfy cost concerns. This would entail the engagement of developing countries in the joint effort to slow, and then reduce, global emissions. The distribution of the burdens and benefits associated with combating climate, more specifically, the basis on which to share the burden of abatement, would not be resolved exclusively by recourse to equity and fairness principles. But equity principles are likely to form at least one part of the solution, while not denying that other factors – market forces, technical expertise, negotiating resources, political and economic influence – will play important roles.

Thus the conclusions drawn from this chapter are that proposals that seek actively to reflect both a balance of fairness principles – responsibility, capability, need – and political and economic realities stand the best chance of being accepted and implemented by both developed and developing countries. It was noted that proposals that reflected a particular dimension of fairness in a very pure form, for instance, contraction and convergence, are partially taken up in more hybrid proposals such as the multistage convergence model. This is understandable. Equality is a powerful notion, and in the long run, convergence of emissions pathways is a geophysical imperative. Overall, the transition to a low-carbon future suggests a moderation of absolute claims and a search for bridging mechanisms. Differentiation will be critical but must be kept within the bounds of what can be managed within the context of multiparty negotiations. At the same time, because hard choices cannot be postponed – a tendency in international negotiations – a future climate regime cannot be everything to all parties: difficult choices have to be made. Visible efforts to reflect a variety of fairness principles would contribute to a shared perception that a new agreement is fair.

The future approach should have universal participation but be flexible enough to accommodate initiatives by a smaller group of countries. Fifteen countries are responsible for almost three-quarters of global emissions. It would be sensible for them to make a concerted effort to seek common ground. In going forward, openness to new proposals and ideas is critical. A simple and immediate extension of absolute targets to developing countries is neither politically feasible nor fair and equitable. A pledge-based system for developing countries, based on SD-PAMs, may be one way to begin including the less economically advanced countries in the developing country category. The review mechanism could build on the existing expert reviews of Annex I communications as well as on models such as the Trade Policy Review of the World Trade Organization, a process designed to facilitate the smooth functioning of the multilateral trading system by enhancing the transparency of countries' trade policies.[92] Differentiation in mitigation actions among developing countries will be important; however, developing countries would need to be convinced that they are not trading group solidarity for an unfair bargain.

Finally, one of the greatest uncertainties in projecting climate change is the course of future economic growth. This uncertainty is greatest for developing countries, whose economies are not yet fully developed. Any assumption of fixed allocations is therefore riskier for developing than industrialized countries, whose growth rates do, over time, vary, but where the basic economic structure is in place and underlying trends (shifts toward services) are ongoing and relatively slow. On the other hand, who can predict exactly the industrial profile and emissions of major emerging economies over the next 5, 10, or 15 years? This argues for flexibility for developing countries, at least in the initial stages, which can be achieved through a variety of mechanisms and policy instruments.

[92] *See* background on the Web site of the World Trade Organization, at http://www.wto.org/english/tratop_e/tpr_e/tp_int_e.htm.

# 7

# Conclusion

Climate change is an enormously complex, multidimensional problem that mixes together science, law, economics, technological advancement, and, recently, security interests in a manner that few other global problems do. The scientific study of climate change has spurred a massive international research effort that has pushed back the boundaries of knowledge about the behavior of, and influences on, the earth system. Successive reports of the Intergovernmental Panel on Climate Change have brought more evidence of human-induced climate change, with the most recent report concluding that warming is unequivocal and that human activities are the dominant cause. Yet the interaction between science and public policy is far from the linear relationship of warning of a grave threat from an authoritative source, followed by an appropriate and timely response. While it provides an authoritative description of the problem and outlines the parameters for a solution, a scientific consensus alone is insufficient to bring about changes in society. In contrast to natural scientists, economists have remained more divided on the costs and benefits of taking early action.[1] Overall, a failure to adequately consider the assumptions underpinning economic analyses of climate change may contribute to obscuring crucial ethical and value choices. Ultimately, our welfare is dependent on the natural system, a reality that is only imperfectly incorporated into our decision-making frameworks. In this context, open articulation of the fairness dimensions can enrich,

[1] *See*, for a notable exception, NICHOLAS STERN, THE ECONOMICS OF CLIMATE CHANGE, THE STERN REVIEW, Cabinet Office, HM Treasury (2006). The central conclusion of the Review was that the costs of inaction outweighed the costs of action to combat climate change. Leading economists immediately criticized the Review's approach. *See* William Nordhaus, *Critical Assumptions in the Stern Review on Climate Change*, 317(5835) SCIENCE 201 (2007).

contextualize, and complement insights gained from economics, international relations, and other modes of policy analysis.

This book set out to analyze and demonstrate the relevance of fairness to understanding and further developing the international climate regime. But are fairness claims in climate change any more than a thin, rhetorical veneer over hard realpolitik? Indeed, for many, international law and the international community lack key attributes of a system in which it makes sense to speak of fairness. The position taken here is that serious engagement with fairness is worthwhile. There exist at least three reasons to take fairness seriously in international climate law and policy. First, fairness in fact features prominently in public discourse concerning climate change and what to do about it. Differing perceptions of fairness constitute a real constraint on the possibilities for international climate policy.[2] But the contested nature of fairness is not sufficient grounds to disqualify it from consideration – rather, it is a reason for deeper engagement. This book has not sought to conclusively define fairness. The approach has instead been to identify several principles – egalitarian, responsibility, need, and capability – that can plausibly contribute to a rough, working consensus on the critical fairness dimensions of climate change. Second, technical analyses can guide, but not determine, options for action. The gravity, scope, and irreversible nature of the climate change problem demand that decision makers as well as citizens acknowledge the ethical and moral dimensions of climate change. As we are reminded, trade-offs will be have to be made, and fairness principles provide the language for reasoned discussion about which differences are relevant and why. Power, wealth and bargaining skills are important, but fairness principles can help set the parameters of acceptable claims. Third, the climate change problem directly concerns the allocation of burdens and benefits – distributing the costs of mitigation and adaptation actions and also allocating shares in the rapidly shrinking absorptive capacity of the atmosphere and natural systems.

There is a tendency for debates on climate change to fracture along the same fault lines as issues of international development and global debates about the unequal relations between states. This presents risks and opportunities. On one hand, superimposing debates on global development,

---

[2] Steve Rayner & Elizabeth M. Malone, *Ten Suggestions for Policymakers*, in 4 HUMAN CHOICE AND CLIMATE CHANGE 109, 116 (Steve Rayner & Elizabeth M. Malone eds., 1999).

which tend to cut along north-south lines, risks miring the climate change negotiations in interminable and possibly irresolvable disputes. On the other, it is an exercise in futility to try to ignore the elephant in the conference room by insisting on a pure, technocratic climate policy. Certainly denying the poorest in the world access to the next rung of the development ladder on the grounds of climate protection would be inequitable and politically entirely unrealistic. The development dimension is a reminder that tackling global climate change will require more than sophisticated, top-down policy instruments such as cap-and-trade schemes. What is needed is an approach that addresses the economic, social, and environmental dimensions of climate change. It is suggested that analyzing fairness provides a language for better understanding these concerns and, it is hoped, framing creative solutions. Fairness principles are not only abstract constituents of the climate change discourse, but they are also embedded in the Framework Convention and its Kyoto Protocol. In particular, the principle of common but differentiated responsibility, a cornerstone of the climate regime, gives effect to fairness principles. Fairness concerns are woven into the fabric of the climate regime, which suggests that a deeper understanding and contextualized interpretation offer insights for the future of international climate policy. The Bali Action Plan, adopted at the Thirteenth Conference of the Parties in 2007, is an example of a forward-looking, balanced interpretation of the basic fairness principles of the Convention. It reaffirmed that mitigation actions by developing countries depend on financial and technological support, that adaptation is a priority for developing countries, and emphasized the need for parties to articulate a long-term vision.

The international community committed itself to concluding negotiations on a post-2012 climate agreement in Copenhagen in 2009. This will not be the last climate negotiation milestone. Looking ahead, what insights could be drawn from the analysis provided in preceding chapters? First, there is an urgent need to establish a long-term vision, whether in the form of a stabilization target or other metric. Second, proposals for a future international response to climate that reflect both a balance of fairness principles and political and economic realities stand a better chance of garnering broad acceptance among both developed and developing countries. A future agreement should encourage universal participation by accommodating different commitment types appropriate for countries with differing national circumstances and at varying stages of economic development. Thus a future climate policy will contain a wider menu of commitment options differentiated along a number of axes: binding or nonbinding; economy-wide or covering only particular sectors; and degree of stringency.

Third, the climate change regime is in a transition phase, from hesitant first steps to a new stage in which the challenge facing the international community is the creation of a truly shared response. As in other transitions, a rigid insistence on particular ethical or moral claims is likely to prove neither helpful nor appropriate – reciprocity and a moderation of absolute claims provide the appropriate touchstones. With respect to fairness, this may entail seeking out principles with the broadest agreement among different groups, which suggests a nuanced understanding of leading principles such as capability and responsibility. Burden sharing should be as consistent as possible with a broad, overlapping understanding of fairness principles. Visible efforts to reflect a variety of fairness principles would contribute to a shared perception that a new agreement is based on a "working consensus" that melds fairness with the requisite dose of political reality. The distribution of the burdens and benefits associated with combating climate change, more specifically, the basis on which to share the burden of abatement, will certainly not be resolved by recourse to fairness alone. But fairness principles will constitute an important part of the solution, while not denying that other factors – market forces, technical expertise, negotiating resources, political and economic influence – will also play key roles.

According to the IPCC, having an even chance of limiting the increase in temperatures to below 2 degrees Celsius requires global emissions peaking by 2015 and falling by 50–85 percent below 2000 levels by 2050. Attaining this will require deep cuts in emissions from developed countries and a significant deviation from the business-as-usual baseline for most developing countries. The urgent need to control emissions from *all* major emitters means that flexibility cannot come at the expense of ambition. Kyoto-style targets are appropriate for industrialized countries and should be tightened in the post-2012 period. The contention advanced here is that binding, Kyoto-style targets remain inapplicable to developing countries, on both fairness and practical grounds.[3] As a matter of fairness, it seems highly

---

[3] *See* Rob Bradley & Hilary McMahon, The Role of Policies and Measures for Climate Mitigation in China, BASIC Project, Working Paper 4, World Resources Institute (2007); Geoffrey J. Blanchard et al., Revised Emissions Growth Projections for

inequitable – not to mention politically unrealistic – to expect that China and India, countries where hundreds of millions of citizens still live in poverty, should assume the type of binding measures that developed countries have only slowly adapted, and not without concerns about impacts on economic growth. From a purely practical perspective, in the emerging economies, the course of economic growth and the unpredictable pace of technological transformation means that absolute emission caps are not suitable policy instruments. Instead, the key policy goal would be to begin slowing the rate of emissions growth and moving decisively away from the business-as-usual emissions scenario. This would be achieved through a concerted effort to improve energy efficiency in all sectors and supporting the deployment of the least emissions-intensive equipment in sectors with long-lived infrastructure, especially the power sector.[4] Mitigation action by developing countries would need to be verifiable and reportable, which, in turn, would trigger financial and technical support. An option that has also been put forward is a pledge-based system for developing countries, based on sustainable development policies and measures. These are policies and measures aimed at meeting the domestic objectives of a developing country but that also bring significant benefits to the climate through reduced greenhouse gas emissions, an example being the Brazilian biofuels program, which was adopted on energy security and economic development grounds.

From the time that climate change began to be of concern to scientists and policy makers, mitigation has received more attention than adaptation to the adverse impacts of climate change. It is telling that although the Convention recognizes the importance of adaptation, and singles out particularly vulnerable groups of countries, the overall design of the Kyoto Protocol is almost entirely aimed at mitigation. Recognition of the need to address current and future vulnerabilities to climate impacts does not stand in opposition to strong mitigation action – it simply recognizes the fact that current greenhouse gas concentrations commit us to some climate change, no matter what. Failure to take adaptation needs seriously is also a failure to address fairness because it is quite clear that the poorest countries are the

CHINA: WHY POST-KYOTO CLIMATE POLICY MUST LOOK EAST, Discussion Paper 2008-06, Harvard Project on International Climate Agreements (2008).
[4] MCKINSEY & COMPANY, PATHWAYS TO A LOW CARBON ECONOMY: VERSION 2 OF THE GREENHOUSE GAS ABATEMENT COST CURVE (2009).

ones that will bear the brunt of the impacts.[5] The benefits of implementing adaptation measures are by definition largely local, not global, so that support for adaptation relies heavily on expressions of solidarity.

Technology is rightly identified as pivotal to addressing climate change. Fundamentally, technological advancement matters because many consider making significant inroads into the other main drivers of emissions – population growth and rising consumption – as neither desirable nor practicable. Nonetheless, questions can be asked about the sustainability of the continuous quest for growth in the regions of the world that have long attained prosperity.[6] What is the potential for technology in bringing us to the low-carbon economy? A standard assumption is that an appropriate mix of public and private funding, incentives in the form of a carbon market, or a combination of both will deliver the necessary clean technologies. Unbridled optimism for the transformative effect of breakthrough energy technologies is probably misplaced.[7] Reliance on advanced, costly technologies automatically raises equity questions. In a carbon-constrained world, will such technologies again reserve access to energy, and decent life, for the fortunate few? On what terms and conditions will new technologies be made accessible? Overall, a pragmatic climate and energy policy should focus on the rapid deployment of a menu of existing technologies – renewables, energy efficiency, and cleaner fossil fuel technologies.

The technology transfer and financing aspects of the climate regime have remained underdeveloped and inadequate. Article 4(7) of the Convention explicitly recognizes that "the extent to which developing country Parties will effectively implement their commitments under the Convention will depend on the effective implementation by developed country Parties of their commitments under the Convention related to financial resources

---

[5] *See* UNITED NATIONS DEVELOPMENT PROGRAMME, HUMAN DEVELOPMENT REPORT 2007/2008, FIGHTING CLIMATE CHANGE: HUMAN SOLIDARITY IN A DIVIDED WORLD (2007).

[6] *See* LESTER R. BROWN, PLAN B 3.0: MOBILIZING TO SAVE CIVILIZATION (3rd ed., 2008), and JAMES GUSTAVE SPETH, THE BRIDGE AT THE END OF THE WORLD: CAPITALISM, THE ENVIRONMENT, AND CROSSING FROM CRISIS TO SUSTAINABILITY (2008).

[7] VACLAV SMIL, ENERGY AT THE CROSSROADS: GLOBAL PERSPECTIVES AND UNCERTAINTIES 129–33 (2003). He catalogues some of the wildly optimistic scenarios that respected experts and institutions predicted for nuclear fission. *Cf.* MICHAEL SCHELLENBERGER & TED NORDHAUS, BREAK THROUGH: FROM THE DEATH OF ENVIRONMENTALISM TO THE POLITICS OF POSSIBILITY (2007).

and transfer of technology." Post-2012 climate policy will need to effectively address the issues of technology and financial resources to support mitigation and adaptation actions in developing countries. A study prepared for the Secretariat of the Convention concluded that estimated global additional investment flows of US$200 billion to US$210 billion would be necessary in 2030 to return global emissions to current levels.[8] To promote the rapid deployment of low-carbon technology in developing countries, mechanisms are required to finance the incremental costs of cleaner technology. It is suggested that several of the existing mechanisms could be reconfigured and given expanded mandates in relation to financing and the transfer of low-carbon technologies. The central pillar of this approach could be the establishment of a mechanism to promote the deployment of clean technology, drawing on the model of the Multilateral Fund under the Montreal Protocol, which would function broadly under the auspices and guidance of the Convention. Linking the mechanism to the Convention could contribute to broader buy-in so that different groups of countries are comfortable participating.

Addressing climate change will be a multigenerational challenge, extending forward in ways we cannot yet fathom. Our efforts thus far have been halting, and we have borrowed a great deal from the future. Open and unabashed engagement with fairness can help nurture a real sense of community, in which basic claims to a decent way of life do not stop short at national borders, and where we can meaningfully articulate our responsibility for a common future. After all, if we look closely, the future is everywhere around us – in our children, grandchildren, and the splendor of the natural world that was, is, and will be, long after we are gone.

[8] UNITED NATIONS FRAMEWORK CONVENTION ON CLIMATE CHANGE, DIALOGUE WORKING PAPER 8 (2007); UNITED NATIONS FRAMEWORK CONVENTION ON CLIMATE CHANGE, REPORT ON ANALYSIS OF EXISTING AND POTENTIAL INVESTMENT AND FINANCIAL FLOWS RELEVANT TO THE DEVELOPMENT OF AN EFFECTIVE AND APPROPRIATE INTERNATIONAL RESPONSE TO CLIMATE CHANGE 2 (2007).

# Bibliography

TECHNICAL REPORTS AND POLICY PAPERS

Agarwal, Anil & Narain, Sunita. *Global Warming in an Unequal World: A Case of Environmental Colonialism.* New Delhi: Centre for Science and Environment, 1991.

Agrawala, Shardul. *Explaining the Evolution of the IPCC Structure and Process.* ENRP Discussion Paper E-97-05. Cambridge, Mass.: Harvard University, Kennedy School of Government, 1997.

Aldy, Joseph E., Barrett, Scott & Stavins, Robert N. *Thirteen Plus One: A Comparison of Global Climate Policy Architectures.* Washington, D.C.: Resources for the Future, 2003.

Baer, Paul & Athanasiou, Tom. *Frameworks and Proposals: A Brief, Adequacy and Equity-Based Evaluation of Some Prominent Climate Policy Frameworks and Proposals.* Global Issues Paper 30. Berlin: Heinrich Böll Stiftung, 2007.

Baer, Paul, et al. *The Greenhouse Development Rights Framework.* 2nd rev. ed. Berlin: Heinrich Böll Stiftung, 2008.

Baumert, Kevin A., et al. *Growing in the Greenhouse: Protecting the Climate by Putting Development First.* Washington, D.C.: World Resources Institute, 2005.

Biermann, Frank. *Science as Power in International Negotiations: Global Environmental Assessments between North and South.* ENRP Discussion Paper 2000-17. Cambridge, Mass.: Harvard University, Kennedy School of Government, 2000.

Bodansky, Daniel. *International Climate Efforts beyond 2012: A Survey of Approaches.* Washington, D.C.: Pew Center on Global Climate Change, 2004.

Bodansky, Daniel & Diringer, Elliot. *Towards an Integrated Multi-track Climate Framework.* Washington, D.C.: Pew Center on Global Climate Change, 2007.

Boisson de Chazournes, Laurence. *The Global Environment Facility as a Pioneering Institution: Lessons Learned and Looking Ahead.* Washington, D.C.: Global Environment Facility, 2003.

Bradley, Rob & McMahon, Hilary. *The Role of Policies and Measures for Climate Mitigation in China.* BASIC Project, Working Paper 4. Washington, D.C.: World Resources Institute, 2007.

Brown, Donald, et al. *White Paper on the Ethical Dimensions of Climate Change.* Philadelphia, Pa.: Rock Ethics Institute, n.d.

Buddemeier, Robert W., et al. *Coral Reefs and Global Climate Change: Potential Contributions of Climate Change to Stresses on Coral Reef Ecosystem.* Washington, D.C.: Pew Center on Climate Change, 2004.

Capoor, Karan & Ambrosi, Philippe. *State and Trends of the Carbon Market 2007.* Washington, D.C.: World Bank, 2007.

Carlson, Curtis, et al. *Sulfur Dioxide Control by Electric Utilities: What Are the Gains from Trade?* Discussion Paper 98-44-REV. Washington, D.C.: Resources for the Future, 2000.

Climate Change Science Program. *Abrupt Climate Change: A Report by the U.S. Climate Change Science Program and the Subcommittee on Global Change Research.* Reston, Va.: U.S. Geological Survey, 2008.

Climate Technology Initiative. *Methods for Climate Change Technology Needs Assessments and Implementing Activities: Developing and Transition Country Approaches and Experiences.* Bonn, Germany: Climate Technology Initiative, 2002.

Committee on Surface Temperature Reconstructions for the Last 2,000 Years. *Surface Temperature Reconstructions for the Last 2,000 Years.* Washington, D.C.: National Research Council, 2006.

Cosbey, Aaron. *Making Development Work in the CDM: Phase 2 of the Development Dividend Report.* Winnipeg, Manitoba, Canada: International Institute for Sustainable Development, 2007.

de Coninck, Heleen C., et al. *Technology Transfer in the Clean Development Mechanism.* Report ECN-E-07-009. The Hague, Netherlands: Energy Research Centre of the Netherlands, 2007.

den Elzen, Michel, et al. *An Analysis of Options for Including International Aviation and Marine Emissions in a Post-2012 Climate Mitigation Regime.* MNP Report 500114007/2007. The Hague: Netherlands Environment Agency, 2007.

Dessai, Suraje. *The Climate Regime from The Hague to Marrakech: Saving or Sinking the Kyoto Protocol?* Working Paper 12. Norwich, U.K.: Tyndall Centre, 2001.

Deutsche Gesellschaft für Technische Zusammenarbeit. *South-North Dialogue on Equity in the Greenhouse: A Proposal for an Adequate and Equitable Climate Change Agreement.* Wuppertal, Germany: Wuppertal Institute for Climate, Energy and Environment, 2004.

Egenhofer, Christian & Cornillie, Jan. *Reinventing the Climate Negotiations: An Analysis of COP 6.* Policy Brief 1. Brussels, Belgium: Centre for European Policy Studies, 2001.

Egenhofer, Christian, et al. *Positive Incentives for Climate Action.* ECP Report 5. Brussels, Belgium: European Climate Change Programme, 2008.

Ellis, Jane. *Evaluating Experience with Electricity-Generating GHG Mitigation Projects.* Paris: Organisation for Economic Co-operation and Development/International Energy Agency, 2003.

Ellis, Jane. *Issues Relating to Implementing "Programmatic CDM."* Paris: Organisation for Economic Co-operation and Development/International Energy Agency, 2006.

Ellis, Jane, et al. *Taking Stock of Progress under the Clean Development Mechanism (CDM).* Paris: Organisation for Economic Co-operation and Development, 2004.

## Bibliography

Ellis, Jane, et al. *SD-PAMs: What, Where, When and How?* Paris: Organisation for Economic Co-operation and Development/International Energy Agency, 2007.
Export-Import Bank of the United States. *Annual Report 2007.* Washington, D.C.: Export-Import Bank of the United States, 2007.
Gitay, Habiba Gitay, et al., eds. *Biodiversity and Climate Change.* IPCC Technical Paper V. Geneva, Switzerland: World Meteorological Organization and United Nations Environment Programme, 2002.
Global Environment Facility. *Investing in Our Planet: GEF Annual Report 2006-2007.* Washington, D.C.: Global Environment Facility, 2008.
Goldemberg, José & Johansson, Thomas B., eds. *World Energy Assessment: Overview 2004 Update.* New York: United Nations Development Programme, 2004.
Hare, Bill & Meinshausen, Malte. *Background Information on Potential Loopholes in the Kyoto Protocol.* Update for COP-6 (Part Two). Amsterdam, Netherlands: Greenpeace International, 2001.
Harris, Paul G. *What's Fair? – International Justice from an Environmental Perspective.* Working Paper. Columbia International Affairs Online, available at http://www.ciaonet.org/conf/hap01/.
Höhne, Niklas & Lahme, Esther. *Types of Future Commitments under the UNFCCC and the Kyoto Protocol Post-2012.* Gland, Switzerland: World Wide Fund for Nature, 2005.
Höhne, Niklas & Moltman, Sarah. *The Distribution of Emission Allowances under the Greenhouse Development Rights and Other Effort Sharing Approaches.* Berlin: Heinrich Böll Stiftung, 2008.
Holtwisch, Christoph. *Asiatisch-pazifische Partnerschaft für umweltverträgliche Entwicklung und Klima – Blockade oder Antrieb für das internationale Klimaregime?* Master's thesis, Fraunhofer-Institut für Umwelt-, Sicherheits- und Energietechnik and the Fern Universität in Hagen, 2007.
Houghton, John, et al., eds. *Revised 1996 IPCC Guidelines for National Greenhouse Gas Inventories, vol. 3, Greenhouse Gas Inventory Reference Manual.* Geneva, Switzerland: World Meteorological Organization and United Nations Environment Programme, 1996.
International Energy Agency. *Biofuels for Transport: An International Perspective.* Paris: International Energy Agency, 2004.
International Energy Agency. *Prospects for $CO_2$ Capture and Storage.* Paris: International Energy Agency, 2004.
International Energy Agency. *World Energy Outlook 2006.* Paris: International Energy Agency, 2006.
International Energy Agency. *Energy Technology Perspectives – Scenarios and Strategies to 2050.* Paris: International Energy Agency, 2006.
International Energy Agency. *Key World Energy Statistics.* Paris: International Energy Agency, 2007.
International Energy Agency. *Renewables in Global Energy Supply: An IEA Fact Sheet.* Paris: International Energy Agency, 2007.
International Energy Agency. *World Energy Outlook 2007.* Paris: International Energy Agency, 2007.

Keck, Alexander & Low, Patrick. *Special and Differential Treatment in the WTO: Why, When and How?* Geneva, Switzerland: World Trade Organization, 2004.

Martinot, Eric & McDoom, Omar. *Promoting Energy Efficiency and Renewable Energy: GEF Climate Change Projects and Impacts.* Washington, D.C.: Global Environment Facility, 2000.

Massachusetts Institute of Technology. *The Future of Coal: An Interdisciplinary MIT Study.* Cambridge: Massachusetts Institute of Technology, 2007.

McKinsey & Company. *Pathways to a Low Carbon Economy: Version 2 of the Global Greenhouse Gas Abatement Curve.* 2009.

Metz, Bert, et al., eds. *Climate Change 2007: Mitigation, Contribution of Working Group III to the Fourth Assessment Report of the Intergovernmental Panel on Climate Change.* Geneva, Switzerland: World Meteorological Organization and United Nations Environment Programme, 2007.

Michaelowa, Axel & Purohit, Pallav. *Additionality Determination of Indian CDM Projects: Can Indian CDM Developers Outwit the CDM Executive Board?* Zurich, Switzerland: Climate Strategies, 2007.

Michaelowa, Axel & Stronzik, Marcus. *Transaction Costs of the Kyoto Mechanisms.* Hamburg, Germany: Hamburg Institute of International Economics, 2002.

Modi, Vijay, et al. *Energy and the Millennium Development Goals.* New York: United Nations Development Programme, 2006.

Müller, Benito. *Equity in Climate Change: The Great Divide.* Oxford: Oxford Institute for Energy Studies, 2002.

Müller, Benito. *Nairobi 2006: Trust and the Future of Adaptation Funding.* Oxford: Oxford Institute for Energy Studies, 2007.

Müller, Benito. *Bali 2007: On the Road Again.* Oxford: Oxford Institute for Energy Studies, 2007.

Müller, Benito & Winkler, Harald. *One Step Forward and Two Steps Back? The Governance of the World Bank Climate Investment Funds.* Oxford: Oxford Institute for Energy Studies, 2008.

Munich Re. *Topicsgeo Annual Review: Natural Catastrophes 2003.* Munich, Germany: Munich Re, 2004.

Netherlands Energy Research Foundation et al. *Potential and Cost of Clean Development, Options in the Energy Sector: Inventory of Options in Non-Annex I Countries to Reduce GHG Emissions.* The Hague: Netherlands, 1999.

Newell, Richard G. & Pizer, William A. *Regulating Stock Externalities under Uncertainty.* Discussion Paper 99-10-REV. Washington, D.C.: Resources for the Future, 2000.

Newell, Richard G. & Pizer, William A. *Discounting the Benefits of Climate Change Mitigation: How Much Do Uncertain Rates Increase Valuations?* Washington, D.C.: Pew Center on Global Climate Change, 2001.

Parry, Martin L., et al., eds. *Climate Change 2007: Impacts, Adaptation and Vulnerability, Contribution of Working Group II to the Fourth Assessment Report of the Intergovernmental Panel on Climate Change.* Geneva, Switzerland: World Meteorological Organization and United Nations Environment Programme, 2007.

Penne, Joyce E., et al. *IPCC Special Report, Aviation and the Global Atmosphere.* Geneva, Switzerland: World Meteorological Organization and United Nations Environment Programme, 1999.

Pew Center on Climate Change. *Beyond Kyoto: Advancing the International Effort against Climate Change.* Washington, D.C.: Pew Center on Climate Change, 2003.

PriceWaterhouseCoopers. *The World in 2050: The Implications of Global Growth for Carbon Emissions and Climate Change Policy,* available at http://www.pwc.com/extweb/pwcpublications.nsf/docid/dfb54c8aad6742db852571f5006dd532.

Royal Society. *Ocean Acidification Due to Increasing Atmospheric Carbon Dioxide.* Policy Doc. 12/05. London: Royal Society, 2005.

Schmidt, Jake, et al. *Sector-Based Approach to the Post-2012 Climate Change Architecture.* Washington, D.C.: Center for Clean Air Policy, 2006.

Sjöberg, Helen. *From Idea to Reality: The Creation of the Global Environment Facility.* Washington, D.C.: Global Environment Facility, 1994.

Sjöberg, Helen. *Restructuring the GEF.* Washington, D.C.: Global Environment Facility, 1999.

Solomon, Susan, et al., eds. *Climate Change 2007: The Physical Science Basis. Contribution of Working Group I to the Fourth Assessment Report of the Intergovernmental Panel on Climate Change.* Geneva, Switzerland: World Meteorological Organization and United Nations Environment Programme, 2007.

Stern, Nicholas. *The Economics of Climate Change.* London: Cabinet Office, H.M. Treasury, 2006.

Sunstein, Cass R. *Montreal versus Kyoto: A Tale of Two Protocols.* Working Paper 06-17. Washington, D.C.: AEI-Brookings, 2006.

UN-Energy. *Sustainable Bioenergy: A Framework for Decision-Makers.* New York: United Nations, 2007.

United Nations Conference on Trade and Development. *Global Warming: Study on a Global System of Tradeable Carbon Emission Entitlements.* Geneva, Switzerland: United Nations Conference on Trade and Development, 1992.

United Nations Development Programme. *The Clean Development Mechanism: An Assessment of Progress.* New York: United Nations Development Programme, 2006.

United Nations Development Programme. *Fighting Climate Change: Human Solidarity in a Divided World.* Human Development Report 2007/2008. New York: United Nations Development Programme, 2007.

United Nations Development Programme & World Bank. *Energy Services for the Millennium Development Goals.* New York: United Nations Development Programme, 2005.

United Nations Development Programme et al. *World Energy Assessment.* New York: United Nations Development Programme, 2000.

United Nations Framework Convention Secretariat. *United Nations Framework Convention on Climate Change: The First 10 Years.* Bonn: United Nations Framework Convention Secretariat, 2004.

United Nations Framework Convention Secretariat. *Investment and Financial Flows to Address Climate Change*. Bonn: United Nations Framework Convention Secretariat, 2007.

Upton, Simon & Doornbosch, Richard. *Do We Have the Right R&D Priorities to Support the Energy Technologies of the Future?* Paris: International Energy Agency, 2006.

U.S. Department of State. *The United States of America's Third National Communication under the United Nations Framework Convention on Climate Change*. Washington, D.C.: U.S. Department of State, 2002.

U.S. Environment Protection Agency. *Inventory of U.S. GHG Emissions and Sinks: 1990–2004*. Washington, D.C.: U.S. Environment Protection Agency, 2006.

World Bank. *Managing Climate Risk: Integrating Adaptation into World Bank Group Operations*. Washington, D.C.: World Bank, 2006.

World Bank. *Clean Energy and Development: Towards an Investment Framework*. Washington, D.C.: World Bank, 2006.

World Bank. *Clean Energy and Development: A Progress Report*. Washington, D.C.: World Bank, 2006.

World Bank. *Clean Energy for Development: The World Bank Action Plan*. Washington, D.C.: World Bank, 2007.

World Bank. *The Welfare Impact of Rural Electrification: A Reassessment of Costs and Benefits, an IEG Impact Evaluation*. Washington, D.C.: World Bank Independent Evaluation Group, 2008.

World Meteorological Organization & United Nations Environment Programme. *Intergovernmental Panel on Climate Change: 16 Years of Scientific Assessment in Support of the Climate Convention*. Geneva, Switzerland: World Meteorological Organization and United Nations Environment Programme, 2004.

World Resources Institute. *Navigating the Numbers*. Washington D.C.: World Resources Institute, 2005.

### JOURNAL ARTICLES

Abbott, Kenneth W. & Snidal, Duncan. *Hard and Soft Law in International Governance*. 54(3) International Organization 421–51 (2000).

Adler, Matthew D. *Corrective Justice and Liability for Global Warming*. 155 University of Pennsylvania Law Review 1859–68 (2007).

Agrawala, Shardul. *Early Science-Policy Interactions in Climate Change: Lessons from the Advisory Group on Greenhouse Gases*. 9(2) Global Environmental Change: Human and Policy Dimensions 157–69 (1999).

Akehurst, Michael. *Equity and General Principles of Law*. 25 International and Comparative Law Quarterly 801–25 (1976).

Alberts, Colin M. *Technology Transfer and Its Role in International Law: A Structural Dilemma*. 6 Harvard Journal of Law and Technology 63–84 (1992).

Barrett, Scott & Stavins, Robert N. *Increasing Participation and Compliance in International Climate Change Agreements*. 3 International Environmental Agreements: Politics, Law and Economics 349–76 (2003).

Baum, Seth. *Beyond the Ramsey Model for Climate Change Assessments.* 7 Ethics in Science and Environmental Politics 15–18 (2007).
Blancoa, María Isabel & Rodrigues, Glória. *Can the Future EU ETS Support Wind Energy Investments?* 36(4) Energy Policy 1509–20 (2008).
Bodansky, Daniel. *The United Nations Framework Convention on Climate Change: A Commentary.* 18 Yale Journal of International Law 451–558 (1993).
Bodansky, Daniel. *Symposium: Customary (and Not So Customary) International Environmental Law.* 3 Indiana Journal of Global Legal Studies 105–20 (1995).
Bradbrook, Adrian J., et al. *A Human Dimension to the Energy Debate: Access to Modern Energy Services.* 26(4) Journal of Energy and Natural Resources Law 526–52 (2008).
Brunnée, Jutta. *COPing with Consent: Law-Making under Multilateral Environmental Agreements.* 15 Leiden Journal of International Law 1–52 (2002).
Buchanan, Allen. *Rawls's Law of Peoples: Rules for a Vanished Westphalian World.* 110(4) Ethics 697–715 (2000).
Bush, Mark B., et al. *48,000 Years of Climate and Forest Change in a Biodiversity Hot Spot.* 303(5659) Science 827–29 (2004).
Byers, Michael. *Custom, Power, and the Power of Rules: Customary International Law from an Interdisciplinary Perspective.* 17 Michigan Journal of International Law 109 (1995).
Caney, Simon. *Cosmopolitan Justice, Responsibility and Global Climate Change* 18 Leiden Journal of International Law 747–75 (2005).
Corfee-Morlot, Jan & Höhne, Niklas. *Climate Change: Long-Term Targets and Short-Term Commitments.* 13 Global Environmental Change 277 (2003).
Cullet, Philippe. *Differential Treatment in International Law: Towards a New Paradigm of Inter-state Relations.* 10 European Journal of International Law 549–68 (1999).
den Elzen, Michel & Berk, Marcel. *Options for Differentiation of Future Commitments in Climate Policy: How to Realize Timely Participation to Meet Stringent Climate Goals?* 1(4) Climate Policy 465–80 (2001).
den Elzen, Michel, et al. *Analysing Countries' Contributions to Climate Change: Scientific and Policy-Related Choices.* 8(6) Environmental Science and Policy 614–36 (2005).
den Elzen, Michel, et al. *Multi-stage: A Rule-Based Evolution of Future Commitments under the Climate Change Convention.* 6(1) International Environmental Agreements 1–21 (2006).
Dickson, Bob, et al. *Rapid Freshening of the Deep North Atlantic Ocean over the Past Four Decades.* 416 Nature 832–37 (2002).
Drumbl, Mark A. *Poverty, Wealth, and Obligation in International Law.* 76 Tulane Law Review 843–90 (2002).
Feely, Richard A., et al. *The Impact of Anthropogenic $CO_2$ on the $CaCO_3$ System in the Oceans.* 305(5682) Science 362–66 (2004).
Fitzgerald, Jack. *The Intergovernmental Panel on Climate Change: Taking the First Steps towards a Global Response.* 14 Southern Illinois University Law Journal 231 (1990).
Grasso, Marco. *A Normative Ethical Framework in Climate Change.* 81(3–4) Climatic Change 223–46 (2007).

Groenenberg, Helen & Van Der Sluijs, Jeroen. *Valueloading and Uncertainty in a Sector-Based Differentiation Scheme for Emission Allowances*. 71(1–2) Climatic Change 75–115 (2005).
Groenenberg, Helen, et al. *Global Triptych: A Bottom-Up Approach for the Differentiation of Commitments under the Climate Convention*. 4(2) Climate Policy 153–75 (2004).
Grubb, Michael. *Seeking Fair Weather: Ethics and the International Debate on Climate Change*. 71 International Affairs 463–96 (1995).
Grubb, Michael & Yamin, Farhana. *Climatic Collapse at The Hague: What Happened, Why and Where Do We Go from Here?* 7 International Affairs 261–76 (2001).
Guston, David H. *Boundary Organizations in Environmental Policy and Science: An Introduction*. 26(4) Science, Technology and Human Values 339–408 (2001).
Hansen, Bogi, et al. *Decreasing Overflow from the Nordic Seas into the Atlantic Ocean through the Faroe Bank Channel since 1950*. 411 Nature 927–30 (2001).
Hoffert, Martin I., et al. *Energy Implications of Future Stabilization of Atmospheric $CO_2$ Content*. 395(6704) Nature 881–84 (1998).
Holtsmark, Bjart J. & Alfsen, Knut H. *PPP-Correction of the IPCC Emission Scenarios – Does It Matter?* 68(1–2) Climatic Change 11–19 (2005).
Hotinski, Roberta, et al. *Solving the Climate Problem*. 46(10) Environment 8–19 (2004).
Jasanoff, Sheila. *Beyond Epistemology: Relativism and Engagement in the Politics of Science*. 26(2) Social Studies of Science 393–418 (1996).
Kammen, Daniel F. & Nemet, Gregory F. *Real Numbers: Reversing the Incredible Shrinking Energy R&D Budget*. Issues in Science and Technology 84 (2005, Fall).
Kaasa, Stine Madland. *The UN Commission on Sustainable Development: Which Mechanisms Explain its Accomplishments?* 7(3) Global Environmental Politics 107–129 (2007).
Keohane, Nathaniel O., et al. *The Choice of Regulatory Instruments in Environmental Policy*. 22 Harvard Environmental Law Review 313–67 (1998).
Kerr, Richard A. *U.S. Bites Greenhouse Bullet and Gags*. 251 Science 868 (1991).
Kinzig, Ann, et al. *Coping with Uncertainty: A Call for a New Science-Policy Forum*. 32(5) Ambio 330–35 (2003).
Koh, Harold. *Review Essay: Why Do Nations Obey International Law?* 106 Yale Law Journal 2599–2659 (1997).
Koskenniemi, Martti. *Hierarchy in International Law: A Sketch*. 8(4) European Journal of International Law 566–82 (1997).
Krasner, Stephen D. *Structural Causes and Regime Consequences: Regimes as Intervening Variables*. 36(2) International Organization 185–205 (1982).
Lankao, Patricia Romero, et al. *Development and Greenhouse Gas Emissions Deviate from the "Modernization" Theory and "Convergence" Hypothesis*. 38 Climate Research 17–29 (2008).
Mace, M. J. *Funding for Adaptation to Climate Change: UNFCCC and GEF Developments since COP-7*. 14(3) Review of European Community and International Environmental Law 225–38 (2005).
Mann, Michael, et al. *Global-Scale Temperature Patterns and Climate Forcing over the Past Six Centuries*. 392 Nature 779–87 (1998).

Matsui, Yoshiro. *Some Aspects of the Principle of "Common but Differentiated Responsibilities."* 2(2) International Environmental Agreements: Politics, Law and Economics 151–70 (2002).

Matsuo, Naoki. *CDM in the Kyoto Negotiations: How CDM Has Worked as a Bridge between Developed and Developing Worlds?* 8 Mitigation and Adaptation Strategies for Global Change 191–203 (2003).

McCaffrey, Stephen. *The Contribution of the UN Convention on the Law of the Non-Navigable Uses of International Watercourses.* 1 International Global Environmental Issues 250–63 (2001).

McIntyre, Stephen & McKitrick, Ross. *Corrections to the Mann et al (1998) Proxy Data Base and Northern Hemisphere Average Temperature Series.* 14(6) Energy and Environment 751–72 (2003).

Michaelowa, Axel, et al. *Issues and Options for the Post-2012 Climate Architecture – An Overview.* 5 International Environmental Agreements 5–18 (2005).

Miller, Clark A. *Hybrid Management: Boundary Organizations, Science Policy, and Environmental Governance in the Climate Regime.* 26(4) Science, Technology and Human Values 478–500 (2001).

Millock, Katrin. *Technology Transfers in the Clean Development Mechanism: An Incentives Issue.* 7 Environment and Development Economics 449–66 (2002).

Nentjes, Andries & Klaassen, Ger. *On the Quality of Compliance Mechanisms of the Kyoto Protocol.* 32(4) Energy Policy 531–34 (2004).

Neumayer, Eric. *In Defence of Historical Accountability for Greenhouse Gas Emissions.* 33(2) Ecological Economics 185–92 (2000).

Nordhaus, William. *A Review of the Stern Review of the Economics of Global Warming.* 45 Journal of Economic Literature 686–702 (2007).

Olmstead, Sheila M. & Stavins, Robert M. *An International Policy Architecture for the Post-Kyoto Era.* 96(2) American Economic Review Papers and Proceedings 35 (2006).

Oreskes, Naomi. *Beyond the Ivory Tower: The Scientific Consensus on Climate Change.* 306(5702) Science 1686 (2004).

Ott, Hermann E., et al. *It Takes Two to Tango – Climate Policy at COP 10 in Buenos Aires and Beyond.* Journal for European Environmental and Planning Law 84–94 (2005).

Ott, Hermann E., et al. *The Montreal Climate Summit: Starting the Kyoto Business and Preparing for Post-2012.* 3(2) Journal for European Environmental and Planning Law 90–100 (2006).

Pacala, Steven & Socolow, Robert. *Stabilization Wedges: Solving the Climate Problem for the Next 50 Years with Current Technologies.* 305(5686) Science 968–72 (2004).

Page, Edward. *Intergenerational Justice and Climate Change.* 47(1) Political Studies 53–66 (1999).

Pan, Jiahua. *Commitment to Human Development Goals with Low Emissions: An Alternative to Emissions Caps for Post-Kyoto from a Developing Country Perspective.* 5(1) International Environmental Agreements 89–104 (2005).

Peng, Shaobing, et al. *Rice Yields Decline with Higher Night Temperature from Global Warming.* 101(27) Proceedings of the National Academy of Sciences of the United States 9971–75 (2004).

Philibert, Cédric. *Climate Mitigation: Approaches for Future International Cooperation.* Paris: Organisation for Economic Co-operation and Development/ International Energy Agency, 2005.

Pogge, Thomas. *Priorities of Global Justice.* 32 Metaphilosophy 9–20 (2001).

Posner, Eric A. & Sunstein, Cass. *Climate Change Justice.* 96 Georgetown Law Journal 1593–94 (2008).

Rahmstorf, Stefan. *A Semi-empirical Approach to Projecting Future Sea-Level Rise.* 315 Science 368–70 (2007).

Raupach, Michael R., et al. *Global and Regional Drivers of Accelerating $CO_2$ Emissions.* 104(24) Proceedings of the National Academy of Sciences of the United States 10288–93 (2008).

Ringius, Lasse, et al. *Burden Sharing and Fairness Principles in International Climate Policy.* 2(1) International Environmental Agreements: Politics, Law and Economics 1–22 (2002).

Roberts, Anthea Elizabeth. *Traditional and Modern Approaches to Customary International Law: A Reconciliation.* 95 American Journal of International Law 757–91 (2001).

Rose, Adam, et al. *International Equity and Differentiation in Global Warming Policy: An Application to Tradeable Emission Permits.* 12(1) Environmental and Resource Economics 25–51 (1998).

Sabine, Christopher L., et al. *The Oceanic Sink for Anthropogenic $CO_2$.* 305(5682) Science 367–71 (2004).

Sands, Phillipe. *The "Greening" of International Law: Emerging Principles and Rules.* 1 Indiana Journal of Global Legal Studies 293–310 (1994).

Schneider, Malte, et al. *Understanding the CDM's Contribution to Technology Transfer.* 36 Energy Policy 2930–38 (2008).

Shue, Henry. *Subsistence Emissions and Luxury Emissions.* 15 Law and Policy 39–59 (1993).

Shue, Henry. *After You: May Action by the Rich Be Contingent upon Action by the Poor?* 1 Indiana Global Legal Studies 343–66 (1994).

Shue, Henry. *Global Environment and International Inequality.* 75(3) International Affairs 533–37 (1999).

Simpson, Gerry J. *Is International Law Fair?* 17 Michigan Journal of International Law 615–42 (1996–1997).

Slaughter Burley, Anne-Marie. *International Law and International Relations Theory: A Dual Agenda.* 87 American Journal of International Law 205–39 (1993).

Springer, Urs. *The Market for Tradable GHG Permits under the Kyoto Protocol: A Survey of Model Studies.* 25(3) Energy Economics 527–51 (2003).

Stavins, Robert N. *What Can We Learn from the Grand Policy Experiment? Lessons from $SO_2$ Allowance Trading.* 12(3) Journal of Economic Perspectives 69–88 (1998).

Stone, Christopher D. *Common but Differentiated Responsibilities in International Law.* 98 American Journal of International Law 276–301 (2004).

Stott, Peter A., et al. *Human Contribution to the European Heatwave of 2003.* 432 Nature 610–14 (2004).

Sugiyama, Taishi & Sinton, Jonathan. *Orchestra of Treaties: A Future Climate Regime Scenario with Multiple Treaties among Like-Minded Countries.* 5(1) International Environmental Agreements 65–88 (2005).

*Symposium on Thomas M. Franck's Fairness in International Law and Institutions.* 13(4) European Journal of International Law 901–1030 (2002).
Tangen, Kristian & Hasselknippe, Henrik. *Converging Markets.* 5(1) International Environmental Agreements 47–64 (2005).
Tasioulas, John. *International Law and the Limits of Fairness.* 13 European Journal of International Law 993–1010 (2003).
Tol, Richard S. J. & Verheyen, Roda. *State Responsibility and Compensation for Climate Change Damages – A Legal and Economic Analysis.* 32 Energy Policy 1109–30 (2004).
Trimble, Phillip R. *Globalization, International Institutions, and the Erosion of National Sovereignty and Democracy.* 95 Michigan Law Review 1944–69 (1996–1997).
Verhoosel, Gaetan. *Beyond the Unsustainable Rhetoric Sustainable Development: Transferring Environmentally Sound Technologies.* 11 Georgetown International Environmental Law Review 49 (1998).
Victor, David G., et al. *A Madisonian Approach to Climate Policy* 309(5742) Science 1820 (2005).
Watanabe, Rie, et al. *The Bali Roadmap for Global Climate Policy – New Horizons and Old Pitfalls.* 5(2) Journal of European Environmental and Planning Law 139–54 (2008).
Weitzman, M. L. *Prices vs. Quantities.* 41(4) Review of Economic Studies 477–91 (1974).
Weyant, John P., ed. *The Costs of the Kyoto Protocol: A Multi-model Evaluation.* Special Issue, Energy Journal (1999).
Wigley, Thomas, et al. *Economic and Environmental Choices in the Stabilization of Atmospheric $CO_2$ Concentrations.* 379 Nature 240–43 (1996).
Wilson, J. Shand. *State Consent and the Sources of International Law.* 86 American Society of International Law Proceedings 108 (1992).
Winkler, Harald. *Measurable, Reportable and Verifiable: The Keys to Mitigation in the Copenhagen Deal.* 8 Climate Policy 534–47 (2008).
Winkler, Harald, et al. *Methods for Quantifying the Benefits of Sustainable Development Policies and Measures (SD-PAMs).* 8 Climate Policy 119–34 (2008).

BOOKS

Adger, Neil, et al., eds. *Fairness in Adaptation to Climate Change.* Cambridge, Mass.: MIT Press, 2006.
Aldy, Joseph E. & Stavins, Robert N., eds. *Architectures for Agreement: Addressing Global Climate on the Post-Kyoto World.* Cambridge, Mass.: MIT Press, 2007.
American Law Institute. *Restatement of the Law, Third, Foreign Relations Law of the United States.* Philadelphia, Pa.: American Law Institute, 1987.
Andersen, Stephen O. & Sarma, L. Madhava. *Protecting the Ozone Layer: The United Nations History.* London: Earthscan, 2002.
Andresen, Steinar, et al., eds. *Science and Politics in International Regimes: Between Integrity and Involvement.* Manchester, U.K.: Manchester University Press, 2000.
Archer, David. *The Long Thaw: How Humans Are Changing the Next 100,000 Years of Earth's Climate.* Princeton, NJ: Princeton University Press, 2008.

Aristotle. *Nicomachean Ethics.* W. D. Ross, trans. Oxford: Clarendon Press, 1908.
Athanasiou, Tom & Baer, Paul. *Dead Heat, Global Justice and Global Warming.* New York: Seven Stories Press, 2002.
Barrett, Scott. *Environment and Statecraft.* New York: Oxford University Press, 2003.
Bedjaoui, Mohammed. *Towards a New International Economic Order.* New York: Holmes and Meier, 1979.
Benedick, Richard Elliot. *Ozone Diplomacy.* Cambridge, Mass.: Harvard University Press, 1991.
Bhaskar, V. & Glyn, Andrew, eds. *The North the South and the Environment: Ecological Constraints and the Global Economy.* Tokyo: United Nations University Press, 1995.
Birnie, Patricia & Boyle, Alan. *International Law and the Environment.* 2nd ed. Oxford: Oxford University Press, 2002.
Boehmer-Christiansen, Sonja & Kellow, Aynsley. *International Environmental Policy: Interests and the Failure of the Kyoto Process.* Cheltenham, U.K.: Edward Elgar, 2002.
Brown, Lester R. *Plan B 3.0: Mobilizing to Save Civilization.* 3rd ed. New York: W. W. Norton, 2008.
Brownlie, Ian. *Principles of Public International Law.* 4th ed. Oxford: Oxford University Press, 1990.
Bruce, James P., et al., eds. *Climate Change 1995: Economic and Social Dimensions of Climate Change, Contribution of Working Group III to the Second Assessment Report of the Intergovernmental Panel on Climate Change.* Cambridge: Cambridge University Press, 1996.
Brunnée, Jutta & Hay, Ellen, eds. *Yearbook of International Environmental Law.* Vol. 9. Oxford: Oxford University Press, 1999.
Canan, Penelope & Reichman, Nancy. *Ozone Connections: Expert Networks in Environmental Governance.* Sheffield, U.K.: Greenleaf, 2002.
Chayes, Abram & Chayes, Antonia Handler. *The New Sovereignty: Compliance with Treaties in International Regulatory Regimes.* Cambridge, Mass.: Harvard University Press, 1995.
Cleveland, Cutler, J., ed. *Encyclopedia of Earth.* Washington, D.C.: Environmental Information Coalition, 2007.
Conway, John K., et al., eds. *Earth, Air, Fire, Water.* Amherst: University of Massachusetts Press, 1999.
Cordonier Segger, Marie & Khalfan, Ashfaq. *Sustainable Development Law: Principles, Practices and Prospects.* Oxford: Oxford University Press, 2004.
Daly, Herman E. & Townsend, Kenneth N., eds. *Valuing the Earth: Economics, Ecology, Ethics.* Cambridge, Mass.: MIT Press, 1993.
Dugard, John. *International Law: A South African Perspective.* 2nd ed. Cape Town, South Africa: Juta, 2000.
Dworkin, Ronald. *Taking Rights Seriously.* Cambridge, Mass.: Harvard University Press, 1977.
Dworkin, Ronald. *Law's Empire.* Cambridge, Mass.: Harvard University Press, 1986.
Ezrahi, Yaron. *The Descent of Icarus: Science and the Transformation of Contemporary Democracy.* Cambridge, Mass.: Harvard University Press, 1990.

Forsyth, Tim. *Critical Political Ecology: The Politics of Environmental Science.* New York: Routledge, 2003.
Franck, Thomas M. *The Power of Legitimacy among Nations.* Oxford: Oxford University Press, 1990.
Franck, Thomas M. *Fairness in International Law and Institutions.* Oxford: Oxford University Press, 1995.
Freestone, David & Streck, Charlotte, eds. *Legal Aspects of Implementing the Kyoto Protocol Mechanisms: Making Kyoto Work.* New York: Oxford University Press, 2005.
Fukuyama, Francis. *The End of History.* New York: Harper Perennial, 1993.
Fuller, Lon L. *The Morality of Law.* New Haven, CT: Yale University Press, 1964.
Gelbspan, Ross. *The Heat Is On: The High Stakes Battle over the Earth's Threatened Climate.* Reading, Mass.: Addison-Wesley, 1997.
Grubb, Michael, et al. *The Kyoto Protocol: A Guide and Assessment.* London: Royal Institute of International Affairs, 1999.
Hackett, Steven C. *Environmental and Natural Resource Economics: Theory, Policy and the Sustainable Society.* New York: M. E. Sharpe, 2001.
Hampson, Fen Osler & Reppy, Judith, eds. *Earthly Goods: Environmental Change and Social Justice.* Ithaca, NY: Cornell University Press, 1996.
Hansen, Michael W., ed. *Managing the Environment across Borders: A Study of TNC Affiliates' Environmental Practices in China, Malaysia and India.* Copenhagen: Samfundslitteratur, 2002.
Hare, R. M. *Moral Thinking.* Oxford: Oxford University Press, 1981.
Hart, H. L. A. *The Concept of Law.* Oxford: Clarendon Press, 1961.
Hasenclever, Andreas, et al. *Theories of International Regimes.* New York: Cambridge University Press, 1997.
Hicks, Robert L., et al. *Greening Aid?: Understanding the Environmental Impact of Development Assistance.* New York: Oxford University Press, 2008.
Holden, Barry, ed. *The Ethical Dimensions of Global Change.* London: Macmillan, 1996.
Holtwisch, Christoph. *Das Nichteinhaltungsverfahren des Kyoto-protokolls: Enstehung-Gestalt-Wirkung.* Berlin: Duncker and Humblot, 2006.
Houghton, John, et al., eds. *Scientific Assessment of Climate Change – Report of Working Group 1 of the IPCC.* Cambridge: Cambridge University Press, 1990.
Houghton, John, et al., eds. *Climate Change 1995: The Science of Climate Change, Contribution of Working Group I to the Second Assessment Report of the Intergovernmental Panel on Climate Change.* Cambridge: Cambridge University Press, 1996.
Houghton, John, et al., eds. *Climate Change 2001: The Scientific Basis, Contribution of Working Group I to the Third Assessment Report of the Intergovernmental Panel on Climate Change.* Cambridge: Cambridge University Press, 2001.
Hurrell, Andrew & Kingsbury, Benedict, eds. *The International Politics of the Environment: Actors, Interests, and Institutions.* New York: Oxford University Press, 1992.
Jasanoff, Sheila. *The Fifth Branch: Science Advisers as Policymakers.* Cambridge, Mass.: Harvard University Press, 1990.

Kaul, Inge, et al., eds. *Providing Global Public Goods: Managing Globalization.* New York: Oxford University Press, 2003.
Keohane, Robert. *After Hegemony: Cooperation and Discord in the World Political Economy.* Princeton, NJ: Princeton University Press, 1984.
Kimball, Lee A. *Treaty Implementation: Science and Technical Advice Enters a New Stage.* Washington, D.C.: American Society of International Law, 1996.
Kleinman, Daniel Lee, et al., eds. *Controversies in Science and Technology: From Climate to Chromosomes.* Vol. 2. New Rochelle, NY: Mary Anne Liebert, 2008.
Kymlicka, Will. *Contemporary Political Philosophy: An Introduction.* Oxford: Oxford University Press, 2002.
Leggett, Jeremy K. *The Carbon War: Global Warming and the End of the Oil Era.* New York: Routledge, 2001.
Lomborg, Bjørn, ed. *Global Crises, Global Solutions.* New York: Cambridge University Press, 2004.
Lovelock, John. *The Revenge of Gaia.* New York: Basic Books, 2007.
Lovelock, John. *The Vanishing Face of Gaia: A Final Warning.* New York: Basic Books, 2009.
Luterbacher, Urs & Sprinz, Detlef F., eds. *International Relations and Global Climate Change.* Cambridge, Mass.: MIT Press, 2001.
Lyons, David. *Forms and Limits of Utilitarianism.* Oxford: Clarendon Press, 1965.
McKibben, William. *The End of Nature.* New York: Random House, 1989.
Meadows, Donella H., et al. *The Limits to Growth.* New York: Universe Books, 1972.
Michaels, Patrick. *The Satanic Gases.* Washington, D.C.: Cato Institute, 2000.
Michaels, Patrick. *Meltdown: The Predictable Distortion of Global Warming by Scientists, Politicians and the Media.* Washington, D.C.: Cato Institute, 2004.
Miller, Clark A. & Edwards, Paul N., eds. *Changing the Atmosphere: Expert Knowledge and Environmental Governance.* Cambridge, Mass.: MIT Press, 2001.
Minzer, Irving L. & Leonard, J. Amber, eds. *Negotiating Climate Change: The Inside Story of the Rio Convention.* New York: Cambridge University Press, 1994.
Morgenthau, Hans J. *Politics among Nations: The Struggle for Power and Peace.* 4th ed. New York: Alfred Knopf, 1967.
Nakicenovic, Nebojsa & Swart, Rob, eds. *Special Report on Emissions Scenarios.* Geneva, Switzerland: Intergovernmental Panel on Climate Change, 2000.
National Academy of Sciences. *Abrupt Climate Change: Inevitable Surprises.* Washington, D.C.: National Academy Press, 2002.
National Academy of Sciences. *Knowledge and Diplomacy: Science Advice in the United Nations System.* Washington, D.C.: National Academy Press, 2002.
Nozick, Robert. *Anarchy, State, and Utopia.* New York: Basic Books, 1974.
Oberthur, Sebastian & Ott, Hermann E. *The Kyoto Protocol: International Climate Policy for the 21st Century.* Berlin: Springer, 1999.
Page, Edward A. *Climate Change, Justice and Future Generations.* Cheltenham, U.K.: Edward Elgar, 2006.
Parfit, Derek. *Reasons and Persons.* Oxford: Oxford University Press, 1984.
Patterson, Dennis, ed. *A Companion to Philosophy of Law and Legal Theory.* New York: Oxford University Press, 1996.

Pogge, Thomas. *World Poverty and Human Rights.* 2nd ed. Malden, Mass.: Polity Press, 2008.
Rajamani, Lavanya. *Differential Treatment in International Environmental Law.* Oxford: Oxford University Press, 2006.
Rawls, John. *A Theory of Justice.* Cambridge, Mass.: Harvard University Press, 1971.
Rawls, John. *The Law of Peoples.* Cambridge, Mass.: Harvard University Press, 1999.
Rayner, Steve & Malone, Elizabeth M., eds. *4 Human Choice and Climate Change.* Columbus, Ohio: Battelle Press, 1999.
Sands, Philippe, ed. *Greening International Law.* New York: New Press, 1993.
Singer, Fred S. *Hot Talk, Cold Science: Global Warming's Unfinished Debate.* Oakland, Calif.: Independent Institute, 1999.
Singer, Peter. *One World: The Ethics of Globalization.* New Haven, CT: Yale University Press, 2002.
Schellenberger, Michael & Nordhaus, Ted. *Break Through: From the Death of Environmentalism to the Politics of Possibility.* New York: Houghton Mifflin, 2007.
Schellnhuber, Hans Joachim, et al., eds. *Avoiding Dangerous Climate Change.* Cambridge: Cambridge University Press, 2006.
Schneider, Stephen H., et al., eds. *Climate Change Policy: A Survey.* Washington, D.C.: Island Press, 2002.
Shelton, Dinah, ed. *Commitment and Compliance: The Role of Non-binding Norms in the International Legal System.* Oxford: Oxford University Press, 2000.
Smil, Vaclav. *Energy at the Crossroads: Global Perspectives and Uncertainties.* Cambridge, Mass.: MIT Press, 2003.
Sorrell, Steve & Skea, Jim, eds. *Pollution for Sale: Emissions Trading and Joint Implementation.* Cheltenham, U.K.: Edward Elgar, 1999.
Speth, James Gustave. *The Bridge at the End of the World: Capitalism, the Environment, and Crossing from Crisis to Sustainability.* New Haven, CT: Yale University Press, 2008.
Stevens, William K. *The Change in the Weather: People, Weather, and the Science of Climate.* New York: Random House, 2001.
Stokke, Olaf Schramm, et al., eds. *Implementing the Climate Regime: International Compliance.* London: Earthscan, 2005.
Toman, Michael A., ed. *Climate Change Economics and Policy: An RFF Anthology.* Washington, D.C.: Resources for the Future, 2001.
Tóth, Ferenc L., ed. *Fair Weather? Equity Concerns in Climate Change.* London: Earthscan, 1999.
Verheyen, Roda. *Climate Change and International Law: Prevention Duties and State Responsibility.* Boston: Brill, 2005.
Victor, David. *The Collapse of the Kyoto Protocol and the Struggle to Slow Global Warming.* New York: Council on Foreign Relations, 2001.
Waltz, Kenneth N. *Theory of International Politics.* New York: McGraw-Hill, 1979.
Weart, Spencer R. *The Discovery of Global Warming.* Cambridge, Mass.: Harvard University Press, 2003.

Weiss, Edith Brown. *In Fairness to Future Generations*. Ardsley, NY: Transnational, 1989.

Weiss, Edith Brown & Jacobson, Harold K., eds. *Engaging Countries: Strengthening Compliance with International Environmental Accords*. Cambridge, Mass.: MIT Press, 1998.

Yamin, Farhana & Depledge, Joanna. *The International Climate Regime: A Guide to Rules, Institutions and Procedures*. Cambridge: Cambridge University Press, 2005.

# Index

activities implemented jointly (AIJ). *See* Joint Implementation
adaptation, 9, 11
　necessity of, 9
　vulnerability of developing countries, 9–10
Adaptation Fund, 99, 220–222
　direct access, 122–123
　governance, 117–119
additionality. *See* Clean Development Mechanism (CDM)
Agenda 21, 174, 185, 186, 210
　technology transfer, 194
Agreement on Straddling Fish Stocks and Highly Migratory Fish Stocks, 176
Alliance of Small Island States (AOSIS), 54, 62
Aristotle, 141
Asia Pacific Cooperation (APEC)
　Sydney declaration of 2007, 113
Asia-Pacific Partnership on Clean Development and Climate, 125

Bali Action Plan
　Ad Hoc Group on Long-Term Cooperative Action (AWG-LCA), 115
　compilation document of views on, 123
　developed country commitments and developing country actions, 115–116
　measurable, reportable and verifiable (MRV), 116–117
　mitigation action contingent on technology and finance, 132, 193
Bangladesh, 32
Berlin Mandate, 61
　carbon taxes, 62
　policies and measures, 62

Brazil, 8
　biofuels program, 265
　Brazilian proposal. *See* historical responsibility
　international fund to address deforestation, 112, 119
　reducing deforestation rate in the Amazon, 124
　role in conceiving CDM, 79
Buenos Aires Plan of Action. *See* Kyoto Protocol
Buenos Aires Programme of Work on Adaptation and Response Measures, 104
Byrd-Hagel resolution, 61

carbon capture and storage. *See* energy: carbon capture and storage
carbon intensity
　increase in, 25
Carbon Sequestration Leadership Forum, 126
carbon tax
　emission trading vs. carbon taxes. *See* emission trading
　harmonized global carbon tax, 231
　price vs. quantity instruments. *See* emission trading
China
　leading share of CDM projects, 82
　member of G77, 61
　per capita emissions, 8
　share of coal in energy mix, 25
　surpassing US as largest emitter, 24
Clean Air Act, 72

285

# Index

Clean Development Mechanism (CDM), 60
  additionality, 77, 80, 81, 206, 207
  balancing efficiency and environmental integrity, 81–82
  effiiency as underlyng logic, 83
  energy efficiency projects, 203
  environmental integrity, 80
  Executive Board, 80–81
  forestry projects, 98
  geographic distribution of projects, 82–83
  project baselines, 205–206
  sustainable development, 80
  technology transfer, 83–84
climate change, 13
  as challenge to society, 13
  biodiversity loss, 13, 29
  Greenland ice cap, melting of, 16
  impacts, 27–29
  safe levels of, 15
  sea level rise, 29–30
  uncertainty, effect of, 33
command-and-control regulatory policies
  command and control, preference for market instruments over, 72
Commission on Sustainable Development, 174
common but differentiated responsibilities, 56, 168, 189
  status as legal principle, 189–190
  under the UNFCCC, 193
compliance
  Compliance Mechanism of the Kyoto Protocol, 85–92, 99, 108
conferences of the parties (COPs), 51
Contraction and Convergence, 242–246
cost-effectiveness. *See also* policy assessment criteria
  in principles of UNFCCC, 3, 55

deforestation
  reduced emissions from deforestation and degradation (REDD), 119–120, 122
Delhi Declaration on Climate Change and Sustainable Development. *See* sustainable development
differential treatment
  categories, 183
  treaties with differentiated provisions regarding implementation, 184
Dworkin, Ronald
  legal rules and principles, 168

economics
  discount rate, ethical issues with, 166
  intergenerational equity and discounting, 166
  nonmarket goods, 165
  uncertainty, impact of on cost-benefit analysis, 167
  welfare economics and ethics, 163
emission trading
  banking and fungibility of Kyoto credits, 101
  emission trading vs. carbon taxes, 74, 231
  European Emissions Trading Scheme (EU ETS), 74
  grandfathering, 145
  international carbon market and private sector, 128
  International Emission Trading, 84–85
  rationale for market mechanisms, 72
energy, 21, 40–48
  carbon capture and storage, 47
  energy and MDGs, 41
  energy efficiency, 25, 44, 45
  energy intensity, 24
  fairness issues, 44
  global energy demand, doubling of, 44
  impact of basic energy access on emissions, 43–44
  Johannesburg Plan of Implementation, 41
  renewable energy, 45–47
  renewable energy, status and trends, 45–46
energy efficiency and conservation. *See* energy
Environmental Integrity Group, 62
equity. *See also* fairness
  definition, 141
  equity and equitable principles international law, 172
European Emissions Trading Scheme (EU ETS). *See* emission trading
European Union (EU)
  Kyoto Protocol negotiations, 62
  reduction target, 71
  renewable energy targets, 124
Expert Group on Technology Transfer (EGTT), 100, 120

fairness, 2
  capability-based principles, 160–162
  contested concept, 133
  cosmopolitan conception of distributive justice, 134

# Index

deal among major emitters, 131
distributive fairness, 15, 16, 18, 136
egalitarian principles, 153–154
equality of opportunity, 135
Franck, Thomas, 146–149
need-based principles, 154–155
procedural fairness, 142, 150–152
REDD, 131–132
responsibility-based principles, 155–160
role of interests, 139, 140
working consensus, 162–163
financial assistance
  CDM, 202–204
  export credit agencies, 201–202
  Global Environment Facility (GEF), 201
financial mechanism, 93
Framework Convention on Climate Change. *See* United Nations Framework Convention on Climate Change (UNFCCC)
Franck, Thomas, 135, 146–149

G-77, 61
G-8
  G-8 plus 5 format, 124
  German presidency, 113, 125
  Gleneagles Dialogue on Climate Change, Clean Energy, and Sustainable Development, 124
  Japanese presidency, 125
General Agreement on Tariffs and Trade, 56
General Assembly
  debate on climate change, 113
Global Environment Facility (GEF), 54
  as a financial mechanism of the UNFCCC, 93–94
  development and structure, 214
Global Triptych proposal, 257–258
global warming. *See* climate change
global warming potential (GWP), 67
Gore, Albert, 33, 114
grandfathering. *See* emission trading
Greenhouse Development Rights (GDRs), 246–249
greenhouse gases (GHGs), 1
  atmospheric concentrations, 22
  carbon cycle, 67
  carbon dioxide, absorption of, 23
  carbon dioxide, sources of, 6, 21–22
  China, 23

cumulative emissions of carbon dioxide, 7
from aviation and marine bunker fuels, 64
main gases, 22
per capita emissions, 24
preindustrial values, 22
United States, 23

historical responsibility, 8, 155–156, 158
  Brazilian proposal, 249–251
hot air, 85

intergenerational justice, 17, 156, 166
Intergovernmental Panel on Climate Change (IPCC), 11, 21, 51
  Fourth Assessment Report, 26
  General Assembly, 51
  origins and mandate, 34–35
  political environment, 37–38
  Second Assessment Report (SAR), 25, 63
  special report on aviation, 65
  summary for policy makers, 36
  thematic working groups, 25
  Third Assessment Report, 26
International Civil Aviation Organization (ICAO), 64
International Emissions Trading. *See* emission trading
International Energy Agency, 44
international law
  customary law, 169–170
  environmental law, 168–169, 171
International Maritime Organization (IMO), 64
international relations
  neo-liberal institutionalism or regime theory, 139
  realism, 138

Joint Implementation (JI), 79
  activities implemented jointly (AIJ), 75
  additionality, 77
  compared to CDM, 76
  eligibility requirements, 76
  impact of EU ETS, 78–79
JUSSCANNZ, 62
justice. *See also* fairness
  difference principle, 144
  distributive justice. *See* fairness
  liberal theories of justice, 135
  libertarianism, 145–146
  Rawls, 145
  utilitarianism, 143–144

Kyoto Protocol, 5–6. *See* compliance,
Compliance Mechanism
  as framework instrument, 92–93
  base year, as acknowledgement of acquired rights, 66
  basket of gases, 22
  basket of gases approach, 66–67
  Buenos Aires Plan, 93
  dialogue on long-term cooperative action, 115
  first commitment period, 6
  flexibility mechanisms, 60
  flexibility under, 72
  historical emissions as basis for targets, 66
  international transactions log, 105
  Marrakech Accords, 93, 100–102, 106, 108, 202
  policies and measures, 53, 62, 64
  process leading to, 60–61
  ratification and entry into force, 59, 103
  review under Article 9, 107
  rules of procedure, 59, 70
  sinks, treatment of, 69
  structure of, 63–64
  subsidiary bodies, 70
  supreme body of, 69
  targets and timetables, proposals by EU on, 65–66
  US opposition, 97–98

leakage, 230
least developed countries (LDCs), 10
Least Developed Countries Fund (LDCF), 99, 217–220

marginal cost of abatement, 72
Marrakech Accords. *See* Kyoto Protocol
McKibben, William, 12
Methane to Markets Partnership, 126
Millennium Development Goals (MDGs), 41, 155, 181
Montreal Protocol, 54, 91, 176–177
multistage and graduation approaches, 251–254

Netherlands, 32
New International Economic Order, 182
Nozick, Robert, 145
nuclear energy
  not eligible under CDM and JI, 98

official development assistance (ODA), 10
  support for adaptation and mitigation, 200–201
OPEC
  adverse effects of response measures, 100
orchestra of treaties proposal, 255–257

policies and measures. *See also* Kyoto Protocol
  sustainable development policies and measures (SD-PAMs), 232–235
policy assessment criteria
  cost-effectiveness, 235
  environmental effectiveness, 232–234
  institutional design, 236–242
polluter pays principle, 6, 66, 155, 250

quantified emissions limitations and reduction objectives, 62

Rawls, John, 134, 144–145, 147
renewable energy. *See* energy
Earth Summit. *See* UN Conference on Environment and Development
rules of procedure. *See* United Nations Framework Convention
Russian Federation, 103

Security Council,
  debate on climate change, 113
Shue, Henry, 136
South Africa, 124
Special Climate Change Fund (SCCF), 99, 215–217
  supported activities, 104
stabilization targets, 39–40, 49
Stern Review, 14, 167
sustainable development, 55
  climate change and sustainable development, 55
  Delhi Declaration on Climate Change and Sustainable Development, 102

targets and timetables, 53
technology transfer
  in MEAs and the UNFCCC, 193–199
  Multilateral Climate Technology Fund, proposal for, 121
  Poznań strategic program on technology transfer, 122

# Index

Umbrella Group, 62
UN Conference on Environment and Development, 50, 173
 differential treatment, 183
UN Conference on the Human Environment, 173
UN Conference on the Law of the Sea
 transfer of technology, 176
UN Convention on the Law of Non-navigational Uses of International Watercourses, 175
UN Convention on the Law of the Sea, 56
UN Environment Programme (UNEP), 51
UN secretary-general
 engagement on climate change, 113, 114
United Nations Framework Convention on Climate Change (UNFCCC), 3, 5
 common obligations under, 57
 COP, powers of, 58
 developed country commitments, 57
 dialogue on long-term cooperative action, 106, 107–108
 General Assembly, role in establishing UNFCCC, 53
 Intergovernmental Negotiating Committee (INC), 50, 53
 inventories and national communications, 57–58
 provision of financial resources and technology transfer, 57
 rules of procedure, 58–59
 ultimate objective, 39, 51, 55–56

UNEP, process of negotiations leading to UNFCCC, 52
United States
 approach to Compliance Mechanism, 52
 approach to Kyoto Protocol. *See* Kyoto Protocol
 Asia-Pacific Partnership on Clean Development and Climate, 125
 Bali Action Plan negotiations, 116
 meetings of major economies on energy security and climate change, 114
 per capita emissions, 8, 24

Vienna Convention for the Protection of the Ozone Layer, 53

World Bank
 Clean Investment Funds (CIFs), 121, 222–223
 Clean Technology Fund (CTF), 222
 energy efficiency projects, 200
 Extractive Industries Review, 199
 renewable energy, 200
 Strategic Climate Change Fund (SCF), 222
World Business Council on Sustainable Development, 126
World Meteorological Organization (WMO), 51
World Summit on Sustainable Development (WSSD), 102, 173–174
 renewable energy, 174
World Trade Organization
 impact of trade on technology transfer, 194
 Trade Policy Review Mechanism, 259

For EU product safety concerns, contact us at Calle de José Abascal, 56–1°,
28003 Madrid, Spain or eugpsr@cambridge.org.

www.ingramcontent.com/pod-product-compliance
Ingram Content Group UK Ltd.
Pitfield, Milton Keynes, MK11 3LW, UK
UKHW011321060825
461487UK00005B/252